S0-BQW-623

TOWARDS A EUROPEAN CRIMINAL RECORD

The success of the four core freedoms of the EU has created fertile ground for transnational organised crime. Innovative, transnational legal weapons are therefore required by national authorities. The availability of data on criminal convictions is at the forefront of the debate. But which mechanism for availability can be used effectively while at the same time respecting an increasingly higher level of data protection at national level?

In the fluid, post-'Reform Treaty' environment, the EU is moving towards the creation of a European Criminal Record which will ultimately secure availability of criminal data beyond the weaknesses of Mutual Legal Assistance mechanisms. Examining the concept of a European Criminal Record in its legal, political and data protection dimensions, this multidisciplinary study is an indispensable exploration of a major initiative in European Criminal Law which is set to monopolise the debate on EU judicial cooperation and enforcement.

CONSTANTIN STEFANOU is a Senior Lecturer at the Institute of Advanced Legal Studies, School of Advanced Study, University of London.

HELEN XANTHAKI is a Senior Lecturer in Legislative Studies at the Institute of Advanced Legal Studies, School of Advanced Study, University of London.

TOWARDS A EUROPEAN CRIMINAL RECORD

Edited by

CONSTANTIN STEFANOU

AND

HELEN XANTHAKI

University of London

CAMBRIDGE UNIVERSITY PRESS
Cambridge, New York, Melbourne, Madrid, Cape Town, Singapore, São Paulo, Delhi

Cambridge University Press
The Edinburgh Building, Cambridge CB2 8RU, UK

Published in the United States of America by Cambridge University Press, New York

www.cambridge.org
Information on this title: www.cambridge.org/9780521866699

First published 2008

Printed in the United Kingdom at the University Press, Cambridge

A catalogue record for this publication is available from the British Library

ISBN 978-0-521-86669-9 hardback

CONTENTS

CONTRIBUTORS

IVANA BACIK (LLB, LLM, BL, FTCD), Reid Professor of Criminal Law, Criminology and Penology, School of Law, Trinity College, University of Dublin.

DR LORENZ BÖLLINGER (Dipl.-Psych., Dr. jur), Professor of Criminal Law and Criminology, Bremen University Law Department, University of Bremen.

ELS DE BUSSER (LLB, MA), Assistant International Criminal Law, Institute for International Research on Criminal Policy (IRCP), Ghent University.

DR JAROSLAV FENYK (PhD), Professor of Law, Criminal Law Department, Law Faculty of the Masaryk University Brno and Law Faculty of the Charles University Prague.

FRANCISCO JAVIER GARCÍA FERNÁNDEZ (Dipl., LLB, LLM), Lawyer, Spain.

DR MARIA GAVOUNELI (LLM, PhD), Lecturer in International Law, Faculty of Law, University of Athens.

DR OSWALD JANSEN (LLB, LLM, PhD), Senior Lecturer, Department of Constitutional and Administrative Law, Law School, Utrecht University.

DR ROBERT KERT (Mag. Iur. Dr. iur.), Assistant Professor, Institute of Criminal Law, University of Vienna.

DR KATALIN LIGETI (LLM, PhD), Docent, Department of Criminal Law of the Faculty of Law, Eötvös Loránd University, Budapest and Advisor at the Hungarian Ministry of Justice and Law Enforcement.

DR VALSAMIS MITSILEGAS (LLB, LLM, PhD), Reader in Law, School of Law, Queen Mary, University of London.

DR ANNA ONDREJOVA (JUDr), Director of the EC and EU Relations Department, The General Prosecutor's Office, Bratislava, Slovakia.

DR DRAGAN PETROVEC (LLD), Associate Professor, Senior Research Fellow, Institute of Criminology, University of Ljubljana.

DR CONSTANTIN STEFANOU (BA, MA, MPhil, PhD), Senior Lecturer, LLM Director, Institute of Advanced Legal Studies, School of Advanced Studies, University of London.

DR KATJA ŠUGMAN (Dipl. Iur., Dipl. Psych., LLM, PhD), Professor of Law, Faculty of Law, University of Ljubljana, Researcher at the Institute of Criminology Ljubljana.

PANTELIS TRAIANOS (LLB, LLM) Attorney-at-law, Athens Bar.

LISA WEBLEY (LLB, PgDipLP, MA), Reader, Department of Academic Legal Studies, School of Law, University of Westminster.

DR ALEXANDRA XANTHAKI (Ptychion, LLM, PhD), Senior Lecturer, Brunel Law School, Brunel University.

DR HELEN XANTHAKI (LLB, MJur, PhD), Senior Lecturer, Academic Director, Institute of Advanced Legal Studies, School of Advanced Studies, University of London.

PREFACE AND ACKNOWLEDGEMENTS

EU criminal law is often misunderstood as an avant garde area of legal integration that lacks legal basis, consistency and legitimacy. This is not necessarily untrue. But any criticisms of that nature should be laid before the EU and national actors who have devised the relevant instruments in the manner observed so far. There is nothing 'strange', inconsistent or illegitimate about EU criminal law as a field of legal integration.

Consequently, research and analysis of aspects of EU criminal law is often presented as a risky business. This is true but again it must be attributed to the scattered, unimaginative and often borderline legitimacy of EU instruments. In an area where unanimity in decision making is often seen as a sanctification of any political and legal position that manages to reach consensus, commentators struggle with requirements of adherence to competence and data protection issues. The European Criminal Record is a paradigm of this state of affairs.

The Reform Treaty may contribute to the unlocking of this vicious circle. The abolition, finally, of the third pillar may, and in a way inevitably will, bring with it increased subsidiarity and proportionality tests and increased controls of competence and legitimacy issues. This is a very fluid, yet incredibly exciting time, for those promoting the EU ideal on a solid basis even in the field of EU criminal law.

This is a time when competencies in the field of criminal law will have to be revisited and defined clearly and concretely. We live in hope.

In view of this environment, the book presented difficulties beyond those commonly faced by academic writers. The balance of academic and practitioner authors is evident in the selection of contributors, as indeed is the editors' success in recruiting authors of exceptional calibre from the majority of EU Member States. Without the difficult questions posed by the authors and the frequent challenge of the editors' initial ideas, the intellectual process toward the completion of this book would have been boring and uninviting; the result would have been mundane and unimaginative. Similarly, without the limitless sources and support of staff of the IALS library awareness of the rather esoteric field studied in the book would have been impossible. The completion of this publication would have been equally impossible without the immense encouragement and support of Professor Avrom Sherr who has the charisma to attribute value even in the darkest intellectual corners of distorted academic minds. The book could not have been conceived, let alone completed, without the immense assistance of Eleni Kouzoupi, Legal Fonctionnaire of the Republic of Cyprus, whose relentless updates on the current state of affairs helped motivate and update the editors further. Last but not least, thanks are due to Mr Anastasios Papaligouras, Minister of Justice of the Hellenic Republic, and his staff for allowing the editors access to legal documentation and national decision-making processes in relation to the European Criminal Record. The editors wish to thank especially the Minister's Legal Counsel, Dr Maria Gavouneli, for that purpose.

Introduction: How did the idea of a European Criminal Record come about?

CONSTANTIN STEFANOU AND HELEN XANTHAKI

1. The necessity of a European Criminal Record: gaps in national criminal records

The concept of a European Criminal Record (ECR) was put forward to the Commission by Dr Constantin Stefanou, serving as the political reviser and horizontal expert in the study on the use of criminal records as a means of preventing organised crime in the areas of money laundering and public procurement funded by the Commission as a Falcone study in 1999.[1] Over a period of two years a multidisciplinary group of fifteen national and three horizontal/comparative experts joined forces to examine and comparatively evaluate the laws on national criminal records in the then fifteen Member States of the European Union (EU) as a means of assessing whether national criminal records are effective and adequate solutions to the problem of increased mobility of persons, services and, consequently, crime in the EU.[2] This multinational, multidisciplinary research revealed that all older Member States maintain databases of convictions imposed on own nationals by national judicial and, at times, administrative authorities; however, the use of national criminal records for the purposes of adhering to the money laundering and public procurement provisions envisaged by the EU in the relevant Directives is not undertaken in a number of countries,[3] including Spain and

[1] H. Xanthaki and C. Stefanou, 'The Use of Criminal Records as a Means of Preventing Organised Crime in the Areas of Money-laundering and Public Procurement: the EU Approach', European Commission FALCONE Study, Ref. No. 1999/FAL/197, IALS, 1999.

[2] H. Xanthaki, 'Cooperation in Justice and Home Affairs', in J. Gower (ed.), *European Union Handbook* (London–Chicago: Fitzroy Dearborn Publishers, 2002), pp. 234–242, at 239.

[3] See H. Xanthaki, 'First Pillar Analysis', in S. White (ed.), *Procurement and Organised Crime* (London: IALS, 2000), pp. 49–71; also see H. Xanthaki, 'Money Laundering in Greece', *CCH Anti-Money Laundering Loose-leaf* (London: CCH, 1999), paras. 90-000–94-000.

Sweden.[4] More crucially, the study reveals discrepancies in national criminal records with reference to three main points: the level of information available in the records, the types of persons with entries in national criminal records and the ground covered in these records.[5]

First, the level of information available in national criminal records varies within Member States as a result of the dramatic differences in the provisions on erasure: in view of the lack of harmonisation in national criminal laws,[6] crimes are punished by diverse levels of sanctions and, therefore, erasure from national criminal records takes place at different time periods. Moreover, the period of time that must elapse after serving a sentence and before the erasure of that sentence from the national records varies between Member States, with very individual and at times even eccentric approaches to criminal punishment and the rehabilitation of ex-offenders. Consequently, erasure and, therefore, the level of data remaining in national criminal records differs between Member States, thus creating a direct discrimination amongst EU citizens based solely on the relevant provisions in their country of origin. Second, the type of persons included in national criminal records varies as a large number of Member States fail to recognise criminal liability for legal persons: crucially, legal persons are not included in criminal records thus preventing their exclusion from further activity, which is often linked to their infiltration by terrorism and organised crime.[7] A similar level of variation in national criminal laws affects the entry of administrative sanctions of a criminal law nature in national criminal records (prominent mainly in the German, Austrian and Polish legal traditions) and disqualifications (whose legal value and equivalence amongst Member States is a rather complex matter). Third, the ground covered by criminal records has important variations in Member States with reference to the data on convictions of own nationals imposed by foreign courts or convictions of foreign nationals imposed by own courts. In other words, where nationality of the convicted and the

[4] H. Xanthaki and C. Stefanou, 'National Criminal Records as Means of Combating Organised Crime in the EU', EU Criminal Law Conference, Brussels, 1–3 December 2000.

[5] H. Xanthaki, 'National Criminal Records and Organised Crime: A Comparative Analysis', in C. Stefanou and H. Xanthaki (eds.), *Financial Crime in the EU: Criminal Records as Effective Tools or Missed Opportunities* (The Hague: Kluwer Law International, 2005), pp. 15–42, at 40–41.

[6] A. Cadoppi, 'Towards a European Criminal Code?' (1996) *European Journal of Crime, Criminal Law and Criminal Justice* 4–7.

[7] C. Stefanou and H. Xanthaki, 'Methods of Preventing the Infiltration of Legal Entities by Organised Crime and Terrorism (study)', European Commission JHA closed tender, Ref. No. DG JAI-B2/2003/01, March 2003.

imposing court varies gaps in data appear with alarming frequency. This is crucial in the combat of transnational crime where variations of nationality of the accused and location of conviction are rather common.[8]

The conclusions that can be drawn from an in-depth comparative analysis of national provisions concerning criminal records are rather useful for the identification of effective and realistic weapons in the fight against transnational organised crime.[9] First, all Member States have already established databases for convictions. The national legislative and administrative structures are already in place and have been tested by judicial and enforcement practices at the national level. Second, national criminal records are, at least in principle, adequate sources of information for convictions imposed by national courts on own nationals. Third, when national criminal records are set against transnational criminals and criminal organisations, they lag behind because of existing discrepancies in substantive and procedural provisions in the national criminal laws of the twenty-seven Member States.

2. Mutual legal assistance: solution or disappointment?

The question is whether national criminal records can stand the test of transnationality,[10] evident in current criminal trends,[11] by use of mutual legal assistance (MLA) mechanisms. National judicial and investigation

[8] C. Stefanou and H. Xanthaki, 'National Criminal Records and the Combat against Organised Crime', 21st International Symposium of Economic Crime: Financial Crime, Terror and Subversion, 7–14 September 2003, Cambridge.

[9] L. Sheeley, 'Transnational Organized Crime: An Imminent Threat to the Nation-State' 48 (1995) *Journal of International Affairs* 463–490, at 484; L. Shelley, J. Picarelli and C. Corpora, 'Global Crime', in M. Cusimano Love (ed.), *Beyond Sovereignty: Issues for a Global Agenda* (Thomson, Wadsworth, 2003), pp. 143–166; National Security Council, 'International Crime Threat Assessment', www.terrorism.com/documents/pub45270/pub45270chapl.html; UN General Assembly, 'Convention against Transnational Organized Crime' (NY: UN Publications, 2001), pp. 25–26.

[10] F. Gazan, 'Commitments and Undertakings under European and International Legal Instruments regarding Trafficking in Human Beings and their Incorporation in National Legislation' in LARA Final Regional Seminar on Criminal Law Reform to Prevent and Combat Trafficking in Human Beings in South-eastern Europe, Proceedings of the Regional Seminar and Final Report, Durrës, Albania, 30 October–1 November 2003, www.coe.int/t/e/legal_affairs/legal_cooperation/combating_economic_crime/3_technical_cooperation/LARA/lara(2003)45.pdf, pp. 95–98, at 96.

[11] C. Resta Nestares and F. Reinares, 'Transnational Organized Crime as an Increasing Threat to the National Security of Democratic Regimes: Assessing Political Impacts and Evaluating State Responses' (1999) *NATO Working Papers Collection* 2.

authorities may be able to complete the data available in the national criminal record with the aid of information received from the national criminal records of other Member States via mutual legal assistance requests. If the reliability of MLA mechanisms can be proven, the search for a transnational solution ends there.

In the EU mutual legal assistance takes place at three levels: the national level, the bilateral/international level and the EU level.[12] A comparative analysis of the legal framework of mutual legal assistance at the national level demonstrates a lack of harmonisation in national approaches.[13] The value of international agreements in the national laws of the Member States remains diverse.[14] Some Member States place international agreements above the Constitution in the hierarchy of sources of national law, some place them below the Constitution and above national laws, whereas others lack any concept of hierarchy in relation to international agreements altogether.[15] Moreover, some Member States require ratification of international agreements whereas others introduce direct and automatic application.[16] Furthermore, some Member States have opted for the introduction of framework laws regulating the issue of legal assistance in a single legal text, whereas other Member States have left the regulation of the matter to a set of scattered provisions found in a number of national legal instruments. However, it must be accepted that gradually more Member States opt for the framework law option. A small number of national laws do not introduce national provisions on mutual legal assistance, leaving this to regulation via international agreements.[17] The picture painted here is

[12] F. E. Dowrick, 'Overlapping International and European Laws' (1982) 31 *International and Comparative Law Quarterly* 59–98.

[13] H. Xanthaki, 'Assessment of the Existing Legislation and Practice for the Promotion of Judicial Cooperation and the Fight against Criminality', in Public Prosecutor's Office of the Court of First Instance of Athens (ed.), *Euro-Joint: The Role of Eurojust against Crime* (Athens: Nomiki Vivliothiki, 2003), pp. 68–79 and 209–218.

[14] J. H. Jackson, 'Status of Treaties in Domestic Legal Systems: A Policy Analysis' (1992) *The American Journal of International Law* 310–340.

[15] L. Wildhaber, 'The European Convention on Human Rights and International Law' (2007) *International and Comparative Law Quarterly* 217–232, at 218.

[16] On monism and dualism, see J. P. Miller and L. Wildhaber, *Praxis des Völkerrechts* (Bern: Stämpfli, 2001), p. 153.

[17] H. Xanthaki, 'The Present Legal Framework of Mutual Legal Assistance within the EU' (2003) 56 *Revue Hellenique de Droit International* 53–90, at 55–56; also see Council of the EU, 'Evaluation Report on Mutual Legal Assistance and Urgent Requests for the Tracing and Restraint of Property': Report on Austria, 14911/00, CRIMORG 170, 22 December 2000; Report on Belgium, 7704/00, CRIMORG 60, 16 May 2000; Report

one of great diversity, obscurity and ambiguity in the provisions on mutual legal assistance at the national level.

At the international level, all Member States are signatories to the European Convention of 20 April 1959 on Mutual Assistance in Criminal Matters,[18] the Additional Protocol of 17 March 1978 to the European Convention on Mutual Assistance in Criminal Matters,[19] the Convention of 19 June 1990 implementing the Schengen Agreement of 14 June 1985 on the Gradual Abolition of Checks at Common Borders,[20] the Council of Europe Convention of 8 November 1990 on Laundering, Search, Seizure and Confiscation of the Proceeds from Crime,[21] the United Nations Convention of 19 December 1988 against Illicit Traffic in Narcotic Drugs and Psychotropic Substances,[22] and the 2001 Second Additional Protocol to the European Convention on Mutual Assistance in Criminal Matters.[23] Moreover, a cluster of Member States are also signatories to the Benelux Conventions[24] and the Nordic Conventions on legal assistance. Figure 1 offers a bird's eye view of the various MLA agreements in Europe.[25]

The complex, often overlapping, provisions of these international agreements[26] plague mutual legal assistance with inherent, and to a degree

on Denmark, 10860/99, CRIMORG 128, 9 September 1999; Report on Finland, 9392/00, CRIMORG 94, 7 July 2000; Report on France, 12000/00, CRIMORG 131, 10 October 2000; Report on Germany, 13365/00, CRIMORG 153, 11 December 2000; Report on Greece, 10596/99, CRIMORG 125, 23 August 1999; Report on Italy, 7254/00, CRIMORG 52, 22 March 2000; Report on Ireland, 9079/99, CRIMORG 70, 18 August 1999; Report on Luxembourg, 5932/99, CRIMORG 21, 15 February 1999; Report on the Netherlands, 10595/99, CRIMORG 124, 18 August 1999; Report on Portugal, 7251/01, CRIMORG 33, 2 April 2001; Report on Spain, 5819/00, CRIMORG 16, 22 March 2000; Report on Sweden, 7250/01, CRIMORG 32, 27 March 2001; Report on Sweden', 7249/01, CRIMORG 31, 26 March 2001; 'Summary Reports on mutual legal assistance', 9501/4/04 REV4 LIMITE CRIMORG 43 and 7917/2/05 REV2 LIMITE CRIMORG 34.

18 http://conventions.coe.int/Treaty/Commun/ListeTraites.asp?CM=8&CL=ENG; CETS 030.

19 http://conventions.coe.int/Treaty/Commun/QueVoulezVous.asp?NT=099&CM=8&DF=5/9/2007&CL=ENG; CETS 099.

20 OJ L 239, 22 September 2000, pp. 63–68.

21 http://conventions.coe.int/Treaty/Commun/QueVoulezVous.asp?NT=141&CM=8&DF=5/9/2007&CL=ENG; CETS 141.

22 http://www.unodc.org/pdf/convention_1988_en.pdf

23 http://conventions.coe.int/Treaty/Commun/QueVoulezVous.asp?NT=182&CM=8&DF=5/9/2007&CL=ENG; CETS 182.

24 Bart de Schutter, 'International Criminal Law in Evolution: Mutual Assistance in Criminal Matters between the Benelux Countries' (1967) 14 *Nederlands Tijdschrift Voor Internationaal Recht* 382–410.

25 Correct on 1 May 2007.

26 C. Schreuer, 'The Waning of the Sovereign State: Towards a New Paradigm for International Law?' (1993) 4 *European Journal of International Law* 447–471, at 461.

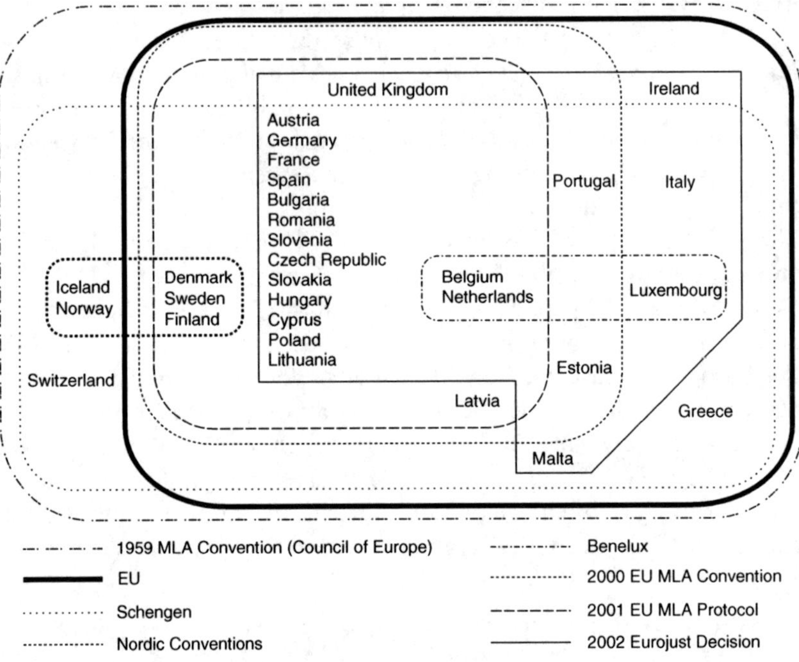

Graph 1: Mutual Legal Assistance for Member States

unavoidable, problems.[27] The correlation of the requested state with the field of application of each of the numerous conventions on mutual legal assistance is the initial hurdle faced by the national authorities of the requesting state. Even when referring to the main international instrument in this area, the 1959 Council of Europe Convention, the identification of the date from which it applies in each Member State and the specific provisions applicable to each Member State after all individual reservations and declarations require a lengthy and detailed study of the law of the requested state. This is rarely possible, especially under the conditions of urgency in mutual legal assistance.

Another hurdle for the requesting state refers to the selection of the international agreement that is applicable in the case of specific

[27] See C. Stefanou, 'Organised Crime and the Use of EU-wide Databases', in I. Bantekas and G. Keramidas (eds.), *International and European Financial Law* (Lexis Nexis Butterworths, 2006), pp. 219–221.

offences.[28] Although the 1959 Convention excludes fiscal, military and political offences, these are covered by the 1972 Protocol and the Schengen Convention. Such offences are not excluded by the 1990 Council of Europe and the 1988 Vienna Conventions. Thus, in the UK, fiscal, political and military offences are not covered by agreements on mutual assistance unless otherwise provided in bilateral agreements with specific Member States. For third countries, and subject to reservations and bilateral agreements, fiscal offences are covered to the extent introduced by the 1972 Protocol and the Schengen Convention which apply in parallel. Political and military offences may afford legal assistance under the Schengen Convention but not under the 1959 Convention. Bilateral agreements complicate things further. In the case of requests related to drug offences, the 1959 and 1988 Council of Europe Convention apply in parallel. As there is no clear hierarchical classification between these two instruments, Member States may pick and choose the Convention which is most useful to them in each particular case. Since it is not necessary to declare under which international Convention one seeks assistance, the execution of the letter rogatory may well be undertaken on the basis of the discretion of the receiving state. In that case, one may pick and choose the field of application, the list of possible actions and the grounds for refusal one prefers. Conflicting provisions as to the use of the dual criminality principle or as to the permissible grounds for refusal complicate the net of provisions that both the requesting and the receiving authorities will have to apply. This situation is further obscured by the common determination of the same central authority for cooperation under most international Conventions in a large number of Member States.

The requirement of dual criminality[29] and the multitude of grounds for refusal of mutual legal assistance[30] under each international Convention present further impediments in obtaining accurate information from

[28] H. G. Nilsson, 'From Classical Judicial Cooperation to Mutual Recognition' (2006) 77 *Revue internationale de droit pénal* 53–58.

[29] S. Murphy, *Principles of International Law* (Thomson West, 2006), p. 408; A. Moore and M. Chiavario (eds.), *Police and Judicial Co-operation in the European Union: FIDE 2004 National Reports* (Cambridge: Cambridge University Press, 2004), p. 24; G. Corstens, *European Criminal Law* (The Hague: Kluwer Law International, 2002), p. 130; M. Joutsen, 'International Instruments on Cooperation in Responding to Transnational Crime', in P. Reichel (ed.), *Handbook of Transnational Crime and Justice* (Sage Publications, 2004), p. 260.

[30] D. McLean, *International Cooperation in Civil and Criminal Matters* (Oxford: Oxford University Press, 2005), pp. 63, 194, 350, 360.

criminal records in other Member States.[31] In order to acquire such data, the offence to which the request refers must be considered a criminal offence in both the requesting and the requested state. Despite convergence in the national criminal laws of Member States,[32] substantive criminal provisions are still notoriously difficult to juxtapose,[33] especially with the variety in the nature and regulation of offences which are not purely criminal.[34] Administrative offences which may lead to criminal prosecution in one Member State may be purely criminal offences in another.[35] With the immense fragmentation in the applicability of the Conventions in this area, dual criminality may well be a more common reason for refusal than one would expect. For example, even when dual criminality is not put forward as a general principle, exemptions as to letters rogatory in relation to the search and seizure of property still apply. Moreover, the wide interpretation of the common grounds for refusal of harm to the sovereignty, security or *ordre public* of the receiving state jeopardises the effectiveness of mutual assistance requests.

There is a final set of practical hurdles to the provision of mutual legal assistance, at the international level that renders its request a tricky exercise. Understanding the request and responding in an adequate manner requires knowledge of the language of both the requesting and requested country. Perhaps more importantly, the provision of data from criminal records via mutual legal assistance mechanisms must be offered in a manner that complies with the national criminal procedural laws of the requesting Member State. Should the procedure for offering data from foreign criminal records clash with the requesting state's national procedural criminal laws then the data kindly offered by the requested state may prove inadmissible, and therefore useless, in criminal proceedings before the requesting state's national courts.[36]

[31] 'Final Report on the First Evaluation Exercise – Mutual Legal Assistance in Criminal Matters', OJ C 216, 1 August 2001, p. 14 points 17 and 19.

[32] H. Askola, *Legal Responses to Trafficking Women for Sexual Exploitation in the EU* (Oxford: Hart Publishing, 2007), p. 12.

[33] For an example of divergent definitions, see A. Wright, *Organized Crime* (Willan Publishing, 2006), p. 13.

[34] C. Harding, P. Fennel, N. Jorg and B. Swart, *Criminal Justice in Europe: A Comparative Study* (Oxford: Oxford University Press, 2002).

[35] K. Yeung, *Securing Compliance: A Principled Approach* (Hart Publishing, 2004), at p. 127; H. Schneider, *The German Stock Corporation Act* (The Hague: Kluwer Law International, 2000), p. 221.

[36] F. Wettner, 'Das allgemeine Verfahrensrecht der gemeinschaftlichen Amtshilfe', in E. Schmidt-Aßmann and B. Schöndorf-Haubold (eds.), *Der Europäische*

Collisions between national legal orders are rather frequent in mutual legal assistance.[37]

As a result, the current picture of legal assistance amongst Member States at the international level is far from satisfactory. Although the example of Italy – which provides favourable assistance to other Member States – is indeed a commendable one, the EU needs a binding legal instrument applicable uniformly in all Member States. The 2000 MLA Convention and its Protocol[38] is the main mechanism for the request and provision of judicial assistance in criminal matters by use of Eurojust.[39] The Convention introduces precise procedures and guidelines to be followed by Member States when sending and servicing procedural documents, transmitting requests of mutual legal assistance, exchanging information spontaneously, transferring persons held in custody for the purposes of investigations, organising joint investigations teams, conducting covert investigations and intercepting communications. The Convention is supplemented by its Protocol of 16 October 2001[40] which introduces mechanisms for dealing with fiscal offences, political offences, requests related to bank accounts and transactions. The two instruments provide a legal basis for requests in most fields of criminal activity as well as a detailed guide for legitimacy in transnational operations against organised crime. However, practice is often not as rosy as theory mainly because of the national legislator's 'removal from European reality'[41] which prevents the prompt and complete implementation of EU law.[42] The 2000 MLA Convention has not been ratified by five Member States: Greece, Ireland, Italy, Latvia and

Verwaltungsverbund – Formen und Verfahren der Verwaltungszusammenarbeit in der EU (Berlin: Mohr Siebeck, 2005), pp. 132–133; A. van Hoek and M. Luchtman, 'Transnational Cooperation in Criminal Matters and the Safeguarding of Human Rights' (2005) *Utrecht Law Journal* 1–39, at 14.

37 E. Jõks, 'Some Problems of International Judicial Assistance from an Estonian Perspective' (1999) *Juridica International* 80–85, at 80–81.

38 Convention of 29 May 2000 on mutual assistance in criminal matters between the Member States, OJ C 197, 12 July 2000, p. 1.

39 See C. Stefanou and H. Xanthaki (2004), 'Memorandum by Dr Constantin Stefanou and Dr Helen Xanthaki', House of Lords, European Union Committee, 23rd Report of Session 2003–04, *Judicial Cooperation in the EU: The Role of Eurojust*, Minutes of Evidence taken before the European Union Committee (Sub-Committee F) 16 June 2004, p. 96.

40 OJ C 326, 21 November 2001, at 2.

41 See M. Jimeno-Bulnes, 'European Judicial Cooperation in Criminal Matters' 9:5 (2003) *European Law Journal* 614–630, at 629.

42 See H. Xanthaki, 'Quality and Transposition of EU Legislation: A Tool for Accession and Membership to the EU' 4 (2006) *European Journal of Law Reform* 89–110.

Luxembourg. The Protocol to the Convention has not been ratified by Estonia, Greece, Ireland, Italy, Luxembourg, Malta and Portugal.[43] In other words, the Convention and the Protocol are not binding on twenty per cent of the Member States – and by extension their national authorities and their investigations and prosecutors.[44] It is disquieting to know that, only in 2005, 155 requests for mutual legal assistance were not addressed by the directness, speed and relative effectiveness provided for in the 2000 MLA Convention and its Protocol, simply because the requesting Member States have refused or omitted to ratify and implement these two instruments. Perhaps it is even more upsetting to know that in the 205 cases of requests reported to have been made to these Member States via Eurojust, the Convention and its Protocol have not been utilised due to the failure or omission of these Member States to ratify them. The effect that non-ratification has on the Member States themselves and on the rest of the EU is pronounced and evident.[45] A further, albeit murkier, debilitating effect of this situation lies with the inevitable fragmentation in the mechanisms for the granting of mutual legal assistance even at the EU level. This leads to a de facto introduction of two speeds in an agency designed to eradicate fragmentation in mutual legal assistance within the EU as a means of enhancing and facilitating cooperation of national authorities. The irony in this case is that these two speeds have not been imposed from above, i.e. the EU, but have been created by the Member States themselves.

3. The Commission proposes

As a result of weaknesses in mutual legal assistance at the national, international and EU levels,[46] the acquisition of data on prior convictions

[43] Council of the EU, 'Addendum to the 'I' Item Note – Implementation of the Strategy and Action Plan to Combat Terrorism', Document No.15266/06 ADD1 REV1, 24 November 2006.

[44] See H. Xanthaki, 'Eurojust: Fulfilled or Empty Promises in EU Criminal Law?' (2006) 8 *European Journal of Law Reform* 175–197.

[45] See H. Xanthaki, 'Drafting for Transposition of EU Criminal Laws: The EU Perspective' (2003) *European Current Law Review* xi–15; also see Helen Xanthaki, 'Assessment of the Existing Legislation and Practice for the Promotion of Judicial Cooperation and the Fight against Criminality', in Public Prosecutor's Office of the Court of First Instance of Athens (ed.), *Euro-Joint: The Role of Eurojust against Crime* (Athens: Nomiki Vivliothiki, 2003), pp. 68–79 and 209–218.

[46] Council of the EU, Third Round of Mutual Evaluation, 'Exchange of Information and Intelligence between Europol and the Member States and among the Member States

imposed either in other Member States or on foreign nationals seems rather difficult to achieve. This was established in a second multinational, multidisciplinary study coordinated by Dr Helen Xanthaki and Dr Constantin Stefanou and funded once again by the European Commission.[47] The study, which constituted the basis of the Institute of Advanced Legal Studies (IALS) ECR study and the proposals on an ECR put forward to the Council and the European Parliament by the Commission,[48] examined the effectiveness of national criminal records in the then twenty-five Member States with specific reference to transnational crime and assessed the feasibility of a centralised database of criminal convictions within the EU. The study also formed the basis of a subsequent research project at Ghent University, which examined the format for an ECR and analysed the competing scenario for the development of a network for existing national records as opposed to the establishment of a centralised unified database.[49] The IALS study started a heated debate on the feasibility of the ECR which continues to the present day and has developed even further than the editors of this book could ever have imagined. It is the feasibility of this concept that constitutes the topic of the book.

The Commission took to the idea of an ECR and presented the concept in its Communication on mutual recognition of final judgments in criminal matters[50] and in measures 2–4 of the Council and Commission programme of measures to give effect to the principle of mutual recognition of decisions in criminal matters.[51] The mutual recognition programme identifies the central role of prior convictions imposed by other Member States in the calculation of sentences in criminal trials and proposes routes for the availability of data on prior

respectively – Report on the Evaluation Visits to 15 Member States (Sweden, Portugal, Germany, Finland, Belgium, France, United Kingdom, Luxembourg, Netherlands, Ireland, Italy, Denmark, Austria, Greece and Spain)', 14292/2/05 Rev 2, CRIMORG 132, 17 January 2006, p. 5.

47 See H. Xanthaki and C. Stefanou, 'A European Criminal Record as a Means of Combating Organised Crime' (study), 2000/FAL/168.

48 See Commission of the EC, 'Communication from the Commission to the Council and the European Parliament on Measures to be Taken to Combat Terrorism and other Forms of Serious Crime, in particular to Improve Exchanges of Information, Proposal for a Council Decision on the Exchange of Information and Cooperation concerning Terrorist Offences', COM(2004) 221 final, 2004/0069 (CNS), 29 March 2004, footnotes 30–31 at 12 and footnote 32, p. 13.

49 See G. Vermeulen and T. Vander Beken, 'Blueprint for an EU Criminal Records Database: Legal, Politico-institutional & Practical Feasibility', Grotius project 2001/GRP/024.

50 See COM (2000) 495 final, 26 July 2000 section 5.

51 See OJ C 12, 15 January 2001, at 10.

convictions to all judicial authorities in the Member States for that purpose. Measure 3 urges the introduction of a unified format for applications for data from criminal records. The programme takes the debate one step forward and pinpoints three possible options for the improvement of data exchanges on convictions, namely facilitation of bilateral information exchanges, networking of existing national criminal records and the establishment of a 'genuine European central criminal records office'.[52]

In 2003 the Italian Presidency conducted a detailed survey of current information systems used by national authorities in investigations and prosecutions as a means of coordinating national technical specifications for effective speedy information exchange and cooperation against organised crime.[53] In the wake of the terrible terrorist attacks in Madrid the Commission called upon the Council for urgent coordination and strengthened cooperation amongst existing national, international and EU networks of information on terrorism, rather than 'losing time destroying existing and creating new procedurally time-consuming institutions and bodies'.[54]

Ten days later the Commission presented a draft Council Decision[55] which aimed to facilitate information exchange against terrorism based on the three IALS studies on national criminal records, on the European Criminal Record and on the infiltration of terrorism in legitimate corporations.[56] In their analysis the Commission linked terrorism with organised crime and presented a holistic approach to the phenomenon of increased transnational criminal activity that flourishes in an enlarged EU plagued by diversities and inefficiencies in mutual legal assistance. The only way to secure accurate, timely and usable data related to investigations, prosecutions and criminal proceedings within the EU is to bypass the process of mutual legal assistance altogether by allowing national authorities direct and automatic access to such information. However, the manner in which this aim can be balanced with data

[52] Ibid.

[53] Council of the EU, 'Answers to the Questionnaire on Information Systems for Fighting against Organised Crime', 9725/03, 12 November 2003, p. 3.

[54] Commission of the EC, 'Commission Paper to the Council on Terrorism providing Input for the European Council', SEC (2004) 348, 18 March 2004, p. 8.

[55] 'Proposal for a Council Decision on the Exchange of Information and Cooperation concerning Terrorist Offences', 8200/04, 5 April 2004.

[56] C. Stefanou and H. Xanthaki, 'IALS Study on Measures in the Member States to Prevent Organised Crime and Terrorist Groups from Infiltrating Legitimate Entities', Study No DG.JAI-B2/2003/01.

protection requirements and proportionality concerns merits further analysis.[57] The window of opportunity provided by the still raw threat of international terrorism pushed the Commission's initiative to fruition, albeit a full eighteen months later.[58] The Council Decision requires the appointment of a specialist law enforcement unit in each Member State, which coordinates transfer of data on terrorist-related prosecutions and convictions to Europol, Eurojust and other Member States via the specially appointed contact point in Eurojust.

4. Competing legislative approaches

In March 2004 Commissioner Vitorino revealed the vision of the Commission in justice and home affairs by announcing legislative proposals for a 'European court record' before the end of 2004.[59] The Commission's proposal for a Council Decision came in October 2004 with a call for urgent measures justified by reference to the terrorist attacks in New York and Madrid and the Belgian paedophilia cases.[60] The basis of additional measures was the gaps and inefficiencies in data exchange mechanisms which function 'randomly and slowly',[61] as demonstrated by the first round of evaluations of mutual legal assistance.[62] The proposal was put forward as the first part of a coordinated policy which would be supplemented by a harmonisation of national criminal records, without prejudice to the Commission's future response to the call of the European Council on 25 March 2004 for a European database of convictions and disqualifications. Own initiative transfer of data on convictions of own nationals to other Member States

[57] Commission of the EC, 'Communication from the Commission to the Council and the European Parliament on Measures to be Taken to Combat Terrorism and other Forms of Serious Crime, in particular to Improve Exchanges of Information; Proposal for a Council Decision on the Exchange of Information and Cooperation concerning Terrorist Offences', COM(2004)221 final; 2004/0069 (CNS), 29 March 2004, pp. 12–14.

[58] Council Decision 2005/671/JHA of 20 September 2005 on the exchange of information and cooperation concerning terrorist offences, OJ L 253/22, 29 September 2005.

[59] 'The Fight against Terrorism: The Commission Proposes Measures on the Exchange of Information and on the European Criminal Record', Press Release IP/04/425, 30 March 2004.

[60] Proposal for a Council Decision on the exchange of information extracted from the criminal record (presented by the Commission), COM(2004) 664 final, 2004/0238 (CNS), 13 October 2004.

[61] Proposal for a Council Decision on the exchange of information from the criminal record, at 2.

[62] OJ C 216, 1 August 2001, at 14.

and standardised forms for transfer of requested data on convictions were the main elements of the Council Decision,[63] which was envisaged to be replaced with a future initiative on a computerised mechanism for transfer of data on convictions. At the same time the Belgian delegation announced their proposal for an ECR.[64] However, in July 2006 the Council Decision was supplemented with a Manual of Procedure,[65] which attempted to address the continuing problem of delays and useless responses to requests for data on convictions undertaken by reference to the Council Decision. For this purpose the Council requested work at two levels: adaptation of internal structures to serious international crime and increasingly intensive discussion of the methods to be put in place for better exchange, sharing and use of existing databases within and between the various existing structures.[66]

Despite the Commission's intention to proceed with the ECR, Member States began to offer alternative solutions. Sweden with the support of the UK presented to the Council a draft Framework Decision viewing the issue of data exchange in a holistic manner that proposed facilitation of information exchange across the boundaries of judicial and police cooperation.[67] Following this trend and within days of the publication of the Council Decision in the *Official Journal*, the Commission presented its proposal for a Council Framework Decision on the organisation and content of the exchange of information extracted from criminal records between Member States, which was introduced as a means of achieving a thorough reform of the national systems of data exchange.[68] Despite the clear focus of the proposal on

[63] Council Decision 2005/876/JHA of 21 November 2005 on the exchange of information extracted from the criminal record, OJ L 322, 9 December 2005.

[64] Proposal for a Council Decision on the exchange of information extracted from the criminal record, 13994/04, 4 November 2004, p. 2.

[65] Council Decision on the exchange of information extracted from criminal records – Manual of Procedure, 6397/3/06 REV 3, 12 July 2006 and 6397/4/06, 28 September 2006.

[66] Council of the EU, 'Third Round of Mutual Evaluation Exchange of Information and Intelligence between Europol and the Member States and among the Member States respectively' – Report on the evaluation visits to 15 Member States (Sweden, Portugal, Germany, Finland, Belgium, France, United Kingdom, Luxembourg, Netherlands, Ireland, Italy, Denmark, Austria, Greece and Spain), 14292/2/05 Rev 2, CRIMORG 132, 17 January 2006, p. 6.

[67] Council of the EU, 'Draft Framework Decision on Simplifying the Exchange of Information and Intelligence between Law Enforcement Authorities of the Member States of the EU', 6888/3/05, 27 July 2005.

[68] COM(2005) 690 final, 2005/0267 (CNS), 22 December 2005.

national criminal records, the Commission made clear reference to the two IALS studies on national criminal records and the ECR,[69] but favoured the approach of a standard European format for conviction records.

In his Opinion on the proposal Peter Hustinx, the European Data Protection Supervisor (EDPS),[70] identified the change of approach from the ECR to the strengthening of data exchanges and commented on the need for additional measures to address the problems on data exchange resulting from differences in language and the technological and legal framework of the Member States. The EDPS articulated the obvious coexistence of competing parallel trends and initiatives that first presented themselves as early as 2004: strengthening bilateral exchanges,[71] introducing a genuine ECR as favoured by the Commission[72] and linking national criminal records in the model realised by the coalition of France, Germany and Spain, now joined by a total of nine additional member states.[73] The coalition now has further countries on board as Belgium, the Czech Republic and Luxembourg have joined the group.[74] Of course, there are those who reject all centralised solutions.[75] At its core the debate concerns the tussle between approximation of legislation and mutual recognition.[76] In fact, the choice of one approach over another is often interpreted as a two-stage approach, where facilitated exchange of data

[69] COM(2005) 690 final, p. 3.

[70] Opinion of the European Data Protection Supervisor on the Proposal for a Council Framework Decision on the organisation and content of the exchange of information extracted from criminal records between Member States (COM (2005) 690 final), 29 May 2006.

[71] 'Roadmap' 2004/JLS/116, http://www.dti.gov.uk/files/file25605.pdf; Commission of the EC, 'White Paper on Exchanges of Information on Convictions and the Effect of such Convictions in the EU', COM(2005) 10 final, 25 January 2005, p. 6.

[72] 'EU rules out Central Criminal Register' *DW-World.DE*, 19 July 2004.

[73] 'EU to Consider Creation of an ECR', e-Government News, 21 July 2004, *IDABC*, EC, 2004; 'Cross-border Paedophile Case boosts EU Cooperation on Criminal Records' *EurActive.com*, 30 October 2006.

[74] J. Macke, 'Exchange of Information on Criminal Records' 3–4 (2006) *Eurcrim* 76–81, at 76–77.

[75] JUSTICE, 'EU Co-operation in Criminal Matters, Response to Specific Proposals', February 2001, para. 5.2.

[76] Luxembourg Presidency Press Release, 'Internal JHA: Strengthening Justice', 28 January 2005, www.eu2005.lu/en/ectualites/communiques/2005/01/2801frieden-justice/index.html; C. Morgan and J. Bateman, 'The EU and the Criminal' (2006) *The Journal of the Law Society of Scotland*, at 34.

constitutes a 'precursor'[77] of a 'computerised database of all criminal records in all EU countries'.[78]

The Commission analysed in detail the advantages and disadvantages of all three scenarios and admitted that bilateral exchanges and a network of national records present major disadvantages, especially with reference to the incredible amount of possible channels and access capacities and the continued problems in use and time of current mutual assistance responses.[79] Further disadvantages of networking, identified by the Council as problems in devising a system of overall project control, were continuing problems with gaps in convictions of non-EU nationals and EU nationals who are not entered in the national criminal records, and the need for multiple consultations for information not filtered by the law of the Member State of origin. The Council balanced its evaluation of this solution with advantages of networking: acceleration and improvement of information exchange, based on existing Council of Europe systems, obviating the need to establish and add to an index with, eventually, the creation of a standardised and comprehensible form of data exchange.[80]

As far as the Commission was concerned, the ECR avoided all disadvantages of bilateral exchanges and a network of national registers but suffered from disproportionality. The doubtful basis of this evaluation was the duplication of effort in entering the same data in both the national and EU record and data protection concerns. Instead, the Commission favoured a hybrid index of convicted persons rather than a proper ECR.[81] The advantages of the index compared to the linkage of national criminal records were identified as acceleration of data

[77] 'Parliament Approves European Criminal Record Swap', *EurActiv.com*, 30 October 2006; also see 'EU: Four Countries Sign Deal to Exchange Records', e-Government News, 7 April 2005.

[78] H. Billings, 'MEPs Back EU Criminal Record Shake-up', *Theparliament.com*, 22 February 2005; also H. Xanthaki and C. Stefanou, 'Initiatives Against Organised Crime: The Use of National Criminal Records as a Means of Combating Organised Crime', The 21st Cambridge International Symposium on Economic Crime, Cambridge 7–14 September 2003.

[79] Commission of the EC, 'White Paper on the Exchange of Information on Convictions and the Effect of such Convictions in the EU', COM(2005) 10 final, 25 January 2005, p. 6.

[80] Council of the EU, 'Policy Debate on the Exchange of Information Extracted from the Criminal Record', 7198/05, 22 March 2005.

[81] Council of the EU, 'Council and Commission Action Plan Implementing the Hague Programme on Strengthening Freedom, Security and Justice in the EU', 9246/1/05 REV 1, 30 May 2005.

exchange, easy identification of Member States where convictions were imposed, use of existing and proven infrastructures (SIS and Eurodac), facilitation of internal operational rules and the possibility of expansion to third-country nationals. Disadvantages of the index are compulsory inclusion in the index without consultation, volume of initial entries in the index and of daily movements and the additional burden for sentencing states.[82]

The Commission's proposal can be viewed as a soothing compromise to Member States that favoured the networking of existing criminal records as maintenance of a shred of sovereignty in the field. In a meeting of experts, which included a closed-doors discussion on the options presented by the Commission before Member States' delegations and experts from the IALS and Ghent University, the Commission presented the index in some detail.[83] The index would only include personal identification data for EU citizens with entries on the Member State where a conviction has been recorded. The idea was that national judicial authorities would access the index, key in the name of the person and acquire a list of countries where an entry in the national criminal record is currently live. The national judicial authority could then contact the relevant countries and seek a copy of the criminal record of that person via the normal channels of communication. Even within the meeting it became evident that the Commission's proposal could not be successful: the concerns of Member States opposing a centralised database were not alleviated by the introduction of a version of a centralised database, whereas Member States supporting or not objecting to a centralised database could not see the added value of the proposal. Indeed, it is difficult to justify the need for an additional legislative and technical burden upon national legislatures and administrations that would be called to make a double entry in the national record and the database with the mere benefit of 'awareness' of a criminal conviction elsewhere for which details could only be received by the generally accepted problematic mutual legal assistance mechanisms. Discontent was expressed by most national delegations and this seemed to put an end to the Commission's index approach. The question is, whether

[82] Council of the EU, 'Policy Debate on the Exchange of Information Extracted from the Criminal Record', 7198/05, 22 March 2005, p. 22.

[83] 'A European Criminal Record: The Future', Experts' Meeting on a European Registry for Disqualifications and Convictions, European Commission, DG Justice and Home Affaires, Directorate D, Internal Security and Criminal Justice, Unit D3/Criminal Justice, 27–28 September 2004.

this terminated discussions on the ECR whose necessity has not been doubted by many.

5. Further EU legislative initiatives

The timid presentation of the index of convictions by the Commission, its discouraging reception by Member States and the split of Member States over a proper ECR seem to have put the Commission's work on a centralised criminal record on hold. However, subsequent measures related to criminal records reveal intense movement in the field and predisposal for further Commission initiatives to be presented when the 'policy window' presents itself at a more opportune time. This tactic is far from unknown to the Commission, especially in cases where the desired core measure stumbles against clashing national legal traditions amongst Member States:

> policy entrepreneurs, such as the Commission, can and do bide their time until they can identify the optimum timing of a proposal. 'Optimum timing' is usually translated to either the removal of a particularly difficult specific hurdle, e.g. another institution or a Member State, or simply the identification of opportunities for political agreement. This 'policy window' is an important element of policy-making and often on it rests the successful or unsuccessful pursuit of a particular Draft.[84]

A measure standardising and recognising disqualifications amongst Member States was sought for a few years in parallel with the ECR,[85] but never came to fruition. For example, the relevant Danish initiative did not flourish, whereas the EU Convention on driving disqualifications has not been ratified by a handful of Member States.[86] This was due to the fact that a number of Member States were unfamiliar with the concept and resented its introduction via an EU legislative measure.

The Commission realised that in the area of the third pillar where unanimity is required, a head-on approach for an express measure on

[84] C. Stefanou and H. Xanthaki, (2000), 'The EU Draft Money Laundering Directive: A Case of Inter-institutional Synergy' (2000) 3 *Journal of Money Laundering Control*, at 337.

[85] The Hague programme adopted on 4–5 November 2004 recognised the crucial importance of disqualifications as sanctions; OJ C 53, 3 March 2005, at 1.

[86] Danish initiative 'with a view to adopting a Council Decision on increasing cooperation between European Union Member States with regard to disqualifications', OJ C 223, 19 September 2002 at 17; EU Convention of 1998 concerning driving disqualifications, OJ C 216, 10 July 1998 at 1 and OJ C 211, 23 July 1999, at 1.

disqualifications would not be successful. The Commission methodically proceeded with the introduction of numerous legislative proposals referring to disqualifications, while refraining from requiring harmonisation at that point. Thus, the Framework Decision on child pornography introduces disqualification of convicted persons from professional activities related to the supervision of children.[87] Similar professional disqualification is introduced in the Framework Decision on corruption.[88] The public procurement Directives demand exclusion from public tendering procedures for natural and legal persons convicted by final judgment for participation in a criminal organisation, corruption, fraud to the detriment of the financial interests of the Communities or money laundering.[89] Under the banking Directive credit institutions that are not of sufficiently good repute are not authorised to perform their duties.[90] The same applies to investment firms, trade in securities, statutory auditing of accounting documents and insurance.[91] A cluster of Directives already settle the issue of mutual recognition of disqualifications imposed by other Member States in the cases of the exercise of the right to vote and stand for election

[87] Article 5(3) Framework Decision 2004/68/JHA on combating the sexual exploitation of children and child pornography, OJ L 13, 20 January 2004, at 44.

[88] Article 4(3), Framework Decision 2003/568/JHA on combating corruption in the private sector, OJ L 192, 31 July 2003, at 54.

[89] Article 45(1), Directive 2004/18/EC of the European Parliament and of the Council of 31 March 2004 on the coordination of procedures for the award of public works contracts, public supply contracts and public service contracts, OJ L 134, 30 April 2004, at 114.

[90] Directive 2000/12/EC of the European Parliament and of the Council of 20 March 2000 relating to the taking up and pursuit of the business of credit institutions, OJ L 126, 26 May 2000, at 1.

[91] Article 9, Directive 2004/39/EC of the European Parliament and of the Council of 21 April 2004 on markets in financial instruments, OJ L 145, 30 April 2004, p. 1; Articles 5 a and 5 b, Council Directive 85/611/EEC of 20 December 1985 on the coordination of laws, regulations and administrative provisions relating to undertakings for collective investment in transferable securities (UCITS), OJ L 375, 31 December 1985, p. 3; Article 3, Eighth Council Directive 84/253/EEC of 10 April 1984 based on Article 54(3)(g) of the Treaty on the approval of persons responsible for carrying out the statutory audits of accounting documents, OJ L 126, 12 May 1984, p 20; Articles 6(1)(a) and 8, Directive 2002/83/EC of the European Parliament and of the Council of 5 November 2002 concerning life assurance, OJ L 345, 19 December 2002, p. 1 and Article 8, Directive 73/239/EC on the coordination of laws, regulations and administrative provisions relating to the taking up and pursuit of the business of direct insurance other than life assurance, OJ L 228, 16 August 1973, p. 3, as amended by Directive 92/49/EC, OJ L 228, 11 August 1992, p. 1.

at municipal and European elections[92] and professional qualifications.[93] Where binding acts could not be agreed upon, resolutions have been put forward as a strong declaration of the need for further legally binding legislative solutions, should self-regulation and common approaches not work. A representative example of this can be traced in the Council Resolution on stadium exclusions which called for the recognition of stadium disqualifications imposed by other Member States.[94] On the basis of these numerous yet fragmented existing legal instruments, the Commission has recently returned to the issue of disqualifications seeking the introduction of a holistic new piece of legislation on the basis of the very strong argument that all relevant measures already passed by the Council have proved ineffective due to the lack of harmonisation of disqualifications.[95]

A similar approach seems to be on the cards for the ECR. This is evident from a number of relevant Commission proposals, some of which are already bearing fruit. First, the Commission's Communication on disqualifications presents fresh initiatives on acquiring data on convictions as a necessary prerequisite for any new proposals on disqualifications. Most crucially, the Commission presented a proposal for a Framework Decision (agreed by Parliament and Council without major difficulties and within just one year) requiring that in the pre-trial, trial and execution stage national authorities take into account convictions for criminal or, where required by national laws, administrative offences imposed in other

[92] Council Directive 94/80/EC of 19 December 1994 laying down detailed arrangements for the exercise of the right to vote and to stand as a candidate in municipal elections by citizens of the Union residing in a Member State of which they are not nationals, OJ L 368, 31 December 1994, p. 38, as amended by Council Directive 96/30/EC of 13 May 1996, OJ L 122, 22 May 1996, p. 14; Council Directive 93/109/EC of 6 December laying down detailed arrangements for the exercise of the right to vote and stand as a candidate in elections to the European Parliament for citizens of the Union residing in a Member State of which they are not nationals, OJ L 329, 30 December 1993, p. 34.

[93] Article 56, para 2, OJ L 255, 30 September 2005, p. 22.

[94] Council Resolution of 9 June 1997 on preventing and restraining football hooliganism through the exchange of experience, exclusion from stadiums and media policy, OJ C 193, 24 June 1997, p. 1; Council Resolution of 17 November 2003 on the use by Member States of bans on access to venues of football matches with an international dimension, OJ C 281, 22 November 2003, p. 1.

[95] Commission of the EC, 'Communication from the Commission to the Council and the European Parliament; Disqualifications arising from criminal convictions in the EU', COM(2006) 73 final, 21 February 2006.

Member States.[96] The Framework Decision is crucial in the ECR debate because it is capable of making Member States appreciate the volume of data required as well as the difficulty of acquiring such data between the time of prosecution and sentencing. As soon as the Framework Decision is received by the national legal orders of the Member States, supporters of a centralised ECR can argue that disproportionality of the ECR – the only argument against it so far – is no longer an issue: in fact, the need for immediately accessible data on prior convictions in all twenty-seven Member States cannot really be fulfilled without the facility of a centralised database of convictions available upon demand from national authorities. The main focus of future debates will, therefore, revolve around the specific elements of the ECR which can guarantee feasibility, legality and proportionality of the instrument, in view of course of the new reality of urgency and necessity.

A number of relevant instruments are also being discussed. In its relevant multinational (twenty Member States), multidisciplinary feasibility study the IALS identified a lacuna in the access of national investigating and prosecuting authorities to foreign databases and recommended the establishment of an EU archive for investigations and prosecutions thus offering quick, accurate and unhindered access to data on investigations and prosecutions in all Member States. This archive could be introduced in two phases: in phase one a European network of national databases for investigations and prosecutions can allow the linkage of national databases in a system comparable to SIS; in the second stage a proper EU database for investigations and prosecutions can serve as the ultimate effective tool for the prevention and combat of serious, organised and transnational crime in the EU.[97] Phase one is currently being put forward to the Council by the Commission, albeit in a reserved and cautious manner.[98]

The second element of the Commission's 2004 strategy on the ECR has already been put into place. The then Commissioner Vitorino linked

[96] Draft Framework Decision on taking account of convictions in the Member States of the European Union in the course of new criminal proceedings, 15445/1/06 REV 1, 24 November 2006; also, COM(2005) 91 final (7645/05 COPEN 60).

[97] H. Xanthaki and C. Stefanou, 'Feasibility Study on the Creation of a Database on Prosecutions and Investigations: The EU Approach', European Commission AGIS Programme Study, Ref. No. JAI/AGIS/ 2003/002, 2003.

[98] Communication from the Commission to the Council and the European Parliament – Towards enhancing access to information by law enforcement agencies, 10745/04, 22 June 2004.

the creation of the ECR with the mutual recognition of judgments in criminal matters.[99] The relevant Council Framework Decision is already in place.[100] The link between the two initiatives is not difficult to identify. The creation of the ECR would inevitably bear the legal question of the value of prior convictions imposed by other EU legal orders for the purposes of sentencing and execution. Recognition of criminal judgments clarifies beyond doubt that the value of foreign criminal judgments is equivalent to that of criminal judgments imposed by the national courts. The Framework Decision on taking into account prior convictions completes the picture by clarifying the purpose and use of these recognised foreign criminal judgments.

In the meantime the Commission extends the debate on the ECR even further. Thus, the creation of a database for third-country nationals is being put into place. In the initial Roadmap the Commission based its proposal once again on the two IALS studies on national criminal records and the ECR and suggested the hybrid solution of the index.[101] Options proposed by the Commission in its recent Working Document[102] include an index of convictions for all crimes, an index of convictions for some crimes and an index of biometrical data at several levels. Moreover, the Commission extends availability of data beyond disqualifications and convictions. On 12 October 2005 the Commission adopted a proposal for a Framework Decision on exchange of information under the principle of availability.[103] The proposal involves the availability of data, such as DNA profiles, fingerprints, ballistic reports, vehicle registration information, telephone numbers and other communication data via online access or by transfer based on an information demand after matching solicited information with index data provided by Member States in respect of information that is not accessible online.

[99] 'EU to Consider Creation of an ECR', e-Government News, 21 July 2004, *IDABC*, EC, 2004.

[100] Council Framework Decision on the application of the principle of mutual recognition to judgments in criminal matters imposing custodial sentences or measures involving deprivation of liberty for the purpose of their enforcement in the European Union, 14040/06, 18 October 2006; also, OJ L 76, 22 March 2005, p. 16–30.

[101] Proposal for a Council Decision on the creation of an index of non-EU nationals convicted in an EU Member State, 2004/JLS/116.

[102] Commission Working Document on the feasibility of an index of third-country nationals convicted in the European Union, COM(2006) 359 final, 4 July 2006.

[103] Proposal for a Council Framework Decision on the exchange of information under the principle of availability, COM (2005) 490 of 12 October 2006.

Furthermore, exchange of data on short-term visas has been proposed recently.[104]

6. Conclusions

The inefficiencies of mutual legal assistance mechanisms have been identified by a number of studies and EU documents. However, the debate on the best possible solution for bypassing the problems of mutual legal assistance at a time of increased demand for accurate information of convictions for EU and third-country nationals is still heated. The IALS proposal for an ECR has been left aside, for now, and the Commission has tried to sell an index of convictions including solely entries of countries where the convictions have been imposed upon EU and third-country nationals. However, the index has proven an unpopular idea mainly due to its inability to bypass the very problems that it is trying to address: inherent hurdles in effective provision of data via a multitude of national databases.

The principle of mutual recognition and a number of recent instruments render the need for immediate access to data available in other Member States more urgent than ever. This has already created an environment that is more receptive towards effective, efficient and proportionate solutions. The ECR debate has not ended. The crucial question is which elements the proposal for an ECR should possess in order to maintain its supporters while alleviating the concerns of its opponents. In the exciting times for EU criminal law that lie ahead, the EU must be ready to respond to this question adequately and persuasively.

[104] Draft Regulation of the European Parliament and of the Council concerning the Visa Information System (VIS) and the exchange of data between Member States on short-stay visas, 11632/06, 13 July 2006.

PART I

2

The European Criminal Record: Analysis

HELEN XANTHAKI

1. Introduction

The details of the European Criminal Record are crucial for its legitimacy under EU law and for its acceptance by the national legal orders of the Member States. The aim of this chapter is twofold: firstly, to assess the current level of standardisation in the use of criminal records as a national means of combating organised crime; and secondly, to evaluate the conditions under which an ECR could be possible in EU law. In order to achieve these aims the chapter will assess the effectiveness of the current use of national criminal records with particular emphasis on their use and effectiveness in cases of cross-border crime; it will then explore the reception of the ECR in the structure of bodies in the area of justice and home affairs and it will, finally, assess which EU legislative instrument could be used for its introduction and under which conditions this introduction could be attempted.

2. The current position

2.1. Content, use, access and erasure

The end of 1999 saw extensive reviews of national laws on criminal records in a number of Member States, most notably Belgium, Denmark, Greece, the Netherlands, Sweden and the UK mainly as a result of EU law on data protection and the Schengen agreement. Moreover, many of the then candidate countries made extensive amendments to their relevant legislation as a means of complying with EU data protection laws. Examples of this practice can be traced in Cyprus, Hungary and Poland.[1]

[1] IALS Studies 1999/FALCONE/197 and 2000/FAL/168 cited in footnote 3, 'White Paper on Exchanges of Information on Convictions and the Effect of such Convictions in the European Union', COM(2005) 10 final, p. 4.

National provisions on the content of criminal records in Member States remain diverse.[2] Although all existing Member States have national databases of criminal decisions having the value of *res judicata*, there is diversity as to the number of relevant archives in each country, the host of criminal records, the content of criminal records and the level of access allowed to them by each national law. In Belgium, Finland, Ireland, Italy and the UK the law allows for parallel local or regional criminal records, whereas in Austria, France, Germany, Ireland and the Netherlands archives including information of particular criminal offences are also kept. In Austria, Ireland, Sweden and the UK criminal record archives are kept by police authorities, whereas in Denmark, Finland, France, Germany, Greece and Spain criminal records are placed with the Ministry of Justice. This renders collaboration amongst national authorities and standardisation of treatment amongst EU citizens a rather unrealistic exercise. In Austria, Belgium, Cyprus, Denmark, Estonia, Finland, France, Hungary, Ireland, Luxembourg, the Netherlands, Poland, Portugal, Slovenia and the UK criminal records include entries on legal persons. In the Czech Republic, Italy, Germany, Greece, Latvia, Lithuania, Malta, Slovakia, Spain and Sweden convictions of legal persons are not included in criminal records. It is worth noting here that Italy and Lithuania recognise criminal liability for legal persons but do not record convictions of legal persons even when imposed by national courts. Thus, even where mutual legal assistance mechanisms are efficient, there is sometimes no information to transfer, even between Member States which recognise criminal liability for legal persons. Further discrepancies arise from erasure. Erasure is unknown in Ireland. In Latvia erasure takes place ten years after the death of the subject. In the other Member States each national law introduces its own period of rehabilitation, ranging from Denmark's ten years running from final discharge to Spain's two years running from the end of the conviction for convictions of up to one year.

Such variations are alarming, when one takes into account the obvious discrimination against EU citizens on the basis of their nationality, as the latter determines the law regulating their rehabilitation. National authorities combating organised crime face the paradoxical obligation of pursuing an EU citizen for a crime that has not yet been erased, while allowing another EU citizen of different nationality sentenced for the same crime at the same time to enjoy a free life in

[2] Commission of the EC, 'Commission Staff Working Paper, Annex to the White Paper on Exchange of Information on Convictions and the Effect of such Convictions in the EU', COM(2005) 10 final, SEC(2005) 63, 25 January 2005, pp. 8–13.

rehabilitation. For example, a German citizen convicted of money laundering acquires a 'blank' criminal record ten years after the imposition of a penalty of one year's imprisonment. In contrast, a Spanish national convicted for the same offence with the same penalty can acquire a 'blank' criminal record two years after the end of conviction, namely seven years before the German citizen. Moreover, German banking institutions would be excused for perceiving the blank criminal record of Spanish job applicants as proof that they have not committed an offence punished by more than one year's imprisonment for at least the last ten years, an assumption which would obviously be untrue under these circumstances. A similar paradox emerges from the real possibility of employment or successful tendering of a convicted Greek money launderer in Spain, where employers and tendering authorities are prevented from access to criminal records of their own and foreign EU nationals.[3]

Unfortunately, these rather depressing conclusions can only be strengthened by reference to the laws on criminal records applicable in the newer Member States. Admittedly, newly passed laws – upon accession – tend to be unanimous in their introduction of a central archive of data on prior convictions imposed on own nationals. However, in Hungary there are five types of archives relevant to criminal convictions, thus placing foreign authorities before a hard 'guestimate' about the most suitable archive for the data sought. In Cyprus, Hungary, the Czech Republic, Poland and Slovenia, there are centralised archives including information on prior criminal convictions. These are commonly kept by the Ministry of Justice, although Cyprus and Hungary differ in that the archive is kept by the Police Crime Record Office and the Ministry of Interior respectively. Thus, in most accession countries approaching the Ministry of Justice for information on criminal records would be a safe, albeit not foolproof, bet. However, the Czech Republic, Latvia and Slovakia do not recognise the criminal liability of legal persons; Lithuania does so, but does not record such convictions. Thus, the problem of lack of information on legal persons remains. The content of criminal records is fairly standard in the new Member States and tends to include full data on convictions, ancillary sentences, suspensions, pardons and sentence expiry. However, in Poland such sentences

[3] H. Xanthaki, 'National Criminal Records and Organised Crime: A Comparative Analysis', in C. Stefanou and H. Xanthaki (eds.), *Financial Crime in the EU: Criminal Records as Effective Tools or Missed Opportunities?* (The Hague: Kluwer Law International, 2005), pp. 15–42, at 19–26.

are only included in the criminal record if the imposing sentence is more than six months' imprisonment, whereas outstanding warrants of arrest are also recorded. Access to data included in criminal records is commonly allowed to the judicial authorities and to the subjects themselves. Apart from this baseline, however, there is a high degree of discrepancy on who is allowed what. In Hungary limited access is offered to the police, the National Judicial Council, and the General Prosecutor for employment purposes. In Poland indirect access is possible but only for reasons of employment in public duty.

2.2. Crimes committed by foreigners

Further discrepancies in the content of national criminal records arise with reference to data recorded on crimes committed abroad or crimes committed by foreigners. As the free movement of natural and legal persons within the EU allows for the unhindered provision of services and establishment in other Member States, it becomes increasingly important for the EU and its Member States to acquire effective weapons in their fight against organised crime. National criminal records, even improved, cannot possibly address the need for updated information on the criminal background of EU citizens, irrespective of where the crimes were committed or where the data is required. Or can they?

The comparative analysis of national laws on the inclusion of entries on convictions of foreign nationals in the host country and on convictions of nationals in other Member States is rather disturbing. All Member States include in their national criminal records all convictions of foreign nationals committed within their jurisdiction. This seems a rather effective weapon for the prevention of organised crime within each Member State, as long as crimes are committed by the same foreign nationals. However, if criminals return to the country of origin or establish themselves in a different Member State, the system offers little protection. In Cyprus, the Czech Republic, Ireland, Poland and the UK national criminal records do not include crimes of their own nationals committed outside their jurisdiction. It is chilling to envisage that criminals may travel abroad, commit serious criminal offences, serve their sentences and then return to their country of origin to resume a life of criminality with a presumption of innocent past behaviour.

Even in Member States, where in principle national criminal records include convictions of own nationals abroad, this exercise is undertaken under sets of conditions that eat into the effectiveness of the system. First, foreign sentences of own nationals are only recorded if they were imposed under the provisions of the European Convention on Human Rights (ECHR). This means that national authorities may select not to record convictions if they consider that the finality of the judgment or the conditions of the trial were not adequate under Article 6 ECHR. Second, some Member States arbitrarily qualify convictions imposed abroad; for example, in the Czech Republic and in Greece foreign convictions are not recorded if the crime is not considered serious. In the case of the Czech Republic the registry administrator makes an arbitrary decision on the seriousness of the crime. Similarly, in Finland and Hungary foreign judgments are only recorded in the national criminal record if the sanctions imposed are recognised by the national law. Perhaps more crucially, it is common practice for convictions imposed abroad to be recorded in national criminal records only if the criminal behaviour is also an offence under domestic law; this is the case at least in Austria, the Czech Republic, Denmark, Germany, Hungary, Luxembourg and Sweden. Even within the EU, where freedom of movement is rather well established, foreign EU nationals have to respect domestic criminal laws: the criminality of behaviour within one Member State is not less if the same behaviour is not a crime in the country of origin. Third, foreign convictions of own nationals are only recorded if the foreign authorities choose and manage to notify the appropriate national authorities. This is the case in Belgium, Greece, Luxembourg, Sweden and the UK. Thus, national authorities maintaining national criminal records are fully dependent on foreign counterparts for the integrity and accuracy of national databases. It is, therefore, conceivable that persons convicted in a Member State other than that of their origin may escape a record of their conviction both in the country of conviction, if its records do not include convictions of foreign persons imposed by national courts, and in the country of origin, if the criminal record there does not include convictions imposed abroad.

For the formation of an accurate image on the past of a person it is, therefore, necessary to ensure that channels of communication amongst national authorities are open. However, it is doubtful that this is the case.

2.3. Mechanisms of collaboration

What mechanisms of collaboration with foreign authorities are there for the exchange of information included in criminal records and are these adequate for the prevention of organised crime?

In Austria the main mechanism of data exchange is the 1959 MLA Convention. Article 13 introduces the obligation of signatory states to communicate extracts from criminal records upon request from the judicial authorities of other signatory states. Under Article 22 contracting states are obliged to communicate all criminal convictions and subsequent measures entered in criminal records. Thus, the Austrian Minister of Justice undertakes automatic exchange of information of criminal convictions with the 38 signatory states of the Convention on an annual basis. Moreover, data exchange takes place on the basis of a number of bilateral agreements with Germany, Switzerland, Italy, Liechtenstein, France, Hungary, the Czech Republic and Slovakia. Exchange of data is generally satisfactory especially with the main countries of cooperation, namely Germany and Switzerland. Furthermore, Austria facilitates data exchange with all other foreign authorities on condition of reciprocity: the Federal Act on International Police Cooperation introduces international police cooperation under data protection requirements. Austria is a party to the Interpol, Schengen and Europol Conventions, thus participating in data exchange from criminal records for criminal police searches only.[4] The system seems to be in place and working rather well. However, there is concern about the effectiveness of the system as it is only foreign convictions for Austrian citizens and residents – not domiciled persons or former residents – that are included in the Austrian criminal records. The complexity of the exchange procedure and delays in responses from foreign authorities are viewed as the main current problems in the system.[5]

In Belgium numerous bilateral agreements for the exchange of data from criminal records are in place. Requests are common from France, Germany, Switzerland, the Netherlands, Austria, Luxembourg and the principality of Monaco, whereas there is significant reduction in the number of requests from Germany, France, the Netherlands, Switzerland, Luxembourg, Italy, Austria, Spain and Greece. The UK has never sent records for Belgian citizens convicted in the UK.[6] Data exchange is also undertaken on the basis of Article 38(2) TEU, the

[4] Council of the EU, 'Evaluation Report on Mutual Legal Assistance and Urgent Requests for the Tracing and Restraint of Property, Report on Austria', 14911/00, CRIMORG 170, Brussels, 22 December 2000.

[5] Robert Kert, 'Report on Austria', IALS Study 2000/FAL/168.

[6] Julie Simone, 'Report on Belgium', IALS Study 2000/FAL/168.

Benelux partnership and the Schengen Convention.[7] General satisfaction with the current state of data exchange is shaded by concerns about the inherent reliance of the system on the national laws of other countries.

In Cyprus data exchange is made on the basis of bilateral and international agreements. The main mechanism for this is Interpol which serves police forces. Cyprus Police maintains an International Relations Office, which is responsible for cooperation with foreign authorities concerning data exchange. Concerns about the effectiveness of the system are focused on the quality of data received and the lengthy time of response.[8] With specific reference to money laundering the newly established Unit for Combating Money Laundering (MOKAS), which constitutes the Cyprus Financial Intelligence Unit, deals with requests for legal assistance from foreign authorities – police and judiciary – through formal letters rogatory and with data exchange with Financial Intelligence Units. MOKAS signed numerous Memoranda of Understanding with its counterpart units in other Member States, such as the Belgian CTIF/CFI and the French TRACFIN.

The Czech Republic uses the 1959 and the 2000 MLA Conventions as the main data exchange mechanisms with foreign authorities. Data exchange is made exclusively with judicial authorities, thus excluding police authorities from criminal records' information. On this basis, exchange of data from the criminal records with Interpol and Europol is not currently possible – although an agreement with Europol is pending (a draft agreement is in place). Yet, even under the draft agreement, exchange of data from criminal records seems rather improbable as the contents of criminal records are not interpreted as operational information of the type falling within the field of application of the draft agreement.[9] Exchange of data is also accomplished through bilateral and multilateral agreements, such as the International Agreement between the Government of the Czech Republic and the Government of the Slovak Republic on the Exchange of Information Found in the Criminal Record.

[7] Council of the EU, 'Evaluation Report on Mutual Legal Assistance and Urgent Requests for the Tracing and Restraint of Property, Report on Belgium', 7704/00, CRIMORG 60, 16 May 2000.

[8] Maria Papaioannou, 'Report on Cyprus', IALS Study 2000/FAL/168.

[9] Jaroslav Fenyk, 'Report on the Czech Republic', IALS Study 2000/FAL/168.

In Denmark any data exchange is undertaken under strict disclosure requirements. The Act on Processing of Personal Data demands an adequate level of data protection as a necessary condition for the exchange of personal data. The field of application of the Act extends to third countries as well as Iceland and Norway which have incorporated Directive 95/46/EC in their laws as a means of guaranteeing data protection. With reference to EU countries disclosure may take place if the subject has given explicit consent to disclosure, if disclosure takes place for the purpose of pursuing private or public interests clearly overriding the interest of confidentiality, if disclosure is necessary for the performance of the activities of an authority or required for a decision to be made by that authority or if disclosure is necessary for the performance of the duties of an official authority.[10] Criminal records are disclosed to institutions belonging to the criminal justice system for the purposes of criminal prosecution and personnel employment. Criminal records are also disclosed to the police, prosecution and courts of the Nordic countries and Council of Europe states for the purpose of foreign criminal proceedings. Disclosure is also permitted to foreign prosecution authorities and courts from countries which are neither Nordic nor Council of Europe members on the discretion of the Police Commissioner. Denmark is part of the Schengen Convention which, however, does not allow transfer of criminal records to foreign authorities, and of the Europol Convention, whose European Information System (EIS) allows for data from criminal records to be stored in Europol databases.[11]

Finland has ratified the 1959 MLA, which constitutes the main mechanism of collaboration with foreign authorities. The main international agreement is signed with the other Nordic countries, namely Iceland, Norway, Sweden and Denmark: it introduces the obligation of signatory states to inform and register any crimes committed by their citizens within their territories, as well as to exchange information when requested.[12] Moreover, extracts from criminal records can be transmitted to Interpol, to police authorities of the International Criminal Police Organisation (ICPO) or to non-ICPO states as long as their duty

[10] Lene Ravn, 'Report on Denmark', IALS Study 2000/FAL/168.

[11] Council of the EU, 'Evaluation Report on Mutual Legal Assistance and Urgent Requests for the Tracing and Restraint of Property, Report on Denmark', 10860/99, CRIMORG 128, 9 September 1999.

[12] Markuu Fredman, 'Report on Finland', IALS Study 2000/FAL/168.

is to serve justice and social order, to uphold public law and to prevent and investigate crime. For any other countries criminal records are accessible only if the information is needed to secure public safety, to prevent harm to life, health or property, and to assist the investigation of a crime which in Finland could result in imprisonment. Furthermore, Finland participates in the Europol and Schengen Conventions.[13]

France is a party to the 1959 MLA Convention and its Protocols, the 2000 MLA Convention and its Protocols, the 2001 Council of Europe MLA and its Protocol, Interpol, Europol and Schengen. Moreover, France has signed bilateral agreements, such as the agreements for closer cooperation with Germany and Switzerland.[14] The system can be efficient when experienced and willing police officers and judges are at both ends of the communication exercise. However, there are delays in the procedure of data exchange and the system can be inefficient with routine checks, such as those involving exchange of data from criminal records.[15]

In Germany the exchange of data from criminal records is regulated by para. 55 BZRG which empowers the German Federal Criminal Record Authority to transmit information to foreign authorities and administrations under German law and international agreements. In practice, this vague provision allows all foreign and international organisations access to data from criminal records upon request.[16] The main instruments used are the 1959 MLA, the 2000 MLA and the 2001 Council of Europe MLA Conventions and their Protocols, as well as a number of bilateral agreements. Even non-signatories to these agreements may seek information from criminal records, but each case is considered ad hoc on the discretion of the German Federal Minister of Justice.[17]

In Greece exchange of information from criminal records is undertaken through MLA Conventions, Interpol, Europol and judicial cooperation

[13] Council of the EU, 'Evaluation Report on Mutual Legal Assistance and Urgent Requests for the Tracing and Restraint of Property, Report on Finland', 9392/00, CRIMORG 94, 7 July 2000.

[14] Council of the EU, 'Evaluation Report on Mutual Legal Assistance and Urgent Requests for the Tracing and Restraint of Property, Report on France', 12000/00, CRIMORG 131, 10 October 2000.

[15] Marc Jobert for Lex Fori, 'Report on France', IALS Study 2000/FAL/168.

[16] Council of the EU, 'Evaluation Report on Mutual Legal Assistance and Urgent Requests for the Tracing and Restraint of Property, Report on Germany', 13365/00, CRIMORG 153, 11 December 2000.

[17] Prof. Lorenz Böllinger, 'Report on Germany', IALS Study 2000/FAL/168.

agreements (such as the South European Cooperation Initiative (SECI), Schengen etc.). Any communication of data is allowed only under conditions guaranteeing the protection of personal data. Thus, the information requested must be adequate, relevant and proportionate to the legitimate purpose for which they are collected; they must only be used for the purpose stated in the request documentation; and the data must only be stored for the period of time deemed necessary for the purpose of the exchange.[18] Greece and Latvia have not implemented the Eurojust Decision. The current system of data exchange is mainly focused on the exchange of information from ongoing operations and investigations rather than routine checks. Thus, although the text of current agreements could allow for a wider interpretation which could include transmission of data from criminal records, this opportunity is not exploited in Greek, and indeed international, practice.[19]

Hungary entrusts its judicial collaboration and mutual assistance to the Department for International Police Cooperation of the Hungarian Police which hosts the Interpol, Europol Project, International Information and International Offices. Moreover, exchange of information with foreign authorities takes place with any national body designated to do so under international bilateral agreements (this is often the case with local or district police offices) as well as with the newly established Coordination Centre for Combating Organised Crime which, though, does not carry international judicial cooperation in its mandate. Formal cooperation is undertaken via Interpol, Europol and international agreements. Unfortunately, SECI and the Central European Cooperation Initiative (CECI) basically duplicate the work of Interpol in Hungary, as they are mainly political initiatives of countries which have already signed the Interpol agreement. Exchange of data from criminal records is adequate but only with reference to police authorities rather than professional associations or tendering authorities.[20]

Ireland's main mechanism of collaboration with foreign authorities is based on Europol through the Liaison and Protection Section of Garda Headquarters in Dublin.[21] There has been an increase in the number of

[18] Council of the EU, 'Evaluation Report on Mutual Legal Assistance and Urgent Requests for the Tracing and Restraint of Property, Report on Greece', 10596/99, CRIMORG 125, 23 August 1999.

[19] Maria Gavouneli, 'Report on Greece', IALS Study 2000/FAL/168.

[20] Katalin Ligeti, 'Report on Hungary', IALS Study 2000/FAL/168.

[21] Council of the EU, 'Evaluation Report on Mutual Legal Assistance and Urgent Requests for the Tracing and Restraint of Property, Report on Ireland', 9079/99, CRIMORG 70, 18 August 1999.

requests received by the Irish Police and the replies sent to foreign authorities. However, there are problems in the current system of information exchange due to inadequate financial resources, the requirement for judicial supervision for investigative powers, the lack of safeguards against abuse, the fundamentally differing structures for the investigation and prosecution of offences in the various states and from the equally fundamental differences in juridical procedure and the lack of access for European contracting authorities to the information contained in the Irish criminal database in order to blacklist tenders.[22]

Italy has signed and ratified several international treaties relating, inter alia, to the exchange of information included in criminal records: all MLA Council of Europe and EU Conventions including their Protocols, the Europol Convention, the Schengen Convention, the Interpol Convention, and various bilateral agreements.[23] Problems observed in Italy include delays in the exchange of information, the confinement of exchange to judicial and investigative purposes and the focus of the current exchange mechanisms to repression rather than prevention.[24]

Luxembourg is a party to Interpol, Europol, EU and Council of Europe MLAs and their Protocols, Schengen and bilateral agreements (such as the 1962 Treaty on Extradition and Mutual Judicial Aid in Criminal Matters between Belgium, the Grand-Duchy of Luxembourg and the Netherlands).[25] The current system of data exchange is reported as inadequate on the basis of delays, complexity and inapplicability of all instruments equally in all Member States.[26]

New Polish legislation on criminal records has paved the way for bilateral and multilateral agreements on the exchange of data from criminal records. Such agreements had not been possible until recently, although data on crimes and investigations were transmitted abroad, provided that the receiving country respects the data protection standards required by Polish law. There are exemptions to this requirement

22 Prof. Ivana Bacik, 'Report on Ireland', IALS Study 2000/FAL/168.

23 Council of the EU, 'Evaluation Report on Mutual Legal Assistance and Urgent Requests for the Tracing and Restraint of Property, Report on Italy', 7254/00, CRIMORG 52, 22 March 2000.

24 Andrea di Nicola, 'Report on Italy', IALS Study 2000/FAL/168.

25 Council of the EU, 'Evaluation Report on Mutual Legal Assistance and Urgent Requests for the Tracing and Restraint of Property, Report on Luxembourg', 5932/99, CRIMORG 21, 15 February 1999.

26 Marc Jobert for Lex Fori, 'Report on Luxembourg', IALS Study 2000/FAL/168.

upon the discretion of the General Inspector for the Protection of Personal Data or if the transmission is indispensable in the 'public interest', necessary for the substantiation of legal claims or essential for the protection of the vital interests of the subject. Transmission can be undertaken by the at least nine different Polish authorities in possession of criminal data such as the Police, the National Security Office, the General Customs Office, the Army Gendarmerie, the Central Bureau for the Protection of the Government, and the Immigration Office. This results in lack of coordination and poor circulation of criminal data, which led the government to the recent proposal for the introduction of the National Criminal Information Centre (NCIC) designed for collecting, analysing and transferring data on current investigation and court proceedings.[27]

Portugal participates in Interpol, Europol, Schengen and all Council of Europe and EU MLA Conventions and Protocols. Reliance on Interpol for exchange of information on data from criminal records and a lack of interest of foreign authorities in information contained in Portuguese criminal records is noted.[28]

Spain collaborates with Interpol, Europol, the EU and Council of Europe MLA Conventions and is a member of the Schengen Group. Under Spanish law, exchange of information is subject to strict judicial control and this applies to most mechanisms of transmission of data to foreign authorities, although in very few urgent cases data is directly released to Interpol.[29]

In Sweden the basis of most collaboration is personal contact although Swedish legislation promotes collaboration. In fact, in October 2000 the Ministry of Justice started a New Central Authority for International Judicial Cooperation.[30]

In England and Wales the basis for cooperation with foreign, non-EU authorities is bilateral agreements for the transfer of information on organised crime and Interpol. These are subject to safeguards ensuring

[27] Prof. Michael Plachta, 'Report on Poland', IALS Study 2000/FAL/168.

[28] Council of the EU, 'Evaluation Report on Mutual Legal Assistance and Urgent Requests for the Tracing and Restraint of Property, Report on Portugal', 7251/01, CRIMORG 33, 2 April 2001; also Pedro Caeiro, 'Report on Portugal', IALS Study 2000/FAL/168.

[29] Council of the EU, 'Evaluation Report on Mutual Legal Assistance and Urgent Requests for the Tracing and Restraint of Property, Report on Spain', 5819/00, CRIMORG 16, 22 March 2000.

[30] Council of the EU, 'Evaluation Report on Mutual Legal Assistance and Urgent Requests for the Tracing and Restraint of Property, Report on Sweden', 7250/01, CRIMORG 32, 27 March 2001.

minimum standards of human rights. With relation to Member States Europol is the main exchange mechanism. Currently the practice is that individual requests are made via Europol who request information via the National Criminal Intelligence Service. It is interesting to note that exchange of information on criminal matters is handled by the Home Office, whereas details about previous convictions and intelligence information (as long as this is not requested for use in proceedings) are handled by the National Criminal Bureau of Interpol at the National Criminal Intelligence Service.[31] The UK resists the trend for a central authority as it is not a unitary state.[32]

The comparative analysis of the national reports on the current mechanisms of collaboration amongst national authorities for the transmission of data from criminal records reveals that there are a large number of instruments introducing exchange mechanisms.[33] The 1959 MLA seems to be the current main mechanism of collaboration amongst national authorities as it is signed by all Member States. At least Austria, Belgium, Cyprus, the Czech Republic, Denmark, Finland, France, Greece, Germany, Italy, Portugal, Spain and the UK make active use of this instrument. The 2000 EU MLA is gaining ground,[34] although Ireland, Italy, Luxembourg, Greece and Malta are yet to incorporate it into their national laws. Similarly, the 2001 EU MLA Protocol is not implemented by Ireland, Italy, Luxembourg, Greece, Malta, Portugal and Estonia. Interpol and Europol are equally popular mechanisms of collaboration although Europol has a narrower mandate since it relates to Member States only. Moreover, the Schengen agreement seems to actively assist exchange of information, although the UK and Ireland have applied the Schengen system only partially and selectively. Most Member States have signed bilateral agreements for the exchange of data related to criminal investigations or prior convictions, whereas Austria, Cyprus and Belgium exchange information on the basis of reciprocity.

[31] Lisa Webley, 'Report on England and Wales', IALS Study 2000/FAL/168.

[32] Select Committee on European Scrutiny, Twenty Third Report, 'Exchange of Criminal Record Information, Draft Council Framework Decision on the Organisation and Content of the Exchange of Information Extracted from Criminal Records between Member States', deposited in Parliament on 18 January 2006, p. 8.20.

[33] Council of the EU, 'Summary Reports on Mutual Legal Assistance', 9501/4/04 REV4 LIMITE CRIMORG 43 and 7917/2/05 REV2 LIMITE CRIMORG 34.

[34] H. Xanthaki, 'The Present Legal Framework of Mutual Legal Assistance within the EU' 56 (2003) *Revue Hellenique de Droit International* 53–90, at 88.

The relatively large number of existing collaboration mechanisms is certainly not a guarantee of effectiveness. On the contrary, there is ineffectiveness in the collaboration mechanism due to a number of factors.[35] Firstly, each of these mechanisms has a limited mandate since all instruments of collaboration do not apply to all national investigative and judicial authorities. Interpol, Europol and Schengen searches, which are the main tools for data retrieval, apply to police searches only. Requests of information from the courts have to be undertaken via the European Convention whereas other national authorities, which do not fall within the field of application of either of these clusters of instruments, are left unable to recover information or with the option of requesting information from the police or court officers whose authority to release the relevant data is rather doubtful. Secondly, some Member States do not participate in some mechanisms. In fact, it can even be argued that it is precisely the existence of so many instruments which renders the system of collaboration, even within the EU, rather unworkable in practice. The problem will continue to exist as long as the exchange of criminal data relies on third pillar instruments or on mere international agreements. Thirdly, reliance on international instruments suffers the unavoidable problem of enforcement. There is little that a country can do if another country delays transmission or refuses transmission altogether, even under the increased cooperation and monitoring mechanisms of Eurojust.[36] Fourthly, there is real concern about the length of time required for the completion of a transmission of data and about the complexity of the procedure. This can be attributed to the focus of the current system on detailed investigations rather than routine criminal record checks. The result of this focus on detailed investigations is discouragement of routine checks introduced by EU instruments related to, for example, public procurement; moreover, the current focus on detailed investigations instigates a 'benign neglect' of prevention and repression of organised crime within the EU. This is in direct clash with the policy of the Commission and the Council in the field of organised crime as clearly stated in Tampere and beyond.

[35] C. Stefanou and H. Xanthaki, *Oral Evidence*, House of Lords, European Union Committee, 23rd Report of Session 2003–04, *Judicial Cooperation in the EU: The Role of Eurojust*, Minutes of Evidence taken before the European Union Committee (Sub-Committee F) 16 June 2004, p. 97; also see M. Jimeno-Bulnes, 'European Judicial Cooperation in Criminal Matters' 9:5 (2003) *European Law Journal* 614–630, at 628.

[36] 'EU Agrees on Crime Data Transfer', BBC News, 6 February 2006, http://news.bbc.co.uk/go/pr/fr/-/1/hi/world/europe/5040812.stm.

Fifthly, the current system of data exchange relies on national laws and procedures which are not even standardised, let alone harmonised. National conditions of reciprocity, data protection or additional safeguards (such as the Spanish requirement for judicial control of any transmission of personal data) introduce further delays to the system, more demand for resources and additional hurdles to the rapid and complete acquisition of data crucial in combating organised crime. The incompatibility of national procedures for the exchange of data in conjunction with additional national inadequacies, such as the Polish lack of coordination amongst the national data possessing units, lead to a discerningly slow, ineffective and complicated procedure whose outcome, content and use can not be foreseen.

3. The ECR as a means of preventing organised crime

3.1. Why a central database?

Alternative routes for addressing the lack of information on prior convictions of own and foreign nationals in the EU have been suggested and explored by the Commission, such as strengthening of bilateral agreements, linking national criminal records and creating an ECR. The advantages and disadvantages of each route have also been explored, albeit solely by the Commission.[37]

Strengthening bilateral and multilateral mutual legal assistance agreements is a route of doubtful effectiveness. The attempt of the EU to address the problems of mutual legal assistance via the 2000 EU MLA Convention and its subsequent Protocol may have encouraged further cooperation between national authorities but it did not solve the problems in the area. Even if the principle of mutual recognition could become absolutely applicable in the future, the current discrepancies in national criminal laws and national criminal procedures rule out any possibility that, in the near future at least, requests for data could arrive in a prompt, complete and useable form; this would require excellent working knowledge of the laws and procedures of the requesting Member State by the authorities of the requested Member State and in an EU of twenty-seven with hundreds of possible bilateral combinations it would require a minor miracle. Moreover, in the current state of EU

[37] Commission of the EC, 'White Paper on Exchanges of Information on Convictions and the Effect of such Convictions in the EU', COM(2005) 10 final, 25 January 2005, p. 6.

law, namely without the Constitutional Treaty which abolishes the three pillars, a new instrument of mutual legal assistance would have to be placed in the third pillar. In other words, it would face the common problem of non-implementation, exactly like the 2000 EU MLA Convention and its Protocol, it would be outside the competence of the European Court of Justice (ECJ) and it would be plagued by doubtful enforceability.

Linking the national criminal records of Member States is a solution that has already been tested to a degree, albeit without much success. The Commission viewed its proposal for an index of convictions as a first stage approach to be followed soon by linkage of national criminal records. The index of convictions has been received negatively by national delegations of Member States to such a degree that the Commission has, at least until now, shelved its relevant proposals. The concept of creating a new database merely with names of persons convicted and the country where conviction was imposed seemed rather disproportionate to the service that the database would offer to national authorities, namely the quick and easy reference to the Member States from which a criminal record should be requested via legal assistance mechanisms. Even the second and last stage of the Commission's preferred route has now been tested. Twelve member states of the EU have already linked their national criminal records. Belgium, the Czech Republic, France, Germany and Spain have already linked their national criminal records. There are advantages to this set up, of course, as access to foreign criminal records is immediate, literally at the tips of the national officer's fingers. However, the quality of information provided can be problematic.[38] Firstly, the data is in a foreign language and the judge or investigator retrieving the data must be able to understand the language of the host database. In a group of four participating counties with three mainstream EU languages, this may not be too burdensome; however, in a group of more than twenty languages and three alphabets (Latin, Greek and Cyrillic), the language of the database will, more often than not, be unfamiliar to the user. Secondly, the data are entered in the terminology of the host legal system; for example, manslaughter in the UK archive would be a term that could either be unusable in the civil law tradition

[38] Even supporters of this solution identify problems of accuracy in the system: J. Grijpink, 'Criminal Records in the European Union, the Challenge of Large-scale Information Exchange' 14 (2006) *European Journal of Crime, Criminal Law and Criminal Justice* 1–15.

or, even worse, would have to be unilaterally and arbitrarily given a national equivalent by the user of the database. Thirdly, access to the data and use cannot be controlled as each national legal order provides for the protection of personal data in a separate manner. A counter-argument at this point could be that the principle of mutual trust entails confidence in the safeguards of quality and the prevalence of the rule of law in other Member States. However, it would be naïve to believe that an environment full of idiosyncrasy in national criminal laws and procedures would allow religious adherence to the procedure required for the admissibility of evidence in criminal trials. At a time when even the definition of judicial authority or criminal proceedings is questionable, access and use cannot be left to the discretion of national officers or to their appreciation of foreign procedures.

The ECR addresses all these problems effectively. A centralised database hosted by an EU institution guarantees accuracy of the system, equivalence of information, equal access to all EU languages, strict and uniformly agreed criteria for access and use. In other words, the ECR is the only route that allows immediate legitimate access to usable data. However, perfection comes at a price. Strict requirements of legitimacy, competence and data protection need to be agreed upon and put into place if the ECR is to be received by the Member States' and the EU's legal order.

3.2. The host: Europol or Eurojust?

It would be disproportionate to place the ECR with a new agency or body created for this purpose. The added value of that new agency would be doubtful, especially since many agencies and bodies are competing for functions in the area of EU criminal law. The European Anti-fraud Office (OLAF), Europol and Eurojust could all host the ECR in theory. In practice, however, the competence of OLAF as an investigation agency dealing exclusively with fraud against the financial interests of the European Communities renders it a bad choice. Eurojust and Europol, however, seem equally appealing.

The first criterion for the selection of the appropriate host for the ECR relates to the nature of the body as a police or judicial authority. The question, therefore, is whether exchange of data from criminal records falls within the area of police or judicial cooperation in criminal matters. It is interesting to note that the Council discussed the proposed Framework Decision on the Registry for Convictions (namely the

Commission's initiative for the index of convictions) at the Council Working Group Justice and Home Affairs, Judicial Cooperation in Criminal Matters. However, the comparative analysis of mutual assistance at the national level in the first part of this chapter revealed a divide between countries that undertook exchange of data from criminal records through police or judicial channels. In fact, the divide can be traced back to the nature of national authorities that maintain the national criminal records: in countries where police authorities maintain national criminal records, exchange takes place under police cooperation, whereas in countries where judicial authorities maintain criminal records, it is the latter that exchange the relevant data. On this basis, placing the ECR with Europol[39] or Eurojust[40] could be equally acceptable, at least prima facie.

In the course of the comparative analysis of national laws, however, one cannot fail to notice that a large cluster of Member States consider the judicial nature of the authority holding and transferring data from criminal records as a condition sine qua non for the legality and admissibility of such data before their national courts. This applies to Belgium, the Czech Republic, France, Germany, Greece, Hungary, Ireland, Italy, Portugal and Spain. Eurojust is a quasi-judicial authority and on the basis of this first criterion Eurojust would be preferable as the host of the ECR;[41] indeed more so since Eurojust is a forum of prosecutors and judges[42] that can successfully handle data exchange for the purposes of investigations and prosecutions as well as for the purposes of criminal proceedings,[43] always with the added guarantees of legitimacy enjoyed by quasi-judicial authorities.

[39] Convention based on Article K.3 of the Treaty on European Union, on the establishment of European Police Office (Europol Convention), OJ C 316, 27 November 1995.

[40] Council Decision 2002/187/JHA of 28 February 2002 setting up Eurojust with a view to reinforcing the fight against serious crime, OJ L 63, 6 March 2002, p. 1; also see Council Decision 2003/659/JHA of 18 June 2003 amending Decision 2002/187/JHA setting up Eurojust with a view to reinforcing the fight against serious crime, OJ L 245/44, 29 September 2003.

[41] J. Sheptycki, 'Patrolling the New European (In)security Field; Organizational Dilemmas and Operational Solutions for Policing the Internal Borders of Europe' 9 (2001) *European Journal of Crime, Criminal Law and Criminal Justice* 144–158, at 154.

[42] Point 46, conclusions of the Tampere European Council of 15 and 16 October 1999.

[43] M. den Boer and P. Doelle, *Controlling Organised Crime: Organisational Changes in the Law Enforcement and Prosecution Services of the EU Member States* (Maastricht: EIPA, 2000), p. 17.

The second criterion for a suitable host refers to the structure for appeals against actions or omissions of the ECR, not least from the subjects themselves. The necessity of a right to appeal arises directly from the Charter of Fundamental Rights.[44] Europol is supervised by its Management Board, composed of one representative from each Member State and reporting directly to the Council.[45] Some additional control is exercised by the European Parliament (EP) through regular reports under Article 34 of the Europol Convention. These accountability mechanisms cannot double as safeguards for the personal data of EU citizens. However, the right to appeal against decisions of Europol related to access to data kept by the agency is foreseen in Article 19 of the Europol Convention which assigns the task of hearing such appeals to the Europol Joint Supervisory Body (JSB).[46] Under Article 24 of the Europol Convention the JSB guarantees legitimacy in the maintenance of data concerning EU citizens and kept by Europol. Thus, Europol already has in place a mechanism for appeals to be heard by an independent JSB.[47] Similarly, Eurojust's handling of personal data is supervised by an independent committee of experts known as the Eurojust JSB.[48] Thus, Eurojust possesses a similar body hearing appeals as Europol, although no appeals have been brought before the Eurojust JSB so far.[49] In fact, even access to documents for the public is regulated in a similar manner within both agencies, as their open policy is a direct implementation of the combination of Article 1 TEU, which states that decisions within the EU are taken as openly as possible, and Article 255 EC, which sets out the right of access to documents of EU institutions.[50] Once again, prima facie both agencies meet the second criterion. However, Eurojust presents numerous advantages as a host of the ECR based on its current structures of appeal against its actions or omissions. Eurojust is an independent body of a judicial nature,[51] which is often viewed as the

[44] OJ C 364, 18 December 2000. [45] Art. 28, Europol Convention.

[46] Also, Arts. 11–28 of the JSB Rules of Procedure.

[47] Until the end of 2006 only five appeals have been received; also, *Europol JSB Activity Report 2002–2004* reporting an increase in the number of appeals, p. 28.

[48] Point 10 of the Preamble and Art. 23 of Eurojust Decision.

[49] Eurojust JSB Activity Report 2004, p. 4.

[50] Council Decision of the of 20 December 1993 on public access to Council Documents, 93/731/EC; also Decision of the College of Eurojust to adopt rules regarding public access to Eurojust documents, 13 July 2004.

[51] Council Decision of 28 February 2002 setting up Eurojust with a view to reinforcing the fight against serious crime, OJ L 63, 6 March 2002.

judicial counterpart of Europol.[52] Indeed, the capacity of Eurojust to offer accurate and prompt legal advice and assistance from the point of view of national and EU law constitutes an excellent basis for being the host of the ECR. Eurojust has the capacity to interpret national criminal records, to evaluate equivalence between criminal offences and sentences and to ensure that entries to national criminal records correspond to those of the ECR. In view of the diversity of crimes, penalties and erasure periods in the legal systems of the Member States, Eurojust's capacity and know-how is an ideal guarantee of legitimacy and capacity. Moreover, Eurojust has the capacity to evaluate requests for information from the ECR, thus ensuring that access is only allowed when so provided for by EU and national laws. Eurojust would be able to deal with concerns from subject and national authorities related to ECR data. Admittedly, the advantage of Eurojust over Europol in its current capacity to consider appeals from EU citizens derives from the capacity and know-how of its personnel and its experience as a College, rather than strictly the set-up for appeals. However, it is exactly this capacity and experience that renders appeals within Eurojust a fairer, learned and, therefore, more effective protective procedure for EU citizens. Therefore, on the basis of the second criterion of this analysis, Eurojust is also a preferred host for the ECR.

The third criterion refers to data protection for citizens whose personal data will be included in the ECR. In July 2001 when Eurojust responded to the study questionnaire by the Institute of Advanced Legal Studies' (IALS) on the ECR it noted that, as things stood then, Eurojust could not keep centralised databases.[53] However, things have changed since then. Although Regulation 45/2001[54] does not apply to activities and institutions of the third pillar, the supervision of the new European Data Protection Officer over activities and bodies processing personal data at the EU level has led Europol and Eurojust to the development of similar data protection structures.[55] Nevertheless, the

[52] Communication from the Commission on the Establishment of Eurojust, COM (2000) 746 final, 22 November 2000.

[53] The response was by Martin Wasmeier – of Eurojust at that time.

[54] Regulation (EC) No 45/2001 of the European Parliament and of the Council of 18 December 2000 on the protection of individuals with regard to the processing of personal data by the Community institutions and bodies and on the free movement of such data, OJ L8, 12 January 2001 at 1.

[55] P. J. Hustinx, 'Data Protection in the European Union' (2005) *Privacy & Informatie* 62–65, at 64.

diverse data protection instruments applicable to the first and third pillar and the fragmentation in the provisions of data protection applicable to each agency of the third pillar have led to calls for the final unification in the level of data protection within the EU.[56] Europol allows all competent national authorities and individual citizens access to personal files under the provisions of the Europol Convention.[57] Its Article 24 introduces Europol's JSB as an independent body with two data protection experts from each Member State whose task is to ensure that the rights of individuals are not violated by the storage, processing and use of personal data.[58] At the national level this task is assigned to National Supervisory Bodies in the Member States. Moreover, individuals request and appeal against their personal files on the basis of inaccuracy. Furthermore, third states and third bodies receive data from Europol under strict express provisions of the Europol Convention and several complimentary Council decisions.[59] The level of data protection offered by Europol is considered adequate in principle, but there is scope for improvement[60] via compliance supervision equivalent to that of the first pillar plus a provision amending Article 24(6) of the Europol Convention and requiring the JSB to prepare and present an annual activity report before the competent committee of the EP.[61] Similar provisions have been introduced with reference to Eurojust. However,

[56] Conference of European Data Protection Authorities, 'Opinion on the Proposal for a Council Framework Decision on the Protection of Personal Data Processed in the Framework of Police and Judicial Cooperation in Criminal Matters', Brussels, 24 January 2006.

[57] Europol, 'Annual Report 2005', p. 20.

[58] Europol JSB, 'The Second Activity Report of the Europol JSB', November 2002–October 2004, p. 10.

[59] Council Act of 12 March 1999 adopting the rules governing the transmission of personal data by Europol to third states and third bodies, OJ C88, 30 March 1999 at 1; Council Act of 3 November 1998 laying down rules governing Europol's external relations with third states and non-EU related bodies, OJ 26, 30 January 1999 at 19; Council Act of 3 November 19998 adopting rules on the confidentiality of Europol information, OJ C26, 30 January 1999 at 10; Council Act of 3 November 1998 adopting rules applicable to Europol analysis files, OJ C26 at 1; also, Act of the Management Board of Europol of 15 October 1998 laying down rules governing Europol's external relations with EU related bodies, OJ C26, 30 January 1999, at 89.

[60] House of Lords, Fifth Report 'Europol's Role in Fighting Crime', 28 January 2003.

[61] J. Apap for the European Parliament, 'Session 2: What Future for Europol? Increasing Europol's Accountability and Improving Europol's Operational Capacity', Brussels, 7 September 2006, p. 5; also, Council of the EU, 'Council and Commission Action Plan Implementing the Hague Programme on Strengthening Freedom, Security and Justice in the EU', JAI 184, 9246/1/05, 30 May 2005, p. 19.

there are obvious advantages to the choice of Eurojust as the host of the ECR. First, Article 15 of its constituting Decision specifies the kind of data that Eurojust is authorised to keep. The data envisaged in this Article are exactly those included in a national criminal record. In other words, Eurojust has already an express authorisation to maintain data for the identification and criminal past of EU citizens. Article 17 of the same Decision introduces a Data Protection Officer who supervises access and use of the relevant data: this officer has long experience of lawful treatment of personal data of EU citizens. Other Articles of the Eurojust Decision specify in detail issues of deletion and correction of data, the process of appeals against such data and access of the subjects, other competent national and EU authorities, and indeed third-country authorities' access to such data. Second, Eurojust's JSB has proceeded to the adoption of new rules of procedure that give emphasis to issues related to data protection and specify the role of the JSB in disputes and appeals.[62] Third, Eurojust has recently adopted new rules of procedure on the processing and protection of personal data at Eurojust.[63] The new rules regulate data protection with specific reference to electronic databases and create a solid framework of access and use under the principles of lawfulness, fairness, necessity and proportionality and on supervision for a Data Protection Officer. Issues such as access, use, erasure and appeals are clearly introduced, thus facilitating uniformity of regulation irrespective of national provisions.[64] It is conceivable, therefore, that the discrepancies in national laws on use, access and erasure from national criminal records could be unified for the purposes of the ECR under the relevant provisions applicable to Eurojust. The robust[65] data protection provisions and existing structures in Eurojust render the agency an ideal host for the ECR.

It seems, therefore, that Eurojust is the best option as a host of the ECR. Its nature as a judicial agency, its procedures of appeal against data held by the agency and its framework for data protection render Eurojust now more than ever a body which is ready to take over the task of a centralised database for convictions. After all, Europol was always considered to have

[62] Act of the JSB of Eurojust of 2 March 2004 laying down its rules of procedure, OJ C 86, 6 March 2004, at 1.

[63] Rules of procedure on the processing and protection of personal data at Eurojust (Text adopted unanimously by the college of Eurojust during the meeting of 21 October 2004 and approved by the Council on 24 February 2005), OJ C 68, 19 March 2005, at 1.

[64] Eurojust JSB Activity Report 2004, p. 5.

[65] Eurojust Annual Report 2005, p. 79.

a supporting and not an independent executive role,[66] mainly limited to crime analysis.[67] However, a number of Member States have failed or omitted to implement the Eurojust Decision,[68] even though the transposition date was set for 6 September 2003. Greece and Luxembourg have still to declare transposition of the Decision, while in Cyprus and Spain transposition took place in late 2006. In its last Annual Report Eurojust identifies Cyprus, Greece and Spain as Member States where transposition has not taken place, whereas in a very recent implementation report the Council reports Greece and Latvia as non-compliant Member States.[69] Clearly there is a discrepancy concerning the Member States that have not transposed the Eurojust Decision. But, leaving this discrepancy aside, the lack of transposition of the Eurojust Decision by some Member States can only be viewed as a danger to the effectiveness of Eurojust as a possible host for the ECR. It is hoped that the matter will be resolved in the future when transposition of the Decision will finally take place, although the future might provide an even more solid structure for the ECR, namely the possibility of Eurojust as a host under the supervision of the European Public Prosecutor (EPP) in a *Corpus Juris* model.[70]

3.3. *Which crimes?*

The choice of host for the ECR has wider implications for the database itself. The competence of Eurojust, and indeed Europol, is limited to specific types of crimes focusing mainly on transnational and organised crime. Thus, under Article 4 of the Eurojust Decision, Eurojust covers all crimes falling within the competence of Europol, plus computer crime,

[66] P. Zanders, 'De Europese Politie-eenheid: Europol' in *Handboek Politiediensten* (The Hague: Kluwer, 1999), pp. 103–104.

[67] W. Bruggeman, 'Policing in Europe: A New Wave?' in M. Den Boer (ed.), *The Implementation of Schengen* (Maastricht, EIPA, 1997), pp. 111–128, at 112.

[68] In her oral evidence to the House of Lords Enquiry Haberl-Schwarz considers this an example of taking political decisions without the willingness to give effect to them; see Questions 132 and 143 in House of Lords European Union Committee, 23rd Report of Session 2003–2004, 'Judicial Cooperation in the EU: The role of Eurojust' Report with Evidence, HL Paper 138, (UK: The Stationery Office, 2004), p. 49.

[69] See 2005 Eurojust Annual Report, p. 15; also see Council of the EU, 'Adendum to the I item note – Implementation of the Strategy and Action Plan to Combat Terrorism', Document No. 15266/06 ADD1 REV1, 24 November 2006, p. 5.

[70] The EPP is already considered as an additional element of the judicial guarantee of investigations conducted by EU institutions; Green Paper on criminal law protection of the financial interests of the Community and the establishment of a European Prosecutor, COM (2001) 715 final, p. 24.

fraud, corruption, crimes affecting the financial interests of the EC, money laundering, environmental crime, participation in a criminal organisation, and any other offences committed together with such crimes. Under Article 2 of the Europol Convention, Europol is competent to deal with money laundering and any related offences, including crimes committed in order to procure means for acts falling within the sphere of Europol, crimes committed to facilitate or execute such acts and crimes committed to ensure the immunity of such acts. Europol also deals with illicit drug trafficking, illicit immigration networks, terrorism, forgery of money, trafficking in human beings and child pornography and illicit vehicle trafficking.

It is interesting to note that the placement of the ECR with existing agencies in the sphere of EU criminal law signifies an inevitable delimitation of the nature of crimes that can be included in this database. Since the creation of a new agency with the mandate to host the ECR does not offer added value, such a proposal would be considered to clash with the principles of proportionality and, possibly, subsidiarity. It seems that the choice of the ECR over the linking of existing national criminal records carries with it thoughts and ambitions on the variety and breadth of crimes that can be included in the proposal. The Commission, in its wisdom, must have considered that the ECR, albeit ambitious and effective, would restrict its competence to transnational and organised crimes. It is possibly with this thought in mind that the more extensive solution of the linkage of national criminal records has been put forward to the Member States. In fact, it is possible that the same thought has prevented Member States from pursuing the network of national criminal records so far. In fact, one has to wonder whether networking national criminal records is indeed a proportionate solution and whether subsidiarity has been observed in this case. As the aim of the proposal is to address the lack of adequate and effective communication between national authorities in their combat against transnational and organised crime, surely the solution sought should refer to such types of crime only. Throwing all types of crimes into the equation requires an unjustified extension of the EU's competence in EU criminal law. After all, national criminal records address national crimes adequately and effectively.

With reference to the choice between Eurojust and Europol, Eurojust presents yet another advantage as the host of the ECR: its competence is wider than that of Europol and therefore more crimes, always transnational and organised, can be covered by the database.

Does that make Eurojust a short-term solution? Could it be that in an attempt to ensure compliance with the current restrictions in the competence of Eurojust, and EU criminal law in general, the span of crimes in the ECR is also constricted even in a possible broadening of this field of law in future? The answer to this legitimate question, which affects the evaluation of the adequacy of a legislative solution putting forward an ECR, lies with the core of intergovernmentalism in the third pillar. Member States can always agree to include further crimes in the ECR, and indeed in the competences of Eurojust, provided that these crimes meet the tests of proportionality, necessity and subsidiarity, which are crucial tests of legitimacy in any legislative proposal at the EU level.

3.4. *Reception from national laws*

The last point of this analysis refers to the type of instrument with which the ECR can be introduced and under which conditions. Although this is a third pillar area, it is suggested that third pillar instruments may not suffice for the introduction of an effective weapon against organised crime. The common area of justice established de jure and de facto through the increasing volume and depth of free movement within the EU demands a unified and harmonised approach against organised crime applicable throughout the EU and the accession countries.[71] Further fragmentation of criminal law could not possibly serve this purpose. A Framework Decision is the best vehicle for the introduction of the ECR, at least at the EU level. Of course in the post-Reform Treaty era, it is doubtful whether Framework Decisions will continue to be used or whether the collapse of the pillars will require the use of a Directive even in the area of EU criminal law. As this point is yet to be clarified by reference to a legal text, the proposal will remain with a Framework Decision as an accurate and realistic solution at the current state of affairs.

The question is whether this Framework Decision could be received by the national laws of the Member States. This question was discussed

[71] C. Stefanou and H. Xanthaki 'Memorandum by Dr Constantin Stefanou and Dr Helen Xanthaki', House of Lords, European Union Committee, 23rd Report of Session 2003–04, *Judicial Cooperation in the EU: The Role of Eurojust*, Minutes of Evidence taken before the European Union Committee (Sub-Committee F) 16 June 2004, pp. 94–95; also W. Schomburg, 'Are We on the Road to a European Law-enforcement Area? International Cooperation in Criminal Matters. What Place for Justice?' 8 (2000) *European Journal of Crime, Criminal Law and Criminal Justice* 51–60.

in detail in the IALS study on the creation of an ECR. In Austria the Decision would not be anti-constitutional; in fact, it would address the necessity for strict statutory legislative introduction of measures tackling fundamental and human rights issues. However, certain conditions must be met for the smooth reception of the ECR: determination of crimes to be included; inclusion of convictions for criminal offences reached under procedures conforming with the rules of EU and international human rights rules only; determination of strict regulation for access to the ECR; delimitation of erasure periods; right of access of the subject to their own entry; and introduction of an appeals procedure. In Belgium the Framework Decision should determine the quality of criminal data and the right to correction; the duration of data maintenance, access details, right of access for the subject; data protection scheme; data access authorisations on the basis of the legitimacy of the request; control of the operation by an independent authority with periodic assessments. In Cyprus the Decision would be received without problems. In view of the Danish scepticism against further EU integration in the third pillar, the ECR seems an unpopular choice – although the need for further measures in the area of exchange of information from national criminal records is acknowledged. In France the Framework Decision on the ECR would be acceptable but only under strict conditions: independent judicial control over the whole operation; limited access to the data; efficient correction procedures; access of subjects to their entries. In Germany no legal objections to the ECR are reported, as long as the problems of accountability, legitimacy and supervision of the host institution are addressed adequately. In Greece reception can be smooth provided that the following conditions are met: strict determination of crimes to be included in the ECR; clear description of authorities with access to the data; indirect access (via the subject) must be excluded at least in the initial phase; effective guarantees for the protection of sensitive personal data via the introduction of what it describes as a 'buffer zone' between judiciary and police.

In Hungary a Framework Decision, rather than any other form of EU legislative instrument, would facilitate the introduction of the ECR in the legal system as it would allow a degree of flexibility to the national laws of the Member States, thus easing the incorporation of the new database to the existing structure of national criminal records. In Ireland the Decision could be accepted without the need for a referendum. In Italy reception of the ECR could be smooth, provided that the Framework Decision determines: the manner of transmission from national authorities to the host institution; the authority and framework for data protection; definition of the use of the data; access to the database. Judicial and administrative authorities should be awarded direct access to the Record, whereas banks and professional associations should have indirect access, namely access via the subject. Luxembourg could receive the ECR, as long as the right to privacy of Article 8 ECHR is respected and access is limited to specific competent authorities. Poland could receive the ECR, although the issue of cost would be of considerable concern for the Polish government. In Portugal the ECR could be received provided that it is introduced via an instrument of the third pillar, preferably a Council Convention. Slovenia would require a clear determination of contents and manner of transmission. In Spain it is doubtful that any database with personal data assigned to a non-judicial body and serving any purpose other than the judiciary could be implemented. The Spanish Office for International Judicial Cooperation of the Ministry of Justice expressed the view that the ECR 'should reinforce the mechanisms that secure the reserved character of the information to be kept and also the preservation of privacy rights of those affected'. Nevertheless, the Decision must comply with the following conditions: determination of the crimes to be included; delimitation of authorities with access to it; introduction of the mechanisms of transmission; determination of its use; introduction of erasure periods. In Sweden the Decision would be acceptable. In the UK strict conditions must be met before the ECR could be received: consistent data protection standards; a common legal basis for databases of this nature; effective remedies for individuals; lawfulness of data (accurate data); right of subjects to access to the data; independent supervision of the operation and regular assessments; judicial control of the operation.

Clearly very few Member States seem to have radical problems with the reception of the ECR in their national legal orders. In fact, Austria, Cyprus, France, Germany, Greece, Ireland, Italy, Luxembourg, Poland, Slovenia, Spain, Sweden and the UK could receive a Framework Decision introducing the ECR without major legal problems, at least from the technical point of view of the transposition of this form of EU legislative text. A group of Member States prefer another type of third pillar instrument, such as a Council Convention. Despite the evidently easier reception of a Council Convention by Member States, the choice of this type of instrument for the introduction of the ECR carries dangers of inadequacy and ineffectiveness. The lack of strict control mechanisms over the implementation of a Convention and the contribution of this measure to the further fragmentation of EU criminal law are two additional factors for the rejection of this suggestion. However, the proposal of a Framework Decision is attractive. It allows the EU to introduce detailed legally binding provisions while at the same time leaving grounds for flexibility as a means of smooth reception of the ECR to the diverse national legal orders of the Member States.

Of course, preference to a Framework Decision is put forward under the current context of sources of EU law. The collapse of the pillar structure in the forthcoming Reform Treaty seems to lead to the abolition of Framework Decisions as a form of EU instruments. Should a unified EU law finally become a reality, the most appropriate form of instrument for the establishment of the ECR would be a Directive. The choice is based on the many similarities in the nature and characteristics of Directives with Framework Decisions.

Nevertheless, national legal orders set six sets of strict conditions for the reception of the ECR from a substantive point of view. First, the Framework Decision must determine with clarity and accuracy the crimes which will fall within the field of application of the Framework Decision. This condition is put forward by the Austrian, Belgian, Greek, Slovenian, Spanish and UK experts that participated in the relevant IALS study. The minimal approximation of crimes and offences poses dangerous problems in the determination of equivalent offences within the legal orders of Member States. For this reason, the Framework Decision should refer to crimes with definitions that are not unduly at variance with or remote from those in national legal orders. It is suggested that the crimes within the competence of Eurojust could be utilised for this purpose.

Second, convictions for crimes in the ECR must have been reached under the ECHR and Article 8 in particular, as this is an express condition for Austria, Germany, Greece, Ireland, Italy, Luxembourg, Spain and the UK. Of course compliance with the Charter of Fundamental Rights is also necessary.

Third, access to the data of the ECR must be restricted, a condition necessary for the Austrian, Belgian, French, German, Greek, Italian, Luxembourg, Spanish and UK national laws. As the purpose of the ECR is to combat organised crime, its use must be limited to authorities and persons whose 'knowledge/information' of the ECR is essential for the performance of their task in the fight against transnational and organised crime. Thus, at the national level only judicial and prosecution authorities are entitled to access. Further restricted levels of access may be offered to police authorities, tendering authorities, some professional associations (e.g. lawyers, notaries, accountants) and banking institutions for employees whose duties touch upon the prevention of organised crime as introduced by money laundering legislation. In view of the diversity of such authorities and associations, a mechanism for the authorisation of the transmission of data to such bodies must be introduced – this is a necessity according to Belgian, German and Italian legislation. Decisions on access requests must be issued within short deadlines in order to avoid unnecessary delays. Access to the data must also be allowed to subjects for their own records – as requested by Austrian, Belgian, French, German, Italian and UK legislation. This would pave the way for effective protection of ECR data as required by the 1995 Data Protection Directive as well as EU and international data protection standards. For the same reason the Italian model of indirect access to the data for tendering authorities, professional associations and banks could be effective and proportionate. At the EU level access must be awarded to Europol, OLAF, the European Public Prosecutor (EPP) and the European Judicial Network. Access upon authorisation and for specific purposes only (such as employment at specific posts within the institutions or participation in public procurement) must be awarded to all EU institutions, although it would be preferable to introduce indirect access though the subject him/herself.

Fourth, there must be judicial control over the host of the ECR. Control of the operations by an independent judicial authority, such as the EPP or Eurojust's JSB, would enshrine data protection safeguards to the ECR. Periodic assessments of the work of the host institution by the supervisory independent judicial body and the EP would enhance accountability and transparency.

Fifth, guarantees of quality and accuracy are necessary requirements for the reception of the ECR by Austrian, French, Spanish and UK law. A mechanism for the correction of ECR data could take the form of a body competent to decide on allegations of error. The EPP could be an ideal body for this purpose as the EPP's access to national criminal records and their data could be possible through the EPP's national officers, whose information would be up to date by the very nature of the EPP's role and tasks. In the meantime, however, Eurojust's JSB is equally suitable for this purpose, as its officers have access to the data in national criminal records and the capacity to control equivalence between entries in the national records and the ECR.

Part of the quality of data in the ECR refers to the sixth condition put forward by Austrian, Belgium, Spain and the UK, namely the introduction of erasure periods for the ECR. One option would be to erase convictions for the ECR as soon as national erasure takes place. However, this would maintain the existing inequality amongst EU citizens and their de facto discrimination on the basis of their nationality. It would also result to further fragmentation of EU criminal law. The second, and preferable, option would be to observe erasure periods introduced by data protection legislation on Eurojust: common erasure periods would contribute to harmonisation of the legal position of erasure in crimes where approximation has been achieved via existing EU laws.

4. Conclusions

Assessment of any legislative measure at the EU level is undertaken on the basis of the five Sutherland criteria:[72] need for action, choice of the most effective course of action, proportionality of the measure, consistency with existing measures, and wider consultation of the circles concerned during the preparatory stages.[73] The ECR is needed to address the increasing problem of transnational and organised crime. The ECR is effective as it will allow competent national authorities and EU institutions immediate access to accurate information on prior convictions imposed by all Member States. The ECR is a proportionate form of action as it involves measures covering transnational crimes only and conditions under which citizens' privacy is protected. Consistency with existing measures is achievable with the ECR which would strengthen data exchange legislation at the international and EU levels. Wider consultation of citizens and Member States can be achieved provided that the Commission continues the debate, public

[72] 'The Internal Market after 1992: Meeting the Challenge', Report to the EEC Commission by the High Level Group on the operation of the internal market, SEC(92) 2044; also Supplement to European Report No. 1808 of 31 October 1992; Commission Communication to the Council and the EP, 'Follow-up of the Sutherland Report', COM(93) 361 final and SEC(92) 2227 fin; Opinion of the Economic and Social Committee of 5 May 1993 'On the Commission Communication on the Operation of the Community's Internal Market after 1992: Follow-up to the Sutherland Report', OJ C 201/59, 26 July 1993; Communication from the Commission, 'Follow-up to the Sutherland Report: Legislative Consolidation to Enhance the Transparency of Community Law in the Area of the Internal Market', 16 December 1993, COM(93) 361 final; Communication from the Commission to the Council, the EP and the ESC 'On the Handling of Urgent Situations in the Context of Implementation of Community Rules: Follow-up to the Sutherland Report', COM(93) 430 final.

[73] H. Xanthaki, 'The Problem of Quality in EU Legislation: What on Earth is Really Wrong?' 38 (2001) *Common Market Law Review* 651–676.

and governmental, drawing attention to competence delimitation, increased data protection and judicial authorisation for the ECR.

Moreover, the new legislative proposal must comply with the equally important principles of subsidiarity, proportionality, adequacy, synergy and adaptability. These are general principles of EC law, which form part of the *acquis* and touch upon all aspects of EU law and policy.[74] The principle of subsidiarity dictates that the highest level of action is justifiable only when lower levels of legislative action are inefficient for the achievement of the goal.[75] The ECR complies with legal subsidiarity as it serves an economy of approaches:[76] it is introduced by a legislative measure in a situation where other forms of regulation would be insufficient. The ECR complies with legislative subsidiarity as it serves an economy of measures: it is introduced via a Framework Decision since lesser forms of measures would be inefficient. Legal proportionality supplements subsidiarity in ensuring correspondence between the choice to legislate and the aim that the proposed legal instrument aims to achieve, whereas legislative proportionality demands that the choice of form of the measure reflects its purpose.[77] The purpose of the ECR is proportionate both with a legislative measure and indeed a Framework Decision, or under a future unified EU law a Directive, for its introduction. The ECR is legally adequate since a legally binding text can achieve common standards in the data on prior convictions available to national authorities. The ECR is also legislatively adequate since a Framework Decision, or a Directive in the post-Reform Treaty era, is capable of achieving common standards, because it imposes minimum levels of data from all Member States and allows national legal orders to receive these standards in a manner that respects the intricacies of national doctrine and practice. The ECR serves synergy, as it promotes coherence and interrelated functioning of diverse fields of law within the national

[74] J. A. Usher, 'The Reception of General Principles of Community Law in the United Kingdom', 16 (2005) *European Business Law Review* 489–510, at 495.

[75] European Commission, Report from the Commission 'Better Lawmaking 2004' pursuant to Article 9 of the Protocol on the Application of the Principles of Subsidiarity and Proportionality (12th report), COM (2005) 98 final and SEC (2005) 364, 21 March 2005, p. 2; also G. Davies, 'Subsidiarity: The Wrong Idea, in the Wrong Place, at the Wrong Time', 43 (2006) *Common Market Law Review* 63–84, at 67.

[76] Ibid., note 18, at 76.

[77] J. Snell, 'True Proportionality', 11 (2000) *European Business Law Review* 50–57 at 50; also G. De Burca, 'The Principle of Proportionality and its Application in EC Law', 13 (1993) *Yearbook of European Law* at 105; J. Jans, 'Proportionality Revisited', 27 (2000) *Legal Issues of European Integration* 239–265.

legal systems of the Member States and a holistic approach of the law on the combat against transnational and organised crime. The ECR respects the principle of adaptability as it promotes flexibility in the choice of the appropriate instrument.[78]

This analysis has demonstrated the clear advantages of the ECR over its competing scenario and has identified the conditions of legitimacy, proportionality and acceptability of the ECR under current EU laws. Moreover, this chapter has presented the substantive and procedural advantages of this legislative solution. However, acceptability at the EU level is only the first step in the creation of the new database. The crucial, so far missing, link is the reception of the ECR by the national legal orders of Member States. This requires further elaboration which will be carried out in later sections of this book, in the form of a detailed presentation of transposition issues under the national legal orders of Member States serving as representative case studies.

[78] H. Xanthaki, 'Quality and Transposition of EU Legislation: A Tool for Accession and Membership to the EU' 4 (2006) *European Journal of Law Reform* 89–110, at 99.

3

The European Criminal Record: Political parameters

CONSTANTIN STEFANOU

1. Introduction

The idea behind the creation of a European Criminal Record was first put forward to the Commission in the political reviser's Report of a Falcone Study on the use of national criminal records, completed in 2000.[1] It was noted in that Report that the existing problems in judicial and enforcement agencies' cooperation across the EU made the use of national criminal records as a means of combating organised crime rather problematic. It was pointed out that practical problems hindered the speed, access and effectiveness of existing methods of cooperation and the creation and use of an ECR was the way forward for the effective combating of organised crime.

Of course, the idea of using databases as a means of combating crime is not new.[2] Practically all enforcement agencies around the world use 'files' (in paper or digital form) on crimes, suspects and methods (*modus operandi*) in an attempt to prevent crime or prosecute criminals. In fact, in recent years digital databases such as the Schengen Information System[3] (SIS) have become the first line of defence against transnational organised crime and plans to update and develop further the system into

[1] FALCONE PROJECT JHA/1999/FAL/197, 'The Use of Criminal Records as a Means of Preventing Organised Crime in the Areas of Money Laundering and Public Procurement: The Need for Europe-wide Collaboration'. The study was also published as an edited book, see: C. Stefanou and H. Xanthaki (eds.), *Financial Crime in the EU: Criminal Records as Effective Tools or Missed Opportunities?* (The Hague, Kluwer Law International, 2005).

[2] See C. Stefanou, 'Organised Crime and the Use of EU-wide Databases', in I. Bantekas and G. Keramidas (eds.), *International and European Financial Law* (LexisNexis Butterworths, 2006), pp. 215–218.

[3] See 'The Schengen Acquis as referred to in Article 1(2) of Council Decision 1999/435/EC of 20 May 1999', OJ L 239, 22/09/2000.

a SIS II are on the way.[4] What makes the proposal for an ECR different is the idea of an EU-wide dedicated database which addresses the problem directly: in other words, a dedicated database which contains information extracted from national criminal records on selected crimes. As already noted in Chapter 1, Mutual Legal Assistance (MLA) has some severe limitations. In this sense the advantages resulting from the creation of a dedicated digital database containing information extracted from national criminal records seem to be self-evident. From the point of view of databases there is heterogeneity in the different national systems for recording data on crimes and criminal activities. In some Member States there are up to three types of such databases (criminal records) at the local, regional and national levels – not necessarily in digital format – while other Member States only have local databases. Moreover, national digital databases are not always compatible and, therefore, migration of data is not always possible. Clearly attempts to coordinate/interlink national databases or cooperation between groups of Member States, such as the Prüm Treaty[5] carries with it the well-known and understood problems of MLA. In the case of the Prüm Treaty, the collapse of the pillar structure (as envisaged in the

[4] See Council Regulation (EC) No 2424/2001 on the development of the second-generation Schengen information system (SIS II) based on Article 66 of the Treaty establishing the European Community; Council Decision 2001/866/JHA on the development of the second-generation Schengen information system (SIS II) based on Articles 30(1), 31 and 34 of the Treaty on European Union; Commission of the European Communities, 'Proposal for a Regulation of the European Parliament and of the Council on the Establishment, Operation and Use of the Second-generation Schengen Information System (SIS II)', COM(2005) 236 final/2; Commission of the European Communities, 'Proposal for a Council Decision on the Establishment, Operation and Use of the Second-generation Schengen Information System (SIS II)', COM(2005) 230 final; Commission of the European Communities, 'Proposal for a Regulation of the European Parliament and of the Council regarding Access to the Second-generation Schengen Information System (SIS II) by the Services in the Member States Responsible for Issuing Vehicle Registration Certificates', COM(2005) 237 final.

[5] Council of the European Union, 'Convention between the Kingdom of Belgium, the Federal Republic of Germany, the Kingdom of Spain, the French Republic, the Grand Duchy of Luxembourg, the Kingdom of the Netherlands and the Republic of Austria on the Stepping up of Cross-border Cooperation particularly in Combating Terrorism, Cross-border Crime and Illegal Migration, Prüm (Germany), 27 May 2005', Council Secretariat, Brussels, Document 10900/05, 7 July 2005. Also see House of Lords, European Union Committee 18th Report of Session 2006–07, 'Prüm: An Effective Weapon against Terrorism and Crime? Report with Evidence', The Stationery Office/House of Lords, 7 May 2007.

forthcoming 'Reform Treaty'[6]) will make such cooperation subject to qualified majority voting and will require a minimum of nine Member States under the principle of flexibility. Given the nature of trans-European organised crime, unless the overwhelming majority of Member States cooperate the MLA limitations will continue to apply.

There are three main problems to consider in assessing the feasibility of an ECR.

- The first concerns the willingness of Member States' national governments and EU citizens to accept in principle an ECR: in other words, acceptance in principle that the establishment of an ECR, in an attempt to combat trans-European organised crime, is desirable and acceptable.
- The second concerns the 'specifics' related to the establishment of an ECR: (a) contents, that is the list of crimes that should be included in this document; and (b) access, that is who should be allowed to view and use this document.
- The third concerns the reconciliation of the need to protect the Union and its citizens from organised crime and the need to protect their human rights and personal privacy concerns.

2. Feasibility of the European Criminal Record

From a practical point of view, the creation of an ECR does not pose major practical difficulties. The Union is already using large scale databases, e.g. the SIS, and by now computerisation has been established in the public sector. Admittedly, some new Member States, specifically mentioned as problem cases in Europol Reports, such as Bulgaria and Romania,[7] also happen to be the ones still lagging behind when it comes to computerisation of the public sector. However, the overwhelming majority of Member States are already using databases at the EU and international levels (e.g. Interpol's I-24/7 communications network[8]) regularly without major problems. Nor would the creation of an ECR dedicated database take up

[6] The new Treaty to replace the ill-fated Constitutional Treaty, see Council of the European Union, 'Presidency Conclusions', Document 11177/07, Brussels, 21/22 June 2007, at 15.

[7] Europol, *2004 European Union Organised Crime Report*, (Luxembourg: Europol, December 2004), at 9–10.

[8] See *Interpol Fact Sheet* G1/03, 'Connecting Police I-24/7', General Information, COM/FS/2006–07/GI-03.

too many staff and resources as most European police forces and judicial authorities have dedicated officers for MLA or international cooperation. Cost and human resources are, therefore, not serious problems. The format of the database will, of course depend on the types of crimes that the Member States would like to include in the ECR. However, the SIS format[9] is a very good guide and the database could produce national 'hits' every time a name with a criminal record is queried. These 'hits' could then become subjects for bilateral data requests or the database itself could reveal immediately the relevant entry from the national criminal record saving judicial authorities from time-consuming correspondence. The latter is particularly important for some types of organised crime (e.g. carousel crime) where successful prosecution often depends on the speed of response from national authorities.

The main 'feasibility' problem stems from the nature of the proposal, i.e. yet another database with sensitive information on some of the Union's citizens – this is an issue that will be examined later in this chapter. But before we proceed let us look briefly at organised crime and

[9] The SIS is the database created by the Schengen Agreement that allows Member States to obtain information concerning persons and property. Information in the SIS database is stored according to the national rules of each Member State and contains the following:

- surname and first name (aliases are recorded separately);
- first letter of the second first name;
- date of birth and birthplace;
- sex;
- permanent physical characteristics;
- nationality;
- information about whether the person in question was armed:
- information about whether the person in question was violent;
- reason for having a record for the person in question:
  - wanted for extradition;
  - undesirable on the territory of a Member State;
  - mentally ill patient, minor or missing with a view to protecting them from their own actions;
  - wanted as a witness to appear before a court or for notification of judgment;
  - serious crime suspects.
- action to be taken by the national authority if the person in question is intercepted.

The SIS also contains records of:

- weapons that have been declared lost, stolen or diverted;
- personal identity documents (or blank personal identity documents) that have been declared lost, stolen or diverted;
- motor vehicles that have been declared lost, stolen or diverted;
- banknotes that have been declared lost, stolen or diverted.

public perceptions of organised crime. The latter is important because public perceptions tend to influence government positions.

2.1 *Organised crime and the EU*

It was the combination of the collapse of Eastern Europe and the establishment of the single market in the early 1990s that started the debate about organised crime in Europe mainly at the national level. There were two sets of problems. The first concerned the impact of the four freedoms (free movement of persons including freedom of establishment, free movement of goods, free movement of capital and freedom to provide services) on organised crime. New criminal organisations emerged as a result of the four freedoms and, because at the time of the establishment of the single market the Member States had not addressed this problem seriously, transnational and organised crime was (and still is) consistently ahead of the law at EU and national levels. Essentially the four freedoms gave trans-European organised crime the choice of territory and jurisdiction, exploiting lack of appropriate legislation or lax implementation. The second set of problems concerned the establishment of the, so-called, eastern European 'mafias'[10] which concentrated their activities on financial crime, e.g. money laundering, banking and the financial system and public tenders. Between 1992 and 1996 organised criminal activity had increased considerably[11] and it was in 1996 that the Commission started to address the issue by organising a number of conferences and seminars on crime and crime prevention.[12] In 1997 the Council created a 'High Level Group' of national officials who focused on organised crime and crime prevention and produced an Action Plan containing recommendations on crime prevention.[13] However, it was

[10] See: European Commission Forward Studies Unit, *Organised Criminality and Security in Europe*, Fondazione Rosselli, Working Paper, 1999.

[11] T. van der Heijden, 'Measuring Organized Crime in Western Europe', Slovenia: College of Police and Security Studies, 1996, www.ncjrs.gov/policing/mea313.htm.

[12] For a detailed description of EU actions and milestones in the field of organised crime see: Commission of the European Communities, 'The Prevention of Crime in the European Union: Reflection on Common Guidelines and Proposals for Community Financial Support', Brussels, COM(2000) 786 final, 29 November 2000, pp. 3–5; also see Commission of the European Communities, *Commission Staff Working Paper*, Joint report from Commission services and EUROPOL, 'Towards a European Strategy to Prevent Organised Crime', SEC(2001) 433, Brussels, 13 March 2001, pp. 3–6.

[13] See: OJ C 251, 15 August 1997. The Action Plan led to a Council Resolution on the prevention of organised crime with reference to the establishment of a comprehensive strategy for combating it on 21 December 1998, OJ 98/C 408/01.

after the official coming into force of the Amsterdam Treaty in 1999 that the Union was in a position to address crime prevention directly as a recognised policy area on the basis of Article 29 (ToA) starting with the well-known Tampere European Council (15 and 16 October 1999) and the birth of an 'area of freedom, security and justice' in the EU.

Most initiatives in the area of freedom security and justice concerned the harmonisation of national legislations in fields included mostly in the EU's third pillar. Harmonisation of national legislations could make a valuable contribution to combating organised crime. However, third pillar harmonisation is notoriously difficult as it requires the harmonisation of twenty-seven different legal traditions. The alternative, action at the EU level, is sometimes regarded by the Member States as an encroachment of national sovereignty and inevitably progress in areas covered by the 'intergovernmental' third pillar suffers ineffective lowest common denominator solutions. Voluntary harmonisation via transposition of EU law is difficult and is 'affected by *institutional, political* and *substantive* factors'.[14] Member States tend to safeguard their autonomy and harmonisation does not always produce the expected results. The best example of this problem in the third pillar, as we have already seen, has been the painstakingly slow progress in the area of MLA, which is central in combating organised crime.

Additional solutions at the international level appeared in 2000 with the 'United Nations Convention against Transnational Organised Crime', which was signed at a celebrated Convention in Palermo during the week of 12–15 December 2000 (Palermo Convention).[15] Indeed the Commission, which is a signatory to the Convention,[16] has urged the Member States to proceed with its ratification.[17] However, compared to EU solutions the Palermo Convention will have to prove itself in the future and

[14] D. G. Dimitrakopoulos, 'The Transposition of EU Law: "Post-Decisional Politics" and Institutional Autonomy' (2001) 7 *European Law Journal* 442–458, at 458.

[15] The Convention now has its own website, see: www.unodc.org/palermo/convmain.html. Also see the UN's website on the Convention www.unodc.org/unodc/crime_cicp_convention.html. For a complete list of the documents see: Draft Convention Against Transnational Organised Crime, www.uncjin.org/Documents/Conventions/conventions.html.

[16] Council Decision of 8 December 2000 on the signing, on behalf of the European Community, of the United Nations Convention against transnational organised crime and its Protocols, OJ L030, 1 February 2001.

[17] 'European Commission Paves the Way for EC Ratification of UN Convention Against Transnational Organised Crime and its Protocols on Smuggling and Trafficking in Human Beings', Press Release, IP/03/1185, 1 September 2003.

should be seen as a complementary initiative rather than the main European initiative in the field.

2.2 Organised crime and the European public

There are, of course, different views when it comes to organised crime: from the sensationalisation of often anecdotal stories in the popular press[18] to major international reports on specific types of organised crime.[19] Some Member States, such as the UK, have annual surveys[20] which offer a reasonably accurate picture of how the public 'feels' about organised crime. In contrast other Member States offer no information at all. Whether or not we can assume that the results from one Member State can be used as a guide for other Member States is a matter of interpretation.[21] The problem with organised crime is that it does not have the same impact on the public and the media as, for example, violent crime or street crime (e.g. car theft) even though such crime might be connected to organised criminal activity – and as a recent Europol Report noted: 'The field of crimes against persons is multi-faceted, often intrinsically linked to other OC activities.'[22] Consequently, it has always been difficult to assess public views. Following Tampere we have seen the steady production of surveys and reports which do take into account public perceptions[23] and show that crime – and aspects of organised crime – is increasingly worrying European citizens.

In the original Falcone Study for the ECR the experts had been asked to provide information about public perceptions of organised crime. According to the national experts' reports (see Table I), organised crime

[18] See for example an article on the sale of human organs: M. Frith and N. Meo, 'Horror of Kidneytown', *Evening Standard*, 18 October 2002, p. 9.

[19] UN Commission on Human Rights, 'Report of the Working Group on Contemporary Forms of Slavery on its Twenty-first Session', E/CN.4/Sub.2/1996/24, 19 July 1996.

[20] See for example the British Crime Survey, www.data-archive.ac.uk/findingData/bcrsTitles.asp.

[21] As the Council of Europe Organised Crime Situation Report 2005 notes for some types of crime, such as cybercrime: 'It would be dangerous to assume that other countries have profiles just like this, but equally, there is no particular reason to think that they are radically different.' See Council of Europe, *Organised Crime Situation Report 2005* (Strasbourg: Council of Europe, 2005), at 76.

[22] Europol, *2004 European Union Organised Crime Report*, at 11.

[23] J. van Dijk, R. Manchin, J. van Kesteren, S. Nevala, G. Hideg, 'The Burden of Crime in the EU: A Comparative Analysis of the European Crime and Safety Survey (EU ICS) 2005' (EU ICS: 2005).

Table I *Is organised crime seen as a serious problem, by the media and the public in Europe?*

Austria	YES (it has become a serious concern in recent years)
Belgium	YES (the creation of an ECR will be seen as positive measure)
Denmark	NO (only certain types of crimes, e.g. human trafficking)
Finland	NO (except from drugs trafficking originating from eastern Europe)
France	YES (but emphasis is on 'street crime')
Germany	YES (emphasis on 'war on drugs')
Greece	YES
Ireland	YES
Italy	YES
Luxembourg	YES (recently it has become a major issue)
Netherlands	N/A
Portugal	YES (there are currently a number of government initiatives on organised crime)
Spain	YES (linked to terrorism)
Sweden	YES
UK (England & Wales)	YES
Cyprus	NO
Czech Republic	YES
Hungary	YES
Poland	YES
Slovenia	YES

is not seen as a major problem in just two Member States (Denmark and Finland) and one accession country (Cyprus). Yet, even in Denmark and Finland experts noted concerns about drugs and human trafficking – mainly from eastern Europe.

While public and media concerns about organised crime do not imply immediate support for the establishment of an ECR it is clear that measures which try to stem the spread of organised crime are likely to be well received by the public and the media. Most experts in the original Falcone Study reported media exaggerations – sometimes even hysteria – which do not really stand up to close scrutiny. However, there is also little doubt that public perceptions are quite important because they are often taken up by political parties. While care should be taken not to support extremist views linked to xenophobia there are strategic advantages for the Commission to be seen to be active in its support of citizens' concerns. Already there are government initiatives in some Member States related to organised crime, terrorism, drugs trafficking and human trafficking. At one stage the Commission examined the idea of an ECR in the form of a European Register of Convictions.[24] However, there were some reservations by Member States and the Commission proceeded with a different version of the ECR in the form of a two-stage[25] European Index of Offenders in which the first stage would follow the SIS format by registering 'hits' to be followed up by national authorities' enquiries at the bilateral level. However, one of the themes of the experts' reports in the original Falcone Study was the difficulty national authorities had in pursuing and prosecuting successfully offenders who, as a result of the free movement of persons, could find refuge – even if it was temporary – in another Member State. By not allowing access to the relevant national criminal record entry such a database would be unlikely to speed up the process considerably.

2.3 *Political opposition to an ECR database*

The question of political acceptability of yet another database is particularly important in Europe because of its past. Especially for the Left

[24] Commission of the EC, 'Communication from the Commission to the Council and the European Parliament on Measures to be Taken to Combat Terrorism and Other Forms of Serious Crime, in particular to Improve Exchanges of Information, Proposal for a Council Decision on the Exchange of Information and Cooperation concerning Terrorist Offences', COM(2004)221 final, 2004/0069 (CNS), 29 March 2004, p. 12.

[25] Commission of the European Communities, White Paper on exchanges of information on convictions and the effect of such convictions in the European Union, Brussels, COM(2005) 10 final, 21 January 2005, pp. 6–7 at 3.2. In this White Paper the Commission quoted the original Falcone Study by the IALS at p. 4.

Table II *Will there be political opposition against the creation of a European Criminal Record either by political parties or by human rights groups?*

Austria	YES (there are concerns about possible human rights abuses)
Belgium	NO (however it must respect existing human rights provisions)
Denmark	YES (because it is connected with *Corpus Juris* and the notion of EU criminal law harmonisation)
Finland	NO
France	NO (it should guard against human rights abuses and should not be entrusted to a police organisation)
Germany	NO (care should taken to guard against human rights abuses)
Greece	NO (personal data issues should be resolved)
Ireland	NO (civil liberties groups might have objections)
Italy	NO (but it should be accompanied by EU criminal law harmonisation)
Luxembourg	NO
Netherlands	N/A
Portugal	NO (although its contents must be consistent with human rights provisions)
Spain	NO (privacy rights should be respected)
Sweden	YES (because of fears of misuse and non-respect of human rights provisions; however, political parties expected to accept the ECR)
UK (England & Wales)	YES (Eurosceptics will raise serious objections to criminal law harmonisation)
Cyprus	NO
Czech Republic	YES (the current government would be in favour but other political parties might object)
Hungary	NO
Poland	NO
Slovenia	NO (safety measures should be put in place to guard against misuse)

in Europe and for citizens of the new Member States (which were often at the receiving end of such practices) keeping files on citizens conjures up images of a totalitarian Europe with dictators, secret police forces and informers keeping files on citizens' actions and political/religious beliefs. This lasting memory seems to have created a strong resistance by some political parties and NGOs to moves by the state which recreate the 'filing' of information on individual citizens. Consequently, any proposal for the creation of a new database must pass this psychological test and alleviate any fears concerning the general use of such data. To put it in more precise terms the citizens must be assured, firstly, that there is a need for such a proposal and, secondly, that there will not be any misuse of information. In order to satisfy this need attention must be placed on three aspects: contents, access and use of the ECR.

As Monnet used to say 'the devil is in the details'. And in the case of the ECR the details are linked to human rights and personal privacy issues. As can be seen in Table II the national experts in the original Falcone Study had noted some possible reservations concerning human rights issues. These reservations are important because it shows that there are fears that the ECR will de facto be used as an instrument of repression.

Although human rights and personal privacy issues will be covered in chapter 4 of this book, broadly speaking, as long as the principles of legality, proportionality and necessity are respected in the content, access and transfer of data personal privacy and human rights issues should not be a problem. Strictly speaking, the EU's Charter of Fundamental Human Rights, the European Convention on Human Rights as well as existing EU and international data protection instruments should ensure that there is adequate protection for the Union's citizens. However, possible objections are important for the acceptability of the ECR and national experts have made it quite clear that such concerns may attract negative attention.

As we have seen already at the moment there are two main suggestions when it comes to models for EU databases: (a) networking of national archives (e.g. the SIS model) and (b) an EU centralised database. As can be seen in Table III, both options have advantages and disadvantages. As is always the case with proposals that involve changes in national administration the logistics of the exercise play an important role. If language and digital data format were not a problem then clearly linking/networking national databases would be the most attractive

Table III *Two models for EU databases*[26]

	Advantages	Disadvantages
Networking of national archives	• National databases exist and function • No need for new provisions on maintenance, access, use and erasure • No need for additional resources (financial, staff training, infrastructure)	• Lack of a common format for data availability so difficult to identify the data • Difficulty in utilising the data as evidence before the courts in common law and Frankish legal systems • Language, terminology, foreign categories of crime, foreign rules on access, usage and erasure
EU centralised database	• Common standard format for data availability • Data directly and immediately available to all Member States • Common rules on maintenance, data protection, access, erasure and use • Centralised control of accuracy, use and data protection • Joint investigations and prosecutions become easier	• Cost • New EU instruments needed • Need to find an appropriate EU host • Resistance from some Member States • Doubts about proportionality in view of duplication of data in the Member States and the EU

option since the coexistence of national and centralised EU databases poses some questions about duplication of data and, therefore, the proportionality of the endeavour. The problems concerning the heterogeneity of existing national databases have been noted by the Commission in its 2005 White Paper on exchanges of information on convictions[27] and clearly there is no easy solution. What the Commission regards as a long-term solution is a two-stage introduction of the ECR, one that links the two models mentioned above. The two stages are: (a) an index of

[26] C. Stefanou, 'Organised Crime and the Use of EU-wide Databases' at 237.
[27] COM(2005) 10 final, 25 January 2005.

convictions and (b) the creation of a European standard format. The Commission's main argument is that the two-stage approach will allow national administrations time to adjust and also allow the Member States time to agree on a harmonised EU standard format for data exchanges.[28]

The Commission's gradualist approach is designed to have immediate results in the sense that it leaves the difficult part of the 'process' for the later stage when, it is hoped, the experience of the first stage will be a positive one, since it will produce results and the Member States will find it easier to take the next step. However, the two-stage approach has some disadvantages. Member States might want more assurances and might stall proceedings until there is more overall progress in European criminal harmonisation. While the need to facilitate data exchange on criminal activity is evident and urgent (indeed the principle of availability of data will form part of EU law by 2008) there is no consensus on the model to be utilised for this purpose. Thus, the Commission's gradualist two-stage method can be explained in two different ways: (a) as a classic functionalist approach or (b) as a fragmented approach that demonstrates either a lack of vision or insurmountable difficulties in national approaches. It should not be forgotten that the creation of EU-wide databases goes side by side with the 'Europeanisation' of national administrations.

Connected to the question of political acceptability is the overall view of the ECR. When the experts in the original Falcone Study were asked about the ECR itself (see Table IV) the majority was in favour while a small minority was against. As to the establishment of an ECR being an unnecessary intrusion into national law, it seems that the majority of experts do not see it as a real problem.

3. Analysis

From a practical point of view the benefits from the creation of an ECR are relatively straightforward: by having specific offences mentioned in the criminal record it is possible to protect the interests of the Member States and the EU from organised crime. Indeed, the benefits do not have to be restricted to organised crime; for example, most of the European public would like to know whether those applying for posts in schools or kindergartens have convictions for paedophilia in other Member States – although this is something that would have to be agreed by the Member States.

[28] Ibid., pp. 6–7.

Table IV *Is the creation of ECR as a positive or negative crime-combating development, a move promoting European integration or merely an unnecessary intrusion into national law?*

Austria	Positive development, but only if it comes after the harmonisation of EU criminal law (*Corpus Juris*)
Belgium	Unsure about this development, but the ECR will be useful only if it is accompanied by further integration in other fields and if human rights issues are taken into account
Denmark	Negative development, Denmark prefers cooperation in this field rather than EU harmonisation
Finland	Positive development, provided that the information in it is regularly updated
France	Positive development, although it is not expected to produce miracles, not intrusive into national law
Germany	Positive development, we should be careful to ensure that human rights aspects are respected, not intrusive into national laws
Greece	Positive development, but it is not a priority and does intrude into national laws
Ireland	Positive development, safeguards are necessary
Italy	Positive development, it should be accompanied by EU criminal law harmonisation
Luxembourg	Positive Development, not intrusive into national laws
Netherlands	N/A
Portugal	Positive Development, not intrusive into national laws
Spain	Positive development, not intrusive into national laws
Sweden	Unsure about this development, but not an intrusion into national laws
UK (England & Wales)	Unsure about this development
Cyprus	Positive development
Czech Republic	Positive development, not intrusive into national laws if principle of proportionality is observed
Hungary	Positive development, in the absence of the more desirable EU criminal law harmonisation
Poland	Positive development that does not intrude into national laws
Slovenia	Positive development that does not intrude into national laws

At the moment the existing MLA system requires cooperation at different levels of government and by different enforcement agencies, to the point that it is so cumbersome that it is seen by some law enforcement agencies as more trouble than it is worth. Anecdotal stories, from enforcement agencies, of requests in one language that was mistaken for another and then sent to the wrong desk or of requests in the right language sent to the wrong enforcement agency abroad because the officer did not quite know where exactly such requests should be sent are many and very familiar to those researching in this field. The general impression they convey is of a system where cooperation is inefficient and seems to work only for the big cases, e.g. terrorism suspects. Effective protection, however, requires more than the occasional successful pursuit and prosecution of offenders across different Member States. The creation of the ECR and the existence of a database which will be accessible by those preventing crime is, therefore, a formidable weapon in the battle against organised crime – indeed one that can be extended to protect European citizens against other types of crimes. There are two obvious problems related to the ECR. The first concerns its content, that is the types of crimes that should be included in it. The second problem concerns access to the ECR. Let us look at them quickly in succession.

3.1 Contents of the ECR

It important to note here that a distinction should be made between existing national databases and the ECR. The former will always contain more data than the latter. In most Member States existing legislation allows for databases that include criminal convictions, investigations as well as personal data. However, some EU citizens and some national authorities would have some doubts about the need for yet another database, such as the ECR. In addition, there might be some concerns about the nature of the data included. The transfer of data from national to centralised EU-wide databases according to national regulations should alleviate some of the fears. In this way national authorities will (a) have control of the information kept on their own citizens and (b) require minimum administrative upheaval. Perhaps more importantly, citizens of individual Member States will still be able to appeal against illegal or false entries by appeal to national courts using national legislation, which they know and understand better. In the case of the ECR the issue of data transfer compatibility might play a role as national authorities often use custom-made rather than commercially available software. Nevertheless, this solution will probably pass the 'psychological' test mentioned earlier. Interestingly, an important additional line of defence is now provided by the European Data Protection Supervisor. A good example of the type of protection that the European Data Protection Supervisor can offer was indicated in 2004 when he issued an Opinion on the Commission's proposal for the exchange of information from criminal records in which he argued that the proposal was not 'proportional', that it should be limited to specific serious crimes and that it should provide precise safeguards to the data subject.[29]

As to the specific list of crimes to be included in the ECR, some experts in the original Falcone Study suggested the crimes mentioned in the *Corpus Juris*. While clearly the protection of the financial interests of the Union is important, the ECR must also include crimes that are relevant to the concerns of the citizens. Otherwise, the creation of yet another database – which challenges personal privacy – solely for the protection of the Union and not the individual citizen might be seen as excessive. Indeed, the creation of an ECR with the sole intention of including *Corpus Juris* crimes would be excessive and would be seen as largely irrelevant to the concerns of the European citizen. Let us not forget that although financial crimes affect all the citizens of the Union they are often seen as abstract and certainly are not perceived by the individual citizen as direct as, for example, street crime. It is therefore recommended that the ECR includes all crimes falling under the definition of organised crime, leaving options open for the expansion of its content with crimes that are perceived by citizens as sensitive and warranting action at the EU level.

3.2 Access to the ECR

Two of the national experts in the original Falcone Study (Spain and Ireland) noted some problems with access. The Spanish expert believed that access should be restricted to the judiciary only, otherwise it would not be compatible with the Spanish legal system. The Irish expert noted that the supervisory body of the ECR should be a Court – rather than Eurojust or the European Public Prosecutor. At the moment, 'access' to national criminal records varies in different Member States. Some Member States allow access to enforcement agencies and judicial

[29] Opinion of the European Data Protection Supervisor on the Proposal for a Council Decision on the exchange of information from criminal records, COM (2004) 664 final, 13 October 2004.

authorities while others allow judicial authorities only. Since the common denominator is judicial authorities, access to the ECR should be restricted to them (which explains why Eurojust rather than Europol is the proposed 'keeper' of EU databases).

One of the problems with access is that when it comes to personal data some Member States offer their citizens a higher level of protection. An ECR database would have to respect these higher levels of protection. However, in doing so it would disadvantage the citizens of Member States that offer lower levels of protection as a higher volume of their data would be transmitted. It is for this reason that the Commission attempted to set out at an early stage issues such as data 'entry', 'erasure' and access to one's own record. But what is the full list of intended users? Given that the ECR should include all those crimes falling within the definition of organised crime the full list should include the following:

- the individual concerned;
- judicial and prosecuting authorities;
- members of the police belonging to units dealing with economic or transnational crime;
- Eurojust;
- Europol;
- OLAF;
- the European Public Prosecutor;
- the European Judicial Network;
- tendering authorities;
- professional associations;
- banks and the EU institutions for employment purposes only.

Let us now turn our attention to a rather sensitive issue, which is how to reconcile the need to protect the Union and its citizens from organised crime and the need to protect their human rights and personal privacy concerns. In recent years the widespread use and misuse of personal data has prompted governmental and non-governmental organisations to look for ways and means to safeguard the rights of individuals. Indeed it is to some degree natural for citizens to feel sceptical about the organised and methodical collection and use of personal data. The comments of some national experts in the original Falcone Study indicated that in order to avoid objections based on form rather than substance we need to take political arguments out of the establishment of an ECR because its aims are practical rather than political. The creation of an ECR is primarily a practical measure aiming to combat organised crime and more generally crimes which the free movement of persons inadvertently facilitates. In other words it does not aim to make a statement about the direction or nature of future EU cooperation in criminal matters and certainly does not intend to trample on citizens' rights. It is unfortunate that proposals to harmonise areas in the third pillar are often also seen as 'political'. What this tells us from a feasibility point of view is that if not handled carefully by the Commission the establishment of an ECR has the potential to become embroiled in political arguments about the future direction or future stable polity of the EU. In fact that is exactly what happened with the two attempts made by the Commission for the introduction of the index of convictions.

3.3 Use of the ECR

How the ECR may be used – e.g. can it be used for employment vetting purposes or assistance in pre-trial proceedings or the detection and prosecution of offenders? – is another point that must be settled. Obviously the use of the ECR must be compatible with existing national provisions concerning use of nationally collected information and must be able to deal with the current constraints in the field of mutual legal assistance. Misuse of the ECR will certainly result in a serious and devastating blow to the European public's confidence. Once again, the issue of supervision becomes crucial to the whole endeavour. If there are too many restrictions then the ECR databases might not be effective enough. If there is too little supervision then the ECR might become the black sheep of human rights groups. A very fine line indeed, but one that the Union will have to tread if the ECR is to remain operational and effective.

4. Conclusion

Judging from the experts views in the original Falcone Study on the establishment of an ECR it is clear that the majority regarded it as a positive development. In most Member States the existence and use of national criminal records is de facto accepted as desirable and necessary and so is the existing exchange of nationally kept data on criminals and suspects based on EU and international agreements. It is, therefore, difficult to argue that the creation of an EU-based database on criminal records will be seen as a major departure from established practices, indeed more so given that the ECR will be subject to the

Table V *Falcone Study experts' views 'at a glance'*

	In view of the free movement of persons within the EU and the increase in organised crime, would such a Directive constitute an effective weapon against organised crime?	Do you foresee political opposition to a move for the creation of an ECR either by political parties or by human rights groups?	Is organised crime seen as a serious problem, by the media and the public, in Europe?	Is the creation of ECR seen as a positive or negative crime-combating development?
Austria	YES	YES	YES	Positive
Belgium	NO	NO	YES	Unsure
Denmark	NO	YES	NO	Negative
Finland	YES	NO	NO	Positive
France	YES	NO	YES	Positive
Germany	YES	NO	YES	Positive
Greece	YES	NO	YES	Positive
Ireland	YES	NO	YES	Positive
Italy	YES	NO	YES	Positive
Luxembourg	YES	NO	YES	Positive
Netherlands	N/A	N/A	N/A	N/A
Portugal	YES	NO	YES	Positive
Spain	YES	NO	YES	Positive
Sweden	Unsure	YES	YES	Unsure
UK (England & Wales)	Unsure	YES	YES	Unsure
Cyprus	YES	NO	NO	Positive
Czech Republic	YES	YES	YES	Positive
Hungary	YES	NO	YES	Positive
Poland	YES	NO	YES	Positive
Slovenia	YES	NO	YES	Positive

more advanced and EU human rights and personal privacy provisions. What remains to be seen is the format the ECR will take. Will it be a single database or an interlinkage of national databases with a standardised template?

As mentioned in the introduction, the need for the creation of an ECR was put forward following a detailed study of the use of national criminal records as a means of combating organised crime and the realisation that under the current conditions organised crime can use the free movement of persons to its advantage. The main political issues related to the establishment of an ECR concern its acceptance by the national governments and citizens, its content, access and human rights connotations. Despite the possible 'political' problems, to which the Commission is anyway well accustomed, the creation of an ECR has great potential to become an important instrument in the fight against organised crime.

The general view of the national experts in the original Falcone Study (see Table V) is that this would be a positive development. From a political point of view the multitude of largely cumbersome and ineffective European and international instruments on the exchange of information concerning organised crime indicate that there can be few 'in principle' objections. Less so given the high standards that the EU has in the areas of human rights and personal privacy protection.

The format that the ECR will take remains to be decided although it is clear that the Commission favours a two-stage interlinkage of national criminal records mainly because some Member States were unsure about yet another centralised database. The Prüm Treaty gave the Commission's two-stage interlinkage of national criminal records a boost. However, at the time of writing this book no final decision has been taken.

4

The establishment of a European Criminal Record: Human rights considerations

ALEXANDRA XANTHAKI

1. Introduction

The previous chapters elaborated on the problems that exist in the current system of exchange of information among Member States regarding criminal convictions. They highlighted the inadequacies in current processes and touched upon the lack of harmonisation of criminal records within the EU. These gaps become more striking, when one considers that knowledge of prior criminal activity would seriously contribute to the combating of transnational organised crime, a category flourishing in Europe. Therefore, changes in the current system appear necessary; such changes should include, the authors of this book propose, the establishment of a European Criminal Record. This chapter assesses the possible compliance of the European Criminal Record (ECR) with human rights standards and identifies the specific conditions that have to be fulfilled so that such compliance is achieved. The chapter analyses the relevant European human rights standards, as codified by the Council of Europe bodies and by the EU, and attempts to apply the principles incorporated therein to the ECR. There has not been specific jurisprudence on criminal records; however, analogies with other measures to prevent crime can be drawn, even though important differences exist between them in the nature and level of interference.

2. General legal framework

2.1 The European Convention on Human Rights

The right to privacy has long been established in Article 8 of the European Convention on Human Rights (ECHR), the main human rights binding instrument of the EU as confirmed by Article 268 of the

Treaty of Amsterdam. Article 8 ECHR recognises the right of everyone to his private and family life. Intrusion on one's privacy violates one's personal autonomy and one's status as a free agent. Chadwick links the right to privacy with notions of individuality, intimacy and liberty[1] and calls it an instrumental freedom, since unless it is respected, especially by the government, all other freedoms are difficult to be exercised.[2] The right to privacy has been an ever-expanding right.[3] The European Court of Human Rights (ECourtHR) has made clear that such a right includes both a negative and a positive aspect; not only should the state refrain from interfering with this right, it should also take positive action to protect the individual.[4] In this respect, the right of Article 8 is wider in scope than the right to privacy recognised in North American jurisprudence.[5]

However, this right is not without exceptions. Paragraph 2 of Article 8 provides that:

> There shall be no interference by a public authority with the exercise of this right except such as is in accordance with the law and is necessary in a democratic society in the interests of national security, public safety or the economic well-being of the country, for the prevention of disorder or crime, or the protection of health or morals, or for the protection of the rights and freedoms of others.

Any access to information contained in national criminal records must satisfy the above conditions. Therefore, any exchange of information included in the national criminal records between Member States must be in accordance with the law, serve one of the specific interests mentioned, be necessary in a democratic society and must not interfere with the rights and freedoms of others.

First, the restriction of the right must be 'in accordance with the law'. In *Malone* v. *United Kingdom*, the ECourtHR interpreted this condition to mean that no right in the Convention can be restricted, unless the citizen knows the basis for such interference through domestic law.[6] In *Copland* v. *United Kingdom*, the Court confirmed that there must be a

[1] P. Chadwick, 'The Value of Privacy' (2006) 5 *European Human Rights Law Review* 495–508.

[2] Ibid., at 497.

[3] H. Fenwick, *Civil Liberties and Human Rights* (London: Cavendish, 2002), at p. 530.

[4] *X and Y* v. *Netherlands* 8 (1985) EHRR 235.

[5] D. Feldman, *Civil Liberties and Human Rights*, 2nd edition (Oxford: Oxford University Press, 2002), at p. 524.

[6] *Malone* v. *United Kingdom* (1985) 7 EHRR 14; *Leander* v. *Sweden* (1987) 9 EHRR 433.

measure of legal protection in domestic law against arbitrary interferences by public authorities with the rights safeguarded by Article 8.1.[7] The condition also requires forseeability, which implies that the law must be sufficiently clear in its terms to give individuals an adequate indication as to the circumstances and the conditions on which the authorities are empowered to resort to any restrictive measures; the law must also be accessible to ensure that individuals can adequately determine with some degree of certainty when and how their rights might be affected. There is no requirement that that law be statutory.[8] Consequently, the establishment of a European Criminal Record cannot take place unless laws at the domestic level specify its modalities.

Secondly, any interference with the right must be directed towards a legitimate aim. Therefore, measures that restrict one's privacy can only be justified if necessary to prevent a specific purpose described in provision 8.2. The list is exhaustive and the state cannot add to these grounds. The establishment of an ECR would clearly aim at the prevention of crime, which is included in this list. The ECourtHR has recognised that the keeping of records relating to past criminal cases can be justified as necessary in a democratic society for the prevention of crime.[9] In *Murray* v. *United Kingdom*,[10] the ECourtHR considered 'the responsibility of an elected government in a democratic society to protect its citizens and its institutions against threats posed by organised crime'. The Court found that neither the collection nor the retention of personal details of an individual suspected of terrorist offences would contravene Article 8. Hence, the establishment of an ECR could take place for a legitimate aim, the prevention of crime.

Thirdly, the restriction must also be 'necessary in a democratic society'. In *Rotaru* v. *Romania*, the ECourtHR stated: 'States do not enjoy unlimited discretion to subject individuals to secret surveillance or a system of secret files. The interest of a state in protecting its national security must be balanced against the seriousness of the interference with the applicant's right to respect for his or her private life.'[11] National security concerns cannot provide the state with unquestioned power to restrict individuals'

[7] *Copland* v. *United Kingdom*, Judgment, 3 April 2007, para. 46.

[8] *Sunday Times* v. *United Kingdom* (1979–80) 2 EHRR 245; *Barthold* v. *Germany* (1985) 7 EHRR 383.

[9] Application No. 13071/61; 9 C.D. 53 referred to in *Friedl* v. *Austria* (1995) 21 EHRR 83, at para. 66.

[10] *Murray* v. *United Kingdom* (1994) 19 EHRR 193.

[11] *Rotaru* v. *Romania* (2000) 8 BHRC 449.

human rights.[12] The jurisprudence of the ECourtHR has interpreted 'necessary' as less flexible than 'indispensable', but more demanding than 'ordinary', 'useful', 'reasonable' or 'desirable'.[13] According to the Court, 'necessary in a democratic society' means that the restriction is based on a 'pressing social need' and is 'proportionate to the legitimate aim pursued'.[14] It is important to keep in mind that national understandings of this principle have not always been in complete agreement with the ECourtHR interpretation of the principle.[15] In *R. (on the application of Daly)* v. *Secretary of State for the Home Department*, the House of Lords explained that the interpretation of the principle by the ECourtHR is stricter than that its interpretation by national courts. The ECourtHR held that the doctrine of proportionality requires the assessment of the balance that the decision-maker has struck rather than the mere examination of reasonableness of the decision. Moreover, proportionality may require attention to be directed to the relative weight accorded to interests and considerations. Also, the intensity of the review is guaranteed by the twin requirement that the limitation of the right was necessary in a democratic society (in the sense of meeting a pressing social need) and the question whether the interference was really proportionate to the legitimate aim being pursued.[16]

The notion of proportionality should be determined on a case by case basis; the Court has identified numerous factors to be taken into account;[17] one of them being the seriousness of the interference to the human right. Criteria for determining the seriousness of the interference might include any inconvenience, embarrassment, pain caused and the duration of the interference.[18] A restriction that would violate the core of any right, its very essence, would almost certainly be disproportionate.[19]

[12] Ibid., in the concurring opinion of Judge Wildhaber.

[13] *Silver* v. *United Kingdom* (1983) 5 EHRR 347, at para.97.

[14] *Olsson* v. *Sweden* (1989) 11 EHRR 259, at para. 67.

[15] For example, in *Smith and Grady* v. *United Kingdom*, the UK Court of Appeal reluctantly rejected a limitation on homosexuals in the army, while the European Court of Human Rights came to the opposite conclusion. See *Smith and Grady* v. *United Kingdom* (1999) 29 EHRR 493.

[16] Lord Steyn, '2000–2005: Laying the Foundations of Human Rights in the United Kingdom' (2005) 4 *European Human Rights Law Review* 349–362.

[17] K. Starmer, *European Human Rights Law* (London: Human Rights Action, 1999), chapter 4.

[18] A. Roberts and N. Taylor, 'Privacy and the DNA Database' (2005) 4 *European Human Rights Law Review* 373–392.

[19] *Rees* v. *United Kingdom* (1987) 9 EHRR 56.

Thus, there should also be consideration of whether there is a less restrictive alternative and the particular measure must be justified on the basis of relevant and sufficient reasons.[20] Of course, the measure taken cannot be arbitrary but should be based on relevant considerations.[21] In *Campbell* v. *United Kingdom*, a blanket rule on the opening of prisoners' mail was found to be a disproportionate response to the problem identified and was, therefore, in breach of Article 8. Although the government argued that the specific measure was necessary to ensure that prohibited material was not contained in the mail, the Court concluded that the same aim could have been reached by opening the mail in the presence of the prisoner without actually reading it.[22] Taylor concludes that it is unlikely that a measure be considered proportionate 'where a less restrictive or intrusive alternative was available'.[23]

Within the EU alternative measures to the ECR have certainly been considered. The variations in the national criminal records, the lack of entries on legal persons and of nationals who have committed crimes abroad and problems of access are important weaknesses to the current system and seriously undermine its effectiveness. A more improved network of national records has been considered, but its major disadvantages, including shortcomings of national criminal records and delays in current mutual assistance responses,[24] have been rather discouraging. The initial enthusiasm for an index of crimes, where the entries would only show the national criminal record where a full entry of a convicted individual would be stored,[25] was curbed too, because of its disadvantages, such as the lack of consultation about the inclusion of data, the sheer volume of the information and the additional burden for the Member States.[26] All these measures have been criticised for lack of efficiency in the prevention of crime. The creation

[20] *Jersild* v. *Denmark* (1995) 19 EHRR 1 at para. 31.

[21] *W* v. *United Kingdom* (1988) 10 EHRR 29.

[22] *Campbell* v *United Kingdom* (1993) 15 EHRR 137.

[23] N. Taylor, 'Policing, Privacy and Proportionality' (2003) Special Issue *European Human Rights Law Review* 86–100, at 88.

[24] Commission of the EC, 'White Paper on the Exchange of Information on Convictions and the Effect of such Convictions in the EU', COM(2005) 10 final, 25 January 2005, at p. 6.

[25] Council of the European Union, 'Council and Commission Action Plan Implementing the Hague Programme on Strengthening Freedom, Security and Justice in the EU', 9246/1/05 REV 1, 30 May 2005.

[26] Council of the European Union, 'Policy Debate on the Exchange of Information Extracted from the Criminal Record', 7198/05, 22 March 2005, at p. 22.

of an ECR appears as the next step, since it would avoid all disadvantages of bilateral exchanges.

Would the establishment of such a centralised record be a proportionate measure? National criminal records prove the widespread belief that the recording of previous convictions is necessary for the prevention of crime. Sedley LJ has noted:

> There is of course nothing which says that those who have never been suspected of anything will not offend, nor that those who have already fallen under justified suspicion but have been acquitted will go on to offend; but the courts know well that among the latter is a significant proportion – markedly higher than the unconvicted population at large – who will offend in the future.[27]

Retention of past convictions is justified on the presumption that among these convicted individuals, a significant proportion will reoffend. Even though one can disagree with the concept of criminal records on the basis that it is punishment following conviction, states currently agree that criminal records play a significant part in their combating of crime.

Even though the retention of criminal records at the national level may seem proportionate to the pursued aim, one can argue that this is not the case with the storage of criminal convictions at the European level. Certainly, since other measures – arguably less intrusive – have been found to be flawed, a centralised record becomes a more attractive option. In essence, proportionality requires a balancing exercise. Feldman cautions that such a balancing is not between the right and the interference but between the nature and extent of the interference and the reasons for interfering.[28] It is arguable whether an ECR for all crimes would be a proportionate measure: storing information across the EU on offences against property seems a rather unnecessary measure. However, for some types of crime the timely availability of previous convictions that the ECR guarantees seems an attractive option. Trafficking, terrorist activities and transnational organised crime are currently on the rise[29] and there is a pressing social need that such crimes be tackled. Timely information among Member States on

[27] As quoted in Roberts and Taylor, 'Privacy and the DNA Database', at 387.

[28] D. Feldman, *Civil Liberties and Human Rights in England and Wales*, p. 57.

[29] See statement by the European Union in http://ec.europa.eu/justice_home/fsj/crime/forum/fsj_crime_forum_en.htm; also see 'UK Organised Crime on Rise', BBC, 6 September 1999, http://news.bbc.co.uk/1/hi/uk/439484.stm.

previous convictions of suspects seems important to combating criminality of this nature. In these cases, an ECR would most certainly be a proportionate measure. More elaboration on other types of crimes that would be included in the record must be done, so that proportionality is satisfied with respect to all entries.

Proportionality also requires an assurance mechanism that would guarantee proper decisions and procedural fairness in making such decisions. In addition, it requires sufficient safeguards against abuse. This was expressed clearly in *Klass* v. *Germany*: 'One of the fundamental principles of a democratic society is the rule of law . . . [which] implies, inter alia, that an interference by the executive authorities with an individual's rights should be subject to an effective control.'[30] This requirement has to be taken into account when discussing the body responsible for the ECR. Eurojust appears a preferable choice, as it possesses the legal expertise and experience to deal with alleged problems and has an adequate appeals system.[31]

2.2 European Union instruments

Proportionality and legality run through EU legislation on personal data. The general right to privacy is protected in Article 286 of the Treaty of Amsterdam. The article establishes that Directives which protect individuals with regard to the processing of personal data and the free movement of such data shall apply to the EU institutions and bodies; it also requires the Council to create an independent supervisory body responsible for monitoring the application of the acts to the community bodies and institutions. In 2004, the European Data Protection Supervisor was established to supervise all EU institutions and bodies on the application of the rules related to the processing of personal data.[32] At the same time, the European Court of Justice (ECJ) has developed a body of fundamental principles that touch upon criminal matters.[33] In these, the principle of proportionality is an important consideration.

[30] *Klass* v. *Germany* (1979–80) 2 EHRR 214, at para. 55.

[31] See chapter 2 for a discussion on this issue.

[32] See Decision No. 2004/55/EC, OJ L 012, 17 January 2004 at 0047–0047; Decision No. 1247/2002/EC, OJ L 183, 12 July 2002 at 0001–0002.

[33] Including legal certainty and actual retroactivity, see P. Craig and G. de Burca, *EU Law: Text, Cases and Materials*, 3rd edition (Oxford: Oxford University Press, 2003), p. 380.

Article 8 of the Charter of Fundamental Rights of the European Union recognises specifically the right to data protection:

1. Everyone has the right to the protection of personal data concerning him or her.
2. Such data must be processed fairly for specified purposes and on the basis of the consent of the person concerned or some other legitimate basis laid down by law. Everyone has the right to access to the data which has been collected concerning him or her and the right to have it rectified.
3. Compliance with these rules shall be subject to control by an independent authority.

Even though the Charter is not a binding instrument, it has been of particular value, especially after it has been cited by the General Advocates, the ECourtHR and national High Courts of Member States.[34] The Charter incorporates the same principles as the European Convention on Human Rights, but also confirms some safeguards that have emerged from the ECourtHR jurisprudence: for example, it explicitly states that the individual has the right of access to information about himself and that his consent is required before any personal data is released. However, the ECourtHR has accepted that this condition can be sidestepped, provided it is justifiable. In *McVeigh* v. *United Kingdom* the taking of fingerprints without consent was held to be a breach of the right to privacy, albeit a justifiable one, as was in *Murray v. United Kingdom*. Article 8 also prescribes that data must be collected 'fairly' and requires a supervisory independent body to overlook the procedure. As seen earlier, Eurojust would satisfy this requirement, if in charge of the ECR.

Other EU instruments have addressed more specific issues related to the exchange of information of criminal records within the EU. The 1959 European Convention on Mutual Assistance in Criminal Matters[35] was the first binding instrument that elaborated issues concerning the exchange of information on criminal matters within the EU. Its Articles set out procedures and safeguards echoing the general instruments on data protection and privacy. Article 13 imposes the obligation of the state to act, when asked for information on criminal matters by the

[34] For more on the Charter and its future, see A. Arnull, 'From Charter to Constitution and Beyond: Fundamental Rights in the New European Union' (2003) *Public Law* 774–793.

[35] Council of Europe, European Treaty Series – 30, adopted in Strasbourg on 20 April 1959.

judicial authorities of a contracting party, in the same manner as it acts when information is requested by its own authorities in similar cases. Requests for information by domestic judicial bodies and request by EU bodies are to be treated in a similar manner and the same principles are to be applied. Article 22 provides that each contracting state must inform the other state of all criminal convictions and other information entered in the national criminal records, while the Ministry of Justice must update and check this automatic communication of information at least once a year. Moreover, criminal convictions must be communicated after they have been entered into the national judicial records. All these guarantees can also be used for the ECR. Unfortunately, the Convention is not as helpful on the issue of storage of criminal records. Such standards though are laid out in Directive 95/46/EC on Rules concerning the Protection of Individuals with regard to the Processing of Personal Data and on the Free Movement of such Data.[36] The Directive allows the processing of personal data if it is necessary 'for the performance of a task carried out in the public interest or in the exercise of official authority vested in the controller or in a third party to whom the data are disclosed' (Article 7e). Also, Article 8.5 reads:

> Processing of data relating to offences, criminal convictions or security measures may be carried out only under the control of official authority, or if suitable specific safeguards are provided under national law, subject to derogations which may be granted by the Member State under national provisions providing suitable specific safeguards. However, a complete register of criminal convictions may be kept only under the control of official authority.

Again, this provision implies that when adequate safeguards are followed, processing of such data by an official authority is possible. The provision does not limit the processing of such data only to a national authority. Its language stresses the importance of proportionality, fulfilled if adequate safeguards are taken. However, it is interesting to note that Article 13 allows for exceptions in the safeguards relating to data quality and informing and access of the individual concerned, if it is a necessary measure for 'the prevention, investigation, detection and prosecution of criminal offences, or of breaches of ethics for regulated professions' (Article 13 d). In this manner, the provision sets the threshold for proportionality lower than previous instruments that required

[36] OJ L 281, 23 November 1995, at p. 31.

extensive safeguards in all cases of personal data. Also, the provision treats the breaches of ethics for regulated professions in a similar way to criminal offences, which opens a question about whether such crimes should also be included in the ECR. The provisions of the Directive are particularly important when one considers that it is a binding instrument, breaches of which bring enforcement procedures that allow the use of established actions in European law (Articles 29 and 30).

Any exchange of information between the ECR would happen automatically; thus, of great relevance is the European Convention for the Protection of Individuals with regard to the Automatic Processing of Personal Data.[37] Again, the Convention focuses on the principles of legality and proportionality: the data must be adequate, relevant and not excessive in relation to the purposes for which they are stored; it should be accurate and up-to-date and preserved in a form which permits identification of the data subjects for no longer than is required for the purpose for which the data is stored (Article 5 of the Convention). The convention also stresses the importance of confidentiality and secrecy (Article 15). These principles must be taken into account when one considers the parties who will have access to the ECR. It is obvious that the ECR cannot be open to all, but only to authorities that need the information specifically for the prevention of crime.

Also, Convention No. 108 stipulates that personal data revealing racial origin, political opinions or religious or other beliefs, health or sexual life and personal data on criminal convictions may not be processed automatically. However, the Convention allows for the processing of such data, if it is provided by law and the processing is a necessary measure in a democratic society in the interests of, inter alia, suppressing criminal offences (Article 9). In other words, the suppression of organised crime justifies the processing of criminal convictions as well as data revealing personal characteristics. It appears that the text implies that information on personal characteristics can help the prevention of organised crime and terrorism. This exception in the name of combating organised crime and terrorism has initiated state policies that raise issues of unjustified discrimination on the basis of racial characteristics. For example, shortly after the terrorist attacks of 9/11, the German Parliament adopted a law requiring the social insurance agencies to pass on their data to intelligence and law enforcement agencies so far as such information was needed for

[37] Council of Europe, European Treaty Series – 108, adopted in Strasbourg on 28 January 1981.

the purposes of a so-called *Rasterfahndung*, a screening method whereby the police search personal data stored by public bodies or private agencies according to the presumed characteristics of suspects.[38] In view of the Islamophobia that has swept Europe after 9/11 and subsequent events,[39] it is important that the EU sets limitations to any – directly or indirectly – discriminatory policies by states. In any case, it is not clear whether this type of information can really prevent such crimes.[40]

The Convention also includes detailed provisions for the exchange of information that are of importance for the ECR: measures must be taken for the protection of the relevant data against accidental or unauthorised destruction or loss, unauthorised access, alteration and dissemination (Article 7). A definite legal basis is required for any disclosure to anyone, including the police.[41] Security measures must take into account the vulnerability of the data, the need to restrict access to the information within the organisation and the long-term storage requirements.[42] Any person must also have the right to correction and erasure and a remedy against errors (Article 8). Any person must be informed of the existence of an automatic data file, of his personal data contained in the system and of communication concerning his personal data. Admittedly, informing the suspect that the authorities have asked for his previous file on ECR would give away any investigation on his activities and would jeopardise any operation. Taking this into account, the Convention allows for the side-stepping of the above requirements for, among others, the suppression of crime, provided the principles of proportionality and legality are satisfied (Article 9).

The protection of the individual is a primary concern of the Convention and of other instruments in this field. Apart from concerns on privacy, concerns on the rights of ex-offenders must also be taken into account when considering the establishment of a European

[38] D. Moeckli, 'Discriminatory Profiles: Law Enforcement after 9/11 and 7/7' (2005) 5 *European Human Rights Law Review* 517–532.

[39] A. Xanthaki, 'Multiculturalism and Extremism: International Law Perspectives', in J. Rehman and S. Breau (eds.), *Religion, Human Rights and International Law* (Dordrecht: Brill Publishers, 2007).

[40] For a discussion on racial profiling, see A. Taslitz, 'Wrongly Accused: Is Race a Factor in Convicting the Innocent?' (2006) 4 *Ohio State Journal of Criminal Law* 121–133; S. Davies, 'Profiling Terror' (2003) 1 *Ohio State Journal of Criminal Law*, 45–102.

[41] J. McBride, 'Disclosure of Crime Prevention Data: Specific European and International Standards', 26 (2001) *European Law Review* 86–102 at 92.

[42] Explanatory Report to Convention No. 108, para. 49, see http://conventions.coe.int/Treaty/EN/Reports/HTML/108.htm.

Criminal Record. Any criminal record of ex-offenders prevents their rehabilitation; having such a record on a European level would maintain the shame that conviction and incarceration generate. Austin writes on the stigmatisation of ex-offenders:

> Roughly speaking, a stigma is a mark or characteristic that designates a person as 'flawed, compromised, and somehow less than fully human'. Stigmatization erects boundaries or barriers between persons who would otherwise belong to the same community. The stigmatized are outcasts who are to be avoided and isolated. They are dehumanized and considered defective or unwholesome. They are discriminated against. Like a contagious disease, stigmas may affect those who are associated with the targeted, including their families, friends, and neighbours.
>
> Stigmas produce significant social and psychological effects. Although anger and arrogance are not unheard of responses to stigmas, stigmas generally induce shame in those who are branded. ... Shame in turn causes silence, secrecy, and concealment. The disrespect of the community leads to self-consciousness, self-doubt, and low self-esteem in the stigmatized'. The imposition of a host of post-conviction penalties, the ready dissemination of criminal records by the state, and the media representations of minority criminals as virtually 'natural born' make the stigma nearly impossible to overcome once it has attached. Rather than shame, some imprisoned minorities may experience anger and indignation as a result of 'reframing' their punishment in less stigmatizing terms. None of this means that minority inmates are without shame. It just may be that whatever shame they experience is a result of their failure to conform to the values of the subgroup of the society from which they come.[43]

Taking this into account, access to the ECR must be very limited and restricted to absolutely necessary occasions. The right of the public to know of serious offenders who live among them has been an issue of discussion recently. Megan's Law in the United States ensures that the public is informed of sexual offenders who live within the community.[44] Some believe that such a law should also be introduced in European

[43] R. Austin, ' "The Shame of it all": Stigma and the Political Disenfranchisement of Formerly Convicted and Incarcerated Persons' (2004) 36 *Columbia Human Rights Law Review* 173–192, at 174–175.

[44] B. Gallagher, 'Now that We Know Where They Are, What Do We Do with Them?: The Placement of Sex Offenders in the Age of Megan's Law' (1997) 7 *Widener Journal of Public Law* 39–85.

states, such as the United Kingdom.[45] However, knowledge of the public would be against proportionality: the restriction of the ex-offender's rights and the danger he will be in, should the public be informed of his previous crime, cannot be said to be proportionate to the prevention of the crime that would be achieved in this instance. This must be taken into account when discussing access to the ECR. All instruments repeat the need for confidentiality.

The concern for the individual whose data is exchanged is especially reflected in the Council of Europe Recommendation regulating the Use of Personal Data in the Police Sector (R(87)15), adopted in 1987.[46] The Recommendation elaborates on rules concerning the collection, storage, use and communication of data for police purposes. Although a useful document, the Recommendation concerns the police sector at the national level and refers to any information, not just extracts from national criminal records, which are already collected and constitute objective materials; still it can be of help for the principles that should run through an ECR. The Recommendation repeats the need for accuracy, use of the data only for the specific purposes; and knowledge of the individual concerned and rights to access, rectification, erasure and appeal.[47] An interesting distinction in the Recommendation is that between storage of facts and storage of opinions or personal assessments; the latter would be unacceptable. The Additional Protocol to the Convention,[48] adopted in 2001, establishes a supervisory body whose decisions can be appealed against through the courts.

Finally, the Organisation for Economic Cooperation and Development (OECD) has adopted Guidelines governing the Protection of Privacy and Trans-border Data Flows of Personal Data, which repeat the same principles.[49] In 2002, the OECD adopted guidelines for the security of

[45] See www.forsarah.com.

[46] Recommendation No. R (87) 15 of the Committee of Ministers to Member States Regulating the Use of Personal Data in the Police Sector, adopted by the Committee of Ministers on 17 September 1987 at the 410th meeting of the Ministers' Deputies.

[47] See the importance that the European Court on Human Rights placed on these requirements in *Leander* v. *Sweden* (1987) 9 EHRR 433; *Kopp* v. *Switzerland* (1999) 27 EHRR 91; *Amman* v. *Switzerland* (2000) 30 EHRR 843 and *Rotaru* v. *Romania*, 4 May 2000.

[48] Additional Protocol to the Convention for the Protection of Individuals with regard to Automatic Processing of Personal Data (ETS. No. 108) regarding Supervisory Authorities and Trans-border Data Flows, ETS. 179.

[49] Organisation for Economic Cooperation and Development, Recommendation of the Council concerning Guidelines Governing the Protection of Privacy and Trans-border Data Flows of Personal Data adopted on 23 September 1980.

information systems and networks[50] (replacing the 1992 guidelines) which confirm the principles of accountability and confidentiality of the bodies managing the information system; the need for awareness of the public of the existence of such system; the regular reassessment of the system; and the principles of proportionality and legitimacy.

In concluding, an ECR could be considered a proportionate measure for the prevention of serious and organised crime, if the principles of privacy and data protection and the guarantees on criminal records set in legal instruments were followed in every step of its establishment and operation. Although several national laws, including Denmark and Germany, give the right of keeping such data only to national authorities, the national legislation can change. Following legality, the ECR would have to be established by specific and prescribed laws, which would set out its detailed legal framework. Such laws would have to explicitly mention the purpose of the ECR, so that in no case would the ERC be used for another reason. The principle of proportionality would necessitate a continuing balancing of the need to prevent organised crime and the conditions of operation of the record. The record should only contain information that is absolutely necessary and be used to the extent that it is necessary.

The rights of ex-offenders must be taken into account: confidentiality, access to one's entry, accuracy, and rights of erasure of data and appeal are essential. Data must be fairly and lawfully collected and processed for the specific purpose of combating organised crime and must be stored, used and disclosed only for the same reason. Information cannot be disclosed for any other purpose, no matter how important it may be. The data contained must be adequate, relevant, up to date and not excessive to the purpose of combating organised crime. It must be accurate and kept in a secure manner for no longer than it is absolutely necessary. Security and confidentiality must be ensured. A lapse of considerable time since the conviction should lead to the erasure of the data from the ECR. The data subject must know of the existence of an ECR and be informed that his/her data will be included. (S)he must have access to the ECR and be able to have his/her personal data erased, rectified, completed or amended insofar as any of the applicable standards are not being observed according to specific procedures set by law. Moreover, there must be a supervisory body

[50] OSCD, Recommendation of the Council concerning Guidelines for the Security of Information and Networks, towards a Culture of Security adopted on 25 July 2002; see www.oecd.org/dataoecd/16/22/15582260.pdf.

that would act as a watchdog for the application of the above standards, whereas the data subject should have the right to appeal with respect to any alleged refusal of his/her rights. The specific measures that the EU will take in order to satisfy the above conditions are at the discretion of the EU bodies, but the system should be periodically reassessed.

3. Specific issues

Although the general safeguards for the ECR have been analysed, some issues require further discussion to ensure their coherence with proportionality.

3.1 Types of crimes included in the ECR

Human rights standards prohibit the inclusion in the ECR of pure suspicions, opinions or personal assessments rather than convictions. In *Amann* v. *Switzerland*, the ECourtHR held that the collection of data merely because it might be useful to enquiries would be too speculative and thus unacceptable.[51] However, in other cases the Court has allowed exceptions to this rule. In *McVeigh, O'Neill and Evans v. United Kingdom*, the Court accepted that the seriousness of the threat that organised crime posed to public safety allowed the retention of personal data where no criminal proceedings were brought.[52] However, the Court has accepted this as a temporary measure, 'for the time being'. The same would apply, according to the Court, when faced with the combating of organised terrorism; such a threat would justify the retention of material concerned, even without the consent of the person concerned.[53] Moreover, the Council of Europe's 1978 Additional Protocol to the European Convention on Mutual Assistance in Criminal Matters[54] requires in Article 4 that states communicate 'a copy of the convictions and measures in question *as well as any other information relevant thereto in order to enable [the State] to consider whether they necessitate any measures at national level*' (emphasis added). According to the Explanatory Report

[51] *Amman* v. *Switzerland* (2000) 30 EHRR 834.

[52] *McVeigh, O'Neill and Evans* v. *United Kingdom* (1981) 5 EHRR 71.

[53] *Mc Veigh* v. *United Kingdom*, Application Nos. 8022/77, 8025/77 and 8027/77 (joined); 25 D.R., paras. 229–231.

[54] Council of Europe, Additional Protocol to the European Convention on Mutual Assistance in Criminal Matters, European Treaty Series – No. 99, Strasbourg 17.III.1978.

to the Additional Protocol,[55] 'subsequent measures' include information on the rehabilitation of the person or some other information relevant to the specific case, while measures consequent upon the sentence include for example, the revocation of a driving licence.

Can it be argued that the language of the Convention allows for the inclusion of such measures in an ECR? It is doubtful whether any information that goes beyond convictions is necessary for the prevention of organised crime. Any restriction to the right to privacy must be interpreted restrictively: the fact that the inclusion of such measures may facilitate the prevention of organised crime is not adequate. The Council of Europe Recommendation regulating the Use of Personal Data in the Police Sector (R(87)15) requires that collection of data should be limited to 'such as is necessary for the prevention of real danger of a specific criminal offence'. I would be very sceptical about the usefulness of such data, even more so at the European level than at the national level. Any inclusion of this information would potentially raise serious issues of discrimination.

Similar principles apply with regard to the types of convictions that would be included in the ECR. It is difficult to accept that any of the grounds in Article 8(2) would justify blanket retention. Indeed, the prevention of organised crime at the European level does not necessitate the inclusion of all crimes, but only of those directly related to organised crime. A European Criminal Record for all crimes would have difficulty satisfying the principle of proportionality. As the ECR would restrict individual freedoms, it is important that such restriction takes place only in absolutely necessary circumstances. Hence, the crimes that would be noted therein should be serious. Indeed, it is not clear how inclusion of petty/trivial crimes to the record would prevent serious crimes. An argument has been made that often offenders move from one crime to another; hence any information on previous offences would be helpful. For example, a past vehicle theft can be related to another more serious past crime committed in another EU country. Yet, as national criminal records would continue to exist, small crimes would be recorded there and access to them would still be possible through the current system of exchange of information. Even if one accepts that their inclusion in the ECR could prevent some crimes, this is such a remote possibility that proportionality is not fulfilled. In this case, the emphasis should be on the strengthening of relevant legal structures, institutions

[55] Additional Protocol to the European Convention on Mutual Assistance in Criminal Matters, Chapter III, para. 20.

and procedures that would improve the mutual flow of information across the Member States.

Certainly, the ECR should include crimes of a transnational dimension. Convictions for transnational drug trafficking, human trafficking, terrorism, illegal trade of art objects, illegal trade of arms and ammunition and other forms of organised crimes would clearly be included in such a record. Offences of a transnational economic character, such as organised crime, corruption, fraud, counterfeiting of money and money laundering should also be included.

It is not clear whether serious crimes of a national dimension should be included in the ECR. Should for example convictions for serious sexual offences, child abuse and violence be included, even though there is no transnational element? Clearly, timely access to such knowledge could be vital for the prevention of other such crimes, but would this serve the purpose of the ECR? Essentially, if the purpose of the ECR is to tackle organised crime, knowledge of such information is not always necessary. If, however, the aim of the register is also to prevent transnational crime in Europe, then serious offences should be included, even if the transnational element is not evident. A common understanding of which crimes are serious would be important. The harmonisation of crimes across the EU, the length of sentences and punishments become even more important if an ECR is to include such information.

Notwithstanding the above discussion, it seems that any blanket decision on the crimes would not be helpful. A case-by-case approach seems necessary to determine which types of convictions would be included in the ECR. The purpose of their inclusion should be defined and the data carefully selected based on objective criteria. A useful exercise in this respect is the study of lists of crimes already prepared for other European instruments. For example, the Convention for the Protection of the Financial Interests of the European Community[56] and its Protocols,[57] the UN Convention against Corruption[58] and the

[56] The Convention on the Protection of the European Communities' Financial Interests (OJ C 316 of 27 November 1995) entered into force on 17 October 2002.

[57] First Council Protocol of 27 September 1996 to the Convention on the Protection of the European Communities' Financial Interests (OJ C 313, 23 October 1996) and Second Council Protocol of 19 June 1997 to the Convention on the Protection of the European Communities' Financial Interests (OJ C 221, 19 July 1997).

[58] Adopted by UN General Assembly Resolution 58/4 of 31 October 2003 and entered into force on 14 December 2005.

Money Laundering Directive[59] all include clusters of crimes that can be included. One list that could prove especially useful as it focused on organised crimes of transnational character would be the one compiled in the course of negotiations for a Framework Decision on the European Arrest Warrant and the Surrender Procedures between the Member States.[60] Article 2 includes the following crimes as long as they are punishable by a custodial sentence or detention order of three years or more: participation in a criminal organisation, terrorism, trafficking in human beings, sexual exploitation of children and child pornography, illicit trafficking in narcotic drugs and psychotropic substances, illicit trafficking in weapons, munitions and explosives, corruption, fraud, laundering of the proceeds of crime, counterfeiting currency, including the euro, computer-related crime, environmental crime, including illicit trafficking in endangered animal and plant species and varieties, facilitation of unauthorised entry and residence, murder, grievous bodily injury, illicit trade in human organs and tissue, kidnapping, illegal restraint and hostage-taking, racism and xenophobia, organised or armed robbery, illicit trafficking in cultural goods, including antiques and works of art, swindling, racketeering and extortion, counterfeiting and piracy of products, forgery of administrative documents and trafficking therein, forgery of means of payment, illicit trafficking in hormonal substances and other growth promoters, illicit trafficking in nuclear or radioactive materials, trafficking in stolen vehicles, rape, arson, crimes within the jurisdiction of the International Criminal Court, unlawful seizure of aircraft/ships, sabotage. Albeit too general, the list of crimes in the *Corpus Juris*[61] could also prove helpful.

Finally, a comment must be made concerning terrorism: in spite of current threats to national security and public safety, the fight against terrorism should not tempt the EU to unlawfully infringe on human rights and individual privacy. The European Court on Human Rights affirmed in *Klass* v. *Germany* (1978) that the European Convention on

[59] Council Directive 91/308/EEC of 10 June 1991. OJ L 166, 28 June 1991 at 77. Directive as amended by Directive 2001/97/EC of the European Parliament and of the Council (OJ L 344, 28 December 2001 at 76). Also see Directive 2005/60/EC of the European Parliament and of the Council of 26 October 2005 on the Prevention of the Use of the Financial System for the Purpose of Money Laundering and Terrorist Financing (OJ L 309, 25 June 2005 at 15).

[60] Council Framework Decision of 13 June 2002 on the European Arrest Warrant and the Surrender Procedures between Member States (2002/584/JHA) OJ L190 of 18 July 2002 at 1.

[61] http://www2.law.uu.nl/wiarda/corpus/art-eng.pdf.

Human Rights does not allow the Member States unlimited discretion to subject persons to secret surveillance. Although an ECR would not involve secret surveillance, an analogy can be drawn here. The Court has always tried to reach a balance between measures fighting terrorism and the rights of the individuals. This should be kept in mind when deciding whether all crimes related to terrorism – even local ones – should be included in a European Criminal Record.

3.2 Issues related to the transfer of data to the ECR

The decision about which national body should regulate the transfer of data to the ECR is important, as this body would have to make decisions that may impact on individuals' human rights. Most Member States keep national criminal records in units allocated within the Ministry of Justice. In Belgium, the national criminal authority is responsible for the collection of information related to convictions, their storage in a computerised system and the transmitting of such information to foreign authorities. In Cyprus, the Crime Record Office, also within the Ministry of Justice, performs the same function with relation to convictions, prosecutions and offences. The Czech Republic, France and Poland also adopt the same approach. In Finland criminal records are under the supervision of the Register Centre, placed within the Ministry of Justice, while in Germany criminal records are regulated by the *Bundeszentralregister* which are located in the office of the Attorney General. Also within the national Ministry of Justice are the Greek General Criminal Record Unit, the Portuguese Administration of Justice Office, the Spanish Central Register Office, the Italian *Casellari Guidiziali* and the Dutch *Centrale justitiële documentatiedienst*, all units responsible for the storage in and transfer information of the national criminal records. However, some states have such units within ministries responsible for the enforcement of the law: in Austria the national criminal register is stored by the Office of Criminal Records, located in the Ministry of Internal Affairs; this is also the case in Slovenia and Hungary. Similar is the approach of Sweden (*Registernämnden)* and the United Kingdom (New Scotland Yard).[62]

[62] Report of the Human Rights Reviser Submitted to the European Commission, Falcone Project on a European Criminal Record as a Means of Combating Organised Crime, Project run by the Sir William Dale Centre for Legislative Studies, IALS and funded by the European Commission (FAL/2000/168).

Human rights standards do not provide a clear answer as to which body should be in charge of transmitting personal data to an ECR. However, the Convention on Mutual Assistance in Criminal Matters prescribes that requests for data exchange should be addressed to the Ministry of Justice and the domestic judicial authorities (Article 14). It seems more appropriate that the body in question would be of a judicial nature or in charge of judicial bodies, so that it can be objective and familiar with the legal principles relevant to transmitting criminal data. A judicial body will have the expertise and knowledge to find difficult balances when there is a clash of interests and to implement the appropriate principles in each case. Alternatively, the body could be placed within the police as long as it has no decision-making powers and the supervisory body is a judicial one. This also conforms to the alternative the convention offers, which suggests that when direct transmission is permitted, it may take place through Europol.

As analysed earlier in this chapter, knowledge of the individual about his/her ECR is paramount. Since the individual would know of his/her entry in the ECR, he/she could be the one transferring the data. This method would give the individual more control and could avoid issues related to incorrect data. However, how realistic this option is can be doubted, since it would create confusion, could allow interference with the data, open the data to pressure manoeuvres and lead to an unreliable register. This is why in most European states entries in criminal records can only be transferred via the relevant authorities. The transfer to the ECR should be provided with very clear procedures, established by statutory law.

A related issue would be whether authorities would have direct access to the ECR or whether they would have to apply for entry. Some states, including Austria, Belgium, the Czech Republic and Portugal, do not currently allow such direct access to criminal records. Rather permission is requested by the national body entrusted with the transfer of data. Only Greece permits the transfer of data to other public authorities, but not to individuals. The full certificate may only be transferred directly to the public prosecutor, foreign embassies, wardens of penitentiary facilities or when required for the appointment of judges, teachers and professors, police officers and students to military schools and police academies.[63] If the transfer of data to the ECR were done directly, changes would need to be made so that national legislations take this into account.

[63] See Article 577, paragraph 1 of the Code of Criminal Procedure.

Transfer of data from the national criminal records to an ECR from authority to authority would provide guarantees of confidentiality and contribute to the protection of the rights of ex-offenders. Such is the transfer envisaged in Article 15 of the Convention on Mutual Assistance in Criminal Matters. Also, the Additional Protocol to the Convention provides that communication on convictions and measures will take place between Ministries of Justice (Chapter III, Article 4, para. 2, 2d section). Sanctions must be imposed for unauthorised transfer and use of data, as provided by the OECD (1992) Recommendation concerning Guidelines for the Security of Information Systems provides that sanctions be imposed for unauthorised use of data.

In addition to the authorities involved, a supervisory body would provide even more guarantees for the correct transfer of data and the protection of the rights of the data subject. The ECourtHR has repeatedly underlined the necessity of having such an independent authority to assess the conformity of data processing operations with Article 8 of the European Convention.[64] The need for an independent authority that would ensure compliance with the rules is also set out in Article 3.3 of the Charter of Fundamental Rights of the European Union and in the Council of Europe's Recommendation R (87)15 regulating the Use of Personal Data in the Police Sector. The latter was more elaborate and specified that any supervisory body should be genuinely independent of police control and have the necessary resources that would ensure its effectiveness. It should be contacted before the introduction of any new form of data processing and its role would be consultative. Although the body would not have the right to exercise veto, failure to follow its advice would raise issues concerning proportionality.[65] Also, the Additional Protocol to Convention No. 108, adopted in 2001, provides that decisions of such a supervisory body can be appealed through the courts. Finally, the data must be retained for as long as needed and then erased from the record.

3.3 Access to the ECR

Even if the above matters were resolved, one of the difficult issues would be determining who would have access to the ECR. Even access of the

[64] For example, *Gaskin* v. *United Kingdom* (1989) 12 EHRR 36 and *Kopp* v. *Switzerland.* (1998) 27 EHRR 91.

[65] See McBride, 'Disclosure of Crime Prevention Data', p. 94.

individual to his own file raises dilemmas. Although it has been established that the individual would certainly need to have access to his own entry, the question whether his access would be full or limited would need exploring. For example, the individual could be able to get a certificate on request when applying for employment and for other reasons. Still, irrespective of the value of the other options, full access would ensure clarity, accountability and openness and would soothe any fears individuals might have about the content of the entries. Certainly, the individual should also have the right to ask for corrections, changes or deletions.

For all other bodies, the main factors to determine access would again be the principles of proportionality and legality. The bodies that should have access to an ECR must be limited, especially taking into account that these bodies could always have access to the national criminal record. The question to ask is for which bodies is access a necessary measure in a democratic society in order to prevent organised crime. The bodies that should have access must be specifically identified in law and their access must not create a possible hindrance to confidentiality and secrecy.

Criminal and judicial authorities should certainly have access to the European Criminal Record. Some state prosecution authorities are not judicial authorities (Spain, Ireland); they should still have access to the ECR as this would help them serve justice better. Police access to the ECR would also be necessary to fulfil the purpose of combating organised crime; however, access should be limited to high-ranking police authority, rather than to all police bodies. High-level national administrative authorities working for the investigation of economic crimes would also benefit considerably by access to the ECR. Some states would have to change their national laws to this end. It appears that some states would probably insist that the above bodies – or some of them – have limited access, for example with specific information from the ECR being forwarded to them after a judicial decision. Taking into account proportionality, it seems to me that such a measure would not be necessary among state authorities of Member States. As long as there are guarantees of confidentiality and guarantees against any abuse of power, such information should be available as necessary to the purpose that the ECR is set to achieve. Laws and guidelines would ensure that information is accessed only when necessary and a supervisory body would ensure the legality of the process.

Different would be the answer on tendering authorities. Although access to such information could be important for the combating of organised crime, access to the ECR would not be necessary and the guarantees would not always be satisfied. For this reason, I believe it would be important that such bodies have access to such information, indirectly, through applying to the body entrusted with the ECR and with a specific question about an individual, rather than complete access to the individual's file. Other options would entail access after the individual's consent or following a court decision or a police statement.

What about authorities that work in particularly sensitive areas? Should, for example, child care bodies or banking institutions and private contracting agencies have access to the ECR? News about ex-offenders of sex crimes working at schools or with children have resulted in heated debates about the right to such information. Current campaigns push for the public knowledge of such information;[66] although public access to the ECR would be impossible from a human rights perspective, such campaigns show the intensity of some quarters' belief that knowledge about previous offences can prevent crimes. Indeed, very few could argue that knowledge of previous sexual offences of an applicant for a child-care job would not prevent, in some cases, further crimes. In a similar way, knowledge of an economic criminal offence committed by an applicant for a job in a bank would be important. Efficient access to such knowledge across the EU has been one of the main reasons for the establishment of an ECR. Yet, ex-offenders have the right to work and the core of this right should not be violated, unless necessary. Even if one focuses on the legal argument that Article 8 binds public bodies, rather than private individuals, the state must take positive measures to protect the individual's right to privacy. The ECJ has recently been examining data protection issues relating to employment.[67] In *Österreichischer Rundfunk and Others*,[68] the ECJ interpreted Directive 95/46 concerning the obligation of public bodies to communicate issues about employees' salaries and pensions. The ECJ held that the communication of data by name relating to an individual's professional income to third parties, 'in the present case a public authority, infringes the right of persons concerned to respect for private life, whatever the subsequent use of the information thus communicated, and constitutes an interference within the meaning of Article 8 of the

[66] www.forsarah.co.uk

[67] E. Szyszczak, 'Social Policy' (2006) 55 *International and Comparative Law Quarterly* 475–482.

[68] Joined Cases C-465/00, C-138/01, and C-139/01 *Österreichischer Rundfunk and Others* [2003] ECR I-4989.

[ECHR]' (para. 74). However, the ECJ also held that such interference can be justified in so far as the wide disclosure is judged to be reasonable by the national courts. In the light of this decision, it is submitted that access to the ECR by bodies that work in such difficult areas must be allowed, only if the access is indirect, discloses only information about the specific crime the individual has committed (rather than full disclosure of his file) and is accessed after the individual's consent. This is more or less the formula used in several states already. For example, in Denmark, disclosure cannot take place in cases of application, e.g. tenders submitted for public procurement, or banking, unless the individual has agreed or disclosure is allowed by law. It is important to reflect further on the link between the purpose of the ECR and the type of bodies that can have access.

In general, public authorities should have access on an ad hoc basis. When a public body deals with a case of serious organised crime then that body would apply for access describing the reasons in a detailed manner. The decision whether and to what extent access should be allowed will be based on the application and interpretation of the legal principles analysed above. It is, therefore, necessary that the body which will decide on such cases will be of a judicial nature, familiar with the legal rules and their application. This process highlights the importance of a judicial supervisory body. The ECourtHR held in *Klass* v. *Germany*: 'In a field where abuse is so easy in individual cases and could have such harmful consequences for democratic society as a whole, it is in principle desirable to entrust supervisory control to a judge.'[69]

This whole formula would be in accordance with existing instruments. The Council of Europe Recommendation R(87)15 provides that communication of data outside the police sector should be exceptional. In case of public bodies, there must be a clear obligation requiring the communication or authorisation by the supervisory authority or a court. In these cases, the supervisory body should be convinced that the need for communication outweighs the data subject's rights, within the framework of the European Convention on Human Rights and the jurisprudence of the European Court on Human Rights.[70] Access to any body must have a specific legal basis and follow the procedures prescribed by law.[71] All requests for communication should be reasoned;

[69] *Klass* v. *Germany* (1979–1980) 2 EHRR 214.
[70] For example, *Campbell* v. *United Kingdom* (1992) 15 EHRR 137.
[71] *MS* v. *Sweden* (1976) 28 EHRR 313.

the quality of data should be verified as far as possible at the time it takes place and the principles of verification, accuracy and completeness should apply.

4. Conclusions

Transfer of information in national criminal records, data collected by surveillance, audio-visual data, even DNA data, are all current practices within Member States. European human rights jurisprudence has tried to be realistic about the transfer of data and allows the transfer of personal data as long as it is necessary for the prevention of crime. The establishment of an ECR would not be against human rights standards as long as the principles of proportionality, legality and confidentially were satisfied at every single step. This would be a difficult exercise that would have to be assigned to a judicial authority. The jurisprudence of Article 8 ECHR and the principles and modalities of national criminal records can act as important guides for the correct pitch of such a measure. The ECR would work next to national criminal records. Only convictions for serious offences of organised crime would be included. More reflection is needed on whether crimes of national nature and serious crimes that fall outside organised crime should also be included. The transfer would have to be made from authority to authority and a judicial supervisory body should be in place to ensure that all principles are satisfied in each case. The individual would have to be aware of the ECR and the information included in his file and would also have the right to access, right of appeal and correction. Frequent assessments of the system will reveal the weaknesses and contribute to finding new and more efficient ways. Finally, criminal and judicial authorities would have direct access and so will police bodies of high rank. However, other public authorities would be able to access the ECR indirectly and get the information necessary for the combating of serious organised crime. Difficult choices will need to be made about access of bodies such as child care and financial bodies; proportionality would be the main guide. Finally, the public would not have access to the ECR. It is envisaged that a system like this would not unjustifiably restrict the freedoms of EU citizens; rather it would improve their quality of life by reducing organised crime in the European Union.

PART II

5

The European Criminal Record in Austria

ROBERT KERT

1. Introduction

The establishment of a European Criminal Record (ECR) seems to be a logical consequence of a unified Europe, especially with regard to transborder and international crime. Criminals can exploit the opportunities of a free market without borders, now open to them as to any EU citizen. Besides its positive aspects, it also opens more possibilities for criminal organisations and organised crime to act in many countries or enables offenders to leave one Member State after a conviction and to start working in another one. In this unified Europe an ECR could offer the possibility to find out whether a person has already been convicted in another Member State.

As usual, enhanced tools for fighting crime, such as the ECR, also bear a risk of abuse and raise questions about adequate human rights protection. Moreover, it is important to ask if the creation of an ECR is possible without harmonisation of criminal law systems. Since the EC does not have a competence to create criminal law, according to the prevailing opinion,[1] twenty-seven different criminal law systems exist

[1] See, for example, S. Thomas, 'Die Anwendung europäischen materiellen Rechts im Strafverfahren' (1991) *Neue Juristische Wochenschrift* 2234; K. Tiedemann, 'Anmerkung zu EuGH 27.10.1992' (1993) *Neue Juristische Wochenschrift* 23; M. Zuleeg, 'Der Beitrag des Strafrechts zur europäischen Integration', in U. Sieber (ed.), *Europäische Einigung und Europäisches Strafrecht* (Köln: Heymann, 1993), pp. 41–60 at p. 43; J. Vogel, 'Die Kompetenz der EG zur Einführung supranationaler Sanktionen', in G. Dannecker, *Die Bekämpfung des Subventionsbetrugs im EG-Bereich,* Schriftenreihe der Europäischen Rechtsakademie Trier (Köln: Bundesanzeiger, 1993), pp. 170–187 at p. 175; W. Bogensberger, 'Strafrecht in der Gemeinschaft' (1995) *Journal für Rechtspolitik* 102; M. Löschnig-Gspandl, 'Gibt es ein "Europäisches Strafrecht"?', in *Strafrechtliche Probleme der Gegenwart* (Wien, Bundesministerium für Justiz, 1997), vol. 25, pp. 25–45 at p. 37; H. Satzger, *Die Europäisierung des Strafrechts* (Köln: Heymanns, 2001), vol. 8, p. 94; R. Kert, *Lebensmittelstrafrecht im Spannungsfeld des Gemeinschaftsrechts* (Wien: Neuer Wissenschaftlicher Verlag, 2004), p. 484.

with different offences, different penalty systems, different systems of criminal records and different periods of erasure. How can one criminal record be created for the whole of the EU, if such fundamental elements for a criminal record are not harmonised? This chapter will analyse these questions and identify possible inputs on the Austrian legislation.

Before discussing the ECR, it is necessary to look at the Austrian legislation on criminal records.[2] The Austrian criminal records have been introduced by the Federal Act on the keeping of criminal convictions – Act on Criminal Records (*Strafregistergesetz*).[3] Section 1 of the *Strafregistergesetz* provides for one criminal record for the whole federal territory, which is kept by the Federal Police Head Office in Vienna (*Bundespolizeidirektion Wien*). When a conviction has the force of *res judicata*, the Federal Police Head Office in Vienna has to be informed about the conviction by the court which has passed the judgment at first instance. A second important provision for the criminal records legislation is the Federal Act on the Erasure of Convictions and the Limitation of Information (*Tilgungsgesetz*),[4] which rules the erasure of convictions and the limitation of access to the criminal record.

2. Existing legal framework in Austria

2.1 Contents of Austrian criminal records

2.1.1 General provisions

Austrian criminal records contain the following:

- all convictions by national criminal courts having the force of *res judicata* and all decisions of foreign criminal courts which have been rendered on the basis of an Austrian conviction;
- all convictions, which have the force of *res judicata*, by foreign criminal courts on Austrian citizens and persons who have their legal domicile or their usual residence (*Wohnsitz oder gewöhnlicher*

[2] For more details concerning the Austrian legislation see R. Kert, 'Criminal Records and Organised Crime in Austria', in C. Stefanou and H. Xanthaki (eds.), *Financial Crime in the EU* (The Hague: Kluwer, 2005), p. 69.

[3] *Bundesgesetz vom 3. Juli 1968 über die Evidenthaltung strafrechtlicher Verurteilungen, Strafregistergesetz 1968 – StRegG*; Bundesgesetzblatt (Federal Law Gazette) 1968 No. 277, amended BGBl 1972 No. 101, 1974 No. 797, 1987 No. 605, 1993 No. 257 and 1996 No. 762.

[4] *Bundesgesetz vom 15. Feber 1972 über die Tilgung von Verurteilungen und die Beschränkung der Auskunft*, Bundesgesetzblatt 1972 No. 68, amended Bundesgesetzblatt 1974 No. 423, 1987 No. 605, 1988 No. 599, 1993 No. 29, 1996 No. 762, I 1999 No. 146 and I 2001 No. 44.

Aufenthalt) in Austria and all decisions of Austrian criminal courts which have been rendered on the basis of such convictions;

- all convictions by foreign criminal courts which have the force of *res judicata*, if the states have an obligation of mutual communication under the International Convention of 5 May 1910 concerning the Suppression of the Circulation of Obscene Publications, under the International Convention for the Suppression of Counterfeiting Currency of 20 April 1929, under the Convention for the Restriction of the Production and the Regulation of the Distribution of Narcotic Drugs of 13 July 1931, and under the International Convention for the Suppression of the Traffic in Women of Full Age;
- all decisions concerning the convictions mentioned above by the Federal President or Austrian criminal courts about (among others):
  - the subsequent setting of a punishment;
  - the subsequent appointment of a probation service;
  - the pardoning of the convicted person, the mitigation, the transformation or new determination of a punishment;
  - the extension of probation;
  - the conditional release from prison;
  - the final release from prison;
  - the cassation or change of a conviction or later decision;
  - the erasure of a conviction.
- all decisions concerning convictions of foreign criminal courts equal to those mentioned above (see section 2 para. 1 *Strafregistergesetz*).

Until now only information on natural persons has been recorded in the criminal records, because criminal responsibility of legal persons did not exist in Austria. On 1 January 2006 the Federal Act on the responsibility of corporations (*Verbandsverantwortlichkeitsgesetz*)[5] came into force and introduced criminal responsibility of legal persons. The plan is to include convictions of legal persons into the criminal records[6] since, until now, a legal basis for that has been missing.

Decisions of administrative penal authorities are not contained in the Austrian criminal records and no central database for decisions in administrative penal matters exists. Only in traffic affairs has a central database been introduced.

[5] *Bundesgesetz über die Verantwortlichkeit von Verbänden für Straftaten*, Bundesgesetzblatt 2005 No. 151.

[6] See the explanations in the Governmental Bill, 994 BlgNR 22. GP, p. 15.

2.1.2. Convictions of foreigners and convictions by foreign courts

Since all final convictions by Austrian courts are included in the Austrian criminal records, crimes committed by foreigners in Austria are also included in the criminal records. The registration of a conviction by an Austrian court is independent from the nationality of the convicted person.

Convictions by foreign criminal courts of Austrian citizens and persons who have their legal domicile or their usual residence in Austria are included in the Austrian criminal records (Section 2 para. 1 fig. 2 *Strafregistergesetz*). There are three conditions for recording a conviction by a foreign court into the Austrian criminal records: (a) The matter was adjudicated by a foreign court; (b) the offence must also be a criminal offence in Austria (under criminal law, not only under administrative law) and (c) the sentence must have been passed in a trial which was conducted in accordance with the principles of Article 6 of the European Convention on Human Rights (ECHR). It is assumed by the jurisprudence that all states, which have signed and ratified the ECHR, fulfil this condition and, in principle, convictions of courts from states members of the Council of Europe are taken into the criminal records without a further examination.[7] This pragmatic approach is, however, problematic since the simple fact that a state has ratified the ECHR does not guarantee that in the specific procedure the principles of a fair trial (Article 6 ECHR) were not violated.[8]

In practice, though, the transmission of information on criminal records works well among all states that are parties to the European Convention on Mutual Assistance in Criminal Matters.[9] Article 13 of the Convention provides that the requested state shall communicate extracts from and information relating to judicial records – requested from it by the judicial authorities of a contracting party and needed in a criminal matter – to the same extent that these may be available to its own judicial authorities in similar cases. According to Article 22 of the Convention, each contracting party shall inform any other party of all criminal convictions and

[7] Oberster Gerichtshof (Supreme Court) 12 September 1990, 1 Ob 8/90. See A. Ellinger and A. Schnabl, *Strafregister- und Tilgungsrecht* (Wien: Verlag Österreich, 1998), p. 19.

[8] See U. Kathrein, in F. Höpfel and E. Ratz (eds.), *Wiener Kommentar zum Strafgesetzbuch* (Wien: Manz, 2006) 2nd edn, § 73 No. 10. See also Verfassungsgerichtshof 25 October 1980, VfSlg 8950. For more details see R. Kert in Stefanou and Xanthaki (eds.), *Financial Crime in the EU*, p. 74.

[9] Bundesgesetzblatt 1969 No. 41.

subsequent measures entered in the judicial records in respect of its nationals. The Ministries of Justice shall communicate this information to one another at least once a year. According to these provisions, there is an automatic exchange of information relating to criminal records between Austria and thirty-eight states[10] that are obliged to communicate all convictions of Austrians to the Office of Criminal Records (*Strafregisteramt*). These convictions are examined by the Office of Criminal Records, if the person is convicted on the basis of an offence which also lies in the competence of the criminal courts in Austria, and if the proceeding corresponds with the principles of Article 6 EHRC and the convicted person is an Austrian national or has permanent residence in Austria.

In addition, there is a number of bilateral treaties which provide for the communication of convictions without any special request. Such treaties exist between Austria and Germany,[11] Switzerland,[12] Italy,[13] Liechtenstein,[14] France,[15] Hungary,[16] the Czech Republic[17] and Slovakia.[18] The treaty between Austria and Germany, for example,

[10] These states are Albania, Belgium, Bulgaria, Croatia, Cyprus, the Czech Republic Denmark, Germany, Estonia, Finland, France, Georgia, Greece, Hungary, Iceland, Ireland, Israel, Italy, Latvia, Liechtenstein, Luxembourg, Malta, Macedonia, Moldova, the Netherlands, Norway, Poland, Portugal, Russia, Slovakia, Slovenia, Spain, Sweden, Switzerland, Turkey, Ukraine and the United Kingdom.

[11] Treaty between the Republic of Austria and the Federal Republic of Germany on the amendment of the European Convention on Mutual Assistance in Criminal Matters, Bundesgesetzblatt 1977 No. 36.

[12] Treaty between the Republic of Austria and Switzerland on the amendment of the European Convention on Mutual Assistance in Criminal Matters, Bundesgesetzblatt 1974 No. 716.

[13] Treaty between the Republic of Austria and the Italian Republic on the amendment of the European Convention on Mutual Assistance in Criminal Matters, Bundesgesetzblatt 1977 No. 558.

[14] Treaty between the Republic of Austria and the Principality of Liechtenstein on the amendment of the European Convention on Mutual Assistance in Criminal Matters, Bundesgesetzblatt 1983 No. 352.

[15] Treaty between the Republic of Austria and the French Republic on the amendment of the European Convention on Mutual Assistance in Criminal Matters, Bundesgesetzblatt 1985 No. 331.

[16] Treaty between the Republic of Austria and the Republic of Hungary on the amendment of the European Convention on Mutual Assistance in Criminal Matters, Bundesgesetzblatt 1994 No. 801.

[17] Treaty between the Republic of Austria and the Czech Republic on the amendment of the European Convention on Mutual Assistance in Criminal Matters, Bundesgesetzblatt 1995 No. 744.

[18] Treaty between the Republic of Austria and the Slovakian Republic on the amendment of the European Convention on Mutual Assistance in Criminal Matters, Bundesgesetzblatt 1996 No. 28.

provides that information relating to criminal records is exchanged between the two states at least every three months.[19] For Austria, the most important states to exchange information relating to criminal records are Germany and Switzerland. With both states the exchange practice is very smooth.

2.2 Mechanisms of collaboration with foreign authorities for the exchange of information included in criminal records

As shown above, there are multilateral and bilateral agreements which provide for mechanisms of collaboration with foreign authorities for the exchange of information included in criminal records. The most important treaty is the European Convention on Mutual Assistance in Criminal Matters, which provides for the obligation to communicate extracts from and information relating to judicial records to the same extent that the other state would make available to its own judicial authorities in similar cases (Article 13).

Section 9 para. 1 fig. 2 *Strafregistergesetz* provides that the Federal Police Head Office in Vienna has to pass information on the criminal records to all foreign authorities, if there is reciprocity.[20] The Federal Act on International Police Cooperation[21] establishes a special regime on the transmission of data. It provides for international police cooperation for purposes of security police, criminal police, passport matters, aliens' police and border control (Section 1 para. 1).[22] The public security authorities have to offer mutual assistance upon a request based on

[19] See Article XVI of the Treaty between the Republic of Austria and the Federal Republic of Germany on the amendment of the European Convention on Mutual Assistance in Criminal Matters.

[20] See Ellinger and Schnabl, *Strafregister- und Tilgungsrecht*, p. 29.

[21] Bundesgesetz vom 19.8.1997 über die internationale polizeiliche Kooperation (*Polizeikooperationsgesetz*), Bundesgesetzblatt I 1997 No. 104.

[22] It may seem strange that international cooperation, a problem on an international level, is ruled by a national law. One reason for the introduction of the *Polizeikooperationsgesetz* was the principle of legality established in Article 18 para. 1 of the *Bundesverfassungsgesetz* (Federal Constitution) which provides that all powers of the authorities must be determined by statutory law. Moreover the *Polizeikooperationsgesetz* provides for measures of legal protection of private persons who are effected by international police cooperation. See H. Drobesch, 'Rechtsfragen internationaler polizeilicher Zusammenarbeit aus der Sicht Österreichs', in M. Baldus and M. Soiné (eds.), *Rechtsprobleme der internationalen polizeilichen Zusammenarbeit* (Baden-Baden: Nomos Verlagsgesellschaft, 1999), p. 206; G. Schefbeck, 'Bundesgesetz,

international treaties, if this serves to carry out a function of security or criminal police by a foreign public security authority or security organisation and if there is reciprocity (Section 3 para. 1). Without a request the security authorities are obliged to offer mutual assistance by the use of data, if there is an international obligation to transfer data or if it is necessary for the foreign security authority to fulfil its functions or if it is necessary to fulfil the criminal police functions of Interpol (Section 3 para. 2). If it is necessary to guarantee the principles of data protection, conditions for the transmission of personal data to foreign public security authorities can be imposed. The transmission of data is prohibited (Section 8) if it is deemed that the public order or other essential interests of the Republic of Austria are violated or if important interests of the concerned or a third person, which are worthy of protection, are violated or if the requesting security authority will not take care of the protection of privacy of the concerned person. In relation to Member States of the Schengen Convention or of the Europol Convention and with regard to international searches on the basis of a judicial order such a supposition must be based on certain facts in the specific case. Moreover, the Federal Act on International Police Cooperation provides for particular regulations for the use of personal data (see Section 8 para. 3 and Section 9).

With Europol and Interpol there is no cooperation in the scope of criminal records, but there is cooperation at police level. The Office of Criminal Records only cooperates with foreign court authorities. On the level of Europol there is an exchange through liaison officers. Problems in the collaboration with Europol and with foreign countries are caused by the different languages and by the fact that there are no harmonised criminal offences. According to the practitioners interviewed, cooperation with all EU Member States is satisfactory in practice but could be improved, in particular when it comes to fighting international and organised crime. However, it is seen as a serious problem that convictions by foreign courts are only included in the Austrian criminal records if the person is an Austrian citizen or has his/her permanent residence in Austria. Practitioners think it is important to also include foreign convictions of foreigners, who have once committed a crime in Austria, in the Austrian criminal records.

mit dem das Polizeikooperationsgesetz erlassen und das Sicherheitspolizeigesetz geändert wird' (1997) *Journal für Rechtspolitik*, at p. 151.

If there is no treaty of reciprocity with another state, the exchange of data is more complicated. In such a case the foreign authority has to send the request to its Ministry of Justice, which has to examine the request and then forward it to the Austrian Ministry of Justice, which examines the request and decides whether or not information will be provided. In its examination of the case the Ministry of Justice verifies if the offence is also a criminal offence in Austria and if the standard of Article 6 EHRC is maintained. If all legal requirements are fulfilled, the Office of Criminal Records is asked to give the information of the criminal record. This proceeding is very complicated and time-consuming.

2.3. *An ECR balanced against privacy legislation and human rights*

Fundamental rights at risk to be violated by the use of criminal records are first of all the right of data protection and the right to privacy provided by Article 8 of the European Convention on Human Rights.

2.3.1. Data protection

The fundamental right of data protection is embodied as a human right in Section 1 of the Act on Data Protection (*Datenschutzgesetz*) which is a constitutional provision. By 1 January 2000 a new Act on Data Protection[23] came into force, which implements the provisions of the EC Directive on the Protection of Data 95/46/EC.[24]

Since the right of data protection is a human right, everybody – not only Austrian nationals – has the right that personal data concerning him be kept private, as far as there is an interest worthy of protection, in particular with regard to the respect for private and family life (Section 1 para. 1 *Datenschutzgesetz)*. Interference with this right is permitted only to safeguard overriding legitimate interests. An interference by a public authority is only permitted on the basis of a statutory

[23] Bundesgesetz über den Schutz personenbezogener Daten, Bundesgesetzblatt I 1999 No. 165.

[24] Directive 95/46/EC of the European Parliament and of the Council of 24 October 1995 on the protection of individuals with regard to the processing of personal data and on the free movement of such data, Official Journal L 281, 23/11/1995 p 31. See K. Feuchtinger, 'Zum Entwurf eines neuen Datenschutzgesetzes', *Österreichische Steuer- und Wirtschaftskartei* (1998), p. 119; A. Duschanek and C. Rosenmayr-Klemenz, 'Datenschutzgesetz – Regierungsvorlage' (1999) *ecolex*, at p. 361.

law – if it is necessary within the limits of Article 8 para. 2 of the European Convention on Human Rights (ECHR). Such statutory laws may provide for the use of data where such data are because of their nature particularly worthy of protection,[25] where the sole purpose is to safeguard important public interests and when there are adequate guaranties for the protection of the affected person's privacy (Article 1 para. 2 *Datenschutzgesetz)*. In cases where the restriction of the right to privacy is admissible, the interference with the fundamental right may only be made in the least invasive way possible. The use of data is always allowed if the person concerned agrees to it. But, despite the consent of the concerned person, the use of data by public authorities for official acts is only admissible if this accords with the functions delegated to them by statutory law.[26]

According to Section 7 of the *Datenschutzgesetz* data may be used as far as the purpose and content of the use of data is covered by the legal competence or statutory powers of the person who processes personal data on behalf of the controller (processor) and if the concerned person's interests warranting protection are not infringed. Data may only be transmitted, if it comes from a permitted use of data application, if the receiver makes his statutory competence or his legal power with regard to the purpose of the transmission credible and if the purpose and content of the transmission does not infringe the interests of privacy of the concerned person.

Section 8 para. 4 of the *Datenschutzgesetz* stipulates that the use of data concerning criminal or administrative offences, especially data concerning suspicion of the commission of a criminal offence and data concerning criminal convictions or preventive measures, does not violate privacy interests of the concerned person which are worthy of protection provided that:

1. there is an explicit statutory authorisation or obligation for the use of such data; or
2. the use of such data is an essential presumption for the processors to exercise a function which is delegated to them by statutory law; or
3. the admissibility of the use of such data derives from statutory diligence or other justified interests of the processor, which outweigh the

[25] These are data concerning natural persons revealing racial or ethnic origins, political opinions, religious or philosophical beliefs, trade-union membership, health or sex life.

[26] H. Drobesch and W. Grosinger, *Das neue österreichische Datenschutzgesetz* (Wien: Juridica Verlag, 2000), p. 100.

interests of secrecy of the concerned person, and the manner in which the data is used ensures the safeguarding of the subject's interests.[27]

According to Section 26 of the *Datenschutzgesetz* every person concerned has the right of access to data concerning him/her. With regard to the subject's access to the criminal records Section 26 para. 9 of the *Datenschutzgesetz* refers to the special provisions of the Act on Criminal Records (*Strafregistergesetz*) concerning a certificate on the criminal records (*Strafregisterbescheinigung*). According to Section 10 of the Act on Criminal Records every individual has the right to obtain a certificate of his or her own registrations in the criminal records. Upon application the mayor or the federal police department has to issue the applicant with certificates with the information held in the criminal record.

Section 27 of the *Datenschutzgesetz*, which defines the right of correction and erasure of data, provides that every controller has to correct or delete data that are incorrect or illegally processed. According to Section 27 para. 9 the rules of the *Datenschutzgesetz* (Section 27 paras. 1 to 8) apply to the criminal records only so far as there are no other provisions under a federal law with regard to an obligation to correct and delete *ex officio*, or provisions regulating the procedure and the competence to decide on applications to correct and erase data on the subject. Section 8 of the Act on Criminal Records provides for a legal protection against registration in the criminal records. Every person who is entered in the criminal records because of a conviction or any other decision has the right to dispute the entry on the basis that the registration in the criminal records was incorrect or inadmissible and also has the right to ask that the content be corrected or annulled or that a fact should have been registered or that the conviction be erased. The Federal Ministry of Interior Affairs has to decide about such applications. If the application is approved, the criminal records must be corrected. If an ECR were to be created, a similar provision should be introduced, to ensure that the right of data protection is safeguarded.[28]

The transference of information on convictions from Austria to a central department, which keeps the ECR, could turn out to be a violation of right to data protection. In principle, Section 12 of the *Datenschutzgesetz* provides that the transfer of data between the EU Member States is free and

[27] Compare Article 8 para 2 fig. 5 of Directive 95/46/EC.

[28] See also Article 12 of Directive 95/46/EC.

unrestricted. However, there is an exception for the transfer of data in matters outside the scope of Community law. The government bill explicitly mentions the use of data for purposes of the third pillar, because these matters do not fall within the scope of Directive 95/94/EC and that would be the condition for a free transfer of data.[29] The reason for this exception is that there is no harmonisation of such matters in the EU. The creation of an ECR should bring such a harmonisation. Section 12 para. 3 fig. 3 of the *Datenschutzgesetz* provides that the transfer of data to another country does not need permission from the Commission of Data Protection (*Datenschutzkommission*), if the transmission of data to another country is provided for in statutory laws which are directly applicable.

2.3.2. Article 8 of the European Convention on Human Rights

In a similar way to the right of data protection, the creation of an ECR could harm the right to respect for private and family life provided for in Article 8 ECHR. It is necessary to mention that the ECHR has the status of constitutional law in Austria. The Commission and the European Court of Human Rights have acknowledged that the collection and storage of data on a person is an interference with Article 8 and such interference needs a particular justification.[30] The Austrian Constitutional Court always reviews an act of processing and transmitting personal data with regard to its compatibility with Article 8 ECHR.[31]

Article 8 para. 2 ECHR allows an interference with the right of privacy by a public authority in accordance with the law and if it is necessary in a democratic society in the interests of national security, public safety or the economic well-being of the country, for the prevention of disorder or crime, for the protection of health and morals, or for the protection of the rights and freedoms of others.

2.3.3. Criminal records: no violation of human rights per se

In Austria the existence and use of criminal records has never been seen as a violation of human rights per se. Even though human rights (right of data

[29] Regierungsvorlage, 1613 der Beilagen zu den Stenographischen Protokollen des Nationalrates 20. GP, p. 42. See also Article 3 of Directive 95/46/EC; A. Duschanek and C. Rosenmayr-Klemenz, *Datenschutzgesetz 2000 – Gesetzestext samt Einführung und Kurzkommentar* (Wien: Wirtschaftskammer Österreich, 2000), p. 58.

[30] J. Frowein and W. Peukert, *Europäische Menschenrechtskonvention (EMRK-Kommentar)*, 2nd edn (Kehl: Engel Verlag, 1996), p. 340.

[31] See for example Verfassungsgerichtshof 30.11.1989, VfSlg 12.228.

protection, Article 8 ECHR) can be affected, criminal records have always been seen as a justified interference with these human rights. However, there is a growing sense of awareness that criminal records should be used with particular caution. There are tendencies to limit access to criminal records.[32] The introduction of the 'diversion' programme to avoid the registration of persons in the criminal records and thus to make their rehabilitation easier was an important development. In fact the triggering case for the introduction of 'diversion' in Austria was a case of illegal transfer of data of criminal records to a potential employer (the access to criminal records was restricted). The result of this illegal transfer was that a young person did not get a job. Such possible abuses of criminal records need to be avoided.

It should not be problematic to argue that the establishment of an ECR is necessary in a democratic society for national security, public safety and the prevention of disorder or crime, if it is seen as a means to combat serious (organised) crime. In the light of Article 8 it could be a problem, if the right of access to information from the criminal record or the erasure of convictions is not regulated strictly enough.[33]

2.3.4. The principle of legality

An important feature of the Austrian constitutional order is the principle of legality. From the Austrian point of view, the principle of legality requires that any interference with a fundamental right must be provided for by statutory law. Article 18 of the Austrian Constitution provides that the whole administration may only be carried out on the basis of statutory laws. This means that statutory laws are the only basis for official acts. For legal provisions such as an ECR, which in principle interfere with fundamental rights, it is necessary that they describe the conditions of the interference very precisely and clearly.[34] The principle of legality is only applicable to acts undertaken by public authorities.

Following this principle the *Datenschutzgesetz* provides that interference with the right of data protection is only permitted on the basis of a statutory law. Article 8 para. 2 ECHR also allows a public authority to interfere with the right of privacy only in accordance with the law. According to the ECHR

[32] Compare M. Flora, 'Die beschränkte Auskunft aus dem Strafregister – eine Neuregelung notwendig?' (1999) *Anwaltsblatt* at 351.

[33] Compare Verfassungsgerichtshof (Constitutional Court) 30.6.2000, B 1117/99–10.

[34] T. Öhlinger, *Verfassungsrecht*, 6th edn (Wien: WUV Universitätsverlag, 2005), p. 258. Verfassungsgerichtshof (Constitutional Court) 12.12.1995 VfSlg 10.737/1985, 29.9.1987 11.455/1987.

this is not necessarily a statutory law. However, the Austrian understanding is that an interference with a privacy law by an authority must be provided for by statutory law. Exemptions from privacy laws are only admissible within the limits of statutory law. Therefore, developing special conditions for acts of authorities in special circumstances on the basis of general 'public interest', especially on the basis of combating organised crime, contradicts Austrian legal tradition. The fight against organised crime cannot justify an extra-statutory action. The powers of authorities in such affairs must be defined by statutory law.

Therefore, many human rights and privacy laws provide for legal reservations, which empower the legislature to specify and restrict fundamental rights by statutory laws. Often these legal reservations (in particular in the ECHR) permit interference by statutory laws only under certain conditions. The interference is only permitted for the purpose of the protection of specifically protected interests and the interference must be necessary to achieve this aim. The Austrian Constitutional Court developed the principle that an interference with a fundamental right is only permitted, if it is proportionate. This means that the interference must be in the public interest, it must an appropriate means of fulfilling the purpose that is in the public interest, the provision must be necessary and there must be an adequate proportion between the public interest and the interference with the fundamental right.[35] This means that the legislature needs to balance the public interest against the interests of the persons concerned.

Therefore, it would be necessary to establish the ECR by statutory law which is directly applicable in Austria.[36] According to the principle of proportionality, it would have to be guaranteed that there is a limited access to the ECR, that the record is only used for the fight against criminality and that the rights of persons affected by the ECR are sufficiently protected. Under the *Strafregistergesetz* the illegal transmission of data is always a violation of a general public interest not to use data from the criminal records in other cases. The data of the criminal records do not lose their secret character, if they are read out in a public trial.[37]

[35] Ibid., p. 284.

[36] W. Mayer, *Das österreichische Bundes-Verfassungsrecht, Kurzkommentar*, 3rd edn (Wien: Manz Verlag, 2002), p. 561.

[37] Oberster Gerichtshof (Supreme Court) 11.6.1981, 13 Os 58/81 = SSt 52/35; 22.9.1983, 13 Os 56/83; 12.2.1985, 10 Os 193/84, SSt 56/11 = EvBl. 1985/147 (p. 660) = RZ 1985/66 (p. 169).

2.3.5. Conclusion

It is important that the interference with fundamental rights is strictly regulated. If the ECR is only a collection of convictions on the European level, which exists beside the national criminal records, there are no insoluble problems with human rights, because it always means that there is a final conviction which is stored by a central department. There are more problems associated with keeping and transferring police data based on mere suspicions.

3. Contents of a European Criminal Record

3.1. A criminal record for a certain type of crimes or for all crimes?

If the ECR is created, the main question will be what crimes should be contained in this central register. An ECR containing only data on crimes with an international dimension would be more readily accepted than an ECR which contains all convictions by the courts of the Member States. It is the common opinion of the interviewees that it would not be useful to enter every minor crime in the ECR, e.g. offences resulting from traffic accidents or minor bodily injuries. Besides the ECR the national criminal records containing all convictions should be maintained.

The question concerning which crimes should be recorded in a ECR is not easy to answer. There is a need for a Europe-wide criminal record, especially for offences which typically have an international dimension. These are, on the one hand, drug trafficking, trafficking of human beings and illicit arms trafficking as well as acts of terrorism or supporting terrorist activities. There are various other proposals of offences which should be included in an ECR: fraud, professional theft, money laundering, counterfeiting and environmental crimes; under certain circumstances, in particularly grave cases, murder and serious bodily injury. One main problem will be how to define the crimes which should be included in the ECR, since definitions of the specific offences are widely heterogeneous among the Member States. Even if we compare the Austrian legislation with the similar one in Germany, we see that there are many differences in detail. If we look for example at the statutory definition of fraud against the Community budget according to the Convention for the Protection of the Financial Interests of the European Communities (PIF Convention), there are many differences between Austrian and German legislation, although there is one common statutory definition of fraud in the PIF Convention.[38]

The difficulty in the establishment of a list of crimes to be included in the ECR is shown by the Council Framework Decision of 13 June 2002 on the European Arrest Warrant and the surrender procedures between Member States,[39] which contains in Article 2 a list of offences giving rise to surrender procedures pursuant to a European arrest warrant without verification of the double criminality of the act. This list is in some respects wide and undetermined.[40] Moreover there are offences in the list, which in some countries, e.g. in Austria, are not criminal offences but administrative penal offences. For example, the term for computer related crime (cyber crime) is wholly indeterminate, although there are European legal provisions which oblige the Member States to create specific criminal offences. But the Member States have the possibility to extend their criminal law beyond these minimum standards. It is possible that in some Member States certain conduct falls under a criminal offence, whereas in another state this conduct is only an administrative offence. Another example is the term 'fraud': although the PFI-Convention harmonises fraud against the community budget, even as between Austria and Germany some differences in the meaning of fraud do exist. Similar difficulties could be seen in the Proposal for a Council Decision on the exchange of information from criminal records.[41] The list was not limited and some categories in this list were fairly unspecific (e.g. road traffic regulations). Therefore, even the offences to be included in the ECR are listed, such a list must always be somewhat unspecific because of the differences in the various Member States.

It is also difficult to define what is organised crime. There are many acts of fraud or bribery which are not organised crime. Not every drug offence is organised crime; often it is a crime to finance the criminal's own addiction. Who decides which offences fall under the term organised crime and which do not? One representative from a political party

[38] See L. García Marqués and R. Kert, 'Strafrechtsänderungsgesetz 1998: Umsetzung des EU-Betrugs-Übereinkommens in Österreich' (1999) *Österreichische Juristen-Zeitung* at p. 213.

[39] OJ L 190, 18 July 2002, p. 1.

[40] See H. Fuchs, 'Europäischer Haftbefehl und Staaten-Souveränität' (2003) *Juristische Blätter*, at p. 405; V. Marschetz, *Auslieferung und europäischer Haftbefehl* (Vienna: Springer 2007), *passim*.

[41] COM (2004) 664 final of 13 October 2004.

emphasized the differences between the statutory definitions of a criminal organisation[42] in the Member States.

It will be difficult to find a common system to define the offences which shall be contained in the ECR since there is no common penal system in the Member States. There are offences that are criminal offences in one Member State but only administrative offences or infringements in another. If an ECR is created, the criminal offences must be defined strictly, since people who have access to the record only see the offence but not the criminal conduct which led to the conviction. If only certain offences are contained in the ECR, a harmonisation of the statutory definitions of offences within the EU will be necessary. Otherwise the ECR will contain information from different Member States that does not have the same meaning. The use of this information is difficult, because the intended users of the information will not know exactly what kind of criminal conduct is the basis for this conviction. For example, drug trafficking can mean that a person was member of a criminal organisation trafficking in drugs but it can also mean that the person only sold a small quantity of drugs to an addict. Since the second case is definitely not organised crime, it is necessary to make clear definitions of the offences contained in the criminal record. The different languages and the different meanings of legal terms are additional problems that must be solved.

In any case it is necessary that only convictions having the force of *res judicata* are contained in the ECR. This requirement stems from the presumption of innocence (Article 6 para. 2 ECHR). This human right can be guaranteed only if final decisions are put into the ECR otherwise those who have access to the ECR might erroneously think that the person has committed the crime.

3.2. Competent authority for the transfer of relevant data to the ECR authority

A crucial question is that of which national authority within the Austrian jurisdiction could undertake the task of transferring the relevant data to a central EU department in charge of the ECR, since this authority has to decide which data is transferred to the central European unit and which data is stored in the ECR. Therefore, it is very important for the responsible use of the instrument of an ECR that this department consists of competent lawyers who verify in every single case whether all the legal requirements to transfer the data are fulfilled.

[42] See Section 278a *Strafgesetzbuch* (Criminal Code).

The Austrian criminal record is kept by the Federal Police Head Office in Vienna,[43] which means that it is kept by the police not by a judicial authority. When a conviction has the force of *res judicata*, the Federal Police Head Office has to be informed about the conviction by the court which delivered the judgment in the first instance. That is why it would be one option that the Office of Criminal Records at the Federal Police Head Office in Vienna would also be responsible for the transfer of data to the ECR. Another possibility would be to establish a department like SIRENE (Supplementary Information Request at National Entry) Österreich,[44] which is competent to coordinate and transfer all relevant data for the Schengen Information System (SIS).

On the other hand, it is worth thinking about giving the competence to transfer the relevant data not to the Ministry of Internal Affairs (police), but to the Ministry of Justice. As the Falcone Project JHA/1999/FAL/197[45] showed, there are only few countries in which the criminal record is kept by the Ministry of Internal Affairs. In Austria it has often been debated whether the Ministry of Justice should keep the criminal record, since only judicial information is kept on the criminal record. The main reason why it is still kept by the police is a practical one, because the judges do not want to undertake the task of keeping and updating the criminal records. However, it would be reasonable to give the power to keep criminal records to the Ministry of Justice. Therefore, the power of the Ministry of Justice to decide which crimes are transferred to the central ECR should be supported. However, the information arises from acts of judicial authorities and it should be in the competence of independent judicial authorities to decide which convictions are transferred to the central department. This would also prevent criminal record data from being mixed with other police data which would facilitate the control. Even if the power to keep the national criminal records remains with the police, judges should have the competence to decide which convictions are transferred to the ECR. Representatives of the political parties deem the existing Office of Criminal Records in the Ministry of Internal Affairs the best solution. However, there should be special control mechanisms to prevent the abuse of data.

[43] Section 1 para. 2 *Strafregistergesetz*.

[44] See Anonymous, 'Sirene Österreich – Das Schengener Informationssystem und seine Auswirkungen auf den Exekutivdienst' (1996) *Öffentliche Sicherheit* 6/96, at p. 19; Anonymous, 'Sirene Österreich' (1997) *Öffentliche Sicherheit* 6/97, at p. 11.

[45] See Stefanou and Xanthaki (eds.), *Financial Crime in the EU*.

3.3. Transfer of data included in criminal records to the ECR authority

In Austria it is prohibited to transfer information included in criminal records to unauthorised persons or departments. It will be compatible with the Austrian legislation, if the transfer of data from an Austrian authority to the ECR authority is provided for explicitly by a statutory law. This statutory law – either an EC Regulation or a national law – would need to determine an authority competent to check which information is transmitted to the ECR. It would be in conflict with the Austrian legislation if a foreign or EC authority were to have direct access to the data. A transfer via the concerned person him/herself seems to be too complicated and not realistic.

3.4. Department at the EU level keeping the ECR

It is an essential and difficult point to decide which department or agency of the EU is best suited to perform the task of keeping and maintaining an ECR. It should be an independent department under the control of a court. The department should be staffed with lawyers familiar with the legislation of the Member States, since they have to verify what is meant by the definitions of crime in the various countries.

Europol would be one option. From the Austrian legal perspective, there would not be a fundamental problem if the ECR were kept by a police authority. On the other hand, the disadvantage of an ECR kept by Europol is that it is not subject to judicial control.[46] Moreover, there must be more transparency in the work of Europol. Therefore, creating an effective control system for Europol would be an important condition before giving them the competence to keep an ECR. It would be necessary to ensure that only data which fulfil the legal requirements are stored in the ECR, that only legitimate persons get access and that data is only used for the purposes provided for by statutory laws. Without these provisions Europol does not seem to be an adequate option. It is also important to establish the necessary technical requirements that guarantee the right of data protection and the right of privacy. Europol is also favoured by most politicians in

[46] See J. Frowein and N. Krisch, 'Der Rechtsschutz gegen Europol' (1998) *Juristenzeitung* 589–597; S. Gleß, 'Kontrolle über Europol und seine Bediensteten' (1998) *Europarecht* 748–764, at p. 764; J. Martínez Soria, 'Die polizeiliche Zusammenarbeit in Europa und der Rechtsschutz des Bürgers' (1998) *Verwaltungsarchiv* 400–438, at p. 432; H. Jung, 'Konturen und Perspektiven des europäischen Strafrechts' (2000) *Juristische Schulung* 417–424, at p. 423.

Austria. But they emphasise that the control of Europol must be seriously discussed due to the reasons outlined above.

It should be considered whether it would not be better to find a separate unit to keep the ECR. This unit could be established at the Directorate-General for Justice and Home Affairs and should be under the control of the European Court of Justice. An EC regulation should govern the competence of this unit, its control etc.

Another option which is more judicial in nature is Eurojust. Its objectives are to coordinate investigations and prosecutions between the competent authorities in the Member States and improve cooperation between the competent authorities. The general competence of Eurojust covers the types of crime which could also be contained in the ECR, such as participation in a criminal organisation, money laundering or fraud and corruption.[47] Because of its objectives, Eurojust would be an alternative to a police authority such as Europol, since it is composed of prosecutors or judges. Since Eurojust already today processes personal data, it has a specially appointed Data Protection Officer and an independent joint supervisory body to monitor collectively the processing of data by Eurojust. In addition to these provisions, if Eurojust became the department to keep the ECR, it would be necessary to place Eurojust under the control of an independent court. Only an independent control body can guarantee that rights of the concerned individuals are respected. Finally, there must be the possibility of appeal for people who are concerned about information contained in the ECR. If this data is not corrected or deleted by the central European department, a remedy from a court must be available.

4. Access to the ECR

The (direct) access to the ECR should be restrictive in order to prevent abuse of data. Austrian law allows that information contained in the criminal records (excerpts from the criminal records – *Strafregisterauskünfte*) is disclosed upon request to all national authorities, all offices of the police, concerned members of the federal army, to the military commanders and to all foreign authorities if there is reciprocity (Section 9 para. 1 *Strafregistergesetz*).[48] Moreover, each person

[47] See Article 4 of the Council Decision of 28 February 2002 setting up Eurojust with a view to reinforcing the fight against serious crime, OJ L 63, 6 March 2002, pp. 1–13.

[48] See Ellinger and Schnabl, *Strafregister- und Tilgungsrecht*, pp. 29–30.

has the right to obtain a certificate (*Strafregisterbescheinigung*) about his or her own registrations in the criminal records. Upon application by an individual mayors or federal police departments have to issue the applicant with a certificate that proves either the convictions of the applicant or that there is no conviction of the applicant (Section 10 *Strafregistergesetz*).

Access to the ECR should also be limited to public authorities. For the Austrian legislation this would mean that judicial and prosecution authorities should always have direct access to the ECR; public tendering authorities and professional associations of lawyers, notaries and accountants too, because they are public authorities in Austria. Banking institutions and private contracting agencies should not have direct access, because they are private institutions. Access to the ECR should not be opened to private actors, since it would make it difficult to oversee who is authorised to access to the data and would facilitate an abuse.

In Austria the lack of direct access to the criminal records by private persons is not really problematic because it is possible for everyone – especially for employers – to demand a certificate about the registrations in the criminal records from the applicant. It is quite usual to have the obligation to bring a copy of your criminal record, when you are applying for a job or a certain permission (e.g. trade permission) or membership. In particular, in applications for professions which require a high reliability, criminal records are often demanded (see e.g. Section 339 *Gewerbeordnung* – Trade Act). For example, Section 67 para. 2 no. 1 of the Federal Procurement Act (*Bundesvergabegesetz*) provides that every tendering authority can demand the tenderer to bring a criminal record or an equivalent document of a court or administrative authority from the state of origin of the tenderer.[49] It would be necessary to enable everyone to obtain a certificate which shows the information about him/herself contained in the ECR. The introduction of an obligation for specific applicants – e.g. tenderers in the proceedings for the award of public contracts or applicants for employment in banking institutions or other professions – to include a copy of their criminal record would not be problematic under Austrian law.

[49] See also Article 45 of the Directive 2004/18/EC of 31 March 2004 on the coordination of procedures for the award of public works contracts, public supply contracts and public service contracts, OJ L 134, 30 April 2004, pp. 114–240.

Another point to be discussed is whether it is necessary to give every public authority access to the ECR. If there is the possibility for every individual to ask for a certificate on his/her criminal record it could be sufficient if only criminal prosecution authorities and authorities that work in particularly sensitive areas (e.g. trade in arms, possession of weapons, production of explosives) or authorities that have to check particular issues of trust concerning certain persons (e.g. of pharmacists, detectives, notaries) had direct access to the ECR. All other authorities in the general administration could ask for a criminal record certificate. This would reduce the possibility of abuse of criminal records. It is interesting to note here that the representatives of the Conservative and of the Socialist party are of the opinion that access to the ECR should – due to the interference with personal rights – be very restrictive. Access to the ECR should be even more rigid in comparison with the access to the criminal record under Austrian legislation.

One important point is to guarantee that only legitimate persons have access to the ECR. Technically in Austria this is guaranteed in the way that each legitimate authority has a unique code number which allows for access to the criminal record. This code number is linked with the address of the authority, so that even if the code number is mistakenly or fraudulently used, the information is sent to the address of this legitimate authority. A similar system of controlled access should be introduced on European level.

It is an important feature of the Austrian criminal record legislation that according to Section 6 of the Act on the Erasure of Convictions and the Limitation of Information (*Tilgungsgesetz*[50]) there is a restriction of information about certain sentences:

- if they do not exceed three months of imprisonment (or of imprisonment in default of payment);
- if the perpetrator was convicted because of an offence which was committed when he or she was a juvenile (under 18 years) or a young adult (under 21 years) and if the sentence does not exceed six months of imprisonment; or
- if committal to an institution for mentally ill offenders is ordered.[51]

[50] Bundesgesetz vom 15. Feber 1972 über die Tilgung von Verurteilungen und die Beschränkung der Auskunft, BGBl 68, amended BGBl 1974/423, 1987/605, 1988/599, 1993/29 and 1996/762.

[51] Flora, 'Beschränkte Auskunft' (1991) *Anwaltsblatt*, at p. 351; Kert, in Stefanou and Xanthaki, *Financial Crime in the EU*, pp. 80–81.

When the sentence exceeds three months, but not six months (or, in juvenile cases, six months, but not one year), the restriction arises three years after the beginning of the term.

If the information is restricted, information on such convictions may only be given to:

- courts, public prosecutor's offices and public security authorities for the purpose of criminal proceedings against the convicted person or someone who is suspected of being involved in the same criminal offence;
- fiscal offence prosecution authorities (*Finanzstrafbehörden*) for the purpose of administrative fiscal offence proceedings against the convicted person or someone who is suspected of being involved in the same offence;
- the authorities in proceedings for pardoning the convicted person concerned;
- authorities according to the Weapons Act (*Waffengesetz*) for the purpose of checking the reliability of persons possessing weapons;
- the public security authorities for the purpose of execution of trade laws concerning the arms trade, the production of and trade in explosives, the production of pharmaceutical products, or concerning professional private investigators;
- passport authorities, citizenship authorities, aliens' police authorities and authorities competent to issue and withdraw residence permissions;
- military authorities for the examination of reliability.

In all other cases such convictions must not be included in excerpts from the criminal records or criminal record certificates and a convicted person is not obliged to indicate such convictions apart from in the case of the mentioned procedures. The main rationale of this provision is to enable a better rehabilitation of the offender and to make recourse to the conviction possible in new criminal proceedings against the same person.[52] Such a limitation of information should also be introduced for the ECR. It enables the courts, the public prosecutor's offices and public security authorities to have access to all data for the purpose of criminal proceedings but not all the other authorities. The limitations on information provided should be less restrictive than under the Austrian legislation. For example, it seems to be possible that every conviction falls within the limitation after five years (after completion of the sentence).[53] Such a provision would make the rehabilitation of offenders, which should always be the aim of criminal sanctions, easier, because the former offenders will have less difficulty in

[52] Flora, *Anwaltsblatt* (1999), p. 351. [53] Ibid., p. 353.

finding employment. On the other hand the fight against organised crime would be facilitated, because courts and prosecution authorities would have access to all information.

5. Use of the ECR

5.1. *The purpose of an ECR in general*

In national legislation the main purpose of keeping the criminal records is the keeping of evidence for the criminal prosecution authorities internally, i.e. the police, the courts and the public prosecutor's offices. The most important purpose of criminal records is to enable judicial authorities to refer to former convictions in later criminal proceedings against the convicted person, providing an indication of the personality of the offender, which is important in sentencing – especially as aggravating circumstances. In Austria criminal records also have an important use outside criminal law. Many authorities use the information for different purposes (e.g. administrative authorities responsible for giving a trade permission/licence), and most employers ask for a criminal record certificate to check the reliability of applicants for a job.

An ECR would make it possible for convictions passed in another Member State to have effects equivalent to those of a national conviction. They could be considered already at the pre-trial stage, e.g. for decisions relating to provisional detention, and then at the trial stage as aggravating circumstance or as reason for excluding a suspended sentence. Moreover, it would be possible to use the information to check the reliability of tenderers or applicants for a job or a permission. In a unified Europe a centralised ECR would enable Member States' authorities to have knowledge about the former criminal career of suspects. In itself this could have a preventive effect, as criminals would know that authorities in other countries would be able to obtain information on former convictions.

5.2. *Is an ECR an effective weapon against organised crime and terrorism?*

The effectiveness of an ECR to combat organised crime and terrorism and to counterbalance the lack of border control within the EU, is seen differently depending on the profession. The police think that an ECR would be very useful, since organised crime activities, particularly in the fields of drug criminality, fraud, trafficking of human beings and money laundering, and terrorism are not limited to one country. It could be useful to see that a person already has prior convictions in another country. Moreover, they think that it could deter criminals if they knew that the authorities of other countries could get information on former convictions. Others, particularly representatives of the judiciary, do not think that an ECR is really a very effective instrument to fight organised crime. The criminal record only contains information on the number and dates of convictions and on the committed crimes, but there is no detailed information about the modus operandi of the crime or other circumstances of the offence. In other words it does not give more extensive data about the person but only presents a first impression. They think that the police have much more information about criminals, because they have also got information on suspected persons. Of course, this last argument could also be used in favour of an ECR. This could result in a transparent use of data on individuals on a correct legal basis. There would be no reason to pass information on individuals to authorities of other countries through informal channels.

6. Critical evaluation

6.1. Implementation into the Austrian legal system

6.1.1. Obstacles to the implementation

From the Austrian perspective there will be no grave and insoluble legal problems with the implementation of an ECR into the Austrian legal system. There are no constitutional problems which could not be solved by legislation. Particularly, it is important that every interference with fundamental and human rights is ruled very strictly by statutory law.

6.1.2. Issues covered by a legal act establishing an ECR

For the implementation of an ECR within the framework of Austrian legislation it is important that some issues are covered by an EC legal act (Directive, Regulation, Framework Decision) establishing an ECR. It must be decided which crimes are included in the ECR: only convictions by criminal courts having the force of *res judicata* should be included in the ECR, but not decisions by administrative authorities. It must be established that only convictions, which are passed in a proceeding being in conformity with the ECHR, should be included in the ECR. If this is guaranteed, there should be no constitutional problems under the Austrian jurisdiction with the establishment of an ECR.

The ECR itself should contain information on the conviction, on the crime committed, on the court that rendered the judgment, on the date of the judgment and on the penalty. As pointed out above, it is necessary that the legal act contains strict provisions about access to the criminal record and the limitation of access. The more access is limited, the easier it will be to implement an ECR into the Austrian jurisdiction, since there are less problems with privacy legislation. To guarantee the right of data protection, the correction and deletion of wrong information must be included. Moreover, it must establish the right of a person concerned to obtain information on all data that is held about him/her. Otherwise it could be seen as a violation of the right of data protection.

One important point to regulate is the erasure of convictions. It is necessary to determine the term of erasure, the beginning of the term, the prolongation of the term because of other convictions, the responsibility for the deletion of convictions etc. In Austria the conviction is erased automatically by act of law upon the expiration of a certain term (*Tilgungsfrist*).[54] A decision by a judge is not necessary.[55] If a conviction is erased, the person is regarded as 'respectable' and he/she is not obliged to give information on an erased conviction. An erased conviction must not be taken into the excerpt of the criminal records and must not be made visible in any other way (Section 1 para. 5 *Tilgungsgesetz*). Erased convictions may neither be seen as aggravating circumstances in the case of a new conviction.

The term of erasure begins when all sentences of imprisonment or fines are executed, are regarded as executed or must not be executed any more. The term of erasure depends on the extent of the conviction and whether it is a juvenile case. Convictions of juveniles without a sentence are erased after three years. Other convictions are erased after five years, if the sentence is not more than one year imprisonment or only a fine, and if it is a juvenile case. Convictions are erased after a time period of ten years, if the sentence is between one and three years of imprisonment, and after fifteen years, if the sentence exceeds three years. Sentences to life imprisonment cannot be erased (Section 5 *Tilgungsgesetz*). If a person is convicted again, before one or more former convictions have been erased, all convictions are erased together

[54] Section 1 para. 1 *Tilgungsgesetz*. See H. Ambrosi, 'Das neue Strafregister – Elektronik im Dienste des Rechts' (1974) *Öffentliche Sicherheit* 4, at p. 1.

[55] An erasure is possible before the end of the legal term of erasure in two cases: on the basis of an act of grace of the Federal President (Article 65 para. 2 lit. c Bundes-Verfassungsgesetz – Federal Constitution) and in the case of an amnesty (Article 93 Bundes-Verfassungsgesetz).

and for the determination of the period of erasure the sentences of all sentences that have not been erased yet are added together (Section 4 para. 1 and 2 *Tilgungsgesetz*). For foreign convictions the terms of erasure are the same. They are also regarded as erased, if they are erased according to the law of the state where they have taken place and if this is certified by a public document. Two years after setting aside the erased conviction and the data about the convicted person must be deleted from the criminal record (Section 12 *Strafregistergesetz*).

These rules of erasure are very complicated and the terms of erasure are too long, because they only start after the execution of the whole penalty. For example, if a fine is paid in instalments, the term of erasure starts with the payment of the last instalment. Also an international comparison of the terms of erasure shows that the Austrian terms are quite long. Shorter terms of erasure would be sufficient for an ECR.

7. Political acceptance

It is difficult to tell if there would be strong political opposition to the creation of an ECR. Representatives of political parties have been sceptical about the need for a creation of an ECR. However, since most of the parties emphasise the aspect of public security, it can be expected that most of them would not be against an ECR.

The spokesperson on justice affairs of the *Österreichische Volkspartei* (Conservative Party) thinks that the competence of Europol according to Article 10 of the Europol Convention could possibly be a sufficient tool in the fight against organised crime. She wonders whether other existing instruments do not have the same effect, e.g. the exchange of information from judicial records on the basis of Article 22 of the European Convention on Mutual Assistance in Criminal Matters or the instruments according to the Europol Convention. With regard to problems in connection with data protection the establishment of new instruments should not have priority, but existing instruments should rather be used and improved.

The representative of the Social Democratic Party also sees the main problem in the possibility of abuse of data contained in the ECR. In recent years there have been some cases of abuse of data by the police (police officers gave private data to politicians). For this reason, it is seen as necessary to establish mechanisms, which enable the protection of rights of the persons concerned. It will be necessary to find a common standard of data protection and protection of human rights and effective control mechanisms before creating an ECR. Opposition is to be expected by human rights groups and the Green Party.

In 2006 the Austrian government supported the idea of an electronic exchange of information on convictions which accelerates the existing system on the basis of Article 22 of the European Convention on Mutual Assistance in Criminal Matters. It supported the introduction of a fast data connection between the national criminal records of the Member States.

7.1. The evaluation of organised crime and terrorism in Austria

Until the beginning of the 1990s, organised crime was not seen as a problem in Austria. In 1997 video surveillance (*großer Lausch- und Spähangriff*) and automatic matching of data (*Rasterfahndung*) were introduced into the Austrian Criminal Procedure as new measures to fight organised crime. The introduction was controversial. And it is interesting that the explanations to the government bill[56] and the report of the parliamentary judicial committee[57] refer to the international development of organised crime and especially to analysis of the criminality in Germany. The reason for this was that in Austria no criminological investigation of organised crime existed, which is an indication that organised crime was not seen as a real problem in Austria. It was in the explanations to this government bill that for the first time after World War II politically motivated terrorism was mentioned, since there were several attacks by letter bombs during this time in Austria.

In the last few years organised crime and, since September 11, terrorism have been seen and discussed as serious problems. There have been many publications and conferences on this subject in recent years.[58]

[56] EBRV 49 BlgNR, 10. [57] JAB 812 BlgNR 20. GP, 1 f.

[58] See for example R. Miklau and C. Pilnacek, 'Optische und akustische Überwachungsmaßnahmen zur Bekämpfung schwerer und organisierter Kriminalität ("Lauschangriff") – Paradigmenwechsel im Verfahrensrecht' (1997) *Journal für Rechtspolitik*, at p. 286; Bundesministerium für Justiz (ed.), *Organisierte Kriminalität – Professionelle Ermittlungsarbeit – Neue Herausforderungen* (Wien: Bundesministerium für Justiz, 1996); M. Edelbacher (ed.), *Organisierte Kriminalität in Europa – Die Bekämpfung der Korruption und der organisierten Kriminalität* (Wien: Linde, 1998); Landesgruppe Österreich der Internationalen Strafrechtsgesellschaft (AIDP) (ed.), *Organisierte Kriminalität und internationales Strafrecht* (Wien: AIDP, 1997); Landesgruppe Österreich der Internationalen Strafrechtsgesellschaft (AIDP) (ed.), *Organisierte Kriminalität und Wirtschaftsrecht* (Wien: AIDP, 1998); E-M. Maier, 'Strafrecht – Kriegsrecht – Ausnahmezustand? Der Rechtsstaat vor der Herausforderung des Terrorismus' (2006) *Journal für Rechtspolitik*, at p. 27.

However, the evaluation of the gravity of the problem differs. Whereas the police see organised crime as a serious problem there is scepticism among specialists in the field and politicians about the seriousness of the problem. The main reason for this might be the estimated number of undetected cases of organised crime.[59] The report of the Federal Government on Interior Security in Austria (Security Report) from the year 2005,[60] which is published by the Federal Ministry of Internal Affairs and the Federal Ministry of Justice, points out that organised criminality has developed into a border-crossing, multinational problem in Austria. It is said that criminal organisations would use the EU as a common action area without any borders. It is seen as a problem that there is a great structural similarity between organised criminality and legal undertakings. The main fields of criminality where criminal organisations are active in Austria are trafficking of human beings, economic crimes, money laundering, international tax fraud, drug trafficking and car trafficking. The Federal Ministry of Internal Affairs says that the role of organised crime in criminality as a whole is significant.[61]

The vulnerable sector is the banking business, especially in connection with money laundering. Moreover, criminal organisations from the Eastern European countries have founded fictitious undertakings and have purchased real estate in Austria. According to the police, (former) leaders of these Eastern European criminal organisations have managed to enter high political and economic positions in Austrian institutions, especially within the context of international societies and trade trusts.[62]

7.2. An ECR as successful instrument to combat organised crime?

There are different evaluations concerning the establishment of an ECR. The police – particularly the Office of Criminal Records – think that the introduction of an ECR is a positive crime-combating development and not an unnecessary intrusion into national law. It is seen as necessary in

[59] See Bundesministerium für Inneres/Bundesministerium für Justiz (eds.), *Bericht der Bundesregierung über die innere Sicherheit in Österreich 2005 (Sicherheitsbericht 2005)* (Wien: 2006), p. 242.

[60] Ibid., p. 236.

[61] Bundesministerium für Inneres/Bundesministerium für Justiz (eds.), *Bericht der Bundesregierung über die innere Sicherheit in Österreich 2001 (Sicherheitsbericht 2001)*, p. 258.

[62] Ibid., p. 269.

an EU with open borders which enable the free movement of persons and also the free movement of criminals. There are problems if someone is conspicuous in a European country, e.g. in Spain, and arrested without documents. If, for example, he says that he comes from Germany, when in reality he is an Austrian, it is impossible for the Spanish authorities to find out whether there are convictions in Austria. The main problems concern drug crimes and trafficking in human beings. Therefore, the idea of a central department which keeps an ECR is supported. The current technical resources should be used. The police think that a model for an ECR could be the Schengen Information System which could help to handle it in practice.

In the judiciary the idea of an ECR is seen quite sceptically, since it is seen as a problem to create an ECR without harmonising the statutory definitions of offences. If the statutory definitions of offences are not harmonised, the criminal record will be very difficult to read, since there are very different meanings of crimes in the various countries. The representatives of the political parties support measures to fight organised crime and terrorism, but they are sceptical about an ECR being the only possibility and the appropriate instrument.

8. Conclusions

The idea of an ECR is certainly an attractive one in a unified Europe with open borders and with free movement of persons. It is obvious that there are cases of organised and border-crossing crime, in which such a centralised criminal record would help to fight against these forms of criminality. On the other hand, the danger that an ECR is in conflict with the right of data protection and privacy rights must always be considered. From an Austrian point of view, the creation of an ECR would be justified by the necessity to guarantee a high level of public safety.

Data held in an ECR are of a sensitive nature. Such data are mentioned in Article 8 para. 5 of Directive 95/46/EC, which says that processing of data relating to offences, criminal convictions or security measures may be carried out only under the control of an official authority or if suitable specific safeguards are provided under national law, subject to derogations which may be granted by the Member State under national provisions offering suitable specific safeguards. According to this provision, a complete register of criminal convictions may be kept only under the control of an official authority. It must always be kept in mind that too wide a dissemination of information kept in a criminal record might reduce the chances of social reintegration of a convicted person. Therefore, a legal act introducing an ECR must contain guarantees that data protection measures are always applied.

An important point is, therefore, that the access to the ECR is strictly limited to persons who need them because of a special profession, e.g. judges and public prosecutors. Moreover, access should be limited to purposes which are necessary for the public safety of the citizens. Under certain circumstances the general interest to combat criminality can make it necessary that third parties also have access to information contained in criminal records, e.g. employers. But these parties should not have direct access, only indirect access.

It seems to be difficult to create an ECR without a harmonisation of the criminal law provisions. Therefore, at this stage it will be difficult to determine which crimes should be contained in the ECR. Moreover, it is necessary to harmonise the extent of penalties. In Europe, there are big differences in the extent of penalties depending on where a crime is committed. For the commission of the same crime, very different sentences are possible. This is shown by many comparisons, for example, between Austria and Germany. But these different penalties can have important consequences for the terms of erasure. In my opinion, these problems are the reason why initiatives of harmonisation and unification of criminal laws, e.g. the *Corpus Juris* project, should come first and should be supported. They are the only way to fight effectively against organised and transnational crime. But I must emphasise that this is my personal opinion and not the opinion of the Austrian government.

If an ECR is introduced, it is important to identify clearly the crimes which are included in a criminal record. It would be problematic, if persons who have not committed grave offences were included in an ECR, because it would make it more difficult to begin a new life in another country. An ECR does not make it easier to begin a new life in another European country. But it will be difficult to make an abstract distinction between grave or organised criminality and 'normal ' criminality. In cases of 'normal' or minor criminality (e.g. fraud cases and drug crimes which are not organised crime) it is not necessary to store them in a Europe-wide criminal record. In these cases, we must always think about the proportionality between the offence committed and the measures which are taken. These measures must always enable rehabilitation of the offender.

In conclusion, believing in a unified Europe, I think that an ECR is necessary in the long term and it is a good idea. At the moment it may be necessary to take some other steps before creating a Europe-wide criminal record, e.g. harmonisation of criminal laws, the establishment of judicial and democratic control mechanisms for Europol and Eurojust, or the establishment of a European Public Prosecutor.

6

The European Criminal Record in the Czech Republic

JAROSLAV FENYK

1. Introduction

The Czech Republic has a central agency responsible for maintaining criminal records (criminal record attached to the Ministry of Justice) and uses a computerised system to store the register of convictions. There is no criminal responsibility of legal persons, and therefore the Czech criminal record contains only natural persons' data.

For the needs of Czech criminal proceedings the system is apparently sufficient. However, the Czech Republic's geographic position is in Central Europe and the country is – without any prejudice – characterised as a transit country for goods, services, people and perhaps more importantly criminals, criminal organisations and their illegal activities. The 'foreign element' is, therefore, presented in more and more criminal cases. Communications and exchanges of information between Member States are inevitable measures for the efficient fight against crime. Current methods (e.g. the 1959 European Convention on mutual assistance in criminal matters) seem to be insufficient and do not fulfil the needs of the EU because of the extensive impact from non-EU states. The practical application of the 1959 Convention embodies the following weaknesses:

- all the parties to the Convention did not establish a record of convictions of foreign courts;
- even for the parties that established a record of convictions it is usually 'occasional practice';
- administration and deletion of data on convictions are subject to national modalities and needs;
- information on non-EU states' citizens can be unavailable;
- it can be difficult to confirm whether a foreigner has or has not been convicted in other Member States.

This chapter reflects on several framework reasons for the use of information from the criminal record database at the national level (criminal law and procedure) and attempts to deploy them in the EU arena (substantive law and procedure points of view):

- the Czech Criminal Code recognises a previous conviction mainly in connection with specific elements of criminal liability in some cases: sentence (aggravating circumstances), suspended sentence, suspended prosecution, settlement, etc.
- the Czech Criminal Procedure Code distinguishes rule-based inadmissibility on the *non bis in idem* principle.
- the Czech Criminal Procedure Code applies coercive measures (when taking an offender into custody recidivism or repeat commission of a crime can be a reason for applying such a measure).

The objective is to improve the quality of exchanged information on sentences/convictions in criminal matters and it is relevant to the Czech Republic (i.e. an obligation to provide comprehensive information on Member State citizens) and to other Member States (i.e. common action at the EU level).

2. Existing legal framework

The law on the Czech Criminal Register (Law no. 269/1994 Coll., as amended) strictly prescribes criminal proceedings. A transcript from the criminal record register ('transcript') is given to bodies active in criminal proceedings (police, public prosecutor, courts) and to the Ministry of Justice at their request. However, there are additional reasons why the data contained in the criminal record are in practice required by the police, the public prosecutor or the court.

2.1 Previous conviction (recidivism, repeated offences) as an essential element of a crime[1]

In some expressly identified instances the Czech Criminal Code (CCC) requires recidivism (repeated offence) as an element of a crime (*nullum crimen sine lege*) or as an inevitable condition for the criminal liability of

[1] Development and characteristic features of recidivism from Czech criminal statistics: number of repeat offenders convicted each year amounts to around 40,000; number of crimes committed by repeat offenders amounts annually to around 60,000, while

natural persons.[2] In those instances recidivism can be ascertained from the database of the criminal record, e.g. Section 121 (CCC),[3] Section 203 (CCC)[4] and Section 247 (CCC).[5]

Recidivism can be considered as an aggravating circumstance in any criminal case and it should be taken as one of the criteria for determining the type and length of punishment, e.g. Section 34 (CCC).[6] When an

the total number of detected crimes amounts yearly to 380.000–400.000 (Source: Governmental Reports on Security Situation in the Czech Republic).

[2] Criminal liability of legal persons has not been introduced in the Czech Republic (a draft law was rejected by the Chamber of Deputies in 2004).

[3] See Section 121 (CCC):

> *Activity detrimental to a consumer*
>
> (1) A person who causes damage which is not negligible to someone else's property by activity which is detrimental to a consumer, in particular by cheating on the quality, quantity or weight of goods, or a person who puts onto the market goods, works or services to a significant extent while concealing substantial defects in them, shall be sentenced to imprisonment for a period of from six months to three years, or barred from business activity or ordered to pay a pecuniary penalty.
>
> (2) An offender shall be sentenced to imprisonment for a period of from two to eight years:
>
> . . . (c) if during the previous five years he/she was convicted, or released from imprisonment, for committing the same type of crime.

[4] See Section 203 (CCC):

> *Torture of animals*
>
> (1) A person who tortures an animal, even though he/she was punished either for a similar misdemeanour in the previous year or sentenced for such crime in the preceding two years, shall be punished by a term of imprisonment of up to one year, prohibition of a specific activity or by a pecuniary penalty.

[5] See Section 247 (CCC):

> *Theft*
>
> (1) A person who appropriates a thing by taking it into his/her possession, and:
>
> . . . (e) was convicted and punished of such act in the previous three years; shall be punished by a term of imprisonment of up to two years or forfeiture of a (specific) thing.

[6] See Section 34 (CCC):

> *Imposition of sentence*
>
> When imposing a sentence, the court shall consider as an aggravating circumstance in particular the fact that the offender:
>
> . . . (k) had already been convicted of a crime; the court is authorised not to consider such fact as an aggravating circumstance according to the

extremely serious crime has been committed, recidivism is one of the elements of obligatory heavy sentencing by the court, e.g. Section 41 (CCC)[7] and Section 42 (CCC).[8]

> nature of the previous offence, particularly in respect of the significance of a protected interest affected by such act, the manner of committing such act and its consequences, the circumstances under which it was committed, the offender's personality, the extent of his culpability, his motives and the period which has passed since his last conviction; the court shall consider whether it concerns an offender who has committed the crime of unauthorised (unlicensed) production and possession of addictive and psychotropic substances or poisons (provision 187a(1)) and whether such offender has committed the said crime because he is addicted to the use of addictive and psychotropic substances or poisons.

[7] See Section 41 (CCC):

Sentencing a particularly dangerous recidivist to a term of imprisonment:

> (1) An offender who repeats an extremely serious premeditated crime, even though he has already been punished for a crime of such type, or for another type of especially serious premeditated crime, shall be considered as a particularly dangerous recidivist (habitual offender) if this circumstance, given the seriousness of the crime and particularly the period since the offender's (previous) sentencing, substantially increases the degree of danger represented by the crime to society.
>
> (2) 'Extremely serious crimes' are crimes stipulated in Section 62 of the Criminal Code and those premeditated crimes punishable by a maximum term of imprisonment of at least eight years.

Section 62 of the Criminal Code refers to: high treason (sec. 91), subversion (sec. 92), terror (sec. 93 and 93a), diversionist activity (secs. 95 and 96), sabotage (sec. 97), espionage (sec. 105), war treason (sec. 114), unlawful crossing of the state border under sec. 171b(3), common danger under sec. 179(2) and (3), putting the safety of an aircraft or a civil vessel at risk under sec. 180a, unlawful taking of an aircraft abroad under sec. 180c(2), unlawful production and keeping of addictive and psychotropic substances under provision 187(4), murder (sec. 219), robbery under sec. 234(2) and (3), hostage-taking under sec. 234a(3), rape under sec. 241(2) and (3), sexual abuse under sec. 242(3) and (4), theft under sec. 247(4), embezzlement under sec. 248(4), fraud under sec. 250(4), genocide under sec. 259, persecution of a population under sec. 263a(3), crime against peace under sec. 1 of the Peace Protection Act, No. 165/1950 Coll.

[8] See Section 42 (CCC):

> 1. In the case of a particularly dangerous recidivist, the maximum term of imprisonment stipulated in the Criminal Code shall be increased by one-third. The court shall sentence a particularly dangerous recidivist to a term of imprisonment in the upper half of the range so determined.
>
> 2. However, the maximum term of imprisonment shall not exceed fifteen years, even after an increase under sub-provision 1. When imposing an extraordinary term of imprisonment of from fifteen years to twenty-five years, the upper limit may not exceed twenty-five years.

2.2 Previous conviction and suspended prosecution, sentence, settlement, etc.

For the purposes of criminal proceedings the criminal record keeps a register of:

- persons whose prosecution was conditionally suspended (Sections 179g–179 h and 307–308 of the Czech Criminal Procedure Code) by the public prosecutor or by the court;
- settlement between victim and offender approved by the public prosecutor or by the court (Sections 309–314 of the Czech Criminal Procedure Code);
- conditionally suspended sentences (Section 58 of the Czech Criminal Code).
- conditional release (Section 61–64 of the Czech Criminal Code);
- stopping of prosecution (Section 172 of the Czech Criminal Procedure Code).

2.3 Previous conviction and non bis in idem *principle*

Section 11 of the Czech Criminal Procedure Code lays a rule of inadmissibility of criminal prosecution (prosecution cannot be started or continued) based in particular on the *non bis in idem* principle.[9]

[9] Section 11 (CCPC):

> *Inadmissibility of criminal prosecution*
>
> (1) The criminal prosecution may not be initiated, and if already initiated, may not be continued and has to be discontinued:
>
> . . . f) in respect of any person against whom there are or have been any criminal proceedings for the same offence that have been concluded through the court verdict coming into legal force, or have been brought to a stop by the court decision or the decision of another authorised body, unless the decision has been cancelled during the said proceedings;
>
> g) in respect of any person against whom there are or have been any criminal proceedings for the same offence that have been concluded through the court verdict on approved settlement coming into force, unless the decision has been cancelled during the said proceedings;
>
> h) in respect of any person against whom there are or have been any criminal proceedings for the same offence that have been concluded through the decision coming into force on assignment of the case with a suspicion that the act is a misdemeanour, another administrative culpable act, or a disciplinary misdemeanour, unless the decision has been cancelled during the said proceedings.

2.4 *Coercive measures in criminal proceedings – custody*

When a court (in criminal proceedings) decides on taking an offender into custody recidivism is one of three reasons for imposing it.[10] After amendment no. 265/2002 Coll., the above-mentioned reasons for custody have been made subject to conditions. It is not possible to take an accused into custody if he/she is prosecuted for an intentional criminal act that carries a term of imprisonment of less than two years or for negligent crime with a term of imprisonment of less than three years. Such a rule is not applied unless one or more of the conditions specified in Section 67 CCPC are present.

2.5 *Ministry of Justice and the criminal record*

The Ministry of Justice can request a transcript from the criminal record database concerning the person with regard to proceedings on:

a) an extraordinary remedy – appellate review to the Supreme Court (of the Minister of Justice to the Supreme Court of the Czech Republic against a court order);
b) an application of a decision of the President of the Czech Republic on amnesty (general pardon);
c) a petition for an individual pardon;
d) a waiver of a sentence of imprisonment or suspension of punishment when a convicted offender is to be extradited to a foreign country or banished;

[10] See Section 67 (CCPC):

> The accused may be taken into custody only if there are concrete matters which justify a concern that he/she will:
>
> a) escape or hide, or go into hiding in order to avoid prosecution or punishment, particularly if he/she can not be immediately identified, does not have a permanent residence or is facing a high penalty (anti-escape custody);
>
> b) influence witnesses or co-defendants who have thus far not been questioned or in other ways obstruct the detection of facts significant to the prosecution (collusion custody); or
>
> c) commit the offence again for which he/she is being prosecuted, complete the criminal act which he/she had attempted or carry out the criminal act which he/she was preparing or threatening to commit (preventive custody).

e) permission for an offender to be extradited to a foreign country for the purposes of a criminal prosecution in that country.

2.6 Criminal record (administrative) legal framework

2.6.1 General legislation

The criminal record agency is a governmental body, having its residence in Prague and being subordinated to the Ministry of Justice. The criminal record is an organisation with its own budget and it is headed by a director, appointed and removable by the Minister of Justice. Regulation of the criminal record is included in Law no. 269/1994 Coll. as amended (no. 126/2003, 253/2006, 342/2006 Coll.) but different remarks on 'the criminal record' can be found in more than 100 laws and other legal norms.[11] The criminal record includes a register in judicial convictions (final sentences) by courts in criminal proceedings as well as a register of significant facts for the criminal process – provided that the law so allows. The data from the register serve for requirements of criminal or administrative proceedings and to prove a person's 'integrity'. So, part of a register in the criminal record consists of data on convicted offenders, the data having been collected in accordance with formerly valid legislation and handed over to the criminal record office on the basis of an international agreement with the Slovak Republic. There are data from criminal files on all finally sentenced offenders by the Czech courts in a register of the criminal record.

2.6.2 International relations

The Constitution of the Czech Republic (Art. 10 of Act no. 1/1993 Coll., as amended) stipulates that the ratified and promulgated international treaties by which the Czech Republic is bound are directly binding and take precedence over the law. Because of the prevailing lack of self-executive provisions of treaties their texts have to be transposed into the national law of the Czech Republic. The Czech Republic is a member

[11] Law no. 140/1961 Coll., the Criminal Code, as amended, law no. 141/1961, Coll., Criminal Procedure Code, as amended, law no. 218/2003 Coll., on Juvenile Justice, law no. 101/2000 Coll., on Personal Data Protection, law no. 634/2004 Coll., on Administrative Taxes, law no. 97/1974 Coll. on Archives, law no. 328/1999 Coll. on Identity Cards, law no. 329/1999 Coll., on Travel Documents, law no. 227/2000 Coll. on Electronic Signature, Law no. 365/2000 Coll. on Information Systems within Public Administration, law no. 133/2000 Coll., on Register of Residents and Personal Identification Numbers, etc.

state of the Council of Europe and the European Union. International (and national) obligations arising from the membership are supplemented by bilateral treaties. The two most important legal documents on cooperation with foreign authorities for the exchange of information included in the criminal record constituting an obligation to provide information from the national database of criminal records are:

1. The 1959 European Convention on Mutual Assistance in Criminal Matters[12] Articles 13, 22 and 26, supplemented by Article 4 of the Additional 13th Protocol from 17 March 1978. These provisions govern the communication of extracts from the criminal records between all the parties to the Convention and require countries to inform each other once a year of all convictions involving each other's nationals. It is traditional for the Convention to apply in all cases; however, application in practice has brought to lights points under dispute. Article 22 of the Convention requires countries to inform each other when non-nationals are convicted; however, it does not require the states (of nationality) to store that information in their own databases. This also applies to the Czech Republic. The Czech legal provisions have strict stipulations on how the criminal records of Czech nationals convicted abroad should be handled. However, the process of obtaining information on previous convictions of non-nationals (according to Art. 13 of the Convention) is not managed smoothly and in practice it tends to lead to delays.
2. The International Agreement between the Government of the Czech Republic and the Government of the Slovak Republic on Exchange of Data from Information Contained in the Criminal Record (26 June1995).[13] Under the text of the Agreement, the parties provide to each other information on the content of the register of the criminal record and on the length of sentence. Formal requests are made on behalf of the Czech Republic from the criminal record in Prague (since 1994 under the Ministry of Justice) and on behalf of the Slovak Republic from the criminal record of the General Prosecution Office of the Slovak Republic in Bratislava. The formal request contains data on the citizenship of the relevant person under the provision of national laws in both countries. Requests for the content of the register of individuals who are not citizens of either the Czech

[12] In power in the Czech Republic since 1992 (no. 550/1992 Coll.).
[13] No. 136/1995 Coll.

Republic or the Slovak Republic are treated on the basis of the same principles mentioned above. Requests and documents under this agreement do not need to be translated (both the Czech and Slovak language are acceptable) while the provision of information on the register is free of charge. The parties to the agreement should ensure the protection of information according to their legislation. The agreement was initially concluded for a period of five years but it is automatically prolonged for one year so long as neither of the parties withdraws from it.

The Czech Republic is an EU Member State and, therefore, it is bound to ratify the Convention on Mutual Assistance in Criminal Matters (2000) and the Protocol (2001) and to apply the Regulation on Exchange Information from Criminal Records.[14]

2.7 Information for and from the criminal record database

In accordance with the requirements of Czech Criminal Law and Criminal Procedure the police, the public prosecutor or a court can request information from the criminal record database. There are principally two kinds of information:

a) a transcript of the criminal record database (required for criminal proceedings, including erased convictions);
b) an abstract of the criminal record database (required for other reasons, such as checking persons applying for certain professions, excluding erased convictions[15]).

[14] OJ L 322/33 (2005). Regulation of the Council leads to improvement of Art. 22 of the Convention on mutual assistance 1959.

[15] On a written (personal) request of a person whose identity has been verified, an abstract from criminal record register the ('abstract') is given over to a person concerned.

Correctness of the facts given in a written request for an abstract and identity of an applicant are verified free of charge by:

a) county public prosecution departments;
b) a municipal office, a town office, the town office of the capital Prague, a district office or local authorities, a town district office; or
c) a town ward office in regional zones of corporate towns, which runs the Birth Record, or entrusted employees of the criminal record office.

Authorities given in a previous paragraph do not return an application after verification of data correctness to an applicant but send it to the criminal record office.

The following information (criminal transcript) is recorded in the national register:

a) personal details of the convicted individual for the purposes of identification;
b) reference to the case number including an index of documents (dossier number);
c) orders on out of court settlements, conviction, penalty (type and extent of sanction), and protective measures (mainly protective medical therapy, reformative training and seizure under the provision on 'Protective Measures' of the Czech Criminal Code) and on execution of such penalties;
d) pardons from the President of the Czech Republic;
e) collective pardons from the President of the Czech Republic;
f) erasure of convictions.

All the information listed above should be provided to the police, the public prosecutor or court and is strictly for use in criminal proceedings. Criminal transcripts, court or public prosecution reports, transcripts and abstracts intended for government bodies (and requests for them) can be transferred in an electronic form.

To create a database, courts and public prosecutors (not the police) should produce (without any delay) special reports on a suspended prosecution for the criminal record, as well as an additional report, commenting on an offender's good conduct during a probation period

An abstract is also provided upon a request by a court for needs other than of criminal proceedings and upon a request by a public administration body where required for proceedings in the case of a petty offence. It is possible to provide an abstract for other purposes if there is provision under specific legislation.

All convictions that have not been deleted including data on execution of the sentence process and on protective measures are included in an abstract unless an offender is regarded, in accordance with any law, as if he was not convicted.

Fees in accordance with a specific legal provision are charged for providing an abstract and for examining a transcript.

Data from a record are enclosed in a transcript; these data are not given in an abstract, not even at the request of a person the subject of the abstract.

An abstract and a transcript are public documents. Therefore the altering or forging of them is a crime under Section 176 (forging and altering a public document) of the Czech Criminal Code (punished by imprisonment for a term of up two years or a pecuniary penalty).

Special forms are used for filing a petition for a transcript and an abstract and for transferring data between courts, public prosecution departments and the criminal record office, which are issued by the Ministry of Justice.

Table 1 *Statistics on frequency of requested criminal transcripts and submitted criminal reports (1995–2006)*[17]

	Criminal transcripts	Reports from courts	EU courts
1995	56 680	58 000	25
1996	59 800	68 180	32
1997	61 770	78 460	46
1998	59 080	104 220	84
1999	68 779	78 838	124
2000	69 535	84 625	340
2001	67 040	94 169	450
2002	72 616	102 680	490
2003	75 865	108 350	520
2004	76 881	112 425	350
2005	76 690	112 815	445
2006	79 279	115 336	669

or that a prosecution continues, as soon as a relevant decision comes into force.[16] It is possible to insert into the criminal record database the above-mentioned data on a sentence by the court of a foreign country but only on condition that a competent Czech court has already decided to recognise a sentence of the foreign court.

The Supreme Court can, on a proposal by the Ministry of Justice, decide to insert data concerning the sentence of a Czech citizen by a foreign court into the criminal record database if the offence is also an offence according to the law of the Czech Republic and the inclusion in the register is justified by the seriousness of the offence and by the length of sentence imposed. There is relevant case law of the Supreme Court of the Czech Republic of 20 March 2000 (No. 11 Tcú 6/2000):

> I. The double criminality condition, under provision 4/2 of Law no. 269/1994 Coll., should be taken into consideration for each individual criminal act included in the conviction by a foreign court. If the subject's behaviour is not a criminal act under the Czech Criminal Code, then the Supreme Court must reject the application of the

[16] Section 55 paras 1, 2 of the Instruction of the Ministry of Justice.

[17] Statistical data from: *Annual Report of the Criminal Record of the Czech Republic* (2006).

Ministry of Justice to record the foreign judgment and the corresponding sentence imposed.

II. The double criminality condition is satisfied if the criminal act that is under foreign criminal provisions qualified as multiply crime is a one crime at least under the Czech Criminal Code.

Special legislation is applied in relation to the Slovak Republic. It is the result of the good relations between the Czech and the Slovak Republics, when, under the former Federation, legislation for both of them was very similar.

Besides International Conventions (see above), according to Section 446 of the Czech Criminal Procedure Code the Supreme Public Prosecutor's Office (preliminary proceedings) or the Ministry of Justice (proceedings before a court) are competent to handle all requests from foreign states to provide information from the criminal record. In the case of an existing international agreement direct cooperation between justice authorities is provided.

Personal data protection The register of criminal records can be kept in digital format. Since the end of 1999, special legislation on personal data protection in information systems applies to keeping the register (Law no. 256/1992 Coll. on protection of personal data in information systems). The most important legislation on personal data protection was included in Law no. 101/2000 Coll. as amended, on personal data protection. Under Section 27 (on transfer of personal data to foreign states) personal data can be transferred to any foreign state only on condition that the legislation of the foreign state is able to protect the data adequately (reciprocity principle); however, there are several exceptions to this rule and data can also be transferred:

a) with the agreement of the person concerned;
b) if it is necessary for the protection of rights or claims of the person concerned;
c) if data is available from publicly accessible evidence or sources;
d) under the terms of a ratified international treaty (agreement or convention);
e) if it is necessary for saving the life or for the health care of the person concerned;
f) if it is permitted under a specific law.

The administrator has a duty to request permission for the transfer of data from the Office for Protection of Personal Data, except in cases where transfer is prescribed by ratified international agreements (treaties or conventions). Unauthorised or illegal transfer of personal data is a criminal offence under Section 178 of the Czech Criminal Code.[18]

3. Contents of a European Criminal Record

Czech criminal procedure would require the provision of all the information (transcript) from a European Criminal Record database.[19] The requirements of Czech criminal procedure direct us to two main problems: (a) What kind of information would it be acceptable to provide? An index of sentenced persons or a full record including other data? (b) Should the Member States provide an abstract, a transcript or both?

Convictions and criminal record definitions at the EU level had been enshrined in a framework decision of the Commission.[20] The EU definition of conviction should be limited to a decision in purely criminal matters. Inclusion of administrative sanctions in criminal records can lead to problems in some countries as, for example, Czech criminal law does not introduce criminal responsibility for administrative misdemeanours. Moreover, procedural definitions (stopping

[18] Section 178 (CCC):

> *Unauthorised disposal of personal data*
>
> (1) Whoever, even through negligence, communicates or allows access to data gathered in connection with the performance of public administration shall be punished by imprisonment for a term of up to three years, or to prohibition of a specific activity or a pecuniary penalty.
>
> A person who acquires data on another person in connection with his profession, employment or office and who, even through negligence, communicates the data to another person, or allows access to such data by another person, thus breaching a duty of confidentiality stipulated by law, shall be liable to sentence under sub-section (1).

[19] These have already been mentioned and are:

- person sentenced, so as he/she could not be confused with another person;
- court and document index (number of 'dossier') of a criminal case;
- decision on stopping prosecution;
- decision on a settlement and suspended prosecution;
- decision on guilt, penalty (including suspended), and protective measures and on their execution;
- individual pardon or similar measure with the same effect;
- participation in a general pardon, or similar measure with the same effect;
- deletion of a sentence.

[20] COM 2005 (91).

prosecution, settlement, transcript, abstract, etc.) are different in different Member States and a common definition is not available. Therefore, the realistic solution would be to consider only a sentence/conviction database.

Following the Hague Programme (2004) and the subsequent White Paper on Exchange of Information, it seems that the most acceptable option can be detailed in the following three successive steps: the European Index of Sentenced/Convicted Persons,[21] a European Standard Form and ultimately the European Criminal Record.

4. Access to the European Criminal Record

If the ECR is indeed created in order to address the information needs of investigation, prosecution and judicial authorities for investigations and prosecutions in the pre-trial and trial stages of the criminal process, it is evident that these authorities should have access to the data. This includes the police, the public prosecution service and the courts. In addition to competent national authorities, Eurojust (particularly because of the potential lack of connection with non-Member States) and Europol[22] would certainly need some access to data for the performance of their missions. Access to further EU institutions should not be excluded.[23]

Current debate revolves around two types of exchange of data on convictions and other elements of criminal proceedings:

a) national level:
   - to improve bilateral exchange of the information;
   - to create connection between national criminal record databases.

b) European level:
   - to establish a European Criminal Record.

The official position of the Czech Republic is that it prefers the national level solution (i.e. a link between national criminal record

[21] The European Index of Sentenced Persons (which is not identical to the European Criminal Record project) can allow specified authorities in all EU countries to obtain extracts of national registers for individuals convicted in any other EU country. The Index itself contains no details on the convictions themselves – see the *European Register of Convicted Persons Feasibility Study* (2005).

[22] Unfortunately – in accordance with Art. 8 of the EUROPOL Convention a database on convicted persons is under preparation.

[23] For example the European Anti-fraud Office – OLAF (which has an administrative–investigative mission). EUROPOL is also acting outside of judicial cooperation in criminal matters, having only police cooperation without operational powers.

databases).[24] It is a compromise position based on the improvement of technical measures and from a legislative point of view it is grounded on old Article 22 of the European Convention on Mutual Assistance in Criminal Matters. The interlinking of national criminal records is a project already phased between France, Germany, Spain and Belgium since the end of 2004 (in electronic format). The Member States taking part in the project invited all other Member States to follow them. The Czech Republic supports the project, but notes that such information cannot be taken as admissible evidence for Czech criminal proceedings; it can only have operational effect.

In the original Report of the Falcone Project, only European level solutions had been taken into consideration. The creation of a European criminal record is most ambitious. From a political, legal and technical point of view it is a difficult and expensive solution. However, ambitious projects require ambitious solutions. There is no doubt that an accurate central database would guarantee a fair and positive impact on criminal proceedings, provided that it is continuously updated, complete, controlled and protected, free of charge for authorised bodies, easily accessible and excluding duplications.[25]

5. Use of the European Criminal Record

Analysis of the many issues related to criminal records leads to the conclusion that attempts to establish a procedurally and substantively acceptable means of exchange of information from national criminal records will come to the forefront of debate on judicial cooperation in criminal matters. With the exception of the trial, criminal procedure is private and confidential and the requirements to be met under Czech criminal law and procedure allowing the sharing of data from this part of the process have been identified in detail. The content of the method of exchange will depend on the agreed common position of EU Member States and require wide debate and consultation. One starting point could be an index of convicted persons.[26] Czech law could accept any

[24] Interviews and consultations with Ministry of Justice civil servants.

[25] See note no. 14.

[26] In the context of the ERCP the 'Index' refers to the central database of the system, which contains a list of all convicted persons that the participating states have decided to include in the system. The Index contains no details in terms of criminal history or details of convictions, only the minimum – see the *European Register of Convicted Persons Feasibility Study* (2005).

solution provided that the use of information of such a nature remains within pending criminal proceedings.

6. Critical evaluation

The idea of establishing a European Criminal Record is very ambitious. On the one hand, it could offer real added value to contemporary judicial (and maybe even police) cooperation in criminal matters. On the other hand, there are obvious difficulties which should be balanced by future advantages. Failing to demonstrate those advantages would jeopardise the implementation of a European Criminal Record.

Points of difficulty include the form in which the European Criminal Record might be introduced. An international Convention and the real possibility of lack of adequate ratifications could offer a slow and inefficient solution, whereas a Framework Decision, despite inherent weakness evident in the transposition of the European Arrest Warrant, is a more efficient legal measure. Another point of difficulty relates to the technical route chosen for the transfer of data from at least twenty-seven national databases into a single one. This requires original and generally acceptable technical choices and agreed budgetary allocation. Difficulties are evident in the necessity of successive steps for the introduction of a single database from the point of view of procedure and continuing improvements of the index of record. Equally, the introduction of a competent body or institution for the administration of the European Criminal Record both at national and EU levels requires new instruments that address conflicting national rules for many operations, including establishment of such a body and agreement on content, use, access, exclusion of overlaps, data protection and financial concerns.

Irrespective of this critique, the idea of a European Criminal Record cannot be discarded. It is, in brief, a crucial component of efforts to facilitate necessary improvements in international cooperation in criminal matters.

7

The European Criminal Record in Germany

LORENZ BÖLLINGER

1. Introduction: basic legal structure of recording crime in Germany

The German constitutional separation of power system and legal order (*ordre public*) provides for a strict separation of police powers in two branches: criminal law enforcement on the justice side and 'defence against dangers' (*Gefahrenabwehr*) on the executive power side. There can be data collection in both branches, but in principle these databases may not be connected or mixed, except in cases of 'immediate danger'. The methods, options, and limits of data collection, data storage in any kind of files, data transfer to other police and public authorities, and deletion (erasure, cancellation) of data from files are all regulated in particular police laws of the sixteen states (*Länder*) of the federal union. All these laws are manifestations of an exemplary federal framework law (*Rahmengesetz*), functioning as a model code and limiting state discretion. Thus, the police are allowed, albeit only in the context of criminal investigation, to collect and store all relevant data concerning the personal identity of a suspect, the alleged perpetration, and necessary additional data. Increasingly police authorities are making use of computer-based data collections for police preventive purposes in the framework of the executive branch. The unresolved legal problem is that there is a lack of legal powers for these practices and an absence of legal remedies for persons whose data are listed. Often data stay in these files even though the investigation has long stopped.

Informally, without regulation, simply for pragmatic reasons and therefore in something of a grey zone, every prosecutor's office in Germany keeps 'name registers' (*Namenskarteien*), containing names of suspects and perpetrators in alphabetical order. Beyond the name they contain the date of birth, address, file number (*Aktenzeichen*), the offence, and remarks on the criminal charges and the subsequent procedure. Nowadays these databases are kept on computers. In some federal states the prosecutors have informally put their digital systems onto a regional network. But there is no official, legal, and technical way of exchanging or transferring these data on a larger scale.

The most important national database institution for police investigation that has relevance for transnational law enforcement is the Federal Criminal Law Enforcement Authority (*Bundeskriminalamt*, BKA), located in Wiesbaden in the state of Hessen, as regulated by the applicable law, the *Bundeskriminalamt-Gesetz* (BKAG).[1] The BKA is the national centre for the collection, storage, and transfer of personal data (Sect. 20 and 8 BKAG). The set of 'basic personal data' that can be legally stored is defined in Sect. 8 BKAG. Legally the BKA is only allowed to collect and store data in connection with actual criminal acts and suspicion. Increasingly and without formal empowerment by law the BKA has turned to collecting data in a purely preventive manner without any solid indication of a criminal act. This is sought to be legitimised by the 'increasing threat of transnational crime'. From legal science and human rights activists there is criticism of this 'mix' of prevention and repression,[2] the breach of the principle of legal empowerment (*Gesetzmässigkeit der Verwaltung*), and the blurring of limits between the executive and justice powers.

Another option for criminal investigation data collection and storage is provided by Sect. 29 of the Federal Police Law[3] *(Bundespolizeigesetz,* BpolG [4]). This concerns personal data that have been obtained in the context of national and transnational matters, border traffic etc. The above-mentioned criticism of blurring power limits also applies here.[5] All of the police authorities are allowed to transfer and exchange data not only nationally, but – on the basis of bilateral accords – also to the police authorities of other states and, based on EU accords and subsequent national legislation, to supranational authorities such as Europol (Sects. 2–4 *Europol-Gesetz*[6]), and Eurojust (Sect. 4 *Eurojust-Gesetz*[7]).

[1] Following reunification, the German federal government intends to transfer the office to Berlin.

[2] P. Siebrasse, *Strafregistrierung und Grundgesetz* (Frankfurt/M: Peter Lang Verlag, 2004), p. 144; Hans-Ulrich Paeffgen, 'Strafprozess im Umbruch, oder: Vom unmöglichen Zustand des Strafprozessrechts' (1999) *Strafverteidiger*, at p. 625.

[3] Law of 19 October 1994 – BGBl. I 1994, p. 2978.

[4] Formerly: *Bundesgrenzschutzgesetz* or *BGSG*.

[5] Siebrasse 2004, pp. 35, 144.

[6] *Gesetz zu dem Übereinkommen vom 26. Juli 1995 auf Grund von Artikel K.3 des Vertrags über die Europäische Union über die Errichtung eines Europäischen Polizeiamts; in der Fassung vom 16. Dezember 1997.*

[7] *Gesetz zur Umsetzung des Beschlusses (2002/187/JI) des Rates vom 28. Februar 2002 über die Errichtung von Eurojust zur Verstärkung der Bekämpfung der schweren Kriminalität – BGBl. I 2004, 105; in der Fassung vom 12.5.2004.*

2. Databases for prosecutions in Germany

There is a central database for prosecutions in Germany, independent of police data records, the *Zentrales Staatsanwaltliches Verfahrensregister* (ZStV), also informally labelled 'SISY' (*Staatsanwaltliches Informationssystem* – prosecutors' information system). It was first introduced to the German Criminal Procedure Code (*Strafprozessordnung* – StPO) in 1994[8] and modified in 1998, and it started operating in 1999. It was created to improve investigation against perpetrators, especially gangs, who work inter-regionally, transnationally and internationally.[9] Its official purpose is to improve the 'operationality of criminal law enforcement' (*Funktionsfähigkeit der Strafrechtspflege*[10]). It is now regulated by Sect. 492–495 StPO.

In accordance with Sect. 492 Para. 5 StPO in 1995 a 'general ordinance for the creation of a national investigation register' (*Allgemeine Verwaltungsvorschrift über eine Errichtungsanordnung für das Länderübergreifende Staatsanwaltliche Verfahrensregister*[11]) was created. In order to avoid double registering these data have to be erased as soon as the fact and the main elements of the verdict are entered in the federal central record (*Bundeszentralregister*, BZR). Other than that there is no connection between the BZR and the prosecutors' information system ZStVR.

According to Sect. 492 Para. 1 StPO the prosecutors' ZStV database is kept nationally and centrally by the same office that keeps the national criminal record, the register of convictions and sentences (BZR). The latter is institutionalised in the office of the Federal General Prosecutor (*Generalbundesanwalt*), who in turn is part of the Federal Ministry of Justice as regulated by law (*Bundeszentralregister-Gesetz* – BZRG). The ZStV database exclusively comprises prosecution data. However, prosecution in German law means any criminal law enforcement activity, starting with a criminal act being registered by the police, and ending with the case being closed in any way. The cause for police registration can either be a report to the police by any citizen or institution, or proactive observance and recognition by the police. Germany applies the legality principle, meaning that every crime that has come to the

[8] See *Einrichtungsanordnung* (implementation directive) in the source materials.

[9] A. Götz and G. Tolzmann, *Bundeszentralregistergesetz, Kommentar, 4*, revised edn (Stuttgart: Kohlhammer Verlag, 2000), Sect. 1 #16.

[10] T. Kleinknecht and L. Meyer-Gossner, *Strafprozessordnung, Kommentar, 47* (München: Beck-Verlag, 2004), Sect. 492, #1.

[11] *Bundesanzeiger* 1995, No. 163 (Federal Journal).

attention of the police in whatever way has to be investigated and every investigative act in the course of criminal law enforcement has to be directed and mandated by the prosecutor. The prosecutor in turn has to be a fully-fledged jurist, equally qualified by legal training and state exams as a judge. In practice, however, average cases and common crimes are primarily investigated by the police. The investigative file is usually handed over to the prosecutor only after the case has been cleared in detail. The prosecutor then decides whether to indict the perpetrator (*Anklageerhebung*) or to drop the case (*nolle prosequi*) if the infraction is a minor one and there is no public interest in prosecuting (Sect. 153 pp. StPO). Only in cases of severe or capital crimes shall the prosecutor be called in immediately by the police in order to formally lead the investigation. In practice this means that, as long as the police investigate without having included the prosecutor, there will be no entry in the national database.[12]

The content of the register is determined by Sect. 492 Para. 2 StPO. The prosecution record ZStV is to contain all personal data necessary for identification, the investigation authority and file number, the date, time, kind and place of the offence. But the data may only be used in criminal proceedings (Sect. 492 Para. 2 Phrase 2 StPO). Compulsory registration pertains to every newly started, current and terminated investigation and prosecution procedure up until the moment of a final court verdict. After that the official criminal record (BZR) 'takes over'. There is no limit as to the intensity or importance of the crime.

The entries into the ZStV have to be erased if they prove to be wrong or as soon as a court verdict has been reached (Sect. 494 Para. 2 #1 and 2 StPO). In case of acquittal the data must be kept in storage for up to two years. They are also kept in the database if before or within these two years another offence by the same person is registered (Sect. 494 Para. 2 Phrase 2–4 StPO).

3. Access to the databases

According to Sect. 492 Para. 3 Phrase 2 StPO Information from the central prosecutors' register (ZStV) may only be given to criminal law enforcement authorities. However, according to Sect. 492 Para. 4 StPO the three German federal secret intelligence services *(Bundesnachrichtendienst, Militärischer*

[12] This was confirmed by all the expert interviewees from the law enforcement organisations.

Abschirmdienst, Verfassungsschutz) are entitled to draw data from the ZStV. Consequentially administrations and administrative courts are not so entitled, not even for the purpose of gaining relevant information for investigating regulatory offences (*Ordnungswidrigkeiten*). But extensive legal interpretation by the commentaries allows for criminal courts to draw from the ZStV beyond the actual case,[13] opening the possibility of unwarranted influence on the sentencing process (Sect. 46 II StGB).[14]

The transnational transfer and exchange of investigation data is regulated by law, especially the International Legal Assistance Law (*Internationale Rechtshilfe-Gesetz* – IRG). Now, according to Sect. 57 BZRG in connection with Sect. 59 IRG as well as Art. 13 Para. 1 of the European Accord about Legal Aid in Criminal Law Enforcement of 12 July 2000,[15] criminal law enforcement authorities of the signatories as well as EU authorities are considered equal to German criminal law enforcement authorities with respect to the right to obtain information from the ZStV.[16]

4. Procedural stages at which data are introduced to or erased from the database

As described above, theoretically, by written law, the data should be introduced as soon as any kind of investigation starts on the basis of 'initial suspicion of a criminal act'. But in practice, unless it is a 'severe case', the police only deliver investigation files to the prosecutor when the investigation is finished. So in practice only then will there be a routine entry to the ZStV. The prosecutor may then either initiate further investigations or decide to indict.

Concerning the erasure of data there are various regulations, depending on whether it is an investigation database kept at the BZR or the personal database kept at the BKA. The general principle for investigation data is that they must be erased at once or within a certain time limit if the investigation has been terminated either by conviction or by acquittal (Sect. 494 Para. 2 No. 2 StPO). Correction of erroneous entries

[13] Kleinknecht and Meyer-Gossner 2004, Sect. 492 #11. [14] Siebrasse 2004, p. 28.

[15] *Übereinkommen vom 29. Mai 2000 über die Rechtshilfe in Strafsachen zwischen den Mitgliedstaaten der Europäischen Union – EuRHÜbk*; OJ C 197, 12 July 2000, p. 3.

[16] See T. Hackner, O. Lagodny and W. Schomburg, *Internationale Rechtshilfe in Strafsachen* (München: Beck Verlag, 2003). Also see Grützner and Pötz, *Internationaler Rechtshilfeverkehr in Strafsachen. Loseblattsammlung. 38, Lieferung zur 2* (Heidelberg: C. F. Müller-Verlag, 1996).

is necessary according to Sect. 494 Para. 1 StPO. The erasure has to be initiated by the prosecuting office that has delivered them to the ZStV. And by Sect. 494 Para. 2 Phrase 1 StPO they must be erased if their registration is not legally warranted or if the proceedings have come to a result – e.g. conviction – that has to be registered in the central federal criminal record for convictions and measures (BZR) in order to avoid double registering. After two years all data have to be erased if the accused (*Beschuldigter*) has been definitively acquitted, if the court has refused to accept the indictment, if the prosecutor has definitely refrained from indictment or if any other criminal investigation against the person is pending. Subsequent minor perpetrations or mere suspicion of minor criminal acts may thus cause protracted registration in the ZStV. If there is only a preliminary stop of proceedings (conditional *nolle prosequi*, Sect. 170 StPO) there is no way to have the entries erased. The authority keeping the register – the BZR office of the Federal General Prosecutor – exerts no control over the content of entries. It is only the prosecutors themselves who monitor the data entries. However, the decision to transfer data is made by the BZR authority in conjunction with the prosecutor in charge (Sect. 495 StPO).

Under certain conditions information included in the data can be blocked in order to protect a persons rights (Sect. 494 Para. 3 in conjunction with Sect. 489 Para. 7 and 8 StPO). This means that the data kept in the registry will not be passed on to criminal law enforcement agencies otherwise entitled, but can still be used to 'prove or disprove' the guilt of the perpetrator. They can also be used for research. Legal scientists consider these provisions to be highly problematic with respect to civil liberties.[17]

5. Purpose of the databases and use in practice

Since the law reforms of 1997–2000 criminal investigation data collection is now finally regulated in Chapter 8, Sect. 474 to 495 StPO. The aim of the law reform was to do away with former obstacles to efficient investigating practices and data transfer in criminal law enforcement, but at the same time provide sufficient data protection for the citizens. Data may only be stored for present and future criminal law enforcement purposes. Sect. 486 StPO provides for the possibility of different agencies and authorities using a data pool. Sect. 489 StPO provides for

[17] Paeffgen 1999, at p. 625.

criteria when data have to be erased – mainly when the reason for storage has disappeared.

The earmarking of data for storage is very flexible as Sect. 492 Para. 6 StPO only limits this to 'any criminal procedure' and the law is interpreted quite extensively.[18] According to the interpretation found in commentaries the data can be used in any criminal procedure – even when it has no connection with the one in the context of which it was originally investigated or obtained. This enables prosecutors to 'pile up' data, which collides with the provisions of Sect. 494 StPO. However, it is common opinion that the general aim should be to avoid double registering and resulting conflicts and contradictions.

The use in practice is mainly that investigation and prosecutions against offenders who have operated inter-regionally are located at different places and can now be pulled together. Petty crimes can also be discarded more easily, helping to concentrate on the important charges, thus economising on resources.

6. Collaboration with foreign authorities for the acquisition of data

The prosecutors who were interviewed unanimously contended that in principle, on the basis of Sect. 483 Para. 2 StPO, they act within the framework of Sect. 57 BZRG, Sect. 59 IRG (International Legal Aid Law) and Art. 13 Para. 1 of the EU Accord for Legal Assistance in Criminal Cases (as passed on 12 July 2000).[19] Therefore, information from the BZRG and the ZStV is voluntarily provided for criminal law enforcement authorities of other states, especially within the EU. However, they say that proactive use of these resources is rarely made due to practical problems – e.g. language problems – and resource scarcity.

Criticism from legal science and civil rights advocates is concentrating on some shortcomings of German national regulation in view of general human rights standards: the legal provisions are considered to be lacking in limitation and precision. They are considered to be in collision with Sect. 17 Para. 2 BDSG (Federal Data Protection Law). They suggest that data transfer should be scrutinised intensely under the auspices of German *ordre public*.[20] One of the shortcomings is the lack of clear and regulated

[18] See, for example, Kleinknecht and Meyer-Gossner 2004. [19] Siebrasse 2004, p. 112.
[20] Götz and Tolzmann 2000, p. 57, Para. 2 No. 6; see also Siebrasse 2004, p. 113.

procedure, the lack of justice review, the arbitrariness of passing on information to foreign countries and especially to EUROPOL.[21]

7. Provisions and restrictions for data sharing between public bodies

Personal data as saved in real and/or digital, electronically operated files are protected against unwarranted access by the BDSG. Other than that, administrations may exchange pertaining data. However, only criminal law enforcement agencies have access to the various criminal registers and records. The sharing of such data increasingly takes place online. The traditional way is to send entire files (folders) or photocopies.

In legal science and in the Supreme Constitutional Court (*Bundesverfassungsgericht*, BVerfGE) jurisdiction problems of this kind of data storage are seen and the issue is raised.[22] Legal discourse centres on the 'basic civil right of informational self-determination' *(Recht auf informationelle Selbstbestimmung)* which is being intensely infringed and actually restricted by the new kinds of data collection (BVerfGE 56, 37; 63, 131; 65, 1 – *Volkszählung*).[23] There is also conflict with the constitutional right to rehabilitation (*Resozialisierungsprinzip*: BVerfGE 35, 202 – *Lebach*) and other basic principles of criminal law (BVerfGE 64, 261 ff.; BVerfGE 45, 187ff.; BVerfGE StV 1997, 30f.; BVerfGE 98, 169ff.). In one decision the Supreme Constitutional Court, in 1973, specifically dealt with data storage in the BZR (BVerfGE 36, 174ff.) and on that occasion it ruled that the regulation, as it stood at the time, was constitutional. However, legal science increasingly expresses doubts and much criticism[24] about the recent extensions as described above and there may be more decisions by the Supreme Constitutional Court concerning this topic in the future.[25]

The strongest criticism concerns the fact that there is no direct way for the individual concerned to find out about the state of personal data

[21] See S. Simitis, *Kommentar zum Bundesdatenschutzgesetz. 5 Auflage* (Baden-Baden: Nomos Verlag, 2002); R. Riegel, *Nochmals: Das Bundeskriminalamtgesetz*, NJW 1997: 3408ff; J. Jacob, 'Datenschutz am Scheideweg – Die neuen Herausforderungen für das Recht des Bürgers auf informationelle Selbstbestimmung', (1997) *Zeitschrift für Innere Sicherheit in Deutschland und Europa*, p. 67.

[22] Paeffgen 1999; Siebrasse 2004, p. 47.

[23] H. P. Bull, 'Verfassungsrechtliche Vorgaben zum Datenschutz' (1998) *Computerrecht*, p. 385; P. Gola and R. Schomerus, *Bundesdatenschutzgesetz Kommentar* (München: Beck Verlag, 2002).

[24] Siebrasse 2004, p. 56. [25] Paeffgen 1999.

storage in the ZStV concerning himself.[26] However, according to Sect. 491 Para. 1 StPO any person involved, in the sense that his or her data are being stored, can demand information from these registers unless this endangers the course of an investigation.

Admissibility and limitations of data transfer as well as the possibility of automated data transfer and automatic online data release are regulated in Sect. 487, 488 StPO. If the purpose is one of those regulated in Sect. 483 StPO – namely, criminal procedure and international criminal legal aid and assistance – then data may be transferred or released to the authorities in charge. This includes, according to current interpretation, investigations and data transfer in the context of Eurojust. The purpose of transfer (Sect. 483 StPO) is not limited to the investigation pertaining to a certain individual case: it extends to other cases, especially past or future cases of the same person or other persons somehow involved in the case, and to the phase of sentence execution (*Strafvollstreckung*). This, as is critically remarked by legal scientists and civil liberties advocates, enables authorities all over Europe to accumulate data that are only minimally related to the investigation they were originally part of.

According to Sect. 487 Para. 2 Phrase 2 in conjunction with Sect. 474 No. 2 StPO information and documents can even be drawn directly from the files and transferred to public authorities if this is deemed 'necessary' (*erforderlich*). According to Sect. 475 StPO even lawyers, private persons, employers etc. can draw data and information, not from the ZStV but from court and police files, if they can prove a 'legitimate interest' *(Berechtigtes Interesse)* and the accused has no legitimate interest in data protection. This regulation enables an employer to circumvent the restrictive regulations of the BZRG: this way he can obtain information which he would not be entitled to via the official extract from the criminal record (*Führungszeugnis)* as regulated by the BZRG. The legal parameters have yet to be rendered more precisely by legal science and the judiciary.

There are no national general principles of law and privacy that prohibit either the creation of national databases on investigations and prosecutions or the use of such data. The basic civil right of 'informational self-determination' (*informationelle Selbstbestimmung*) as interpreted by the BVerfG is guaranteed by Art. 2 Para. 1 and Art. 1 Para. 1 GG (Federal Constitution). Personal data protection in principle, as regulated by the BDSG (Federal Data Protection Law), extends to any data stored in any

[26] See Siebrasse 2004, p. 140 with further references.

electronic or other file kept by public authorities, and represents the manifestation and specification of this right.[27] The laws allowing for creation of public registers and files have to comply with the BDSG.

There are no formal exemptions to these laws, even under extreme conditions or security threats. However, the BZRG (Federal Central Record Law), the BKAG (Federal Criminal Law Enforcement Authority Law) and Chapter 8, Sect. 474 – 495 StPO provide for restrictions of this civil right of informational self-determination. According to basic constitutional principles, any civil liberty can only by restricted by federal law. The restriction – by constitutional law doctrine – may not surpass the 'core' or essential of the basic constitutional right. By weighing the conflicting interests the authority can, under exceptional conditions, render the privacy laws practically ineffective.

8. Linking national databases as an effective weapon against transnational crime?

Measure 12 of the Mutual Recognition Programme[28] has been welcomed by all interviewees. However, there is also agreement that there should be as little additional bureaucracy and as many rule of law safeguards as possible. Therefore linking national databases on investigations and prosecutions in a network is considered to be the method of choice, being one logical precondition and consequence of mutual recognition. One basic principle of German national registering of criminal law data is to avoid violation of data protection principles (qualitative aspect) and the double storing of data (quantitative aspect). Establishing one central EU database would automatically imply such double storage. EUROPOL and EUROJUST should be restricted to administering data access and exchange. Given the means of information technology this would not in the least impair efficiency as most of this will take place online.

None of the interviewees sees much sense in establishing an extra and central EU database: it is considered an unnecessary duplication of effort and expenditure while at the same time doubling the risk of mistakes and even abuse. For example: they see the danger of one agency keeping a database being left out in favour of the superior one – leading to incompleteness of one of the databases. On the other hand, the process of erasure would be much more complicated. They all support

[27] Bull 1998; Gola and Schomerus 2002. [28] See OJ C 12, 15 January 2001, p. 10.

a linear and hierarchical system inside a Member State with 'head station' databases of the EU Member States being interconnected online.

Furthermore the use of a central database in the EU is estimated to be limited as the data that could possibly be obtained from it would be quite restricted. As in the national investigation database the EU database could only include names of perpetrators, the date and time of the offence and the legal definition. The prosecutors in charge would, within the legal framework of the International Legal Assistance Law (*Gesetz über Internationale Rechtshilfe*, IRG), still have to inquire directly in order do find out details about the case. The problem is also that this kind of information is not considered to be admissible proof in a criminal court. Some experts think that the introduction of the EU database could reduce the need for inquiries in the framework of the IRG. But this kind of 'security advancement' could just as well be achieved by networking the national investigation databases.

9. Acceptability of a central EU database

Data on citizens under surveillance – usually probation (*Bewährungshilfe*, Sect. 56 StGB) or tight supervision (*Führungsaufsicht*, Sect. 68 StGB) data which are in Germany administered by the justice authorities – are to be kept in the BZR (federal central record), accessible to all law enforcement agencies and authorities. As said before, all the interviewees consider it preferable to link up national databases as well. This, of course, presupposes that all the Member States have similar data bases.

The main concern shared by most interviewees and by myself is that the high standards of data protection as established and accepted in Germany could possibly be lowered by a central EU database. It is foreseen that the creation of such a database would force the Member States to homogenise their applicable laws, resulting in a downgrading of German rule of law standards under the principle of the 'minimum common denominator'. The almost universal aim is to keep national authority over databases and allow for certain divergences between Member States.

10. Possible use of EU database supply

According to German procedural law (StPO) the basic constitutional principles of direct (*Unmittelbarkeit*) and oral (*Mündlichkeit*) procedure have to be heeded, especially in evidence taking. This means that EU database data can only be introduced in the way provided for by the

StPO: witness evidence (*Zeugenbeweis*) and documentary evidence (*Urkundsbeweis*). Print-outs from the EU database would be admissible as the latter. However, in practice the function of the EU database would probably be to provide for 'soft intelligence' – supporting the national law enforcement agencies. Increasingly the admissibility of videotaping evidence is becoming accepted and regulated.

As said above, the basic approach in Germany is to prefer the linking-up of national databases. The exchange and transnational online accessibility of these data should be limited to crimes of a certain quality: either crimes directed against the interest of the EU, or very severe crimes and organised crime. Other than that, a regard for the specific national legal cultures should remain, leaving room for difference and variation. The general consideration is that it is not necessary to homogenise substantive crime definitions beyond a certain 'core' of important and 'severe' crimes. At any rate, specific safeguards would have to ensure that the transfer of data from German national authorities to the EU database does not clash with German national law. Data exchange is legally permissible under the European Accord for Legal Assistance in Criminal Law Enforcement of 12 July 2000 (EURhAbk). So if these stipulations are adhered to there should be no clash.

The BZR would be the national authority in charge of providing the content of the ZStVR; the BKA would also provide information from the police investigation register (personal data offences). Under the premise that such a EU database is created – which is not wanted by the German interviewees – the same persons and authorities would have access to it as regulated by German law.

When looking for a EU agency as a suitable host for the EU database, Eurojust (pursuant to Article 14 of the Eurojust decision) would be the logical place to establish a database for investigations and prosecutions that includes relevant data on EU citizens, supervised by a judicial/quasi judicial authority acceptable to the national legal orders. However, in view of the free movement of persons within the EU and the increase in crime, a central EU database would not significantly improve the situation in comparison with the linking of national databases.

11. Assessment of political feasibility in Germany

Predictably some Human Rights Groups and NGOs as well as the Free Democratic Party (FDP), the Green Party (*Die Grünen*) and parts of the Social-democratic Party (SPD) would oppose such a development as there are strong feelings and opinions – grounded partly in the totalitarian Nazi experience – that there should not be too much state control and data registering. As mentioned above any kind of data storing is considered to be interfering with the right to privacy. The argument is for keeping these matters as decentralised as possible in order to avoid the formation of a vast bureaucracy.

This is very much the view of liberal intellectuals, however. According to popular surveys 'crime' is seen as a serious problem by the average member of the public, albeit 'only' third in rank below the issues of 'unemployment' and 'national security'. The parties very much orient their policies along these surveys. The more tabloid the media, the more emphasis on the issue of crime and the lesson factual orientation. Research shows, for example, that the number of sexual crimes has decreased by 30 per cent since 1980. In the same time period the number of media reports of a certain length about sexual crimes has increased tenfold.

There had been a strong movement towards the reduction of police powers and the promotion of the rehabilitation of ex-offenders in the 1970s, resulting in significant changes in criminal policy and criminal law. However, since the 1990s there has been a strong populist swing of the pendulum towards more punitive forms of reaction – measurable in figures of imprisonment and commital to intra-mural forced treatment as well as in an increase of duration of detention and a decrease in probation releases. For the time being, especially under the influence and impression of the terrorism scare, the general public tends to call for even more detention, less rehabilitation and more police powers. It can be concluded, therefore, that there would not be much popular or political opposition against a move towards an EU central database.

12. Conclusions

The German *Zentrales Strafverfahrensregister* (ZStV – central criminal investigation register)[29] started in June 1999, based on an ordinance of August 1995. Until then the means of prosecutors to gain information from decentralised databases and investigation registries were considered to be unsatisfactory. Police information systems were also not very instrumental as the police collect data predominantly under danger prevention aspects. Meanwhile practically all the offices and authorities that are entitled to use it have been connected electronically to the ZStV. It is estimated that there

[29] It can be accessed online: www.vrp.de.

are around 70–80,000 memos (*Mitteilungen*) and 40,000 inquiries *(Anfragen)* per day. It is expected that in the long run there will be a continuity of around 30–40 million entries. Data exchange is administered exclusively via e-mail or direct data and file transfer via so-called 'head offices' (*Kopfstellen*), meaning interchanges in every State which dispose of high-performance computer services 24 hours per day. So far there has been little public and legal science attention and interest in this new institution and in the overall increases in effectiveness. It remains to be seen and evaluated whether the hopes and aims connected to the reform will materialise. At any rate it can be said that modern technology and online systems have considerably increased efficiency of the law enforcement system and, along with it, the intensity of control and infringement of individual civil rights. Further centralisation at the EU level could result in counterproductive effects on both levels: it could prove to reduce efficiency in comparison with less bureaucratic models and it could reduce trust of the relevant public in state institutions. One example of this kind of ambivalence is the introduction of DNA analysis in the law enforcement system. In Germany, since 1998 DNA analysis in the framework both of current and future criminal investigation is legal. Under Sect. 81g and Sect. 2 DNA-FG (*DNA Identitätsfeststellungsgesetz* of 9 July 1998) a DNA register is kept at the BKA, enabling data to be stored even for possible future investigations – which is new to the basic understanding of criminal law in only dealing with delicts already committed (Sect. 16 BKAG). The only criterion to be legally interpreted and subsumed is 'the danger of future criminal acts' *(die Gefahr zukünftiger Straftaten)*. This is considered to be very problematic by rule of law standards as well as legal doctrine and methodology. According to Sect. 3 Phrase 4 BKAG these data may be disclosed and transferred to any investigating authority nationally and in the framework of international criminal law assistance. There is no time limit to this kind of data storing. However, the data have to be erased when the subject has been acquitted (Sect. 8 P. 3, Sect. 32 BKAG). On the part of legal science and civil liberties activists this increase of control intensity, the intrusion into the innermost human intimacy sphere is heavily criticised.[30] The question remains whether this kind of security advancement adequately balances the loss in privacy and trust.

[30] Siebrasse 2004, pp. 29, 153, 164.

8

The European Criminal Record in Greece

MARIA GAVOUNELI AND PANTELIS TRAIANOS

1. Introduction

The legal status and regulation of criminal records in Greece followed a two-tiered approach, common in most European legal orders. Originally, the criminal record constituted nothing else but a tool for the detection of crimes and a parameter for the determination of the penalty to be imposed upon conviction. A prevention parameter, in the sense that an ex-offender should not be given the chance to indulge in criminal conduct, was also considered inherent in the criminal record function. The emphasis, however, remained clear: the criminal record was an instrument of state policy, a public document freely used by the courts and law enforcement agencies. It was only in the 1980s, and in view of technological developments and the subsequent emerging need to shield the individual both from the increasing use (and misuse) of personal data by the national administration within a state and the unhindered transnational flow of such information to be freely used by anybody, that the criminal record also became a personal file, replete with sensitive information pertaining to that particular individual. The tension between the criminal policy tool, to be owned and used by the state at its discretion, and the personal data file, to be safeguarded from interference or even use by third parties, is eloquently reflected in the regulation of the criminal record in the Greek legal order.

In 1951 the Greek Code of Criminal Procedure (CCrP) came into force and criminal records were regulated in its Articles 573–580.[1] Subsequently, Law 1805/1988 provided an overhaul of the criminal

[1] For an overview of the Greek criminal legal system see: A. Kontaxis, *Code of Criminal Procedure* (Athens: Ant. N. Sakkoulas, 2006) pp. 3503–3520 [in Greek]; D. D. Spinellis, 'Criminal Law and Procedure', in K. D. Kerameus and P. J. Kozyris (eds.), *Introduction to Greek Law* (2nd revised edition, The Hague/Athens: Kluwer/Ant. N. Sakkoulas, 1993), pp. 339–365. See also A. Karras, *Criminal Procedure* (2nd revised edition, Athens: Ant.

record-keeping[2] system and the supporting administrative services.[3] Articles 6–15 of Law 1805/1988 modified Articles 573–580 of the Greek CCrP, and in essence brought about three innovations:

- the introduction of two types of copies or excerpts of the criminal record ('for judicial use' and 'for general use') with the original being always kept with the central authority;
- the introduction of different categories of recipients, to whom each type of copy is to be made available (individuals and agencies of the public and private sector); and
- the modification of the conditions under which entries to and erasure from the criminal record are made.

The implementation of the new Articles 573–580 CCrP was repeatedly suspended[4] before they finally entered into force on 1 January 2002. Further amendments to the system may be introduced by presidential decrees.[5] Regulations pertaining to criminal records may also be found in other statutes, notably Law 2472/1997 on the protection of the individual from the processing of data of a personal character,[6] a statute adopted in implementation of both the 1981 Council of Europe Convention for the Protection of Individuals with regard to the automated processing of

N. Sakkoulas, 1999), pp. 806–808 [in Greek]. Articles 573–580 CCrP were repeatedly modified by Legislative Decree 3425/1955; the Royal Decree of 16 April 1957 'on certificates, criminal records etc. in the case of destruction of registries'; articles 22–29 of Legislative Decree 1160/1972; and the Royal Decree 330/1973.

[2] Articles 6–13 of Law 1805/1988, *Government Gazette* A 199, 31 August 1988.

[3] Articles 14–15 of Law 1805/1988.

[4] Article 2 of Law 1851/1989 (*Government Gazette* A 122, 16 May 1989); Article 22 of Law 1868/1989 (*Government Gazette* A 230, 10 October 1989); Article 18 of Law 1916/1990 (*Government Gazette* A 187, 28 December 1990); Article 32.2 of Law 1968/1990 (*Government Gazette* A 150, 11 October 1991); Article 45 of Law 2109/1992 (*Government Gazette* A 205, 29 December 1992); Article 43 of Law 2172/1993 (*Government Gazette* A 207, 16 December 1993); Article 16.11 of Law 2298/1995 (*Government Gazette* A 62, 4 April 1995); Article 4 of Law 2408/1996 (*Government Gazette* A 104, 4 June 1996); Articles 21.1. and 25 of Law 2721/1999 (*Government Gazette* A 112, 3 June 1999).

[5] Article 573 of the Code of Criminal Procedure.

[6] *Government Gazette* A 50, 10 April 1997; the full text in English and in French is available at 50 *Revue Hellenique de Droit International* 1997, pp. 645–706. For an overview see L. Mitrou, 'The Greek Law on the Protection of Personal Data' in L.-A. Sicilianos and M. Gavouneli (eds.), *Scientific and Technological Development and Human Rights* (Athens: 2001), pp. 143–157.

personal data[7] as well as Directive 95/46/EC on the Protection of Individuals with regard to the processing of personal data and on the free movement of such data.[8] In that respect Article 28 paragraph 1 of the Greek Constitution provides that 'the generally accepted rules of international law as well as international treaties, once ratified by law and entered into force according to their specific terms and conditions, constitute an integral part of the domestic legal order and supersede any other contrary statutory provision'.[9] As a result, the general provisions on criminal records may be amended or simply set aside by subsequent international obligations undertaken by the Greek State – and that has often been the case.

Moreover, the application of the system in practice is subject to human rights guarantees, best exemplified in the protection of private life under Article 8 of the European Convention on Human Rights[10] and the corresponding freedom to receive and impart information without interference by public authority and regardless of frontiers under Article 10 thereof as well as the relevant case law of the European Court of Human Rights.

2. Existing legal framework

Criminal records in Greece are kept in local record registries attached to the office of the Public Prosecutor in the Court of First Instance of the subject's place of birth. In the Ministry of Justice there is an independent Department of Criminal Records[11] operating as a central authority and having overall supervision of the criminal records system.

[7] ETS no. 108, adopted on 28 January 1981; ratified by Law 2068/1992 (*Government Gazette* A 118). For an overview of the international legal framework on the protection of personal data see J.-P. Jacqué, 'La Convention pour la protection des personnes à l'égard du traitement informatisé des données à caractère personnel', 26 (1980) *Annuaire Français de Droit International* at 773; L.-A. Sicilianos, 'International Protection of Personal Data: Privacy, Freedom of Information or Both?', in L.-A. Sicilianos and M. Gavouneli (eds.), *Scientific and Technological Development and Human Rights* (Athens: 2001), pp. 123–141.

[8] OJ L 281, 1995, p. 31.

[9] For a general overview of the relationship between the Greek legal order and international law see M. Gavouneli, 'The Jurisprudence of Greek Courts on Public International Law' 48 (1995) *Revue Hellenique de Droit International* 351–391.

[10] ETS no. 5, 1950. Greece, a contracting party since 1952, ratified (again) the European Convention on Human Rights by legislative decree 52/1974, *Government Gazette* A 259, after the brief interlude of the *affaire grecque* (1968–1974).

[11] Presidential Decree 36/2000 (*Government Gazette* A 129, 14–17 February 2000).

Every certificate of criminal record consists of two parts: the first concerns the identification of the subject and the second the content of their 'criminal past behaviour'. According to Article 574.2 CCrP every certificate must record the following:

a) information necessary for the identification of the subject;
b) the full list of any irrevocable[12] convictions issued by a court or a judicial council for felonies or misdemeanours for which a custodial penalty or a pecuniary sanction has been imposed, including any supplementary penalties or measures of security;
c) the full list of any decisions imposing confinement to a correctional institution or educative (reformative) measures on a minor;
d) the full list of any convictions issued by foreign courts, if they involve an act constituting a felony or misdemeanour under Greek criminal law;
e) the full list of any decisions acquitting the accused on the basis of incapacity to stand trial due to lack of culpability, including any security measures that replace the main sentence, provided that the offence was punishable by a minimum penalty of three months' imprisonment;
f) the full list of any court or judicial council decisions acquitting the accused for reasons of practical repentance, provided that the offence was punishable by a minimum penalty of three months' imprisonment; and
g) any decisions suspending a custodial penalty.

Under Article 574 paragraph 3 CCrP the certificate of criminal record also records any pardons lifting the consequences of conviction; prescriptions of the act or the penalty as prescribed by law; suspensions of sentences as provided by law; conditional releases from imprisonment; amendments or waivers of measures of security or educative (reformative) measures; and decisions under Articles 550 and 551 CCrP on penalties for multiple convictions for the same or different crimes respectively. Under Article 574.4 CCrP any custodial sentence in excess of three months imposed for a felony or an intentional misdemeanour must also be recorded.

Under Article 578 CCrP certificates of criminal record cease to be in effect in the following cases only:

[12] Order of the Public Prosecutor at the Athens Court of First Instance 82/2006, (2006) *Poiniki Dikaiosyni* [=Criminal Justice], at 1003.

- when the subject dies or reaches 80 years of age;
- in cases of certificates concerning entries of correctional or educational/reformative measures imposed on minors, as soon as the minor reaches 17 years of age;
- when the conviction is quashed by a subsequent final decision, when amnesty is awarded, or when, by virtue of an explicit provision of a subsequent statute, the act ceases to be punishable;
- when the conviction carries a suspended sentence under Article 99 of the Criminal Code, the suspended sentence is erased from the record five years after the period of suspension has lapsed, provided that such suspension has not been lifted or revoked;
- if the certificate was issued after a conviction imposing on a minor confinement to a correctional institution, the certificate of criminal record ceases to be in effect five years after the sentence has been served provided that the minimum confinement imposed did not exceed one year; and eight years after the sentence has been served for confinement that exceeded one year; unless a new conviction has been imposed. If the person is subject to conditional release, the deadline of five or eight years starts from the completion of the time spent under conditions.
- if the conviction imposed a pecuniary sentence or a sentence of imprisonment up to one month for an offence committed with intention or a sentence of imprisonment up to two months for an offence committed by negligence, the certificate of criminal record ceases to be in effect ten years after serving the sentence provided that the offender has not been convicted again for a felony or a misdemeanour.

The registries responsible for the maintenance of criminal records are supposed to dispose of all certificates that ceased to be in effect once every six months; it seems that this rarely happens in practice. Disputes arising from errors in entries[13] are resolved by order of the Public Prosecutor at the Court of First Instance of the subject's place of birth. In the case of persons born abroad the competent authority is the Public Prosecutor of the Athens Court of First Instance.[14] Appeal is possible before the competent Judicial Council of First Instance within one month.

[13] On the meaning of 'dispute' in a criminal record see Athens Court of First Instance 809/2006, (2006) *Poinika Chronika* [=Criminal Chronicles], at 739.

[14] Article 580 CCrP. For more see K. Sofoulakis, 'Disputes and Corrections of Erroneous Entries in Criminal Records Certificates and their Copies pursuant to Article 580 of the Code of Criminal Procedure' 2 (2000) *Poinikos Logos* 903–904 [in Greek].

Data referring to criminal charges or convictions constitute 'sensitive data'[15] and their collection and processing is in principle forbidden.[16] The creation and operation of such a file is possible only upon a special permit by the Data Protection Authority,[17] provided that such 'processing is necessary for the purposes of criminal or correctional policy when carried out by a public authority and pertains to the detection of offences, criminal convictions and security measures'.[18] The constitutional basis of this position lies with 9 A of the Greek Constitution, as supplemented by the latest 2001 amendment: 'All persons have the right to be protected from the collection, processing and use, especially by electronic means, of their personal data, as specified by law. The protection of personal data is ensured by an independent authority, which is established and operates as specified by law.'[19]

3. Contents of a European Criminal Record

The provisions on criminal records in Greece refer to 'persons', without any further qualification as to nationality or domicile. However, under Article 573 paragraph 2 CCrP, the central Criminal Records Unit keeps criminal records for persons born abroad: it follows that both crimes committed abroad by Greek nationals and foreigners residing in Greece are included in the national criminal records. Furthermore, under Article 574 CCrP, the criminal record also includes foreign criminal convictions. Such notification is usually carried out in the course of mutual judicial assistance or when the convicted person is not a national of the state where the offence was committed. According to these constitutional principles, from a Greek point of view the ECR could record only data on crimes with an international dimension. A list of these

[15] According to the definition included in Article 2(b) of Law 2472/1997 on the protection of the individual from the processing of data of a personal character (*Government Gazette* A 50, 10 April 1997).

[16] Article 7 paragraph 1 of Law 2472/1997.

[17] The Data Protection Authority is an independent administrative authority, established by Articles 15–20 of Law 2472/1997 as amended by Law 3471/2006 (*Government Gazette* A 133/2006), which further transposed Directive 2002/58/EU of the European Parliament and of the Council of 12 July 2002 on Data Protection. Full information may be found in the website of the Authority.

[18] Article 7 paragraph 2(e) of Law 2472/1997.

[19] For a thorough overview see V. Sotiropoulos, *Constitutional Protection of Personal Data* (Athens: Sakkoulas, 2006) [in Greek].

crimes could probably be the one used in the Framework Decision on the European Arrest Warrant[20] and subsequent instruments.

Greece already participates in the Schengen Information System (SIS), created under the Convention applying the Schengen Agreement, as subsequently repeatedly amended.[21] The SIS was created to facilitate the transnational flow of data necessary for the efficient control of external borders and the adoption of necessary security measures within the Schengen area. The uninhibited flow of data is not necessarily incompatible with the protection of such sensitive data. Under Article 126, paragraph 1 of the Schengen Convention 'with regard to the automatic processing of personal data transmitted pursuant to this Convention, each contracting party shall, no later than the time of entry into force of this Convention, adopt the national provisions requisite to achieve a level of protection of personal data at least equal to that resulting from the principles of the Council of Europe Convention of 28 January 1981'.[22]

[20] Council Framework Decision 2002/584/JHA of 13 June 2002 on the European Arrest Warrant and the surrender procedures between the member States, OJ L 190, p. 1, 18 July 2002.

[21] 'Convention implementing the Schengen Agreement of 14 June 1985 between the Governments of the States of the Benelux Economic Union, the Federal Republic of Germany and the French Republic on the gradual abolition of checks at their common borders', OJ L 239, pp. 19–62, 22 September 2000; to which acceded Italy, ibid., pp. 63–68; Spain, ibid., pp. 69–75; Portugal, ibid, pp. 76–82; Greece, ibid., pp. 83–89; Austria, ibid., pp. 90–96; Denmark, ibid., pp. 97–105; Finland, ibid., pp. 106–114; and Sweden, ibid., pp. 115–123.

[22] On the SIS data provisions see in general L. F. M. Verhey, 'Privacy Aspects of the Convention applying the Schengen Agreement' in H. Meijers et al., *Schengen. Internationalisation of Central Chapters of the Law on Aliens, Refugees, Security and the Police* (The Hague: Kluwer, 1991), pp. 110–34; B. Schatenberg, 'The Schengen Information System: Privacy and Legal Protection', in H. G. Schermers et al. (eds.), *Free Movement of Persons in Europe* (Dordrecht/Boston/London: Martinus Nijhoff, 1993), pp. 43–51; P. Billaud, 'La protection des données informatiques dans le cadre des accords de Schengen', in A. Pauly (ed.), *Les accords de Schengen: Abolition des frontières intérieures ou menace pour les libertés publiques?* (Maastricht: EIPA, 1993), pp. 27–38; N.K. Sakellariou, *The Schengen Information System* (Athens: Ant. N. Sakkoulas, 1995) [in Greek]; V. Hreblay, *Les accords de Schengen, Origines, fonctionnement, avenir* (Bruxelles: Bruylant 1998); Chistian Chocquet, 'Le système d'information Schengen: un double défi' 418 (198) *Revue du marché commun et l'Union européenne* 294–298; M. Colvin, 'The Schengen Information System: A Human Rights Audit' (2001) *European Human Rights Law Review* 271–279; N. Wichmann, 'The Participation of the Schengen Associates. Inside or Outside?' 11 (2006) *European Foreign Affairs Review* 87–107.

Further information contained in a criminal record may also be supplied to another state on the basis of the Prüm Convention.[23] Greece did not participate in the original convention but has repeatedly stated recently that it intends to do so, either as a direct participant or in the context of EU action in that respect. It is worth noting that the Prüm Convention covers exchange of information, including criminal records and other personal data, not only for purposes of combating terrorism, cross-border crime and illegal migration but also 'for the prevention of criminal offences and in maintaining public order and security for major events with a cross-border dimension, in particular for sporting events or European Council meetings'.[24] To the extent that such cooperation between national authorities is ensured not only upon request but also *proprio motu*, on their own accord, the Greek participation in the new system would also constitute a qualitative change.

4. Access to the European Criminal Record

In the domestic legal order access to criminal records revolves around two fundamental considerations. First, whether such 'sensitive' data could be subject to processing; and, second, the origin of such data, the purpose of processing and who is to be responsible for it.[25] Several Greek statutes require the furnishing of copies of criminal records. The Greek CCrP sets the rules according to which access to criminal records is possible. The full certificate for judicial use may only be transmitted directly to the competent authority requesting such information. A summary criminal record certificate may be widely available for general use.

According to Article 577.1 of the CCrP a copy of the criminal record for judicial use can only be supplied to:

[23] The Convention was concluded on 27 May 2005 between Belgium, Germany, Spain, France, Luxembourg, the Netherlands and Austria, all members of the European Union, 'without prejudice to the provisions of the Treaty on European Union and the Treaty establishing the European Community' and 'in observance of the fundamental rights deriving from the Charter of Fundamental Rights of the European Union, the European Convention for the protection of Human Rights and Fundamental Freedoms and the constitutional traditions common to the States concerned, particularly in the awareness that the supply of personal data to another contracting party requires a reasonable standard of data protection on the part of the receiving contracting party'; second and fourth preambular paragraphs, respectively; the full text is available at Council of the European Union document 10900/05, CROMORG 65, ENFOPOL 85, MIGR 30, 7 July 2005.

[24] Article 14 of the Prüm Convention.

[25] Thus also Sotiropoulos, *Constitutional Protection of Personal Data*, at p. 125.

a) the Public Prosecutor who conducts an ordinary investigation or the competent prosecutor in a military tribunal and solely for judicial use;
b) the directors of prisons or other penitentiary institutions or clinics for convicts who serve a custodial penalty or are subject to a security measure following a final (irrevocable) conviction;
c) foreign authorities exercising criminal jurisdiction that are subject to mutual legal assistance agreements;
d) public services, civil, military and church authorities, legal entities of public law, statutory companies and banks;
e) foreign embassies and consulates;
f) authorities in charge of judges, teachers of all grades of education and members of security forces, as well as candidate students for police academies and military schools.

Article 577.3 CCrP further provides that a presidential decree, issued upon recommendation of the Minister of Justice, may stipulate that copies for judicial use can be issued for appointments to any other public office or legal body in public law. The copy of criminal record 'for judicial use' is officially transmitted to the competent authorities after a request made by the subject. It is not handed to the subject themselves. Already, under the rules of electronic transmission of official data, the criminal record of applicants for appointment by the civil service or in education is transmitted to the authority concerned directly.[26]

According to Article 575 CCrP whenever there is a statutory requirement for a copy of the criminal record, a copy for general use will be supplied unless a full copy is expressly required. According to Article 576.3 CCrP a copy of the criminal record for general use includes all available entries with the exception of pecuniary sentences or custodial penalties of less than six months after a lapse of three years; and custodial penalties in excess of six months or confinement to a psychiatric institution after a lapse of twenty years. The copy for general use is handed only to the subject. The right of subjects to access all of their data is protected fully by Article 12 of Law 2472/1997. The Data Protection Authority has developed case law on access to such information, which has impacted significantly upon administrative practices.

[26] See Joint Ministerial Decision 2458/2005 of the Minister of Public Order and the Home Minister.

Access to personal data, including criminal records, is regularly provided for in all the bilateral conventions on mutual legal assistance. The obligation to exchange information, including criminal records, constitutes a standard provision of such agreements concluded with Albania, Armenia, Australia, Bulgaria, Canada, China, Croatia, Cyprus, the Czech Republic, Egypt, Georgia, Hungary, Lebanon, Poland, Romania, Russia, Slovakia, Slovenia, Syria, Tunisia and the United States. Greece is also a contracting party to the 1959 European Convention on Mutual Assistance in Criminal Matters[27] and the 1990 Council of Europe Convention on Laundering, Search, Seizure and Confiscation of the Proceeds of Crime.[28] At least the most recent among them typically include a provision stating that such exchange of information is subject to domestic data protection legislation, including the right of subjects to access to their criminal records. Often agreements stipulate that the domestic law most favourable to the protection of personal data, including criminal records, prevails.

5. Use of the European Criminal Record

5.1 Judicial use

Current legislation introduces an exhaustive list of individuals and authorities that have the right to be supplied with a copy for judicial use of a person's criminal record.[29] The same rules apply to the right of foreign authorities exercising criminal jurisdiction to request a copy for judicial use of a person subject to their jurisdiction.

An issue arising from the judicial use of criminal records concerns the attachment of the defendant's criminal records to the judicial file for the purpose of the determination of sentence under Article 577.2 CCrP. The certificate is inserted in a sealed opaque envelope to be opened only once the verdict has been reached.[30] A note of this is

[27] ETS no. 30, 20 April 1959; ratified by legislative decree 4218/1961.

[28] ETS no. 141, 8 November 1990; ratified by Law 2655/1998. Greece has also signed but not as yet ratified the Council of Europe Convention on Laundering, Search, Seizure and Confiscation of the Proceeds of Crime and the Financing of Terrorism, CETS no. 1998, 16 May 2005.

[29] Article 577.1 of the Code of Criminal Procedure.

[30] According to I. Anagnostopoulos, 'Certificate of Criminality, Certificate of Criminal Record and Impartial Judgment' 49 (1999) *Poinika Chronika* 5–10: 'The prohibition of access to the content of the criminal record until the accused is pronounced guilty, apparently aims at the creation of a clear judicial conviction, based on the evidence of the case in question and the prevention of the danger of its corrosion by elements of

entered in the transcripts of the trial. In appeals the criminal record certificate is reinserted in an opaque envelope and sealed. Responsibility for the correct inclusion of the certificate to the file lies with the court clerk, who is subject to disciplinary sanctions in case of errors in the procedure. The previous system did not include these safeguards.

5.2 Use for future employment and admission to schools and associations

It is widely accepted that the main aim of criminal records is to ensure that individuals, whose past behaviour is considered questionable or unsuitable, are not appointed to positions involving a certain degree of authority[31] and responsibility. Normally copies of criminal records must be submitted with most applications for employment. The entire criminal record is submitted for vetting purposes in the case of applications for employment in a variety of public services, generally considered as 'sensitive',[32] including civil and military authorities, legal bodies in public law, statutory companies and banks. It is also needed for the appointment of judges, teachers and professors and members of the security forces, as well as candidate students to police and other military academies, also when the criminal record concerns 'sensitive' positions in the public services. In Greece there is no legal requirement for the submission of a copy from the criminal record of applicants for employment in the private sector; however, it is demanded in practice.[33]

Under Article 575 CCrP copies for general use may be supplied for prospective members of the Bar, future notaries and chartered accountants. A copy of their criminal record is a prerequisite for the registration of lawyers with the Bar of their choice.[34] The inability to produce a

previous convictions' [in Greek; translation by the author]. On the same point see also *Areios Pagos* 389/2006 (2006) *Poinikos Logos*, at 251.

[31] See Opinion 3/1989 of the Prosecutor at the Patras Criminal Court of First Instance 37 (1989) *Nomiko Vima* [=Law Tribune – NoB], at 1103.

[32] Council of Europe, European Committee on Crime Problems (CDPC), 'Report on the Criminal Record and the Rehabilitation of Convicted Persons' (Strasbourg: CoE, 1984), pp. 13–55.

[33] See European Offender Employment Group, *Models of Good Practice in Europe: What Works* (UK: NIACRO, 1995), at 47.

[34] Legislative Decree 3026 of 6/8 October 1954 introduces the obligation of all prospective members of the Bar to submit a 'blank' (empty) criminal record. See also Legislative Decree 3329 of 21/25 August 1955 on 'The Formation of a Body of Chartered Accountants', as amended; and Article 2 paragraph 1 of the Decision of the Body of Chartered Accountants no. 2377 of 16/26 August 1965 (*Government Gazette* B 554/1965), as codified in Presidential

'blank' copy leads to ineligibility for office. The ECR could invite looser use: for example, assignment to public service could be prevented only in case of convictions for crimes related to the type of work applied for.[35]

6. Protection against organised crime

Information is certainly the most important currency in the fight against organised crime. Indeed, the European system of exchange of information in the context of police cooperation, from the early days of the Schengen Information System to the exigencies of the Prüm Convention, was created with a view to enhance the system of judicial protection against organised crime. This a goal to which Greece adheres fully. However, the adoption of relevant instruments is commonly delayed because of intense parliamentary scrutiny of civil liberties issues, including the treatment of sensitive data such as criminal records. As a typical example, Greece has not yet ratified the UN Palermo Convention on Transnational Organised Crime in spite of the repeatedly expressed intentions of the Minister of Justice to do so.

Although information on criminal records is necessarily included in any exchange of information system, the importance of criminal records must not be exaggerated. After all, a criminal record refers only to convictions rendered *irrevocably* by a court of law and not to prosecutions or police investigations in general. As a result, the coordinated fight against organised crime would necessarily require a much more extensive system of joint action than access to a criminal record system, however complete, may provide.

Of course one must not lose sight of the capacity of the criminal record to act as a very effective obstacle to the rehabilitation and social reintegration of ex-offenders: cases of recidivism are certainly more possible when the person released remains without an occupation after the penalty has been served.[36] The guarantees inherent in the keeping of criminal records nowadays purport to vitiate any risk of mismanagement, or at least to mitigate the continued effects of a criminal conduct

Decrees 226/1992 (*Government Gazette* A 120, 14 July 1992) and 341/1997 (*Government Gazette* A 232, 21 November 1997), respectively.

[35] S. Giovanoglou, 'Criminal Record: A Historical Continuum of Unfulfilled Reform' (2005) *Poiniki Dikaiosini*, at p. 1212 [in Greek].

[36] Northern Ireland Association for the Care and Resettlement of Offenders, *Regulating the 'Yellow Ticket'. The Laws, Policies and Practices which affect the Employment of People with Criminal Records in the European Union* (Belfast: 1996), at p. 4.

for which the lawful sanction has been applied and served. As a result, all national criminal record systems and presumably also the ECR would also include erasure provisions. In the organised crime context, however, the continued existence of a criminal record may also impact upon the status of the individual involved as a victim or collaborator of justice, thus covered by the special protection accorded to such individuals by national and European rules on the protection of whistleblowers.

7. Critical evaluation

The Hellenic system of criminal record keeping has been subject to an extensive overhaul in recent decades. Addressed as an integral parameter of the judicial system, it suffers from the common organisational defects of public administration. The latest step in this long saga is the complete computerisation of the justice system, with priority given to the data-processing system. The general idea of a central, autonomous criminal record registry, which will function in parallel with regional criminal registries in the land, remains a slowly nearing goal.

The existence of a fully operational computerised system would be instrumental in order to achieve an ECR, which can only be accomplished when national criminal records have reached a common level of organisation and are interconnected or at least interconnectable. Nevertheless, given the strong emphasis placed by the Greek polity and citizenry on issues of personal freedom and protection of personal data, it is unlikely that an ECR would be easily accepted in Greece unless it is accompanied with strong civil liberties guarantees. Consequently, the preconditions for the establishment of any central criminal record registry should necessarily include a detailed list of crimes with international characteristics recorded and full personal data protection guarantees before and after their entry.

The creation of the ECR presupposes the basic harmonisation of several different national procedures and the exchange of information in an area of justice, public security and freedom, with special emphasis on the effective protection of the human rights of the European citizens.

9

The European Criminal Record in Hungary

KATALIN LIGETI

1. Introduction

The legal framework of maintaining criminal records and access to the entries contained in these records, including cooperation with foreign authorities, has been recently modified by the Hungarian legislature. The prevailing legislation treats separately the types and contents of the criminal records on the one hand (*first unit*), and the use of them for the purpose of international cooperation in criminal matters on the other hand (*second unit*).

Accordingly, the *first unit* of the current regulatory framework is laid down in Act No. 85 of 1999 on the Criminal Record (Criminal Record Act or CRA). The CRA sets out the rules on criminal registers, including the types of register, the content and the accessibility of entries, the duty to provide data, as well as the surveillance body and data protection principles. The CRA is supplemented by a number of ministerial decrees, which regulate the technical aspects of the registers. For example Decree No. 6 of 2000 of the Minister of the Interior on the issue of extracts, Joint Decree No. 7 of 2000 of the Minister of the Interior and the Minister of Justice[1] on the body in charge of keeping and maintaining criminal registers and the rules governing access to data contained therein and, lastly, Decree No. 8 of 2000 of the Minister of the Interior on photographs and DNA profiles.

The *second unit* of the regulatory framework includes Act No. 54 of 1999 on the cooperation and exchange of information with Europol and Interpol (Europol–Interpol Act), Act No. 14 on the promulgation of the Europol Convention, Act No. 34 of 1994 on the police (Police Act) and Joint Decree No. 4 of 2002 of the Minister of the Interior and the Minister of Finance on

[1] This Joint Decree has been amended by Decree No. 8 of 2007 of the Minister of Justice and Law Enforcement on reshaping certain administrative duties.

the Centre for International Criminal Cooperation (Decree on CICC). To some extent the Police Act serves as background legislation in respect of international cooperation defining the mainframe of exchange of information. The Decree on CICC is a supplementary to the Europol–Interpol Act providing for general layout, tasks, duties and procedure of CICC itself. Although CICC is the main body in charge of facilitating international police cooperation, there are other authorities and bodies on which the law confers certain tasks in this context. In addition, there are some law enforcement agencies that, though not empowered by force of law, do take part in international exchange of criminal information. I specify both kinds of bodies and their tasks and duties under the relevant sections of this chapter.

2. Types and content of the Hungarian criminal registers

The CRA distinguishes five sorts of criminal registers. All five registers are kept, maintained and managed by the Office of Administrative and Governmental Electronic Public Services.[2] The CRA provides for each type of register separately both in respect to its content and to those administrative and other governmental or non-governmental bodies which are entitled to access the entries.

The CRA stipulates that criminal registers shall be kept and maintained for the purpose of crime prevention and the enforcement of criminal laws; tasks that require up to date information on possible suspects and on offenders. Due to the lack of criminal liability of legal entities, all above-mentioned registers contain data exclusively on natural persons.[3] For the sake of data protection the registers are supposed to be kept separately. There are strict rules on the accessibility and interchangeability of their contents. Under the CRA there are a number of criminal register regimes, which we will now proceed to examine.

[2] Until 2006 all administrative tasks related to the criminal registers fell within the jurisdiction of Central Data Processing Office of the Ministry of the Interior [Central Office]. Yet as the Ministry of the Interior has been disbanded and its duties split up among the Ministry of Regional Development and the Ministry of Justice and Law Enforcement, the Central Office had to be moved to the Chancellery. Once its constitutional position changed, the Central Office was united with other administrative registries, such as the National Register of Vehicles, the Register of Domiciles, etc. This is why this new administrative body in charge of these registries is named the Office of Administrative and Governmental Electronic Public Services.

[3] Hungarian law provides for imposing certain criminal measures against legal entities without acknowledging the criminal liability of legal entities. For details see Act No. 104 of 2001 on criminal measures against legal entities.

2.1. *Register of offenders*[4]

The Register of offenders (RO) registers all persons against whom any Hungarian criminal court has imposed criminal sanction of any kind; against whom the public prosecutor suspended the charges or imposed an admonition or reprimand; who have been pardoned or exonerated; against whom criminal proceedings have ceased or been terminated; who have been found guilty by a foreign criminal court if the foreign judgment has previously been declared to have the same effects as domestic judgments or if the Hungarian authority is executing the enforcement of the foreign judgment.

The RO covers two types of entries: those related to the offender's person and the crime committed and those related to the enforcement of the judgment (resolution) or sanction. In the first category fall the offender's personal data (name, place and date of birth, ID number, address) including nationality and domicile or residence, the crime committed, the mode of perpetration, if the perpetrator is a repeat offender of any kind and, in case of conviction, the criminal sanction or sanctions. Criminal courts and offices of the public prosecution involved in the criminal proceedings and conviction are also recorded, as well as filing and other electronically generated case numbers. Entries related to the enforcement of the sanctions include details of when a term of imprisonment began and ended, data on early release, duration of probation, community service or fine, and information on any pardon.

Full copies of the RO containing all such listed entries are provided exclusively to: (i) the courts, the offices of the public prosecution and other criminal law enforcement agencies; (ii) the Minister of Justice and Law Enforcement in order to manage applications for pardon or to provide international assistance in criminal matters; (iii) national security agencies; (iv) foreign criminal law enforcement agencies, prosecuting offices, courts and international judicial or prosecuting bodies in accordance with the laws on international cooperation in criminal matters; (v) The CICC; and (vi) in respect of immigration affairs, immigration offices.

Access to extracts of the RO including only the first category of data shall also be granted to: (a) the police, for the purposes of administrative and surveillance duties; (b) the High Council of the Judiciary in order to examine the criminal registers in respect to judges to be appointed; (c) the Prosecutor General in order to examine the

[4] Paras. 9–19a of the CRA.

criminal registers in respect to public prosecutors to be appointed. Access to extracts of the RO including only certain given parts of the first category of entries shall also be granted in accordance with the laws and for the purposes of: (1) the issue of licences to carry firearms and ammunition; (2) the appointment of lay judges; (3) the appointment of public notaries; (4) the issue of passports; (5) granting immigration permits; (6) admission to the Bar; and (7) in further cases where Hungarian law provides so.

Entries of the RO shall be deleted after the elapse of a certain period of time depending on the type of sanction applied and whether the offence was committed deliberately or negligently. Consequently, entries are deleted:

- after fifteen years upon release in cases of imprisonment for offences committed deliberately;
- after ten years upon release in cases of fines and community service for offences committed deliberately;
- after five years upon release in cases of imprisonment for offences committed negligently;
- after three years upon release in cases of fines and community service for offences committed negligently;
- after the offender's thirtieth year of age in cases of juvenile offenders, etc.

2.2. Register of persons under coercive measures[5]

The Register of persons under coercive measures (RCM) registers those offenders who have been in pre-trial detention, under home arrest, under a banning or restriction order, under restriction of dwelling area or in preliminary compulsory medical treatment (the latter applies to mentally ill offenders). The RCM contains the individual's personal data (see above), the crime he or she is suspected to have committed and the duration of the coercive measure. Those having either full or partial access to the RO, have the same kind of access with respect to the RCM. Special access is granted to passport offices, childcare offices and public guardianship authorities – the latter in respect of a subject's unaccompanied children. Entries in the RCM shall be deleted upon termination of the coercive measure.

[5] Paras. 20–24 of the CRA.

2.3. *Register of persons subject to criminal proceedings*[6]

The Register of persons subject to criminal proceedings (RCP) contains data about persons suspected or accused of criminal offences. The RCP also covers the identification of criminal law enforcement agencies in charge of the criminal proceedings and the exact date and time when such proceedings are launched. Entries in the RCP shall be deleted upon final adjudication of the criminal case or upon termination of the criminal proceedings or the criminal investigation.

2.4. *Register of photographs and dactyloscopy (Fingerprints)*[7]

The Register of photographs and dactyloscopy (RPD) contains personal data, fingerprints, palm-prints and portraits of offenders who are the subject of well-founded criminal charges for having committed an intentional crime. Access to the RPD is regulated in the same way as for RO, RCM and RCP. Entries in the RPD shall be deleted:

- in cases of offences committed deliberately: if the offender was sentenced to a period of imprisonment, twenty years after the date of release; or if the court imposed coercive measures, probation or compulsory medical treatment (the latter for mentally ill offenders) upon the date of prescription of the sentence;[8]
- upon termination of the criminal proceedings or the criminal investigation;
- upon prescription of the sentence for the criminal offence if fingerprint samples have been gathered at a crime scene.[9]

2.5. *Register of DNA profiles*[10]

The Register of DNA profiles (RDP) contains the offender's personal data and the information related to the crime committed as specified in relation to the RO. The RDP also contains a code with the offender's DNA profile in order to identify him/her. The RDP registers only those offenders who are subject to well-founded criminal charges for having committed certain types of serious crimes such as: (1) crimes to be

[6] Paras. 25–29 of the CRA. [7] Paras. 30–37 of the CRA.
[8] Subsection A of Para. 36 of the CRA. [9] Subsection C of Para. 36 of the CRA.
[10] Paras. 38–46 of the CRA.

punished with a minimum of five years' imprisonment; (2) crimes in connection with cross-border criminality; (3) sex offences; (4) crimes against children; (5) drug offences; and (6) forgery, money laundering, terrorism or offences against the sovereignty of the state.

Access to entries of the RDP is granted exclusively to: (1) the courts, the offices of public prosecution and the criminal law enforcement agencies; (2) national security agencies; (3) foreign criminal law enforcement agencies, foreign offices of public prosecution, foreign courts and international judicial or prosecuting bodies in accordance with the laws on international cooperation in criminal matters; and (4) the CICC. No full access is granted in general; only parts of the DNA profile inevitable for the identification of the person shall be accessed. Entries in the RDP shall be deleted:

- in cases of sentences of imprisonment, twenty years after the date of release;
- if the court imposed coercive measures, probation or compulsory medical treatment (the latter for mentally ill offenders) upon the date of prescription of the sentence;[11]
- upon termination of the criminal procedings or the investigation;
- upon prescription of the sentence for the criminal offence if the DNA samples were gathered at a crime scene.[12]

All five types of criminal registrer shall be scrutinised by the Minister of Justice and Law Enforcement, the Data Protection Ombudsman and the competent office of public prosecution. In respect of data protection, these authorities have full access to the registers even if such access would not have otherwise been granted to them.

2.6. *Extract*[13]

There is an additional type of criminal register, the extract, which is provided exclusively to the very person to whom it refers. The extract contains the person's identification data and a statement that he/she is either unsentenced, has already been released, is not registered in the RO (i.e. clean register or clean extract); or includes the conviction and the details of the imprisonment or the correctional and security measures applied against him/her. The extract is a document needed in general to enter employment in the public sphere and in certain cases in the private

[11] Subsection A of Para. 45 of the CRA. [12] Subsection C of Para. 45 of the CRA.
[13] Paras. 57–59 of the CRA.

economy too (e.g. GPs, private detectives, lifeguards, higher positions in economic associations, private entrepreneurs, etc.).

3. Crimes committed by foreigners and crimes committed by nationals abroad

As is clear from the description in the previous section all five types of criminal registers contain the offender's nationality. Therefore, crimes committed by foreigners in Hungary are registered in one of the Hungarian criminal registers, though they are not kept separately. Separating any entries for foreigners from those of Hungarian nationals would place anti-discrimination principles into doubt. This means that there is no separate criminal register for foreigner offenders, but upon inquiry the automated database will show the offenders' nationality together with any other personal data.

The only record in Hungary that treats foreigners separately is kept by the immigration office. That record lists all police measures (including fines for petty traffic offences) imposed upon persons who had been granted a temporary or a permanent residence permit in Hungary.[14]

It is worth noting that in addition to the criminal registers listed above, courts have their own register on the cases they try (court statistics);[15] offices of prosecution authorities also register the charges they bring (statistics on charges);[16] and police forces have a unified criminal register of police and prosecution[17] recording all investigations they have carried out. These records serve, however, merely for statistical purposes. They show the total number of foreigners tried in Hungary or the total number of convicted foreigners in Hungary as well as the total number of foreigners accused of a crime in a given year. These records, however, refer only to the

[14] Registry on Foreigners, introduced by Para. 75 of Act No. 39 of 2001 on foreigners' right to enter and to reside in Hungary.

[15] Regulation No. 113 of 1974 of the Minister of Justice on the rules of court statistics.

[16] Regulation No. 5 of 1982 of the Prosecutor General on the introduction of a digitalised register of information on prosecutorial actions perfected before criminal courts.

[17] As the name Unified Criminal Register of Police and Prosecution shows, offices of the prosecution also add their contribution to police investigation in this regime for recording information. This register has been introduced by Joint Regulation of the Minister of Interior and of the Prosecutor General No. 0011 of 1963. In fact, a statistical reform has been launched to redraft legislation laying down a Uniform Register, as a result of which this joint regulation is going to be rendered null and void on 31 December 2007. A possible new regulatory framework for the Uniform Register shall be introduced in an act to be voted on by the parliament.

nationality and do not contain any personal information on the offender. Therefore, these statistical records cannot be used for the purpose of international judicial cooperation.

There are no records kept on foreign convictions of Hungarian nationals. The Hungarian authorities are aware of convictions of Hungarian nationals abroad only if the foreign authority has informed them. There is no such obligation, it happens on a voluntary basis. Foreign authorities usually inform their Hungarian counterparts if they need certain information concerning the Hungarian offender. Information on foreign convictions of Hungarian nationals can be introduced into the RO only if the foreign judgment has been declared to have the same effects as a domestic judgment or if the Hungarian authorities have undertaken the execution of the foreign judgment.

4. Mechanisms of international criminal cooperation

In order to describe the mechanism of cooperation with foreign criminal law enforcement bodies available in Hungary for the exchange of information contained in criminal records, three sub-questions have to be answered: (i) which Hungarian authorities are entitled to forward information to foreign authorities, (ii) which cooperation mechanisms are available, and (iii) what is the actual exchange mechanism like.

4.1. Authorities entitled to forward information to foreign authorities

The Europol–Interpol Act, the Europol Convention and the Decree on the CICC specify which authorities are entitled to forward information to foreign authorities. It has to be underlined that the CICC was introduced prior to Hungary's Accession to the European Union. As a result, the CICC does not fully comply with the provisions of the Europol Convention. Meanwhile Hungary became an EU Member State and joined the Europol Convention. Nevertheless, the Decree on the CICC was not amended and, therefore, the prevailing legal framework on criminal cooperation with other Member States and the EU itself is to some extent controversial. Still, with some fine tuning the CICC works reasonably well and according to Hungarian practitioners it has managed to fit into the new structure of cooperation.

The CICC comprises the following four units :

- Europol National Unit (ENU);
- Interpol Hungarian National Unit;

- International Information Exchange Office; and
- SIRENE Project Unit.[18]

The CICC is a semi-independent section of the National Police Headquarters being scrutinised by the Ministry of Justice and Law Enforcement. The CICC is in charge of undertaking all the necessary tasks in order to enhance cooperation with Interpol and to collaborate with Europol, other regional cooperation networks, units of the Schengen Network (SIS) and any other parties of bilateral or multilateral agreements on police cooperation duly signed and executed by Hungary.[19] The CICC also collaborates with OLAF.[20] The CICC hires officers of the Border Guard and of the Customs Office, for both of these agencies do have some criminal law enforcement duties under Hungarian criminal legislation.[21] Some CICC officers do work as liaison officers residing abroad at the headquarters of the CICC's partners, such as Europol, Interpol and OLAF.[22] Though the CICC is the central authority for cooperation with foreign criminal law enforcement authorities, it does not eliminate direct bilateral contacts between parts of the Hungarian police and their foreign partners. Such direct bilateral cooperation is most significant at lower levels, between the police departments of the border districts and also in respect of the Office of the Prosecutor General.

Since organised crime is conceived in Hungary as a major threat against public order, the Coordination Centre for Combating Organised Crime (Centre) was established by Act No. 124 of 2000. This body's main task ought not to interfere with police coordinating activities, in particular gathering and analysing information on suspects and perpetrators of organised crime and their collaborators. In the course of performing its tasks, the Centre forwards information to other law enforcement agencies. Yet the Centre is not supposed to exchange criminal information on the international level. Still, some senior CICC officers allege that the Centre often provides information to

[18] Para. 2 of Decree on the CICC. SIRENE is an abbreviation of Supplementary Information Request on the National Entry. The SIRENE Project Unit is in charge of the preparation of Hungary's accession to the Schengen Information System.

[19] Paras. 6–7 of Decree on the CICC. [20] Para. 2 of Europol–Interpol Act.

[21] Subsections C and D of Para. 3 of Decree on the CICC; as regards criminal law enforcement duties of the Customs Office and of the Border Guard, see Para. 36 of Act No. 19 of 1998 on the Criminal Procedure.

[22] Para. 3 of Decree on the CICC.

foreign police departments, a practice that clearly violates the law and interferes with the competence of the CICC.

4.2. Cooperation systems

As far as cooperation with foreign authorities is concerned, it is worth noting that Hungary is a member of global, regional and bilateral cooperation systems. The main exchange route of information is the Interpol Hungarian National Unit. Exchange of information with the 180 partner offices is undertaken via round the clock telecommunication network. The scope of information exchanged between the partner offices extends, inter alia, to stolen vehicles, the search for fugitives or suspects, the search for works of art or antiquities and information on narcotic substances or money laundering.

Hungary's Europol National Unit was established in 1999 (at that time it was called Europol Project Office). Hungary ratified and promulgated the Europol Convention, therefore, CICC functions as a fully fledged Europol National Unit. All types of information and data pertaining to criminal offences or well-founded suspicion thereof which fall within the competence of Europol according to Subsections (1)–(5) of Section 2 of the Europol Convention are being registered in Hungary. The Hungarian Europol National Unit does cooperate with Europol within the framework of cooperation processes foreseen under section 4.3. below.

The CICC is also in charge of participating in regional police cooperation networks.[23] Hungary is at present party to the South European Cooperative Initiative (SECI) and the Central European Initiative (CEI). Both regional networks are political initiatives in the first place and not professional ones like Interpol, therefore their actual use is rather limited. They both aim at effectively combating cross-border organised crime in the region.

- The SECI was set up by an international agreement in 2000.[24] Its aim is to facilitate police and customs cooperation between the parties for

[23] Point c./ of Para. 6 of the Decree on the CICC.

[24] The Participating States of the Southeast European Cooperative Initiative held an inaugural meeting in Geneva on 5–6 December 1996 and formally adopted the SECI Statement of Purpose on 6 December 1996. The SECI Participating States include: Albania, Bosnia and Herzegovina, Bulgaria, Croatia, Greece, Hungary, Moldova, Romania, Slovenia, The Former Yugoslav Republic of Macedonia, Turkey and, as of December 2000, the Federal Republic of Yugoslavia.

combating cross-border crime, in particular to facilitate the exchange of information related to the illegal transport of goods and services and to organise mutual training programs. The SECI has its head office in Bucharest consisting of the liaison criminal police and customs officers from the members. According to the interview with the director of CICC, there is no actual exchange of information in the SECI system, since all member countries are Interpol members. Consequently, SECI duplicates the number of information channels between its members. As a result, the SECI is intent on becoming a regional Europol network.[25]

- The CEI was launched in 1989 on the initiative of Hungary.[26] It gathers all countries of the CEE region, but it also has two western European members (Italy and Austria). CEI is also mainly a political initiative, being aimed at strengthening cooperation between the member countries and enhancing integration in the region. The CEI working group for combating organised crime was set up in 1998 and started working in 1999. There is no actual exchange of information between the CEI countries; the working group only prepares studies on the features of organised crime in the member countries.

According to an interview with the director of the CICC, Hungary has extensive and intensive police cooperation with its neighbouring countries, and with Germany, the United Kingdom, the Netherlands and the USA.

4.3. Exchange mechanisms

As far as the exchange of information contained in criminal registers is concerned, the underlying principle is that Hungarian criminal registers shall by no means be directly accessed by any foreign law enforcement

[25] See: European Commission, 'Assessment of the SECI Regional Centre for Combating Trans-Border Crime', Bucharest, August 2004.

[26] The origin of the CEI lies in the agreement signed in Budapest on 11 November 1989 by Italy, Austria, Hungary and Yugoslavia, establishing a platform for mutual political, economic, scientific and cultural cooperation called Quadragonal Cooperation. In May 1990 with the admission of Czechoslovakia, it became the Pentagonal Initiative, and in 1991, following the adhesion of Poland, it was renamed the Hexagonal Initiative. Following the dissolution of the former Yugoslavia, the Vienna Summit in July 1992 admitted the Republics of Bosnia and Herzegovina, Croatia and Slovenia, and approved the renaming of the grouping as the Central European Initiative. With the dissolution of Czechoslovakia in 1993, both its former parts, the Czech Republic and the Slovak Republic, were admitted to the CEI. At the Budapest Summit in 1993 a proposal for the admission of Macedonia (the tenth member of the Initiative) was approved.

agency or other branch of the foreign judiciary. All communication is perfected via the CICC. The CICC normally works as the transmitter of requests coming from abroad to national law enforcement agencies, and vice versa. It receives requests originating from foreign criminal law enforcement agencies, including Interpol, Europol or OLAF, and forwards them to competent Hungarian criminal law enforcement agencies. The same happens to requests coming from Hungarian authorities.[27] Requests are executed within a reasonable period of time, though no exact time limits are set by the applicable legislation. Transmission and other international communications are done via the CICC's round the clock telecommunications network available for both foreign and domestic law enforcement agencies.[28]

A special regime of international cooperation in criminal matters covers cross-border controlled transports (CCT). If CCT is supposed to cross Hungary's state borders, CICC shall be consulted and involved. Representatives of the criminal law enforcement agencies of those foreign countries that are involved in CCT shall be granted a permit to take part in the CCT's surveillance group.[29]

The existing legal framework of cooperation mechanisms has recently been modified by the implementing legislation of the Council Framework Decision on simplifying the exchange of information and intelligence between law enforcement authorities of the Member States of the European Union[30] (Council Framework Decision or FD). Although the FD entered into force on 30 December 2006,[31] Hungary still lags behind the requirements. Hungary has not done anything so far to implement what the FD envisages and provides for.

The FD stipulates very strict time limits for executing a request concerning criminal information. As regards crimes included in the so-called catalogue of the Council Framework Decision introducing the European arrest warrant,[32] urgent requests should be responded to within eight hours, and non-urgent ones within one week. In respect of any other offences requests should be responded to within two weeks. The FD fails to introduce a scheme of direct access to national criminal registers of the Member States. Entries and other contents of such

[27] Para. 7 of Decree on the CICC. [28] Para. 8 of Decree on the CICC.
[29] Para. 17 of Decree on the CICC. [30] 2006/690/JHA, 18 December 2006.
[31] See Article 13 of the Council Framework Decision.
[32] See Article 2(2) of the Framework Decision 2002/584/JHA on the European arrest warrant.

registers shall be exchanged via requests forwarded to competent national authorities. In this respect, the FD does not alter the prevailing legal framework of exchange of information in criminal cases. Still, providing for strict time limits is a great improvement compared to the existing mechanisms. At the time of writing this chapter Hungary has not undertaken any steps in order to make the Hungarian system compatible with the time-frames prescribed in the FD.

Although Hungary does not comply with the FD, it has proclaimed its willingness to join the Prüm Convention,[33] which introduces a completely different understanding of cross-border cooperation in criminal matters also involving direct accessibility to criminal records by the signing parties. Fulfilling this target would require substantial changes in Hungarian data protection provisions (see below). An additional hindrance within the mechanisms of exchange of criminal information flows from Hungarian confidentiality provisions. The Police Act sets out that police intelligence obtained by secret or undercover measures by detection or investigation agencies of the Hungarian police forces shall be deemed as state secret.[34] Even some of the senior officers of the CICC say that this confidentiality provision is wholly unreasonable. Such an understanding of state secrecy is anything but in line with the path followed by other Europol members. Nonetheless, information qualifying as state secret is not supposed to be exchanged unless entitled by a duly authorised person in charge of revising confidentiality provisions and clauses. This provision is a clear obstacle to criminal cooperation within the EU.

To sum up, most of the actual information exchange happens via the Hungarian National Interpol Unit, which is part of CICC. The Europol National Unit started its operations as of 1 January 2007, therefore it has not had much practice so far. Since CICC has full access to the entries of all five criminal registers described above in detail, and with regard to the fact that it operates a round the clock telecommunications network, there is no reason to believe that the exchange of these entries will not be effective. However, the time taken for such exchange often exceeds what would normally be considered optimal, let alone what the FD sets out.

[33] Convention between the Kingdom of Belgium, the Federal Republic of Germany, the Kingdom of Spain, the French Republic, the Grand Duchy of Luxembourg, the Kingdom of the Netherlands and the Republic of Austria on the stepping up of cross-border cooperation, particularly in combating terrorism, cross-border crime and illegal migration.

[34] Subsection (2) of Para. 63 of the PA.

5. Hungarian privacy legislation and data protection

According to the Hungarian Constitution everybody has the right to privacy and to the protection of his/her personal data. This constitutional right is enshrined in Act No. 63 of 1992 on the Protection of Personal Data and the Access to Public Records (Data Protection Act or DPA). The DPA respects the following principles:

- legality: data has to be fairly and lawfully processed;
- purpose: data has to be processed for a limited, and clearly stated purpose;
- proportionality: data must be adequate, relevant and not excessive;
- accuracy: data must be accurate;
- subject's rights: data must be processed in accordance with the data subject's rights;
- limited transfer: data must not be transferred to others without adequate protection;
- supervision: there has to be some independent oversight of data protection. In the case of Hungary, it is the Ombudsman for Data Protection.

Hungary also ratified the Council of Europe Convention for the Protection of Individuals with regard to the Automatic Processing of Personal Data in 1998 (DPC) and implemented it in Hungarian law by Act No. 6 of 1998. Both DPC (Art. 6.) and DPA (Art. 2) provide that personal data relating to criminal convictions constitutes a special category of data that deserves a higher degree of protection. Consequently, Art. 6. of DPC states that personal data relating to criminal convictions may not be processed automatically unless domestic law provides for appropriate safeguards. Such safeguards are contained in the DPA. According to the latter, if the unauthorised use of information causes any damage to the data subject, he/she is entitled to compensation. Moreover, the data subject may claim breach of his/her inherent rights and file a law suit for indemnification.

Further safeguards are set out by Art. 177/A of the Hungarian Criminal Code providing for the criminalisation of illicit use of personal data:

> (1) Anybody who, acting in breach of laws providing for the protection of personal data:
>
> a./ processes personal data without adequate authorisation or for unauthorised purposes
>
> b./ omits to fulfil its obligation on informing data subjects
>
> c./ omits data security precaution

> and as a result thereof causes considerable harm or injury to another or to others, commits a misdemeanour offence and shall be punished with imprisonment of a maximum of one year, community service or a fine.
>
> . . .
>
> (3) Punishment shall be imprisonment of a maximum of three years for a felony in so far as illicit use of personal data is committed in respect of special data.

Criminal law protection of data processing has become very narrow. Prior to the latest amendment of these provisions, the mere fact of unlawful announcement or use of the criminal record qualified as an offence. Moreover, harm to the individual involved or illegal benefit on behalf of the perpetrator or third persons had not been necessary. According to the former text of the provision, perpetrators of the crime could only be employees working for the central registers. The current criminal legislation on the one hand makes anybody criminally liable if illicitly processing data even if not acting in his/her profession, while on the other hand criminal liability as such is curtailed to causing harm to others.

From this brief presentation of the relevant Hungarian legislation it becomes evident that the Hungarian legislature demonstrates little tolerance for unlawful use of criminal records even if criminalisation is cut back. The strictness and accuracy in the provisions of the Hungarian Criminal Code concerning criminal records – special data – is a clear expression of the balance envisaged by the Hungarian legislature between the general public interest – the protection of the public from convicted criminals – and the right of such persons to rehabilitation after having been released from prison.

The right of the convicted person to get over past mistakes and seek employment without the burden of a stained reputation is further realised in relation to the accessibility of entries contained in the criminal record. It is evident from the description under section 1 of the present chapter that Hungarian law introduces three different levels of access to the criminal record:

- full access is granted to prosecuting and investigating agencies (both national and international), the courts, etc.;
- partial access is granted to the High Council of Judiciary, the General Prosecutor, the Minister of Justice, etc., only for performing a certain task;
- limited access as provided for by the law shall be granted on a case by case basis.

These three different levels of authorisation are the result of the legislature's eagerness to achieve as accurate a balance as possible, ensuring that employers are aware of as much detail as necessary for the selection of a suitable employee while at the same time confining the data to what is absolutely inevitable to provide a fair opportunity for rehabilitation for convicted persons.

Data protection and privacy legislation concerns emerging from the processing and management of criminal registers are also relevant with regard to international criminal cooperation. The Hungarian Data Protection Ombudsman is also in charge of surveillance and scrutiny of the CICC and its exchange of special information with foreign law enforcement agencies. The Ombudsman in his annual report of the year 2006[35] claimed that the CICC is continuously disrespecting provisions of its own statute. The Decree on the CICC foresees that the CICC shall prepare and follow a Data Protection and Security Handbook[36] which it has so far failed to adopt.

The Ombudsman has also made some remarks concerning Hungary's whish to later join the Prüm Convention. The Prüm Convention's endeavour to introduce a European-level direct accessibility to national criminal records in the future is, in the Hungarian Data Protection Ombudsman's view, by no means welcome for data protection and data security reasons. In the Ombudsman's opinion, direct accessibility ought to be replaced by cooperation of national contact points such as the CICC. The major objection of the Hungarian Data Protection Ombudsman against joining the Prüm convention is that the latter is not part of the *acquis communautaire* and, therefore, no community dispute resolution bodies have jurisdiction to settle claims arising from the Prüm Convention. At the same time, the denial of direct accessibility to information contained in Hungarian criminal registers puts in doubt the concept of a functioning and effective European Criminal Record.

[35] Annual Report of 2006 of the Parliamentary Commissioner on Data Protection, Budapest, 2007, Office of the Parliamentary Commissioner on Data Protection.

[36] Para. 19 of Decree on the CICC.

10

The European Criminal Record in Ireland

IVANA BACIK

1. Introduction

The purpose of this Chapter is to examine the feasibility of a European database for convictions from the national perspective of Irish law. The existing legal framework for recording criminal convictions in Ireland is set out below.

2. Existing legal framework

2.1. Recording and maintenance of information about criminal convictions in Ireland

An Garda Síochána is the Irish national police force. There has been recent extensive legislative reform of the Garda with the passing of the Garda Síochána Act 2005. Records of criminal convictions have traditionally been held by An Garda Síochána, and not by the Department of Justice (now the Department of Justice, Equality and Law Reform). The management of the statutory Habitual Criminal Registry (which was later renamed the Dublin Criminal Registry) was devolved after Irish Independence to An Garda Síochána in 1929. In 1973, the Dublin Criminal Registry was amalgamated with the administratively instituted Criminal Records Office (Dublin) to form the current institution, the Garda Criminal Records Office. In 2000, a new computerised system for recording convictions and court outcomes (i.e. sentences, disposals under the Probation of Offenders Act etc.), was introduced. This computerised system is called PULSE (Police Using Leading Systems Effectively). In 2002, the Garda Central Vetting Unit was formed on an administrative basis, and it liaises with the Criminal Records Office where required.[1]

[1] *Report of the Working Group on Garda Vetting*, February 2004.

The Garda Criminal Records Office now has computerised systems for the storage and retrieval of intelligence information. The Crime Reporting and Recording Systems Manual contains instructions for individual members of An Garda Síochána in the mechanics of recording crime, but this is an internal confidential document, so it is not possible to access it.

The criminal record contains information on each conviction; the offence type, the date on which it was committed, the date of conviction and the type of sentence imposed. Since PULSE was introduced, the way in which offences are recorded has been changed from the previous manual system. Each individual's record is now filed under a PULSE identification number, and includes the name, address and date of birth of the individual and the number of domestic convictions. There is space in the record for recording the number of foreign convictions, and where information on this is available through Europol it is included under this heading.[2] Each individual's skin colour, eye colour, facial shape, approximate height, hair colour and approximate weight are also recorded, as are any marks, scars or tattoos.

An Garda Síochána thus holds information on all natural and legal persons who have been convicted of organised crime offences. The databases which are held by the Gardaí contain information on all criminal activities and convictions (fraud, large scale theft, trafficking in arms, persons, drugs and corruption). This record is held by the Gardaí as information relating to the security of the state. However, there is no database in existence in Ireland which holds data exclusively on legal or natural persons who have been convicted of organised crime, transnational crime or serious economic crime. These are all included in the general centrally maintained PULSE system.

In July 2004, the Expert Group on Crime Statistics produced a Report on Crime Statistics for the Minister for Justice, Equality and Law Reform which was critical of some aspects of the PULSE system.[3] The Group noted that the introduction of the system represented a significant step forward but further noted that it created a discontinuity in the recording of national crime statistics with figures produced from the previous manual system.[4] The Group identified a number of specific shortcomings with the PULSE system, notably the absence of a criminal history repository to provide

[2] Verbal communication from the Garda Criminal Records Office, April 2007.

[3] *Report of the Expert Group on Crime Statistics* (Dublin: Government Publications, 2004).

[4] See letter from the Chairperson of the Expert Group on Crime Statistics to the Minister for Justice, Equality and Law Reform, 27 July 2004 (www.justice.ie).

comprehensive data across the system, and the unavailability of any data related to crimes prosecuted by authorities other than An Garda Síochána (such as the Health and Safety Authority, for example, which prosecutes companies and individuals for breaches of health and safety legislation).

According to the Garda Criminal Records Office, records are generally kept in the PULSE system on crimes committed by nationals and non-nationals in the jurisdiction of Ireland. Where information is available through Europol, details of foreign convictions are also entered on the PULSE record system.

The Sex Offenders Act 2001 introduced provisions requiring convicted sex offenders to notify the Gardaí of their names and addresses and any change of address. Section 26 of the 2001 Act makes it an offence for a convicted sex offender to apply for work or to perform a service (including state work or service) which involves having unsupervised access to, or contact with children or mentally impaired people, without telling the prospective employer or contractor that that person is a sex offender. Other than these provisions, the Garda Central Vetting Unit, established in 2002, deals with requests to vet certain prospective employees; namely prospective full-time employees of the Health Service Executive (HSE), or any agencies that it funds where the work involves access to children and vulnerable adults. The Child Care (Special Care) Regulations 2004 provide that the HSE or other body maintaining or providing a special care unit must ensure that staff or others who have access to children are appropriately vetted.

The Data Protection Act 1988 and Data Protection (Amendment) Act 2003 together provide various safeguards for the accessing of data on criminal records. The Data Protection legislation applies to criminal records, so anyone wishing to apply to see their own criminal record must make application to the Data Protection section in the Garda Criminal Records Office under section 4 of the legislation ('Right of Access'). This application must be made in writing and must include payment of a small fee. There are certain obvious restrictions on the information that may be provided; in particular, a person who is a suspect in a criminal investigation does not have the right to see the information held about him or her by An Garda Síochána, where that would impede the process of the criminal investigation.

2.2. *Irish legislation and practice on mutual assistance*

Ireland is a signatory to the European Convention on Mutual Assistance in Criminal Matters 1959 and additional Protocols 1978. Aspects of these have been implemented in Ireland through the Criminal Justice Act 1994. In addition, the Europol Act 1997 and Europol (Amendment) Act 2006 contain other mechanisms of collaboration with foreign authorities in criminal law. Generally, criminal legislation which provides for an element of collaboration with foreign authorities includes the following:

- Europol Act 1997 (to give effect to the Convention on the Establishment of a European Police Office of 26 July 1995);
- Europol (Amendment) Act 2006 (to give effect to the 2000, 2002 and 2003 Protocols to the 1995 Convention on the Establishment of a European Police Office, and to amend the 1997 Act accordingly);
- Child Trafficking and Pornography Act 1998 (Joint Action concerning action to combat trafficking in human beings and the sexual exploitation of children, 24 February 1997);
- Transfer of Sentenced Persons Act 1995 (Council of Europe Convention on the Transfer of Sentenced Persons, 25 May 1987);
- Criminal Justice Act 1994 (EC Directive 91/308 on Prevention of the Use of the Financial System for the Purpose of Money Laundering);
- Extradition Act 1987 (European Convention on the Suppression of Terrorism, 1977);
- Criminal Justice (Theft and Fraud Offences) Act 2001 (an Act which, among other things, was introduced to give effect to provisions of the Convention on the Protection of the European Communities' Financial Interests of 26 July 1995, and the three Protocols to that Convention).

The Criminal Justice Act 1994 makes provision for the enforcement in accordance with Irish law of confiscation or forfeiture orders issued in some other jurisdictions in respect of property or proceeds associated with drug-trafficking or other serious criminal offences. However, strict conditions apply to the application of these provisions.[5]

The Liaison and Protection Section of Garda Headquarters in Dublin (formerly the International Liaison Office) is the contact point for Europol.[6] This Section is headed by a Detective Chief Superintendent and handles a range of matters relating to international law enforcement. Garda Liaison Officers are posted at Europol Headquarters in the

[5] See further D. Walsh, *Criminal Procedure* (Dublin: Thomson Round Hall, 2002), pp. 100–103.

[6] See D. Walsh, *The Irish Police* (Dublin: Round Hall, 1998), pp. 424–431.

Netherlands and Spain. Personnel from the Security and Intelligence Section of the Garda attend meetings of all major EU police cooperation bodies. A Mutual Assistance Section also exists within the Crime Administration Section.

A particularly well-established procedure in Irish criminal law for collaboration with foreign authorities is that of extradition. This is the legal procedure whereby a person is detained in one jurisdiction and delivered into the custody of another jurisdiction for the purpose of being charged and tried for a criminal offence alleged to have been committed there. Ireland is a party to several multilateral treaties on extradition, and some unilateral treaties with some other individual jurisdictions for reciprocal arrangements.

Thus there are a number of mutual assistance mechanisms in place currently in Ireland to facilitate transnational police cooperation. However, the first Director of Public Prosecutions, Eamonn Barnes, has written that several main factors exist which limit the development of police cooperation, namely:

- inadequate financial resources;
- the fact that investigative powers require judicial supervision;
- the lack of safeguards against abuse;
- the 'fundamentally differing structures for the investigation and prosecution of offences in the various states and from the equally fundamental differences in juridical procedure';
- the lack of access for European contracting authorities to the information contained in the Irish criminal database, in order to blacklist tenders.[7]

Thus, current collaboration mechanisms and current provisions for the exchange of data are regarded by some commentators as not being wholly adequate for the prevention and detection of organised crime, nor for the purposes of public procurement law and the fight against organised crime in that area.

2.3 Proposed mutual assistance legislation

Ireland is not currently a signatory to the 2000 Convention on Mutual Assistance in Criminal Matters between the Member States of the

[7] E. Barnes, 'Criminal Law and Procedure in the European Union', in G. Barret (ed.), *Justice Co-operation in the European Union* (Dublin, Institute of European Affairs, 1997), p. 64.

European Union; nor to the Protocol of 2001. However, in December 2005 the Minister for Justice, Equality and Law Reform published the Criminal Justice (Mutual Assistance) Bill 2005. This Bill is aimed at giving effect to seven mutual legal assistance instruments, as follows:

- the Convention on Mutual Assistance in Criminal Matters between the Member States of the EU;
- the Protocol to the Convention on Mutual Assistance in Criminal Matters between the Member States of the EU;
- the Second Additional Protocol to the European Convention on Mutual Assistance in Criminal Matters;
- the mutual legal assistance aspects of the Agreement between the EU and the United States of America on Extradition and Mutual Legal Assistance;
- the Council Framework Decision on the execution in the European Union of orders freezing property or evidence;
- the Agreement between the EU and the Republic of Iceland and the Kingdom of Norway on the application of certain provisions of the 2000 Convention on Mutual Assistance in Criminal Matters and the 2001 Protocol thereto;
- the mutual legal assistance aspects of the Schengen *acquis*.

The Bill is also intended to provide for certain amendments to the Criminal Justice Act 1994, and if enacted will transpose the Criminal Justice Act 1994 (Section 46(6)) Regulations 1996 into primary legislation. The main new forms of mutual assistance provided for in the Bill, in respect of which Ireland will be taking part if the Bill is enacted, are as follows:

- The provision of financial information to other states for criminal investigation purposes in relation to transactions on bank accounts and the monitoring of such accounts.
- The provision of assistance, in accordance with national law, in relation to the interception of telecommunications in the context of criminal investigations in EU Member States.
- The hearing of witnesses and experts in other countries by video conference or by telephone conference.
- The mutual recognition and enforcement of orders for freezing property or evidence from other Member States of the EU.
- Obtaining identification evidence for criminal investigations both inside and outside the state.

- Provision for the establishment of joint investigation teams with the USA.
- Provision of a legal basis for the restitution of articles obtained by criminal means to their rightful owner and for controlled deliveries in the state and participation in such deliveries in other EU and Council of Europe member states.[8]

The Bill was passed by Seanad Éireann (the upper House in the Irish Oireachtas or Parliament) on 10 May 2006, and was referred to a Select Committee of Dáil Éireann (the lower House in the Oireachtas) on 28 September 2006.[9]

The Irish Human Rights Commission has expressed various criticisms of the Bill.[10] Notably, the Commission expressed concern at the inadequate consideration of human rights issues in the course of drafting the source EU legislation upon which the Bill is based. In particular, the Commission pointed out the way in which the remit of the EU Convention had been extended to cover not only mutual legal assistance between judicial authorities, but also mutual legal assistance between police and customs authorities. They expressed concern at the absence of democratic scrutiny and accountability in the drafting process at EU level while this extension was being decided upon.[11] Their criticisms should also be taken into consideration in any debate on the creation and establishment of a European Criminal Record.

3. Contents of a European Criminal Record

If a European Criminal Record (ECR) were to be introduced, it would be important that its scope should be restricted to those crimes with a transnational organised dimension. The crimes included in the ECR should comply with the condition of transnationality as a requirement of the principles of subsidiarity, necessity and proportionality applicable in new EU legislative proposals. This does not necessarily mean that data

[8] See Press Release from the Minister for Justice, Equality and Law Reform dated 5 December 2005, www.justice.ie.

[9] As of 30 April 2007. The current Dáil was dissolved on 29 April 2007 and a General Election called for 24 May 2007, with the result that the Bill may now lapse.

[10] Irish Human Rights Commission, *Observations on the Scheme of the Criminal Justice (International Co-operation) Bill 2005* (Dublin: 10 May 2005), at www.ihrc.ie.

[11] Ibid., p. 5.

contained in the ECR could not include information on crimes committed within one State; but it does mean that the ECR must be limited to those crimes which by their nature tend to have an international or transnational element; such as terrorist-related activities, money laundering or EU-level fraud.

Any European legislation introducing the ECR would have to clearly specify the nature of the crimes which would fall within its field of application. Convictions for crimes which could legally be recorded in the ECR would have to be obtained in accordance with the protections set out in the European Convention on Human Rights (specifically Articles 5 and 6). Crimes harming the financial interests of the EU could therefore be included, but the ECR could also include convictions for other transnational crimes considered to be a priority for the EU. These could include organised crime; crimes of terrorism; and sexual offences against children (e.g. where evidence exists of an organised transnational paedophile ring). However, before such crimes could be included in the ECR, it would be important that clear definitions for those specific crimes, acceptable to each Member State, would be adopted and agreed. Such definitions would have to include the requirement that the crime concerned should have a transnational dimension, even where committed in a single Member State.

Similarly, the ECR could only include information on convictions confirmed after final decisions of the national courts, and after any appeal mechanisms within the national criminal justice system had been exhausted, with due regard to the principles of *res judicata* applicable within the national legal order.

Finally, it should be stipulated in any European legislation purporting to create an ECR that information could not be held in the ECR in respect of convictions obtained against any individual who was under 18 at the time convicted, that is before they had reached the age of adulthood.

4. Access to the European Criminal Record

Under the Europol Convention (1995), each Member State is obliged to ensure that its laws governing the processing of personal data in data files covered by the Convention ensure a standard of data protection which at least corresponds to the principles enshrined in the 1981 Council of Europe Convention on Data Protection. In Ireland, this is achieved primarily by extending the provisions of the Data Protection

Act 1988 to the Europol Convention, subject to the necessary modifications (Europol Act 1997, section 6, as amended by section 3 of the Europol (Amendment) Act 2006). Section 7 of the Europol Act 1997 designates the Data Protection Commissioner as the national supervisory body in Ireland. This is in accordance with the obligation in the Convention that each Member State must designate a national supervisory body to monitor, independently and in accordance with national law, the permissibility of the input, retrieval and any communication to Europol of personal data by the Member State concerned (Article 23). Under the Europol Convention, individuals are also given a limited right to access their personal data held within Europol, or to have such data checked (Europol Convention, Article 19).

If an ECR were to be created, the same data protection provisions that currently apply to national criminal records should also be applied to its content. Thus, all natural and legal persons should have the right to inspect their own entry on the record, and to have access to information kept about them within the record. They should also have recourse to an appeal mechanism where the information kept about them is inaccurate in some way or is wrongfully disclosed to third parties.

In terms of disclosure of the content of the record to third parties, then since the object of the creation of an ECR is to prevent the increase of organised transnational crime in Europe, policing authorities should have access to the record, but only under strict conditions (see further below). It would be essential that any access to the ECR for other public authorities would be carefully controlled and subject to scrutiny by a court. Private institutions, such as banks or insurance companies, for example, should not be permitted to have access to the record.

Protection for the right to privacy afforded in Article 8 of the European Convention on Human Rights would have to be observed in any provisions about access to the data contained in the ECR.[12] This would be an express condition for Ireland before an ECR could be acceptable.

In short, clear restrictions would have to be placed upon the persons and bodies permitted to access the data contained in the ECR. This would be a condition necessary for Irish law before the ECR could be introduced. As the purpose of the ECR is to combat organised crime with a transnational dimension, access to the data it is to contain must

[12] See for example S. Farran, 'Recent Commission Decisions and Reports concerning Article 8 ECHR' 21 (1996) *European Law Review* 14–28.

be limited to those agencies or individuals for whom it is essential for the performance of their task in the fight against transnational organised crime.

Thus, at the national level access should be limited to judicial and prosecution authorities, as well as to the individual subjects upon whom the data is kept. Access to police authorities in other Member States might be justified only if it were made to high level sections or divisions within national police authorities which specialise in serious, transnational and organised crime.

At EU level, again very restrictive conditions should be placed upon access to the data contained in the ECR. Access could be allowed to Eurojust and the European Public Prosecutor.

Indirect access to further agencies and bodies at the national and EU levels could be afforded indirectly and exclusively via the subject, following authorisation from the independent judicial supervisory body. But it would be imperative that direct access should not be afforded to any private bodies or agencies such as banks or insurance companies. Finally, it would be important that the ECR should be kept and maintained by an independent authority under the control of a European Court, in order to ensure appropriate levels of accountability and transparency in the process.

5. Use of the European Criminal Record

At national level in Ireland, the obvious authority to undertake the task of using and coordinating the use of the ECR would be the Garda Criminal Records Office, referred to above. Those protections already existing in relation to transfer of information to Europol should be extended to cover any transfer of information to a European Criminal Record authority.

At European level there would have to be judicial control over the host of the ECR, with periodic assessments of the work of the host institution by a supervisory independent judicial body and the European Parliament. Guarantees of quality and accuracy would also be necessary requirements for the reception of the ECR into Irish law. A mechanism for the correction of ECR data, and appeal processes for any persons aggrieved by the operation of the ECR, would have to be provided.

The issue of erasure periods (or 'spent convictions') for the ECR is a particular cause of controversy. It would be important for any legislation introducing the ECR to include provision for the erasure of entries to the ECR, in the interests of the potential rehabilitation of ex-offenders. However, there is at present serious inequality existing among EU citizens on grounds of their nationality, because erasure rules differ so widely between Member States. In particular, in Ireland there are no national rules on erasure of criminal convictions, so that at present any criminal convictions recorded in respect of an individual remain on that individual's record indefinitely. The Data Protection Commissioner has criticised this, pointing out that it is a requirement of the Data Protection legislation that information should not be kept for longer than is necessary for the purpose for which it was obtained, and that the indefinite retention of information about (often) minor convictions 'does not appear to accord with the spirit of that requirement':

> But since Irish legislation makes no provision for 'spent' convictions, the Gardaí have no guidance on how long they should retain such records. The issue that arises here comes down to the balancing of law enforcement needs with the privacy interests of the individual, taking account of the realities of information technology . . . I believe it is in keeping with the spirit of the Data Protection Act for me to raise this issue in my Report, and recommend that it be given consideration by the appropriate authorities.[13]

One option suggested elsewhere in the text of this book for erasure provisions within the ECR would be to provide that convictions for the ECR are erased in accordance with national rules. But this is unworkable in Ireland, where there are no national rules on erasure. Thus, from an Irish perspective, it would be preferable if the ECR contained some common provision for the observation of erasure periods, such as those introduced by data protection legislation on Eurojust, for example.

6. Critical evaluation

The question of a European Criminal Record involves significant political as well as legal considerations. First, it would have to be established that the need exists in reality for the introduction of an ECR. In the view of this writer, this has not yet been done. Instead of introducing an ECR, it would be possible for example to extend the current mutual assistance

[13] http://www.dataprotection.ie/docs/Case_Study_13/96.

provisions, and to expand the mechanisms for cooperation among national police forces via the Europol processes, in order to ensure greater protection against the spread of organised transnational crime.

However, if an ECR is to be proposed, then any procedures introduced to facilitate the application of the ECR must contain sufficient safeguards to ensure that the human rights and civil liberties of individual citizens of the European Union are not unduly encroached upon. Such safeguards should be aimed at protecting the essential civil policing tradition, the traditions of an adversarial criminal legal system based upon common law principles such as the presumption of innocence; and the Irish separation between the prosecution role and the judicial role. Establishment of an ECR simply could not succeed without such safeguards being included. There is already considerable disquiet at the absence of democratic accountability in the continuing expansion of the criminal jurisdiction and powers of the EU and of EU-level agencies.[14]

Thus, the inclusion of substantive safeguards for the protection of human rights would be essential in any legislation providing for an ECR. As leading Irish commentator Paul O'Mahony has written in a similar context,

> It is likely that, in the absence of such systems for the protection of fundamental rights and for the gathering, analysis and dissemination of information . . . the ordinary citizen will increasingly feel him or herself to be the impotent subject of a Kafkaesque system of unintelligible complexity and insidiously sinister powers.[15]

How then might such safeguards best be incorporated into any legislative framework providing for a European Criminal Record? Legal basis for the safeguards might be found in the European Convention on Human Rights, incorporated in Ireland by the European Convention on Human Rights Act 2003, together with the EU Charter of fundamental rights. These documents clearly offer some measure of protection to individuals against the various encroachments upon human rights and civil liberties that could easily result from the creation and establishment of a European Criminal Record. In Ireland, these

[14] See for example B. Hayes, *The Activities and Development of Europol: Towards an Unaccountable 'FBI' in Europe* (London: Statewatch, 2002).

[15] P. O'Mahony, 'The Impact of the Third Pillar on Irish Civil Liberties', in E. Regan (ed.), *The New Third Pillar: Co-operation against Crime in the EU* (Dublin: Institute of European Affairs, 2000).

protections coexist with the existing fundamental rights provisions contained in Articles of the Irish Constitution, Bunreacht na hÉireann.

At European level, O'Mahony has argued that further protections could be introduced through the establishment of an Independent Monitoring Agency on Civil Liberties within the EU structures.[16] Such an agency, he suggests, would offer stronger protection against potential abuse of powers than currently exists through documents like the European Convention. This proposed agency could be charged with monitoring the actual impact of the new forms of cooperation in police and criminal law matters provided for under the New Third Pillar. The agency would have to be independent of all Member State and EU institutions, and could inform the individual citizen of their rights, process specific complaints and inform citizens of the remedies available: 'As a disseminator of information and a repository of complaints, such an agency could usefully inform the policy makers in adopting more refined and effective systems which guarantee fundamental rights in the EU.'[17]

To date, there has been no serious move towards the establishment of an independent monitoring agency of this kind. However, many new EU measures aimed at combating organised crime have already been introduced, without any consultation with civil society organisations or human rights groups, and apparently with inadequate regard for their implications for human rights or the liberties of individuals.

As the Irish Human Rights Commission has argued, significant extension of the criminal jurisdiction of the EU has been achieved in the absence of adequate democratic scrutiny and accountability processes at European level. Before any substantive steps towards the creation of any form of ECR are taken, therefore, it is vitally important that extensive consultation as to its desirability and feasibility should take place, not just with judicial and prosecuting authorities in the Member States, but also with those representing accused persons; with organisations, both non-governmental and state agencies, and with citizens' groups and individuals.

Extensive consultation would be particularly necessary, because of the serious effect that the creation of an ECR would have upon the protection of the individual right to privacy at European level. Case law from the European Court of Human Rights has established that any interference with the private life of the individual, such as the storing and

[16] Ibid. [17] Ibid., p. 176.

release of personal data, falls within the application of Article 8 of the Convention. Any interference must be in accordance with law; 'pursue a legitimate aim' and must be 'necessary in a democratic society'.[18] In order to be considered necessary in a democratic society, storage or disclosure of personal data must be proportionate to the legitimate aim pursued. In particular, adequate and effective safeguards should be put in place in order to regulate and control the storage and disclosure of such data, so as to ensure the minimum impairment of the Article 8 right to respect for private life.[19]

The establishment of some procedure at European level to ensure greater consistency in the exchange of data on organised transnational crime convictions at national level could represent a positive development in the campaign against transnational crime. However, if such a record were to be introduced, it would have to be done in the context of a full public debate with extensive participation from all those groups and individuals potentially affected, to ensure greater democratic scrutiny and accountability in the drafting process.

Any legislation introduced as a consequence of the participatory public debate would have to include the appropriate safeguards and protections to ensure that the creation of an ECR or similar model does not create unnecessary encroachments on the fundamental human rights and civil liberties of individual citizens of the EU.

[18] See for example *Amann* v. *Switzerland*, ECHR, 16 February 2000.

[19] *MS* v. *Sweden*, ECHR, 27 August 1997.

11

The European Criminal Record in the Netherlands

OSWALD JANSEN

1. Introduction: The legal framework

In November 2002 the Dutch Act on Judicial and Prosecutorial Data (*Wet justitiële en strafvorderlijke gegevens*) was published in the Dutch Bulletin of Acts and Decrees (*Staatsblad*).[1] The Act, which entered into force on 1 April 2004,[2] replaced the 1955 Act on Judicial Documentation and the Certificate of Behaviour.[3]

Although the Dutch regulation of criminal records is closely related to the Act on the Protection of Personal Data (*Wet bescherming persoonsgegevens*), the Act on Police Files (*Wet politieregisters*), the Act to Improve the Assessments of Integrity of Public Administration,[4] which entered into force on 1 June 2003, and the Act on Records on Companies (*Wet documentatie vennootschappen*), which entered into force on 8 May 2003, this chapter restricts itself to a discussion of the Act on Judicial and Prosecutorial Data. I will discuss the way criminal data are defined and who has access to them. I will also describe the way Council Decision 2005/876/JHA of 21 November 2005 on the exchange of information extracted from the criminal record[5] has

[1] Act of 7 November 2002, [2002] *Staatsblad* 552. To be precise, the Act was first entitled Act on Criminal Data (*Wet justitiële gegevens*). By Act of 30 June 2004, [2004] *Staatsblad* 315 which entered into force on 1 September 2004 (Decision of 3 August 2004, [2004] 390) the title changed into the current one.

[2] Decision of 25 March 2004, [2004] *Staatsblad* 129.

[3] *Wet op de justitiële documentatie en op de verklaringen omtrent het gedrag*, [1955] *Staatsblad* 395.

[4] *Wet Bevordering Integriteitsbeoordelingen door het Openbaar Bestuur*, Act of 20 June 2002, [2002] *Staatsblad*, 347. See also The BIBOP-order (*Besluit* BIBOP), [2003] *Staatsblad*, 180 and as far as the date of entry into force is concerned the [2002] *Staatsblad* 502 and [2003] *Staatsblad* 216.

[5] OJ 9 December 2005 L 322/33.

been implemented by amending the Order on Criminal Data (*Besluit justitiële gegevens*).[6]

As mentioned above, the Act on Judicial and Prosecutorial Data replaced the Act on Judicial Documentation and the Certificate of Behaviour. The Dutch government provided some reasons for replacing the Act on Criminal Records. The Act on Criminal Records stems from the 'paper era' and in order to introduce the desired automated processing of criminal records and to centralise this process, the existing legislation needs to be altered. Current legislation makes a distinction between the general register of criminal documentation (*algemeen documentatieregister*) and the register of punishments (*strafregister*). The main function of this distinction is to divide the sort of access third persons can have to criminal data. The proposed Act on Criminal Data[7] brings regulation in line with practice: only one registration exists in fact. The Act has the following structure. The first section (Title 1) consists of one article with definitions of judicial data,[8] prosecutorial data,[9] personal file,[10] legal person,[11] judicial

[6] Order of 25 March 2004, [2004] *Staatsblad* 130. The Order entered into force on 1 April 2004 (Decision of 25 March 2004, [2004] *Staatsblad* 129). The amendment has been done by the Order of 26 January 2007, [2007] *Staatsblad 40*, which entered into force on 7 February 2007.

[7] Later the title of the proposed act changed into its current name: Act on Judicial and Prosecutorial Data.

[8] Judicial data (*justitiële gegevens*) is defined as: data to be described by *Algemene maatregel van bestuur* (a regulation to a certain extent comparable with an Order in Council) on natural as well as legal persons in relation to the execution of criminal law and criminal procedure (*justitiële gegevens of gegevens: bij algemene maatregel van bestuur te omschrijven gegevens omtrent natuurlijke personen en rechtspersonen inzake de toepassing van het strafrecht of de strafvordering*).

[9] Prosecutorial data (*strafvorderlijke gegevens*) is defined as: data on natural as well as legal persons obtained within the framework of a criminal investigation which the Public Prosecutor's Office (*Openbaar Ministerie*) processes in a criminal file or in a automated way (*gegevens over een natuurlijk persoon of rechtspersoon die zijn verkregen in het kader van een strafvorderlijk onderzoek en die het openbaar ministerie in een strafdossier of langs geautomatiseerde weg verwerkt).*

[10] Personal file (*persoonsdossier*) is defined as: a dossier which contains the reports submitted to the judicial authorities on inquiries of the behaviour or the circumstances of the life of a natural person due to criminal proceedings against him, the execution of sentences against him or his rehabilitation.

[11] Legal person (*rechtspersoon*) is defined as: a legal person as defined in the second Book of the Dutch Civil Code as well as the entities equated to legal persons as defined in Article 51 of the Dutch Penal Code.

documentation,[12] documentation of personal files,[13] and the important legal terms which are used in the Act on the Protection of Personal Data, such as personal data,[14] processing of personal data,[15] data subject,[16] and the provision of personal data.[17] Articles 2–39, Title 2, contain provisions on the processing of personal data (*de verwerking van justitiële gegevens*). These provisions are divided into general provisions (Section 1, Articles 2–7), provisions on the provision of judicial data (*het verstrekken van justitiële gegevens*) (Section 2, Articles 8–17), provisions on the rights of the data subject (*betrokkene*) to be notified whether his personal data are processed and to rectify (Section 3, Articles 18–26), provisions on the regulation by the Data Protection Commission (*College bescherming persoonsgegevens*) (Section 4, Article 27),[18] and

[12] Judicial documentation (*justitiële documentatie*) is defined as: a coherent collection of judicial data of various persons processed in an automated way.

[13] Documentation of personal files (*documentatie persoonsdossiers*) is defined as: a coherent collection of defined personal files on various persons processed in an automated way or contrived with a view to their efficient referral.

[14] Personal data (*persoonsgegevens*) is defined in Article 1 (a) Dutch Act on the Protection of Personal Data as: any information relating to an identified or identifiable natural person.

[15] Processing of personal data (*verwerking van persoonsgegevens*) is defined in Article 1 (b) Dutch Act on the Protection of Personal Data as: any operation or any set of operations concerning personal data, including the collection, recording, organisation, storage, updating or modification, retrieval, consultation, use, dissemination by means of transmission, distribution or making available in any other form, merging, linking, as well as blocking, erasure or destruction of data.

[16] Data subject (*betrokkene*) is defined in Article 1 (f) Dutch Act on the Protection of Personal Data as: the person to whom personal data relate.

[17] Provision of personal data (*het verstrekken van persoonsgegevens*) is defined in Article 1 (n) Dutch Act on the Protection of Personal Data as: the disclosure or making available of personal data.

[18] Article 27, para. 2, declares the following provisions of the Dutch Act on the Protection of Personal Data applicable:

Article 51, para. 2:

The Commission shall be asked to issue an opinion on bills and draft texts of general administrative regulations relating entirely or substantially to the processing of personal data;

Article 60

1. The Commission, acting in an official capacity or at the request of an interested party, may initiate an investigation into the manner in which the provisions laid down by or under the Act are being applied with respect to the processing of data.
2. The Commission shall present its provisional findings to the responsible party or the group of responsible parties concerned, and allow them to give their views. The Commission shall present these findings also to the Minister concerned, where they relate to the implementation of any law.

provisions on the certificate of behaviour (*Verklaring omtrent het gedrag*) (Section 5, Articles 28–39). Articles 40–51, Title 3, contain provisions on personal files (*persoonsdossiers*). Articles 52–79, Title 4 (*slotbepalingen*) contain diverse provisions, such as the general obligation to keep certain data confidential and changes in other legislation.

The Order on Judicial Data has the following structure. The first Chapter consists of one Article with a number of definitions, one of which is that of Central Authority according to Council Decision 2005/876/JHA. The second Chapter consists of two sections, the first of which, Articles 2–9, contains provisions on the detailed description and definition of judicial data (*justitiële gegevens*), the second, Articles 10 and 10a, on the allowed origin of judicial data (*afkomst justitiële gegevens*). The third chapter contains detailed provisions on the provision of judicial data, divided into five sections: section 1, Articles 14–22, on the provision of data in order to execute certain governmental tasks (*verstrekking ten behoeve van het uitoefenen van de taak*); section 2, Articles 23–28, on the provision of data for the aim of hiring or dismissal of personnel (*verstrekking ten behoeve van het*

3. In the case of an investigation initiated at the request of an interested party, the Commission shall inform the said party of its findings, unless providing such information would be incompatible with the purpose of the data processing or the nature of the personal data, or unless important interests of parties other than the requester, including the responsible party, would sustain disproportionate harm as a consequence. In the event that the Commission does not inform the interested party of its findings, it shall send the said party such information as it deems appropriate.

Article 61

1. [Responsibility for the supervision of compliance referred to in Article 51(1) lies with the members and special members of the Commission, the officials of the Commission secretariat and the persons designated by decision of the Commission.
2. The persons referred to under (1) are authorised to enter a residence without the consent of the resident.
3. The persons referred to under (1) require the express and special authority of the Commission for the purposes of exercising the powers defined under (2), without prejudice to Article 2 of the General Act on the entry of premises (*Algemene wet op het binnentreden*).
4. The Commission is authorised to apply administrative measures of constraint pursuant to Article 5:20(l) of the General Administrative Law Act, provided that this concerns the obligation to provide assistance to an official designated by or under (1).
5. No appeal is possible on the grounds of a confidentiality obligation, where information or assistance is required in connection with the involvement of the person concerned in the processing of personal data.
6. Upon request, the Commission shall provide every assistance to the supervisory authorities of the other Member States of the European Union, where this is necessary for the performance of their work].

aannemen en ontslag van personeel); section 3, Articles 29–30f, on the provision of data for the aim of advice, recommendation or nomination of persons (*Verstrekking ten behoeve van advies, aanbeveling of voordracht van personen*); section 4, Article 30a, on the provision of data to foreign authorities; and the last section, Articles 30b-30f, on the provision of data to the authority of an EU Member State by the Dutch Central Authority, the *Justitiële Informatiedienst.* The fourth Chapter, Articles 32 and 33, contains provisions on the Certificate of Behaviour (*Verklaring omtrent het gedrag*). Chapter 5, Articles 34 and 35, contains provisions on the origin of reports from personal files (*afkomst van de rapporten die persoonsdossiers vormen*), Chapter 6 consists of Article 36 on the costs charged for the provision of certain declarations by the competent authorities and Chapter 7, Articles 37–54, provides for the withdrawal and changes of numerous other orders.

2. General provisions on judicial documentation

The Ministry of Justice processes judicial data in judicial documentation in the interest of good criminal procedure (Article 2 para. 1). Articles 2–9 of the Order on Judicial Data of 25 March 2004,[19] which is an *algemene maatregel van bestuur*[20] demanded by Article 2 para. 2 of the Act, define in a detailed manner all kinds of data with a detailed list of crimes, decisions, etc., to be registered. The judicial data concern all serious offences (*misdrijven*) and the minor offences (*overtredingen*) mainly described in Article 4 para. 2. These minor offences concerned are, for example, all economic offences, offences in the field of weapons, foreigners, fraud, protection of species and plants, and so on. According to Article 7 of the Order on Judicial Data judicial personal data are data such as forename, surname, address, the place of birth, the country of birth, identification numbers, nationality; on legal persons these data are the name, the legal form and statutory and factual seat of the legal person, as well as its registration number.

Similarly to the Act on the Protection of Personal Data Article 3 provides that the Minister of Justice takes the measures necessary, with regard to the purposes for which they are processed, to ensure that the data is correct and accurate. The Minister shall correct the data when they appear to him to be incorrect or incomplete.

[19] *Besluit justitiële gegevens*, Order of 25 March 2004, [2004] *Staatsblad* 130.

[20] A regulation to a certain extent comparable with an Order in Council. It is a regulation which has a rank in the legal order just below formal statute (Acts of Parliament) and above a ministerial decision (*Ministerieel besluit*).

The Minister shall also implement effective suitable technical and organisational measures to secure judicial data against loss or any form of illegal processing. Taking into account the current state of technology and the costs, these measures shall ensure a level of security which is in conformity with the risks of the processing of and the character of judicial data (Article 7 para. 1). Article 49 paras 1, 2 and 3, as well as Article 50 para. 1, of the Act on the Protection of Personal Data (*Wet bescherming persoonsgegevens*) also apply. These provisions read as follows:

> Artical 49
>
> 1. Where any person suffers harm as a consequence of acts concerning him which infringe the provisions laid down by or under this Act, the following paragraphs shall apply, without prejudice to other legal provisions.
> 2. For harm that does not comprise damage to property, the injured party has the right to fair compensation.
> 3. Responsible parties are liable for harm resulting from non-compliance with the provisions referred to under (1). Data processors are liable for this harm where this was incurred as a result of their actions.
>
> Artical 50
>
> 1. Where responsible parties or data processors act in contravention of the provisions laid down by or under this Act and other parties sustain, or may sustain, harm as a consequence thereof, the courts may, at the petition of the other parties, impose a ban on such conduct and order them to take measures to remedy the consequences of that conduct.

Judicial data will be removed from the judicial documentation after 30 years, or 20 years after the person concerned has died (Article 4 para. 1). The period starts the day after the case – whose judicial data is processed – has become *res judicata* (Article 4 para. 1). If the judicial data concern serious offences against public decency (*misdrijven tegen de zeden*) under Articles 240b-250[21] of the Dutch Criminal Code the data will be removed 20 years after the person concerned has died (Article 4 para. 2). According to Article 4 para. 3 of the Act the Order on Judicial Data determines in Article 17 para. 2, that these judicial data will be available to the *Reclassering* (social rehabilitation service), the *Raad voor de kinderbescherming* (organisation on child care) and certain behavioural scientists.

The period of 20 years shall be extended by the length of the unconditional prison sentence if this penalty is longer than three years and with

[21] Examples are indecent assault or rape.

the length of the *Terbeschikkingstelling* (detention at Her Majesty's pleasure) (Article 5 para. 1). In cases where this provision applies, the period will be extended by another ten years if the penalty concerns a criminal act of which the maximum sentence is eight years or more (Article 5 para. 2). This provision concerns the severest criminal acts. The data will in all cases be removed after the person involved has reached his or her 80th birthday (Article 5 para. 3).

Data on minor offences (*overtredingen*) will be removed after five years (Article 6 para. 1), unless a prison sentence, or an obligation to do community service (*dienstverlening*) instead of a prison sentence, was imposed, in which case the period shall be ten years (Article 6 para. 2). If a legal person was convicted for a minor offence to a fine of the third category or higher, which is EUR 4500 or more, the same longer period of ten years applies (Article 6 para. 3). The provisions in Article 4 paras. 2 and 3, also apply.

3. The regulation of the provision of judicial data

Judicial data shall be provided to Dutch judicial officials (*rechterlijke ambtenaren*) and judicial officials from Aruba and the Netherlands Antilles for the purpose of justice (*rechtspleging*) and to the Minister of Justice for the purpose of criminal justice (*strafrechtspleging*) (Article 8 paras. 1 and 2). It is also possible to provide judicial data related to economic offences to persons or agencies which have the power to make a compromise for economic offences on the basis of Article 37 of the Act on Economic Offences (Article 8 para. 3). According to Article 8 para. 5, of the Act the Order on Judicial Data regulates the provision of data to other judicial officials or authorities resulting from international agreements. Article 30a of the Order[22] demands that data are only provided to foreign, mainly non-EU authorities, if the public prosecutor authorises this. Article 30b–30f of the Order regulate the provision of data to the Central Authority of any other Member State by the *Justitiële informatiedienst*, which is the Dutch Central Authority. As far as these data concern citizens of the Member State of the foreign Central Authority (who do not have Dutch nationality), the data will be provided immediately (Article 30c of the Order). In other cases these data can be provided upon request if

[22] In Dutch: *Ter uitvoering van een op een verdrag gegrond verzoek kunnen justitiële gegevens door tussenkomst van de officier van justitie aan de bevoegde buitenlandse autoriteiten worden verstrekt ten behoeve van strafrechtelijke doeleinden.*

the aim is in conformity with the aims of the Act and the Order and if the public prosecutor approves (Art. 30d of the Order). According to Article 30d para. 2, limitations can be set on the processing or continued processing of these data. The *Justitiële informatiedienst* shall answer to a request immediately but at least within 10 working days (Article 30d para. 3, of the Order).

Whereas Articles 8 and 8a regulate the provision of judicial data for justice purposes, Articles 9–15 regulate the provision of judicial data for other purposes.[23] According to Article 9 the Order on Judicial Data authorises the provision of this data on the basis of public interest and regulates the processing (*verwerking*) and the continued processing (*verdere verwerking*) of judicial data. The only judicial data which can be provided on the basis of Article 9 are data relating to verdicts which are *res judicata* and where a prison sentence has been imposed (Article 10 para. 1) or if a legal person was convicted for a minor offence to a fine of EUR 4500 or more (Article 11 para. 1).

Nevertheless, no such judicial data can be provided in the three sets of circumstances described in Article 10 para. 2 and Article 11 para. 2, where: (i) a verdict was reviewed after it had become *res judicata* and no punishment or measure was imposed, or (ii) if four years have passed since the verdict became *res judicata*.[24] This period shall be extended by the length of the prison sentence which had been imposed unconditionally[25] and by the length of probation (Article 10 paras 4 and 5, Article 11 para. 4).[26] (iii) The third set of circumstances concerns natural persons only, namely where a foreign court has passed a sentence relating to a criminal act which is not a serious offence under Dutch law – unless the

[23] Article 12 provides for the provision of judicial data in relation to juveniles and the limitations to that. I will not discuss these provisions.

[24] Article 10 para. 2 (a) and (b), Article 11 para. 2 (a) and (b). This period will be eight years, and this can only involve punishments imposed on natural persons, if the verdict imposed an unconditional liberty-depriving sanction or a conditional liberty-depriving sanction of which, due to breach of one of the conditions, the execution was ordered wholly or in part (Article 10 para. 3). A similar extension of this period is possible if the verdict concerns legal persons if it imposed an unconditional fine or a conditional fine of which, due to breach of one of the conditions, the execution was ordered wholly or in part (Article 11 para. 3).

[25] According to Article 10 para. 7, community service imposed instead of an unconditional liberty-depriving sanction is equated with an unconditional liberty-depriving sanction.

[26] The time limit will not end so long as the time limit of any verdict which is *res judicata* not has ended (Article 10 para. 6, Article 11 para. 5).

punishment is a prison sentence which must be served in the Netherlands (Article 10 para. 2 (c)).[27]

If serious public interest (*zwaarwegend algemeen belang*) requires it – and to the extent necessary for the correct execution of the task by the person to whom the judicial data will be provided – it is possible for the Order to designate persons and authorities as mentioned in Article 9 to whom more data can be given than provided for in Articles 10–12. It can also determine the data that can be provided and can set rules on the processing and the continued processing. The provision of Article 9 para. 2 applies as well. It is prohibited to use these data for purposes other than those for which they had originally been provided.

According to the provisions just mentioned the Order on Judicial Data regulates the provision on request of judicial data to the national secret services (*Algemene Inlichtingen- en Veiligheidsdienst* and the *Militaire Inlichtingen- en Veiligheidsdienst*), the central authority entrusted with the execution of the Act to Improve the Assessments of Integrity of Public Administration, the *Bureau bevordering integriteits-beoordelingen door het openbaar bestuur* (Articles 14 and 15 of the Order), and a list of authorities with a description of the tasks for which the provision is allowed and the conditions involved (Articles 16–30 of the Order).

In special cases of important public interest the Minister of Justice can permit the provision of the judicial data described by him in conformity with the rules and conditions set by him. The Minister shall send a copy of his decision to the Data Protection Commission (*College bescherming persoonsgegevens*) (Article 14 para. 1). Unless the Minister determines differently, the data shall not be used for purposes other than those for which they had originally been provided. The Minister can also set rules on the processing and continued processing of this data (Article 14 paras 2 and 3). Save for an exemption by the Minister of Justice, judicial data can only be used for scientific research or statistics in such form that the possibility to identify individual persons from it can reasonably be prevented. The Minister of Justice can set conditions to the processing and continued processing of this judicial data (Article 15). Judicial data can also be provided by means of telecommunication (Article 16 para. 1).

[27] According to Article 10 para. 8 the time limit of foreign verdicts which were or are executed in the Netherlands starts the day after it became *res judicata*. The length of the time limit shall be determined on the basis of the verdict or decision by virtue of which the punishment or measure became executable in the Netherlands.

The recipient of this data shall not save or copy them in an automated way, unless this is necessary for the execution of a certain task approved by the Minister of Justice. More detailed rules to secure privacy in relation to the provision of data by means of telecommunication can be set by an administrative measure (*Administratieve maatregel van bestuur*). The Minister shall report the names of the persons or organisations to which judicial data has been provided on an annual basis (Article 16 para. 1 of the Data Protection Commission). This report shall also mention the number of requests by these persons or organisations. A fee can be required for the provision of judicial data on the basis of Articles 9, 13, 14 and 15. This fee shall not exceed the limits set by the Order on Judicial Data (Article 17 of the Act, Article 36 of the Order).

4. Regulation of personal files

The Minister of Justice shall process personal data in personal files, registered in the personal files documentation[28] for the purpose of enhancing the proper execution of criminal law (Article 40 para. 1). The Order on Judicial Data determines the way the reports that form the personal files shall be obtained (Article 40 para. 2; Articles 34 and 35 of the Order). A report in a personal file shall be removed after ten years have passed. This time limit will start on the day the report has been closed. If a sentence longer than ten years was imposed the period will equal the length of this sentence. A personal file will be removed in any case as soon as the subject has died or has reached his 80th birthday (Article 41).

The Minister of Justice can use copies of the report in a personal file for the purpose of handling a pardon request or for research purposes according to Article 28, and in order to issue the certificate of behaviour (Article 42 para. 1). If requested and for the purposes of good justice, the prosecution and the punishment of criminal acts, the execution of punishments and measures or to give an opinion on a request for pardon, the Minister of Justice can provide copies of a report from a personal file to Dutch judicial officials, judicial officials of Aruba and the Netherlands Antilles and to other judicial officials determined by the Minister (Article 42 para. 2). Article 42 also regulates the provision, on request, of copies of reports for other purposes. These are:

[28] According to para. 3, Articles 3 and 7 also apply.

- the selection and treatment of prisoners to penitentiary consultants (*penitentiaire consulenten*) and the heads of the institutions where a punishment or measure imposed on a natural person is executed (Article 42 para. 3);
- the preparation of any report or the execution of any form of supervision of probationers or convicted persons to the directors of the Dutch after-care and resettlement organisation, to probation officers or to the directors of the Dutch Council on child protection.

The Order on Judicial Data defines other persons or organisations who can receive copies from a personal file and the type of information that they can receive (Article 42 para. 5 of the Act; Articles 34 and 35 of the Order). If requested for the purposes of scientific research or statistics, copies of reports can only be provided in a form that reasonably prevents the identification of individual natural persons, except by dispensation of the Minister of Justice, who can set conditions to this provision of data (Article 42 para. 6). If requested, the Ministry of Justice shall inform an individual within four weeks whether reports on him or her have been entered in the documentation of personal files. The Minister shall not notify in written form, unless he refuses to notify. More detailed rules on the way data can be inspected can be made under Article 43 by ministerial regulation (*Ministeriële regeling*).[29] Every provision of a copy of reports from personal files according to Article 41 shall be registered and kept for at least one year. The Minister of Justice shall inform anyone, upon request, whether copies of reports from personal files that concern him or her have been provided according to Article 42 in the year preceding the request (Article 44). Article 20 applies to the handling of the requests according to Article 43 para. 1 and Article 44 para. 2.

An individual who has been notified of reports that concern him or her, can lodge a written request to correct, add, remove or screen personal data in these reports, if they are incorrect, incomplete or irrelevant in relation to the purpose of the processing or if they are processed in conflict with a rule. The request should also contain the changes to be made (Article 46). The decision on the requests according to Articles 44 and 46 is considered to be a decision according to Article 1:3 para. 2, of the Dutch General Administrative Law Act. If the Minister of Justice has corrected, added, removed or screened off personal data in

[29] A *Ministeriële regeling* is a regulation set by a Secretary of State (*Minister*).

reports then he will notify the person and organisations concerned as soon as possible unless it is impossible to do so or if such notification carries a disproportionate cost (Article 48).

An individual whose judicial data has been processed can lodge a complaint on the basis of special personal circumstances. The Minister of Justice shall decide within four weeks, after hearing from the Public Prosecutor's Office whether he considers the protest to have legitimate grounds; if so the Minister will terminate the processing immediately.

5. The certificate of behaviour

The certificate of behaviour (*Verklaring omtrent het gedrag*) is a declaration by the Ministry of Justice that their investigations on the natural or legal person concerned did not lead to concerns about any risks for society which could be relevant to the purpose for which the declaration was requested. The interests of the person concerned are also taken into account (Article 28). The subject may apply for a declaration to the mayor of the municipality where they are registered (Article 33). The application shall state the name and date of birth of the subject and a description of the purpose for which the declaration is requested (Article 32 para. 1). If the application concerns a legal person, it shall include the formal name, the registration number of the legal person by the Chamber of Commerce or, if there is no registration, its formal name, legal form, statutory or real seat, as well as name, address and date of birth of each of the directors and owners of the legal person, and the name of the person applying for the declaration (Article 32 para. 2). In an appendix applicants must also include a written description of the subject for whom the declaration is requested as a means of assessing any relevant risk to society (Article 32 para. 3).

The mayor and the Ministry of Justice confirm that the application is complete and that this is the true identity of the applicant. The mayor then immediately sends the application to the Ministry (Article 30 para. 2). The mayor may advise the Ministry of any special circumstances relating to the particular municipality but this must be done within ten days from the receipt of the application (Article 31). The Ministry of Justice may ignore the application altogether, if consideration of the applicant's behaviour seems unnecessary for the limitation of any risk to society. The mayor must be informed that this is the case (Article 34). According to the General Administrative Law Act (GALA), the decision not to respond to the application for a declaration constitutes an order

(Article 1:3 para. 1 GALA). This means that an appeal against it is possible before the administrative judge after a notice of objection.

In the investigation of the behaviour of a natural person, the Ministry of Justice can use existing judicial data in the judicial documentation on the applicant as well as data from police files (*politieregisters*), as defined in Article 1(c) of the Act on Police Files. However, the Ministry of Justice is refused access to data not available to the applicant as confidential. This would be the case with state security interests under Article 21. If the investigation concerns a legal person, the Ministry of Justice can access existing judicial data in the judicial documentation, data from police files (*politieregisters*) as defined in Article 1 (c) of the Act on Police Files, as well as data from the registry of companies maintained by the Ministry of Justice (Article 36 para. 2). Judicial data concern criminal acts registered in the name of the legal person, as well as judicial data on every director or owner (*bestuurders, vennoten, maten* or *beheerders*) of the legal person and data on criminal acts on the basis of Article 51 para. 2 of the Dutch Criminal Code (Article 36 para. 2). The Ministry of Justice shall not base the declaration on data on criminal acts for which the accused has been acquitted in a verdict that is *res judicata* (*onherroepelijke vrijspraak*) (Article 35 para. 3).

The Ministry shall decide within four weeks from the date of receipt of the application in case of declarations for natural persons, and within eight weeks for declarations for legal persons (Articles 37 and 38). The Ministry of Justice will refuse to issue a declaration if its research on the applicant identifies that the applicant had committed a criminal act, which – if repeated – would risk the execution of the task or activities in relation to which the declaration was requested. The decision on the application is considered as a decision under Article 1:3 para. 2 GALA (Article 29). This means that the rules on research and drafting, balance of interests, legal justification and the system of legal protection of general Dutch administrative law are also applicable in this case. Moreover, judicial review of this decision is possible before the administrative courts after a notice of objection sent to the Minister of Justice.

6. The rights of the subject to information and correction of erroneous data

Upon request of the subject, the Minister of Justice must notify the subject of any data registered in the judicial documentation and its content within four weeks. The Minister will not notify in a written form. Only refusals to notify must be made in writing. More detailed rules on the request and the way notification of data is undertaken can be introduced by ministerial regulation (*Ministeriële regeling*) (Article 18).[30] Every provision of judicial data on the basis of Articles 9, 13 and 14 shall be registered and kept for at least one year. If requested, the Secretary of Justice shall also notify subjects of entries on them provided in the year preceding the request (Article 19). There will be no notification under Article 18 para. 1 and Article 19 para. 1 if this is necessary for the protection of state security.

If the request concerns minors younger than 16 or persons who have been made a ward of court, it shall be submitted by their legal representative. If it concerns legal persons, the request shall be made by its representatives. It can also be made by an attorney to whom the subject has given specific authorisation for the exercise of the subject's rights on the basis of the Act on Judicial Data and who submits the request in the interests of the client alone.[31] The Ministry of Justice shall take all necessary steps to confirm the identity of the representative (Article 20).

Subjects who have been notified of entries in judicial documentation that concern them may request that the Minister of Justice corrects, adds, removes or screens all personal data in these reports on the basis that they are incorrect, incomplete, irrelevant to the purpose of processing, or if they are processed in breach of a legal rule. The requests must contain in detail all requested changes. Within four weeks from the receipt of the request, the Minister of Justice will notify the subject whether he intends to comply with the request.

Article 22 para. 2 also states that Article 37 of the Dutch Personal Data Protection Act applies in this instance. Where an important interest of the applicant so requires, the responsible party shall reply to the request referred to in Articles 35 and 36 in a form, other than in writing, which takes due account of this interest. The responsible party shall make sure that the identity of the applicant is properly established. In the case of minors who have not yet reached the age of 16 and of persons placed under legal restraint, the requests referred to in Articles 35 and 36

[30] The Secretary of Justice can require a fee which cannot exceed the amount set by or on the basis of the Order on Judicial Data. The fee shall be refunded if the Secretary has decided to correct, add, remove or screen the data as a result of a request, a recommendation by the Data Protection Commission or an order by a judge, or if the request is denied according to Article 21.

[31] More detailed rules on the specific authorisation can be given by *Ministeriële regeling*. As far as I know such a regulation does not exist.

shall be made by their legal representatives. Data shall also be provided to the legal representatives. A decision on the request according to Articles 18, 19 or 22 is considered to be a decision under the GALA (Article 23 para. 1). This makes judicial review possible before the administrative courts. General rules on the preparation of decisions, the right to be heard, the weighing of interests and motivation apply here also. Article 23 para. 2 declares Articles 47 and 48 applicable. Thus, within the time limits provided for, in appeals under the GALA or Article 46(2), the subject may request from the Data Protection Commission to mediate or give its opinion on any disputes or to make use of the provisions concerning the arrangement of disputes in a code of conduct which has been the subject of a declaration as referred to in Article 25(1). In that case, notwithstanding Article 6:7 GALA, the appeal may still be lodged or the court proceedings provided for in Article 46 still be initiated after the party concerned has received notice from the Data Protection Commission, or further to the provisions concerning the arrangement of disputes in a code of conduct which has been the subject of a declaration as referred to in Article 25(1) that the case has been dealt with, but no more than six weeks after that time. During the period when the appeal and the proceedings are in process, bodies responsible for dealing with the dispute may obtain the opinion of the Data Protection Commission. The bodies responsible for dealing with the dispute shall send a copy of their verdict to the Data Protection Commission.

If the Minister of Justice has corrected, added or erased judicial data, the Minister shall inform the persons and organisations mentioned in Article 8 paras. 5, 9, 13 and 14. Bodies or persons who had access to the wrong data from the year preceding the request must also be notified of these changes as soon as possible, unless this is impossible or requires disproportionate effort (Article 24 para. 1). If requested, the Minister shall inform the applicant or their legal representative who has been notified of the agreed changes. The subject can protest against their entries on the basis of special personal circumstances. The Secretary of Justice shall decide within four weeks, following the opinion of the Public Prosecutor's Office (*Openbaar Ministerie*), whether the protest is considered legitimate. If so, the Minister will terminate the processing of this data with immediate effect.

12

The European Criminal Record in Slovenia

KATJA ŠUGMAN AND DRAGAN PETROVEC

1. Introduction

Ideas of mutual recognition[1] and mutual trust[2] in connection with a central criminal record authority are not recent. As we know, the need for a more effective exchange of criminal record data was emphasised in the European Council Declaration on Combating Terrorism (March 2004)[3] and confirmed by the Hague Programme (November 2004).[4] In October 2004 the first Proposal for a Council Decision on the exchange of information extracted from criminal records was adopted. It was followed by the White Paper on exchanges of information on convictions and the effect of such convictions within the European Union (January 25 2005)[5] and the Council Decisions on the exchange of information extracted from the criminal record.[6] Among the three possible options for a mutual recognition programme proposed in the White Paper the Commission obviously chose a middle option between

[1] The concept of mutual recognition was launched in March 1998 by the UK Home Secretary during the UK presidency. It further developed during the Tampere Council in October 1999 (in connection with the abolition of the extradition procedures and the introduction of the European Arrest Warrant) and was mentioned in the conclusions as the cornerstone of judicial cooperation in both civil and criminal matters. See H. G. Nilsson, 'Mutual Trust or Mutual Mistrust?', in G. De Kerchove and A. Weyembergh (eds.), *La confiance mutuelle dans l'espace pénal européen* (Bruxelles: Institut d'études Européennes, 2005), pp. 29–45.

[2] The idea of mutual trust appeared in the Programme of Measures to implement the principle of Mutual Recognition in November 2000 (2001/C 12/02) and was considered a tool for achieving the mutual recognition principle. See S. Alegre, 'Mutual Trust – Lifting the Mask', in G. De Kerchove and A. Weyembergh (eds.), *La confiance mutuelle*, pp. 41–47.

[3] http://consilium.europa.eu/uedocs/cmsUpload/DECL-25.3.pdf.

[4] http://ec.europa.eu/justice_home/news/information_dossiers/the_hague_priorities/index_en.htm.

[5] COM(2005) 10 final, 25 January 2005.

[6] Decision 2005/876/JHA, 21 November 2005.

networking of national criminal record offices. This solution was presented in the Proposal for a Council Framework Decision on the organisation and content of the exchange of information extracted from criminal records between Member States in December 2005.[7]

The purpose of this chapter is to give an overview of the recent Slovenian legal framework regarding criminal records and the transfer of data from the criminal records. This will be done in order to enquire into the legal obstacles to implementing the last EU document on the topic, namely the Proposal for a Council Framework Decision on the organisation and content of the exchange of information extracted from criminal records between Member States.

2. Existing legal framework

2.1. General legal framework

A legal framework for keeping criminal records can be found in various acts. The most detailed ones and at the same time the ones that contain most of the relevant provisions are the Rules on Criminal Records (RCR) issued by the Ministry of Justice.[8] There is, however, a broader legal framework contained in the more general provisions of the Code of Criminal Procedure (CCP),[9] the Criminal Code (CC),[10] and the Personal Data Protection Act (PDPA).[11] Slovenia has also ratified the European Convention on Mutual Assistance in Criminal Matters (July 1999),[12] including the Additional Protocol to the European Convention on Mutual Assistance in Criminal Matters.

The Code of Criminal Procedure provides for the general rules of criminal record-keeping, while the CC provides for the general framework of a criminal records 'philosophy', namely the rules on when criminal records could be disclosed and when convictions should be erased from the criminal records according to the process of rehabilitation.

2.2. General rules

Article 135 CCP provides for the duty of the Ministry of Justice to keep the criminal records and records of educational measures (for minors)

[7] COM(2005) 690 final, 22 December 2005.
[8] Official Journal of the Republic of Slovenia (O. J.) No. 34/2004.
[9] O. J. No. 32/2007. [10] O. J. No. 95/2004.
[11] O. J. No. 86/04. [12] O. J. MP No. 25/99.

and for the obligation of the Minister of Justice to prescribe the manner of keeping the records. Therefore, the register is centralised by the Ministry of Justice.

The Criminal Code contains general rules on what a criminal record should contain: personal data on people convicted of criminal offences; information on the sentences,[13] safety measures, suspended sentences and judicial admonitions imposed, the remitted sentences referring to the convicted persons of which the record is being kept, as well as the legal consequences incident to such sentences and measures,[14] and later alterations of convictions contained in the criminal record. It must also contain information on the serving of sentences and on the annulment of records of wrongful conviction (Art. 105(1) CC). There is a special criminal record for minors (Art. 105(2) CC). It includes personal data on juvenile offenders, information on the educational measures applied and carried out, as well as all the other information relating to the implementation of educational measures.[15]

The Criminal Code also provides for the rules on when and who may request the information from the criminal record to be disclosed or exchanged. Firstly, information from the criminal record may be given only with respect to convictions that have not been removed and secondly, they may only be released to the court, state prosecutor, police dealing with criminal proceedings against a previous offender, bodies responsible for the implementation of criminal sanctions and bodies involved in the procedures for granting an amnesty or pardon, or for removing a conviction (Art. 105(3) CC). Thirdly, information on a conviction that has not been removed may be released to the state authorities, legal persons and private employers upon substantiated

[13] For details of the Slovenian sentencing system see K. Šugman, M. Jager, K. Filipčič and N. Peršak, *Slovenia: Criminal Justice Systems in Europe and North America* (Helsinki: Heuni, 2004), pp. 52–68.

[14] The legal consequences of conviction are defined in Articles 99–101 CP. The types of legal consequences are: termination of the performance of certain public functions or official duties, debarment from the performance of certain public functions or official duties, debarment from entering a certain profession, debarment from obtaining certain permits. They may not be applied to a juvenile offender. They may not remain in effect for more than five years. See as well a detailed analysis in V. Jakulin, 'Pravne posledice obsodbe v kazenskem pravu' (Legal Consequences of Conviction in Criminal Proceedings) (1992) 52 *Zbornik znanstvenih razprav* 55–72.

[15] See a comprehensive monograph on educational measures in Slovenia in B. Dekleva (ed.), *Nove vrste vzgojnih ukrepov za mladoletnike* (New Forms of Educational Measures for Minors) (Ljubljana: Inštitut za kriminologijo, 1996).

request only if the legal consequences of the conviction are still in effect or if such persons demonstrate a legitimate and legally grounded interest in the possession of such information (Art. 105(4) CC).[16] Upon his/her own request, an individual may be given information on whether he/she was convicted (Art. 105(5) CC). Slovenia, therefore, exercises the system of indirect access – any authority that has a right to access to a criminal record has to contact the Ministry of Justice and get information from the Ministry.

Article 86 CC provides for the rules regarding access to the criminal records for minors. It is only allowed to: the courts, state prosecutors, police in connection with criminal proceedings against a juvenile offender and to the social service and institutions where the juvenile educational measures are carried out.

Regarding the possibility of access to criminal records, the rules of the Personal Data Protection Act (PDPA) should also be considered. The fundamental principle is to prevent any illegal and unjustified disturbance of personal privacy in the course of data-processing, the securing of databases and the use thereof. All the personal data-collection should be carried out following the principle of proportionality (Art. 3 PDPA). Personal data can be processed only when the law so provides or an individual gives his consent (Art. 8 PDPA). The law has to provide as well for the purpose of data-collection and processing. There are even stricter rules for the processing and use of so-called sensitive personal data, among which criminal convictions can definitely be placed (Art. 13 PDPA). In cases where especially sensitive personal data is transferred by means of telecommunication, it must be processed with cryptographic methods and an electronic signature in order for their confidentiality to be protected during the transmission (Art. 14(2) PDPA). Personal data must be collected only for the purpose provided by law and processed only in accordance with this purpose (Art. 16 PDPA). Upon the request of a person whose personal data is being collected that person may be given information on his personal data collected and processed by the

[16] After the conviction is removed, the information of the conviction must not be released to anyone. The benefit of such a solution is that offenders may be rehabilitated and reintegrated into society by avoiding stigma. Arguments, of course, exist as well for the other solution: namely, that the data on criminal convictions should always be publicly available, especially for employment purposes. See *Public Access to Criminal History Record Information: Criminal Justice Information Policy* (Washington D.C.: US Department of Justice, 1988).

data collection agencies.[17] He/she also has a right to amend, correct, block or delete data that is not complete, correct or was collected without his consent (when this was necessary) or contrary to the purpose provided by law (Art. 32 PDPA).[18]

The CC also provides for a general rule on the legal rights of the convicted person after his/her sentence is served. Article 102 states that after the sentence of imprisonment or juvenile detention has been served, remitted or barred by the statute, the convicted person shall enjoy all the rights contained in the constitution, laws and other regulations, and may exercise all the rights other than those which he is deprived of owing to the application of safety measures or the legal consequences of the conviction. This rule also applies to offenders released on parole.

Article 103 CC provides for the rehabilitation and consequently the annulment of conviction. After a certain time, depending on the severity of the offence (according to the sentence passed), the entry of the conviction has to be removed from the criminal record, the legal consequences of the conviction cease to apply and the offender has to be deemed as if he/she had never been convicted. The entry is erased from the record at a specified time after the sentence was served (barred by statute due to prescription or if the sentence was discharged, unless the convicted person commits another criminal offence).[19] The time limits for erasure from the record are:

(1) one year from the judgment in which a judicial admonition was administered;
(2) three years, for a fine, accessory sentence, a prison sentence not exceeding one year;
(3) five years, for a prison sentence of between one and three years;
(4) eight years for a prison sentence of between three and five years;
(5) ten years for a prison sentence of between five and ten years;
(6) fifteen years, for a prison sentence of between ten and fifteen years;
(7) a prison sentence of twenty years shall not be removed from the criminal record.

[17] For more details see N. Pirc Musar (ed.), *Zakon o varstvu osebnih podatkov s komentarjem* (Ljubljana: GV Založba, 2006), s.v. Arts. 29–31.

[18] Ibid., s.v. Arts. 32–33.

[19] See Z. Kanduč, 'Zastraševanje in rehabilitacija' 47 (1996) 3 *Revija za kriminalistiko in kriminologijo* 228–240.

A prison sentence of more than fifteen years is never deleted from the record and the conviction may not be removed for as long as safety measures apply to the offender.[20]

2.3. Rules on Criminal Records

Rules on the Criminal Record (RCR) contain detailed provisions on the topic. In Slovenia criminal records are kept for any perpetrator of a criminal offence (private or legal person) convicted in the Republic of Slovenia, including sentences passed on Slovenian citizens by foreign courts, if the sentences were transmitted to the judicial authorities of the Republic of Slovenia (Art. 3(1) RCR). There is a special record for minors who have committed criminal offences and a special record for people convicted of misdemeanours (petty offences).

Criminal records contain (Art. 9 RCR):

(1) personal data of the convicted person containing the surname and forename – in the case of married women, their maiden name – nickname and, if applicable, false identity;
(2) personal ID number;
(3) place of birth, name of the local district of birth – for a convicted person born in a foreign country, the name of the country of birth – and date of birth;
(4) citizenship;
(5) permanent or temporary residence – specifying the address at which the convict was living at the time he was sentenced;
(6) name and address of the court which passed the sentence – for foreign courts a name of the state to which the sentencing court belongs – the number and date of judicial decision of the court of the first instance, the date on which the judgment became final or the date of the decisions of the Court of Appeals in case it reversed the court of first instance's decision;
(7) legal qualification of a criminal offence with a citation of the article and paragraph of the Criminal Code;

[20] The maximum prison sentence in Slovenia is 30 years (Art. 37 PC). Recently there has been very intensive debate between equally engaged sides: one arguing for an increase to a life sentence and the other for a reduction to a maximum penalty of 20 years. D. Petrovec, *Kazen brez zločina* (Ljubljana: Studia Humanitatis, 1998).

(8) type of criminal sanction, educational measure or safety measure that has to be put in the record, and the duration of the sentence;
(9) all subsequent modifications of the data in the record including the mentioning of the authority that passed this decision.

Criminal records also contain data on the sentences or educational measures imposed by foreign courts on citizens of the Republic of Slovenia and on foreigners with a permanent residence in the Republic of Slovenia (Art. 10(1) RCR).

Criminal records for minors have to contain the same data as for adults, including data on educational measures passed or previously served by the minor in question (Art. 4(2) RCR). The misdemeanour record contains:

(1) personal data of the convicted person containing surname and forename – in the case of married women, their maiden name – nickname and, if applicable, false identity;
(2) personal ID number – for foreigners date of birth;
(3) permanent or temporary residence;
(4) Legal qualification of a misdemeanour with a citation of the article and paragraph of the legal act;
(5) the number and the date of the decision passed by the court;
(6) the sanction and its duration;
(7) all the subsequent changes regarding the above mentioned data.

Criminal records for legal persons contain the full name and the place where a legal person is registered, the legal person's ID number, data on convictions passed, safety measures and legal consequences of the convictions and all the subsequent modifications of the data in the record (Art. 3(3) RCR).

Records are kept for criminal judgments that have become final (Art. 14 RCR). All the relevant data has to be sent within 15 days after the judgment becomes final to the Ministry of Justice, which enters the data about the criminal conviction into the criminal record (Art. 15(2) RCR). The Ministry of Justice is also in charge of removing the data from the criminal record. The removal is made on the basis of the final decision by which the court decides, according to the legally prescribed terms, that the conviction has to be removed (see above rehabilitation, Art. 103 CC). The Ministry of Justice has to check (*ex officio*) the criminal records regularly and when noticing that a certain conviction has to be removed from the record informs the court that has jurisdiction to issue a decision on this alteration from the record (Art. 18. RCR). The records removed are kept in the archives (Art. 19 RCR).

Criminal records are of a secret nature and access to the data is restricted and given only to authorised authorities (see above 2.3).[21] The data on convictions passed by foreign courts may be given only to the court, state prosecutor, police dealing with criminal proceedings against a previous offender, bodies responsible for the implementation of criminal sanctions and bodies involved in the procedures for granting an amnesty or pardon, or for removing a conviction (Art. 25 RCR).

2.4. *International instruments*

Article 514 CCP provides for the general rule that international aid in criminal matters is administered pursuant to the provisions of the CCP unless otherwise provided by international agreements. As far as mutual legal aid is concerned it is necessary to mention that the Act of ratification of the European Convention on Mutual Assistance in Criminal Matters, which was adopted in September 1999 including the Additional Protocol to the European Convention on Mutual Assistance in Criminal Matters. Therefore, the exchange of information from the criminal record is now governed by this Convention. In addition to the channels provided by the Convention there is an intense cooperation with Interpol and national agencies and/or the judicial system in a number of countries according to the bilateral and multilateral agreements.

3. Contents of the European Criminal Record

With regard to the contents of the European Criminal Record (ECR) as proposed by Article 11 of a Proposal for a Council Framework Decision on the organisation and content of the exchange of the information extracted from criminal records between Member States (PCFD), they are very similar to the contents of the national criminal record (see 2.3).

(1) Information on a convicted person required by the PCFD is practically the same as in national legislation: first name, surname, date of birth, place of birth, possible nickname or pseudonym, gender, nationality and citizenship, and for legal persons name and

[21] J. Čebulj and J. Žurej, *Varstvo osebnih podatkov in informacije javnega značaja* (Ljubljana: Nebra, 2005).

registration data. The most important information, given here for the purposes of the PCFD, is obviously nationality or citizenship. Slovenia would have no problem implementing the solutions of the PCFD as far as the major requirement of Article 4 is concerned – ensuring that all convictions handed down in its territory are accompanied by the nationality of the convicted person, especially if they are a national of another Member State.

(2) National records also contain information on the nature of the conviction (name and address of the court which passed the sentence, number and date of the judicial decision).

(3) For the legal classification of a criminal offence, Slovenian law requires only that a citation of the relevant article and paragraph of the Criminal Code be entered into the record. However, since the PCFD demands 'information on the facts giving rise to the conviction' (Art. 11(2) (c) PCFD), it also requires the information on the factual side of the case. If the PCFD is truly referring to the factual side of the criminal conviction in question, this might require change in our legislation and could cause some implementation problems since our criminal records contain only the legal side of the case (i.e. legal classification) namely the CC article in question.

(4) The Slovenian record includes all the necessary information on the contents of the conviction: type of criminal sanction, educational measures or safety measures, and subsequent decisions affecting the enforcement of the sentence.

Generally, the implementation of the PCFD would not pose a big problem for Slovenia. The major change required to implement the PCFD is the inclusion of more detail on the facts of the case. Another important thing to be borne in mind is that Slovenia will have to inform other Member States of the time limits for the erasure of entries from the criminal record (Art. 103 CC, see 2.2). Special care will have to be taken about the possible alteration or deletion of sentences or other measures (Art. 5(2) PCFD).

4. Access to the European Criminal Record

Slovenia already has a central authority which keeps and transmits criminal records: the Ministry of Justice. An obvious solution would, therefore, be to designate the Ministry as the central authority for the purposes of PCFD and Council Decision 2005/876/JHA of 21 November on the exchange of information extracted from the criminal record. Slovenia would, therefore, have to provide for a way for the national central authority to inform the central authority of a convicted person's nationality with regard to a conviction passed in Slovenia.[22]

For the national law now in force, the rules for the transmission of the criminal records are as described above. The transfer of such data would not be in conflict with Slovenian legislation, since such transfers already exist among different authorities. It would only be necessary to include the European Criminal Record under a specific jurisdiction (the Schengen Information System for instance) capable of ensuring a quick and secure system for the exchange of information. Another possibility is an electronic transmission of scanned documents. The chosen solution will obviously depend on what will be decided at a European level.

According to the national rules (see Section 2.2.) information from the criminal record may be given only with respect to convictions that have not been removed (rehabilitation, see Section 2.2). The list of bodies enumerated in the first paragraph of Article 105 CC contains only criminal justice authorities, including the police. They are limited to accessing information only when dealing with criminal proceedings against a previous offender. Both limitations make it obvious that the information required under that paragraph has to be used only for the purpose of criminal proceedings. In cases where the central authority of a Member State will require information for the purpose of criminal proceedings, Slovenian legislation would have to be amended to ensure that a central authority of another Member State will be listed among the authorities that are able to submit requests for information from the national criminal record.

As far as requests for any purposes other than criminal proceedings are concerned (Art. 7(2) PCFD), the situation is more complex. National legislation does provide for the possibility of certain bodies getting information from criminal records in such cases but under some

[22] Such a solution is in accordance with the principle of the availability (introduced by the Hague programme, see note 4) stating that: 'throughout the Union, a law enforcement officer in one Member State who needs information to perform his duties can obtain this from another Member State and that the law enforcement agency in the other Member State which holds this information will make it available for the stated purpose.' The Hague Programme does not generally recommend the creation of centralised European databases, but sets out the option that the national databases can be reciprocally addressed.

relatively strict conditions. Firstly, information from the criminal record may be given only with respect to convictions that have not been removed; secondly, bodies are limited to state authorities, legal persons and private employers; thirdly, they have to submit a reasoned request; and fourthly, they have to demonstrate a legitimate and legally grounded interest in the possession of such information or the legal consequences of the conviction must still be in effect (Art. 105(4) CC). The latter is of particular interest to employers since one of the legal consequences can also be a prohibition from entering a certain profession or from performing certain public functions. Again, Slovenian legislation would have to be amended in such a way that the central authority of another Member State will be listed among the authorities that are able to submit requests for the information from the national criminal record for purposes other than that of criminal proceedings. But in that case, according to the national legislation, they would have to submit a reasoned request and demonstrate a legitimate and legally grounded interest in the possession of such information.[23]

Since Slovenian law already provides for the possibility of a citizen requesting information on his own convictions (Art. 105(5) CC) national legislation is already in accordance with the demands of the PCFD (Art. 6(2)).[24] However, it does not provide for the explicit possibility of a resident (non-national) requesting such information. Article 24(1) RCR, which is considered *lex specialis* to the CC explicitly provides only for the right of a citizen to request information of his own conviction or non-conviction. National legislation will, therefore, have to be changed so that it allows a non-national resident of the Republic of Slovenia to be able to exercise the same right.

The Slovenian Personal Data Protection Act contains rules on how personal data can be transferred to third countries; such a transfer is possible only on the basis of the decision of the state supervision authority, which establishes that the state to which the data is to

[23] The implementation of the principle of availability has to fulfil some conditions such as: the exchange may only take place in order that legal tasks may be performed; supervision of respect for data protection and appropriate control prior to and after the exchange must be ensured. See M. den Boer, 'New Dimensions in EU Police Co-operation: The Hague Milestone for what they are worth', in J. W. de Zwaan and Flora A. N. J. Goudappel (eds.), *Freedom, Security and Justice in the European Union* (The Hague: Asser Press, 2006), pp. 223–224.

[24] E-vloga za pridobitev potrdila iz kazenske evidence izrečenih vzgojnih ukrepov za fizične osebe, (2004) 23 *Pravna praksa*, 21, 13.

be transferred provides for the appropriate level of data protection (Art. 63(1) PDPA). However, the PDPA provides that when the data is transferred to the manager of a data register in one of the Member States the above-mentioned rule does not apply (Art. 62(1) PDPA). Therefore, from the perspective of data protection provided in the PDPA there is no legal obstacle preventing the transfer of criminal records into other Member States.

5. Use of the European Criminal Record

Slovenian national law provides for the use of criminal records in few cases. Therefore, according to recent legislation, the European Criminal Record could be used in a same way. The most common and frequent way of using the data from the criminal record is while trying a person for another criminal offence or more precisely, when imposing a sentence. It is the regular practice of the court to acquire information from the Ministry of Justice on possible previous convictions of a defendant. The CCP requires that in his first interrogation the accused should be asked, inter alia, whether he has been convicted and the sentence has not yet been deleted, whether he has served a sentence and, if so, when and for what criminal offence and whether criminal proceedings against him for some other offence are in progress (Art. 227(19) CCP). Such information can be used for sentencing.

Generally the perpetrator can be sentenced within the limits of the statutory terms provided for the offence a perpetrator is charged with. The decision on what sentence shall be passed is made having regard to the gravity of the offence and the perpetrator's culpability (Art. 41(1) CC). In passing the sentence the court must consider all the mitigating and aggravating circumstances, among which the perpetrator's past behaviour including possible criminal convictions is taken into consideration (Art. 41(2) CC).

There are special provisions regarding recidivists (repeat offenders) requiring that the courts take special care when imposing a sentence. In deciding the sentence of a perpetrator who committed a criminal offence after he had already been convicted or had served his sentence (or in some similar situations such as after the implementation of his sentence had been barred by time or after his sentence has been remitted) the court must consider whether the earlier offence is of the same type as the new one, whether both offences were committed for the same motive and the time which has elapsed since the former conviction or since serving, withdrawing, remitting or barring the sentence (Art. 41(2) CCP). In cases where the perpetrator intentionally committed a criminal offence for which the imposition of a prison sentence is prescribed by the law the court may even extend the prescribed term of his sentence under certain circumstances, which imply that he is a multirecidivist. If, for example, the perpetrator has been sentenced to more than one year's imprisonment for an intentional criminal offence of the same type at least twice before or less than five years have passed from the day when he was discharged from the penal institution where he served his previous sentence, the court can extend his sentence from the day on which he committed the criminal offence in question. In deciding whether to extend the prison sentence, the court must consider in particular the similarity of the offences committed, the motives and any other circumstances indicating that the perpetrator is likely to recommit such an offence (Art. 46 CC).

In cases where the PCFD has been adopted and especially if the Proposal for a Council Framework Decision on taking account of convictions in new criminal proceedings[25] is also adopted, convictions that have been passed by another Member State could be given equivalent effect by a Member State to convictions that were passed by the national court against the same perpetrator in the course of a new criminal proceeding.

Our law also provides the possibility of certain other bodies requiring information on convictions in criminal procedure. As shown above, only information on a conviction that has not been removed or erased may be released. The bodies that may ask for it are the state authorities, legal persons and private employers upon substantiated request, but only if the legal consequences of the conviction are still in effect or if such persons demonstrate a legitimate and legally grounded interest in the possession of such information (Art. 105(4) CC). The law does not provide any more detail as to what 'legally grounded interest' might be.

6. Critical evaluation

There is no doubt that the PCFD provides for a much quicker and a great deal more efficient procedure for exchanging criminal record data. Generally, one cannot object to the idea of each Member State centralising information on convictions handed down to its own nationals. It is

[25] COM(2005) 91, 17 March 2005.

only fair that courts, when passing a sentence, should be aware of all the previous criminal offences of a perpetrator, not just those committed in the convicting Member State itself. However, great care has to be taken regarding the possible abuse of such an important and sensitive database, especially if, in the future, it will develop into a true central European Criminal Record.

Firstly, a question that will have to be addressed now and in the future is that of the scope of the criminal record exchange or of a possible centralised European Criminal Record. Should it contain all criminal offences, and if so what are the criteria for an act being characterised as a criminal offence? Should this be decided by the national law of the convicting Member State, the national law of Member State of convict's nationality or even some third solution? The recent PCFD adopts a solution by which conviction means:

> any final decisions of a criminal court or of an administrative authority whose decisions can be appealed against before a court having jurisdiction in particular in criminal matters, establishing guilt of a criminal offence or an act punishable in accordance with the national law as an offence against the law (Art. 2(1) PCFD).

As we can see, the PCFD adopts a very wide definition of a criminal offence. As much as a broad definition of a criminal offence is welcome in the context of the protection of human rights (e.g. the European Court of Human Rights),[26] it might nevertheless be dubious in the context of data exchange. A very broad interpretation of the PCFD would allow for the data transmission of very minor offences (e.g. misdemeanours) and the question arises as to whether such transfers are in true accord with basic legal principles such as the principle of proportionality.[27]

Secondly, I want to address the question of access to the criminal record. This question can be divided into two sub-topics: (i) who can access criminal records? and (ii) for what purpose? For protecting the

[26] In its judgments the European Court of Human Rights defined the meaning of the 'criminal' charge or being 'charged with a criminal offence' as provided by Art. 6(2) and 6(3) of the European Convention of Human Rights. The leading case is *Engel and others* v. *Netherlands*, Judgment of 8 June 1976, Ser. A, No 22; (1979–80) 1 EHRR 647. See S. Trechsel, *Human Rights in Criminal Proceedings* (Oxford: Oxford University Press, 2005), pp. 14–36.

[27] K. Šugman and M. Jager, 'The Developing EU Criminal Law and the *ultima ratio* Principle', in Petrus Van Duyne (ed.), (forthcoming).

rights of the citizens, especially the right to social rehabilitation, it seems that the use of information transmitted under the PCFD should be strictly limited to the course of criminal proceedings. This means, firstly, that the access should only be allowed to the bodies involved in the criminal justice system (e.g. prosecutors, courts). Any person can, of course, demand information on his own criminal record. And secondly, any information extracted from criminal records should only be used for the purposes of criminal proceedings. However, we should also consider the option of allowing criminal records to be accessed on the basis of other well-founded reasons.[28] Such options should be restrictive and very carefully regulated.

The question, therefore, is whether the solution adopted by the PCFD is really appropriate. In other words, is it acceptable that the use of information from criminal records for any purpose other than criminal proceedings should be decided purely in accordance with the national law of the requesting and requested state (Art. 7(2) PCFD)? Since the national laws of Member States differ a lot in this respect,[29] the rule that personal data may be used by the requesting Member State solely for the purpose of the particular proceedings they were requested for, does not provide for enough data protection. According to the White Paper, most countries do not allow third parties to access criminal records, but some do. Therefore, it is highly questionable whether such sensitive data should freely be used for other purposes (e.g. banks, employment, security service etc.) and the regulation of this should be left to national legislations. This is especially true since Member States will not be dealing only with data acquired in their own states but also with data from other Member States. The fact that EU ambitions regarding criminal records (e.g. the eventual creation of a centralised European Criminal Record) are even higher makes such a solution even more worrying.

Thirdly, there is the question of identity fraud. Identity fraud means that 'somebody with dishonest intentions deliberately passes himself off under an identity that does not belong to him by using the identity of

[28] One of them could be employment purposes, especially very sensitive ones: e.g. teachers, youth workers etc. This was demonstrated by the Fourniret case, where a convicted French serial murderer and paedophile Michel Fourniret got a job as a supervisor in a Belgian school and continued with his criminal activities. See http://news.bbc.co.uk/2/hi/europe/5410518.stm.

[29] See White Paper on exchanges of information on convictions and the effect of such convictions in the European Union, COM(2005) 10 final, 25 January 2005, 2.1.7.a.

another existing or fictitious person'.[30] The possibilities of false identity are increasing with the introduction of sophisticated computer techniques[31] and the growth of cyberspace which allows people to assume false or double identities.[32] If criminal offenders succeed in creating a false identity, criminal records become incorrect and innocent people may suffer because of wrong entries. By creating a common EU database the problem could be aggravated as there is less chance to actually identify a mistake in a large database and less likelihood of being able to verify an identity in a database detached from its national origins.[33]

Fourthly, there is, of course, the question of data protection. Generally it would be better to wait with any further developments on the criminal record field since the Council Framework Decision on data protection[34] must surely be adopted before any centralised criminal record database can be established. For now, we can do nothing more then exercise the mutual trust principle and rely on other Member States' data protection.

[30] J. Grijpink, 'Criminal Records in the European Union: The Challenge of Large-scale Information Exchange' (2006) 14 *European Journal of Crime, Criminal Law and Criminal Justice*, at 9.

[31] Use of other people's credit cards, photos, identity documents etc. At a European Arrest Warrant Conference (Krakow, Poland, 2 November 2006) the Czech prosecutor reported of a case, where another Member State requested the surrender of a Czech national who was a suspect in a criminal case, but it turned out that someone was using his identity since the requested Czech national was in prison and could not have committed the alleged criminal offence.

[32] See Y. Jewkes (ed.), *Dot.cons: Crime, Deviance and Identity on the Internet* (Cullompton: Willan Publishing, 2002).

[33] Grijpink, 'Criminal Records in the European Union', pp. 9–10.

[34] Such as the Council Framework Decision on the protection of personal data processed in the framework of police and judicial cooperation in criminal matters (COM2005) 475 final, 4 October 2005.

13

The European Criminal Record in Slovakia

ANNA ONDREJOVA

1. General Information

1.1 The criminal record system in the Slovak Republic – national legal framework

The activity of the Register is governed by the Act on Register of Criminal Convictions[1] that the Slovak National Council passed on 3 November 1999 and which became effective on 1 January 2000. The Act on Residence of Foreigners, as amended,[2] was the means to introduce changes related to the protection of the state with some new penal law rules, the establishment of the National Security Authority and new powers granted to municipalities. In particular, a new provision has been introduced which allows citizens to be issued with copies from the Criminal Register. The Act on Representation of the Slovak Republic at Eurojust,[3] as amended, regulates the relations between the Criminal Register and any Eurojust National Member when providing information from the Register.

As an EU Member State the Slovak Republic is obliged to apply decisions of EU authorities or to take the necessary implementing legislative and organisational measures on the basis of such decisions. The Council Decision on the exchange of information extracted from the criminal record (hereinafter referred to as 'Decision')[4] imposes an obligation on all Member States to designate a central authority for receiving and sending information on convictions and related decisions or measures and for the mutual exchange of such information. This is a

[1] Law No. 311/1999, Coll., on Register of Criminal Convictions.

[2] Law No. 48/2002, Coll., and No. 418/2002, Coll., on Residence of Foreigners.

[3] Law No. 530/2004, Coll., on Representation of the Slovak Republic at Eurojust.

[4] Council Decision 2005/876/JHA of 21 November 2005 on the exchange of information extracted from the criminal record, OJ L 322, 9 December 2005.

new task beyond the scope of Article 22 of the European Convention on Mutual Assistance in Criminal Matters and the Additional Protocol to the European Convention on Mutual Assistance in Criminal Matters of 20 April 1959.[5] A specific Act has to be passed in order to authorise the General Prosecutor's Office of the Slovak Republic to fulfil this task.

Both the Criminal Code[6] and the Code of Criminal Procedure[7] represent significant change in relation to the way the Criminal Register operates. In these legal regulations several new kinds of sanctions and protective measures as well as new legal rules of a substantive and a procedural nature have been devised that may be applied only upon the basis of a specific Act in regulating the operations of the Criminal Register.

1.2 The content of the criminal record

The criminal record system in Slovak Republic is centralised. It includes convictions by penal courts as well as courts' and prosecutors' decisions to suspend conditionally criminal prosecutions or to approve extra-judicial settlements. Registration of administrative penalties is partial and decentralised. The Slovak Republic has only one central database where any final criminal conviction executed by the Slovak criminal courts is registered. Moreover, any case where either the prosecutor or the courts have conditionally discontinued the criminal prosecution is registered in this database. Information on extra-judicial settlements approved within criminal proceedings is also included in the database and so are Supreme Court rulings on the recognition in Slovak territory of judgments of foreign courts. Notifications made by foreign courts on the final conviction of a Slovak national or on the final conviction of a person permanently residing in Slovakia are also entered in this registry including notifications sent pursuant to Article 22 of the European Convention on Mutual Assistance in Criminal Matters as amended by the Additional Protocol to the European Convention on Mutual Assistance in Criminal Matters of 20 April 1959 as well as notifications

[5] Article 22, European Convention on Mutual Assistance in Criminal Matters, publication in the SK OJ, no. 550/1992, Coll.; Additional Protocol to the European Convention on Mutual Assistance in Criminal Matters of 20 April 1959 publication in the SK OJ, no. 12/1997, Coll.

[6] Law No. 300/2005, Coll., Criminal Code.

[7] Law No. 301/2005, Coll. Code of Criminal Procedure, as amended.

delivered pursuant to Article 22 of the UN Convention against Transnational Organised Crime of 15 November 2000, etc.

Criminal records on persons finally convicted by a court as well as any other notifications of a court are kept there for 100 years from the date of birth of the person concerned.

Under current Slovak law, a legal person cannot commit a criminal offence. There is no centralised register of administrative sanctions imposed on legal persons. Public bodies keep registrers of the sanctions that they have imposed (Ministry of Finance, Ministry of Environment, territorial self-governing bodies etc). There is no separate register for convictions of minors, but the specific data are registered and kept in the register of previous convictions. There is no separate register of infringements of traffic regulations (criminal offences). The local traffic police (within the police force) keep registrers of administrative sanctions imposed for violations of traffic regulations within respective districts according to the address of a driver. Registration of criminal convictions is uniform.

The registration of criminal convictions is made according to the names of convicted persons and not according to the criminal offences. The data on criminal offences may be obtained from judicial statistics. Pursuant to the Criminal Code, criminal acts are divided into several groups as follows: criminal offences against life and health (Chapter I), against freedom and human dignity (Chapter II), against family and youth (Chapter III), against property (Chapter IV), economic criminal offences (Chapter V), generally dangerous and against the environment (Chapter VI), against the Republic (Chapter VII), against order in public affairs (Chapter VIII), against other rights and freedoms (Chapter IX), against conscription, civil service, service in the armed forces and defence of the country (Chapter X), military criminal offences (Chapter XI) and against peace and humanity (Chapter XII).

The Criminal Code knows eleven types of sanctions. Some of them may also be imposed cumulatively:

a) sentence of deprivation of liberty;
b) house arrest;
c) mandatory community work;
d) pecuniary punishment;
e) forfeiture/confiscation of property;
f) forfeiture/confiscation of a thing;
g) disqualification from a professional activity;

h) prohibition of abode;
i) deprivation of titles of honours and awards;
j) deprivation of a military or other rank;
k) sentence of banishment.

The Criminal Code foresees the possibility of conditional suspension of a conviction imposing deprivation of liberty or pecuniary punishment of juveniles. Often, sanctions imposed with a conditional suspension of their execution are perceived to be another type of sentence compared to the actual sanction imposed without conditional suspension.

The database described above is called 'criminal records', it has been created in electronic form and it is managed by a special unit within the General Prosecutor's Office of the Slovak Republic. The operation of the criminal records is governed by the Act on Criminal Records.[8]

The records are kept on the basis of the names of the persons concerned. The application for an extract or for a copy of the criminal record as well as the registry of convicted persons includes 16 categories of data about every person and the following data are included: first name, second name, date of birth, birth identification number (any citizen born in Slovakia is given a birth identification number), sex, nationality, ID number or passport number (for foreigners), permanent residence address (place where a citizen is registered by the police as resident), father's name and surname, and mother's name, surname and maiden name.

Any government body has the duty to inform the criminal records about any change of name or surname of a person over the age of 15 made under special regulation. If no data are found on such a person in the criminal records then the General Prosecutor's Office shall keep such notification in a special register with the view to make the appropriate changes to the names of persons kept in the criminal records register in the future, in accordance with the legal status. If required for the fulfilment of his duties the General Prosecutor's Office may obtain data from other registrers, such as the citizens' register, ID register, travel documents register and from the register of births, marriages and deaths, by means of an IT device.

[8] Law No. 311/1999, Coll., as amended by the Act no. 48/2002, Coll., Act no. 418/2002, Coll. and Act 530/2004, Coll.

1.3 Criminal record extracts

The data from criminal records can be used for criminal proceedings, administrative proceedings and for security checks (i.e. to prove that a person does not have a criminal record) to prove the person's reliability.

Copies of criminal records are made available to prosecutors in charge of criminal proceedings wherever they so request. To the police force, it is delivered for the purposes of deciding on a foreigner's application for a residence permit, pursuant to a special regulation. A copy of a person's criminal record is also provided to the Office of the President of the Slovak Republic in proceedings for an application for a pardon. Upon its request, a copy is sent to the Ministry of Justice in proceedings where an individual complains of administrative illegality. Copies of criminal records can be obtained for purposes of recruitment by the following government bodies or their armed units: the Slovak Information Service (intelligence agency), the National Security Office (protection of classified information), Military Intelligence, the Ministry of Interior, the Ministry of Justice and the Ministry of Transport, Posts and Telecommunications.

On the basis of international treaties by which the Slovak Republic is bound, and subject to legally defined terms, the General Prosecutor's Office may issue copies and extracts of criminal records as well as other information and send them to the judicial authorities of the contracting parties upon their request where such information is necessary for the purposes of a criminal matter. The extent of the information provided to foreign judicial authorities is identical to what is provided to the Slovak national authorities in similar cases (in accordance with Article 13 of the European Convention on Mutual Assistance in Criminal Matters).

The General Prosecutor's Office issues copies, extracts and other information from criminal records that is necessary for a criminal matter if so requested by a Eurojust national member or by a person acting on behalf of the applicant under special regulation.

A copy of a person's own criminal record is issued upon his/her application; verification of the applicant's identity has to be stated in the application. The copy contains the following information: data on every conviction of the person concerned (including spent convictions and erased convictions), on the length of a sentence, on execution of protective measures and on convictions considered as spent upon a court's decision or pursuant to a law; information on a court's or on the prosecutor's final decision to conditionally discontinue criminal prosecution as well as on their final decision to approve extra-judicial settlement. Data on final convictions of Slovak Republic nationals (or persons permanently residing in the Slovak republic territory) from criminal records sent by foreign courts are also included in the copy of criminal records.

An extract from criminal records is issued upon a person's written application and verification of the person's identity has to be stated in the application. Upon their request, the extract is also provided to the courts and other authorities (pursuant to special regulations) for the purposes of judicial proceedings in other than criminal matters. The following information is included in the extract of criminal records: any sentences that have not been spent including information on the length of sentences imposed, and protective measures and appropriate restrictions, unless a perpetrator is regarded by the law as not having been convicted. No information on final conditional discontinuance of criminal prosecution is stated in the extract from criminal records.

The judgments of foreign courts are included in the extract if they were executed in the Slovak Republic in accordance with an international treaty by which the Slovak Republic is bound and if they have not been expunged. An application for an extract from criminal records may also be filed from abroad – in the Slovak Republic Embassy which will verify the data contained in the application.

Pursuant to special regulations, individuals pay a fee for verification by municipal authorities or by notary of data when applying for a copy or for an extract of criminal records as well as for the issue of a copy or an extract from criminal records. Moreover, further changes have been made in the legal order of the Slovak Republic that either directly or indirectly influence the operation the Criminal Register. There are 230 generally binding legal rules (including international treaties and implementing regulations) where the Criminal Register is mentioned. Through numerous legal rules, the obligation is imposed on citizens to submit a copy or an extract from the Criminal Register (mostly in connection with the need to prove a person's suitability by a statement/certificate stating that he/she has no criminal record).

In several legal rules the copy or extract from the Criminal Register is considered as the only document which can prove the integrity of a natural person. However, these documents only prove whether or not a person was sentenced by a court or whether criminal proceedings against him/her have been conditionally discontinued, or whether conciliation has been approved concerning an act he/she committed, or whether a foreign court has notified Slovak authorities of a sentence against the person in question. The individual's integrity or reliability/trustworthiness is examined also on the basis of other different materials and information and does not merely result from the criminal records information. The fact should be taken into consideration that the Slovak legal order defines the notion of integrity/probity only for the purpose of a specific law/Act. There is no uniform definition for this notion; as a result, it contains various connotations. For example, an individual carrying out certain legal professions is not deemed incorrupt (without a criminal record) even if his/her conviction has been expunged a long time ago (so-called zero tolerance principle). However, a person is considered blameless if he/she has not been convicted of a criminal act related to a certain professional activity or vocation even though he/she has been convicted of an extremely serious crime.

A citizen is entitled/has the right to apply for a copy or an extract of his/her criminal records, with no obligation to state the purpose of the application (e.g. when applying for a new job and if a new employer requires such information). This way, it is often the case that a business entity in the private sector gains more information on a job applicant than it should have on the basis of privacy protection. This is also the case for foreign businesses to which Slovak nationals apply for seasonal work. The broad and benevolent approach to the content of criminal records copies is dangerous and sometimes clashes with a citizen's right to protect his/her privacy.

Despite several investments made since 1999 to improve technical equipment, the Criminal Register is still overloaded as a result of the legal regulation on citizens' obligation to prove their integrity by means of copies or extracts from criminal records. Annually, more than 635,000 extracts and 294,000 copies from the Criminal Register are issued, and more than one million documents are processed.

Since 1999, the technical equipment of the Criminal Register has been significantly improved and important progress has been made. In the majority of cases, the information exchange is carried out via electronic channels between authorised domestic and foreign institutions. In the near future, finalisation of the establishment of direct electronic interconnection systems between district prosecution offices may be expected with a view to enabling citizens to submit their applications addressed to the Criminal Register.

The purpose of the Criminal Registry has been and still is to keep files on individuals who have been finally sentenced by the courts, on the criminal acts they committed, on the sanctions imposed and on the length of sentence. After 2000, data on valid sentences imposed by foreign courts and recognised by the Slovak court's decision are gradually being included. Also included are data resulting from foreign courts' notifications on valid convictions of Slovak nationals or on valid convictions of persons permanently residing in the Slovak territory, as well as data on the conditional discontinuance of criminal prosecution and on conciliation that may be decided not only by a court but also by a prosecutor. Currently there is a requirement to broaden the subject of the files to be used by other Member States as well.

1.4 The transnational exchange of criminal record information

These are extracts also used for the purpose of transnational exchanges of information. On the basis of international agreements by which the Slovak Republic is bound, the General Prosecutor's Office issues extracts, copies and other information from the register of previous convictions upon requests made by the contracting parties' judicial authorities and pursuant to the terms stipulated by law. This information is used for the purposes of criminal proceedings and is issued to the same extent as if it was provided to the national bodies in similar cases. For example, Article 13 of the European Convention on Mutual Assistance in Criminal Matters as amended by the Additional Protocol to the European Convention on Mutual Assistance in Criminal Matters of 20 April 1959. It also applies to bilateral agreements, e.g. the agreements with Afghanistan, Bulgaria, Cyprus, Greece, Yemen, Cuba, Hungary, Poland, Syria, Italy and Vietnam. Pursuant to the Constitution of the Slovak Republic, any state authority (in contrast to citizens) may carry out only the acts expressly permitted by law. Outside criminal proceedings provision of the information from the registry of previous convictions to foreign authorities is not regulated by the laws in force.

The Slovak Republic is a party to the following international agreements on legal assistance:

- Notification of the Federal Ministry of Foreign Affairs that on 20 April 1959 the European Convention on Mutual Assistance in Criminal Matters has been agreed at Strasbourg. Article 13(1) notes that the requested party shall send the copies and information from the register of previous convictions to the contracting party upon request by judicial authorities of the party where they are necessary for criminal proceedings to the same extent as this information is provided to its own judicial authorities in similar cases.[9]

- In one case, the bilateral agreement on legal assistance expressly defines 'the mutual provision of copies from the Register of Previous Convictions' (with Bulgaria); in another case (with Poland) it is rather ambiguous as the word 'extracts' is used in the heading of the agreement but in the text the phrase used is 'full information from the Register of Previous Convictions'.
- Regulation of the Ministry of Foreign Affairs on the Agreement between the Czechoslovak Socialist Republic and the Bulgarian Socialist Republic on Legal Assistance and on Regulation of Relationships in the Civil, Family and Penal Matters: 'Copies from the register of previous convictions. The contracting parties' authorities responsible for registration of penal convictions shall provide copies from the register of previous convictions to the judicial authorities of another Party upon their request.'[10]
- Regulation of the Ministry of Foreign Affairs on the signing of the Agreement between the Czechoslovak Socialist Republic and the People's Republic of Poland on Legal Assistance and on Regulation of Legal Relationships in Civil, Family, Work and Penal Matters. Article 85 states: 'Extracts from the register of previous convictions. Upon request, the parties shall send full information from the register of previous convictions to each other concerning the nationals of another party as well as the information on subsequent decisions concerning these convictions, if such conviction is subject to entry into the register pursuant to the legal order of that party the court of which had rendered such decision.'[11]
- Notification of the Federal Ministry of Foreign Affairs on the signing of the Agreement between the Czechoslovak Socialist Republic and the Republic of Italy on Legal Assistance in Civil and Penal Matters. Article 29 states: 'Extracts from the register of previous convictions. Upon request, one party shall send extracts from the register of previous convictions to another party for the

[9] Article 13, and Article 22, European Convention on Mutual Assistance in Criminal Matters, publication in the SK OJ, no. 550/1992, Coll. Additional Protocol to the European Convention on Mutual Assistance in Criminal Matters of 20 April 1959 publication in the SK OJ, no. 12/1997, Coll.

[10] Article 88 No. 3/1978 Coll. [11] Article 85 No.42/1989 Coll.

purposes of criminal proceedings within which legal assistance may be requested.'[12]

- Notification of the Federal Ministry of Foreign Affairs on the signing of the Agreement between the Czechoslovak Socialist Republic and the People's Democratic Republic of Yemen on Legal Assistance in Civil and Penal Matters. Article 51 states: 'Extracts from the register of previous convictions. Upon request, the Parties shall send the extracts from the register of previous convictions to each other.'[13]
- Notification of the Federal Ministry of Foreign Affairs on the signing of the Agreement between the Czechoslovak Socialist Republic and the People's Republic of Hungary on Legal Assistance and Regulation of Legal Relationships in Civil, Family and Penal Matters.[14]
- Regulation of the Ministry of Foreign Affairs on the Agreement between the Czechoslovak Socialist Republic and the Syrian Arab Republic on Legal Assistance in Civil, Family and Penal Matters.[15]
- Regulation of the Ministry of Foreign Affairs on the Agreement between the Czechoslovak Socialist Republic and the Socialist Republic of Vietnam on Legal Assistance in Civil and Penal Matters.[16]
- Regulation of the Ministry of Foreign Affairs on the Agreement between the Czechoslovak Socialist Republic and the Republic of Greece on Legal Assistance in Civil and Penal Matters.[17]
- Regulation of the Ministry of Foreign Affairs on the Agreement between the Czechoslovak Socialist Republic and the Republic of Cyprus on Legal Assistance in Civil and Penal Matters.[18]
- Regulation of the Ministry of Foreign Affairs on the Agreement between the Czechoslovak Socialist Republic and the Democratic Republic of Afghanistan on Legal Assistance in Civil and Penal Matters.[19]
- Regulation of the Ministry of Foreign Affairs on the Agreement between the Czechoslovak Socialist Republic and the Republic of Cuba on Mutual Legal Assistance in Civil, Family and Penal Matters.[20]

[12] Article 29 No. 508/1990 Coll. [13] Article 51 No. 6/1990 Coll.
[14] Article 92 No. 63/1990 Coll. [15] Article 11 No. 8/1986 Coll.
[16] Article 79, para. 2 No. 98/1984 Coll. [17] Article 48 Law. 102/1983 Coll.
[18] Article 47 No. 96/1983 Coll. [19] Article 51 No. 44/1983 Coll.
[20] Article 79 para. 2 No. 80/1981 Coll.

1.5 *Proposal for new legal regulation*

Having looked at the current state of affairs, the need for new legal regulation seems to be justified since amendment and completion of the law/Act in force does not seem sufficient.

A proposal is to be tabled to entrust the Criminal Register of the General Prosecutor's Office with the responsibilities of the central authority pursuant to the Council Decision on the exchange of information extracted from the criminal record,[21] i.e. with transmission of data from its own files to other Member States on its own initiative or upon reception and handling of requests for such information made by competent authorities of the Member States.

Legal regulation is only beginning to reach some degree of uniformity on the contents of criminal records files in the Member States. Nevertheless, within the fight against crime and its most extreme forms, there is an imperative need for efficient information exchange on perpetrators of criminal activities. Pursuant to international agreements and treaties, the information from the registries is provided to the competent foreign authorities to the same extent as to the prosecuting and adjudicating bodies of the Slovak Republic. However, the registries are sending only information on convictions to the central authorities of other Member States.

A bill is to be tabled stipulating that both the extract and copy from the Criminal Register should have the nature of an official document so that penal protection could apply in order to prevent falsifications/forgery or misuse. Having regard to the purpose of data transmission from the Criminal Register, a proposal has been made to change the procedures substantially.

An extract will be issued from the Criminal Register to a citizen upon his/her application and the payment of a fee. While submitting his/her application, the citizen has no obligation to state the purpose for which his/her application is made. The conditions under which a citizen may inspect his/her own criminal file are modified as well. It can be reasonably assumed that a citizen will apply for an extract primarily as a result of a legal obligation imposed on him/her in order to prove his/her

[21] Council Decision 2005/876/JHA of 21 November 2005 on the exchange of information extracted from the criminal record, 13994/04, 4 November 2004, Articles 1 to 3. Council Decision on the exchange of information extracted from the criminal record – Manual of Procedure, 6397/4/06, 28 September 2006.

integrity. However, he/she will not be allowed to prove his/her integrity by means of a copy from the Criminal Register.

Neither the state nor its authorities may be deprived of their right to execute their powers of protecting public order and their duty to protect the security of the State and its citizens. It is also in the interest of transparency in public life that only individuals that have not been convicted may carry out professional responsibilities and professional positions as defined by the law. For this reason the proposal has been made that only legally designated state authorities and legally designated professional associations should be authorised to request a copy of criminal records and solely for legally defined purposes. The state authorities, as well as public administration authorities, shall have the right to request an extract from criminal records for the purposes of a special procedure. It is hoped that this proposed bill will prevent the possible misuse and dissemination of personal data contained in the files of the Criminal Register.

The proposed bill also responds to the government's Resolution on the establishment of a uniform contact points network in the Slovak Republic.[22] The aim of this network is to simplify intra-EU market access for businesses via the creation of centres where all administrative procedures in the field of provision of services will be brought together. The proposed bill contains separate provisions on the activity of the Criminal Register in relation to other Member States in the field of providing information from its files. If the Criminal Register was given the status of a central authority, it could have the right to issue such information on its own initiative to other EU competent authorities concerning other EU nationals, to receive information on convictions of Slovak nationals in other Member States and to handle other issues falling within the responsibility of these central authorities. In this way a legal framework could be defined to give the Criminal Register the right to provide information on the basis of international treaties and on the basis of Council Decisions or decisions by other EU authorities.

The proposed bill regulates the procedures to be followed by the Criminal Register, by applicants, by entitled and competent authorities in all respects concerning the maintenance and provision of criminal record data. The proposed bill also contains amendments to all laws that

[22] Government's Resolution No. 324 of 19 April 2006 on the draft conception of establishment of a uniform contact points network in the Slovak Republic.

require a citizen to submit a copy of criminal records for the purpose of proving his/her integrity.

The bill complies with the Constitution of the Slovak Republic, the constitutional laws, the international treaties which the Slovak Republic has signed and with existing legislation while it is in step with the laws of the EC and the EU.

1.6 Relation to the European Criminal Record

The Slovakian Criminal Register represents an exhaustive base of data collected over more than 150 years. Pursuant to the effective legal regulation, the Slovak General Prosecutor's Office keeps information about different convicted individuals together with a number of their personal data so that a convicted person shall be unambiguously identified. These data are permanently monitored and changes of personal data are updated in cooperation with other state bodies (changes of name, surname, birth identification number, permanent residence address, nationality, data on parents etc.). To keep the database updated, concerted cooperation of a large number of national government authorities and bodies is needed in order to permanently collect great amounts of protected personal data.

The Criminal Register is used by numerous government bodies that are so entitled pursuant to a law including security and intelligence units which verify a person's reliability in the event that he/she applies for employment in such units. Many national state authorities use criminal records for the purposes of their own activities provided that they shall keep confidential what information they do obtain. The law provides that data on certain persons (e.g. the President of the Republic within the term of his/her office) shall not be provided to anybody. Prohibitions in the performance of a professional activity are not kept in the Criminal Register if such penalties were not imposed as a result of criminal proceedings but within either administrative or civil proceedings.

Pursuant to the Act on Register of Criminal Convictions[23] official forms (issued by the General Prosecutor's Office) are necessary for an application for copies or extracts of criminal records as well as for the transmission of these data between courts, different prosecution offices and the General Prosecutor's Office. This means that the Slovak judicial

[23] Section 9, para. 5, Law No. 311/1999, Coll., on register of criminal convictions.

authorities have no direct access to the entries in the criminal records. Instead they need to send a specific application to the General Prosecutor's Office of the Slovak Republic that manages the criminal records. In this way the General Prosecutor's Office prevents unjustified inspection of criminal records.

2. Proposed new legislation

New legislation will create statutory conditions for the collection, processing, protection of data and provision of information on individuals finally convicted by courts in criminal proceedings, on persons subject to conditional cease of criminal prosecution, on persons under approved conciliation and subsequent discontinuation of criminal prosecution, and on subsequent decisions and measures related to these decisions by courts or prosecutors.

For Slovak nationals and permanent residents of Slovakia the imposition of such decisions and convictions by foreign courts, including courts of other Member States, is immaterial. Decisions and convictions of foreign courts, including courts in other Member States, are treated in the same manner as equivalent measures and convictions imposed by Slovak courts. In contrast, for foreigners, only a Slovak court's judgment of conviction is included in Slovak records. Final conditional discontinuation of criminal prosecution, approval with conciliation and discontinuance of criminal prosecution (decisions taken by a prosecutor of the Slovak Prosecution Service or by a court of the Slovak Republic) do not have the nature of a judgment of conviction, but it is necessary to enter this information in the Register so that the judicial bodies can use it for the purpose of possible new criminal prosecutions of the same individual and for examining an individual's 'integrity' (by the competent authorities).

Approval of confessions and agreements on guilt and punishment have the legal value of a judgment of conviction. Conditional discontinuance of criminal prosecution also means conditional discontinuance of criminal prosecution of an accused who gives assistance to the process of justice.

The decision of a court or prosecutor becomes final if eligible persons fail to apply for a remedial measure within due time or if a remedial measure is dismissed by a competent authority. However, the Code of Criminal Procedure also recognises extraordinary relief by means of which a final decision may be cancelled or altered. Furthermore, changes may also be made as a result of the right of the President of the Slovak Republic to grant a pardon or amnesty or as a result of the release of a convict from serving his/her term or of suspension of – or conditional release from – serving a sentence of deprivation of liberty. For these reasons, any related decisions and measures are subject to entry into the records as well.

Statutory conditions are being created allowing the Criminal Register to process other facts – but only if so provided by a law, international treaty or special rule, i.e. legal act of the European Communities and European Union. There are reasonable grounds to suppose that measures are to be taken within the fight against international organised crime, terrorism and extremism.

Entry of data into the Criminal Register is not an end in itself. The objective is the use of these data primarily in the activities of prosecuting and judicial bodies with the aim of fighting and preventing crime. Provision of data concerns not only the authorities of the Slovak Republic but also the central authorities of other Member States and the authorities of third states if so provided by an international treaty by which the Slovak Republic is bound. In the area of crime prevention, it is primarily aimed at the perpetrators of extremely serious criminal activities.

The data extracted from the criminal records are also necessary in proceedings on administrative infractions. The need for such information may also not be excluded from other kinds of administrative proceedings or within proceedings governed by Code of Civil Procedure.

There are a number of legal rules imposing the obligation to prove the blamelessness or reliability (security checks) of natural persons by means of data extracted from the Criminal Register. In this way, the legal framework is created for a prosecutorial authority to discharge such task/responsibility.

Special provisions are proposed in relation to an authority that will keep the data and ensure their protection against destruction, theft, loss, damage, unauthorised access, alteration or unauthorised dissemination.

The Register of Criminal Records is a special organisational unit within the General Prosecutor's Office and it carries out these tasks pursuant to the Act on Public Prosecution Service.[24] The requirements resulting from the Council Decision on the exchange of information

[24] Article 40, para. 2, (d) Law No. 153/2001, Coll., on public prosecution service.

extracted from the criminal record represent grounds for more detailed definition of its status. The Register of Criminal Records of the General Prosecutor's Office should discharge the responsibilities of the central authority receiving and transmitting to competent authorities of other Member States any information about convictions and related decisions or measures.

For a long time the Register of Criminal Records has carried out these tasks upon a request from the authorities of the Slovak Republic. At the moment, this unit is built and supported in such a manner that it can fulfil the new task much better than any new office that might be created.

It would be logical to foresee persons and bodies to whom the data extracted from the Criminal Register would be available solely upon authorisation, as well as persons and bodies with direct rights of access of data from the Register. From a Slovak point of view the former category should include natural persons and bodies authorised by law to receive data on convictions. Current limitations of access for bodies authorised by law could apply also to access to data from the Register.

As for courts and judicial bodies of foreign countries, the information extracted from the Criminal Register shall be transmitted on the basis of an international treaty. Pursuant to a special rule, the information extracted from the Criminal Register will be provided to a central authority of other Member States. Any person or body can request data but the data will be exclusively available to persons and bodies included in the restrictive list stated in the established instrument of the Criminal Register. The Register will reject requests from unauthorised individuals and entities.

It would be reasonable to suggest changes in the contents of the criminal record and the formal elements of the documents by means of which the courts, the prosecution service or the competent EU body transmit to the Criminal Register data on criminal acts.

The Criminal Register carries out its activities in accordance with the Act on Personal Data Protection as amended and with the Convention for the Protection of Individuals with regard to Automatic Processing of Personal Data.[25] While performing its activities, it can use the information and communication technologies and within the extent necessary to fulfil its tasks it also may obtain data extracted from the register of

[25] Law No. 482/2002, Coll., on personal data protection, as amended. Convention for the Protection of Individuals with regard to Automatic Processing of Personal Data (publication in the SK OJ, no. 49/2001, Coll.).

citizens, the ID register, the travel documents register and register of births, marriages and deaths. Thus, the possible use of technical means as well as information sources is regulated. However, any information is based on the decisions issued by courts and prosecutors.

Information is transmitted to the Criminal Register via several documents:

- information from the court on conviction and sentence imposed and information from the court about the course or alteration of the execution of a sentence;
- a report by a court or by the prosecution service about conditional discontinuance of criminal prosecution and an additional record on the course of any probationary period;
- a report from a court or the prosecution service on approval of extra-judicial settlement (conciliation) and on discontinuance of criminal prosecution.

These documents are sent to the Criminal Register from the courts and the prosecution offices that have decided cases at first instance and they are also sent after any appeal proceedings or the grant of extraordinary relief or if an amnesty applies to the convict or after a pardon granted to him/her.

The information transmitted from a central authority of another Member State is entered into files in accordance with the Council Decision on the exchange of information extracted from the criminal record as well as the foreign court's decision on the conviction of a Slovak national or on the conviction of an individual permanently residing in the Slovak Republic if that results from an international treaty by which the Slovak Republic is bound.

There has been a proposal to list expressly the documents to be delivered by courts and prosecution offices to the Criminal Register in order to remove any possible doubts or confusion about the precise documentation to be transmitted. There has also been a proposal to impose an obligation on the courts and prosecution service to deliver the documents immediately so that there is timely updating of files. If, within the time limit imposed by the Criminal Code or Code of Criminal Procedure, a court or a prosecution service fails to comply with the obligation to provide information whether a convicted or accused person has demonstrated good behaviour during the probationary period it is proposed that the Criminal Register should request an additional report. This proposal aims to protect an individual who has fulfilled the statutory conditions of the probationary period but no decision has been made about him/her or because no certificate of good conduct was sent to the Criminal Register (irrespective of the reason). There is one more reason for including such a regulation: Article 92, para. 2 Law No. 300/2005, Coll., Criminal Code has linked erasure with the execution of sanctions of all types except for a sentence of deprivation of liberty. Another proposal concerns the imposition of an obligation on the register of births, marriages and deaths to inform the Criminal Register about any change of name or surname of any criminally liable individual where such change was made pursuant to the Act on Name and Surname;[26] the same applies to the obligation to provide information about the death of such individual. If such individual is not found in the files, the information shall be withdrawn from the files.

Data concerning natural persons are maintained on file for a period of one hundred years starting from the date of the subject's birth. As criminality amongst the elderly is low, files kept on the elderly are of minor significance. However, data can be erased provided that it refers to final judgments that have been cancelled within subsequent proceedings as well as data on deceased persons. These documents can be kept in archives or withdrawn. Any data from the archives are provided upon written request to authorised individuals only.

According to the proposal submitted, the extract from criminal records is expected to be the only document issued to a citizen upon his/her written application and payment of a fee (as determined by law). By means of an extract from the criminal records, a citizen shall not prove his/her 'integrity' but merely whether or not he/she has been convicted and if so whether or not the conviction is still in effect at the time of issue of the extract. The concept of 'integrity' shall not be equivalent to the concept of 'not convicted'. In his/her application for issue of an extract from the Register, a citizen will not be obliged to state the purpose for it. It is expected that, in the majority of cases, the obligation to submit the extract will be imposed by a legal rule (e.g. a procedure conducted by a state administrative or self-governing body, such as a job application); it is, however, possible that a citizen might apply on his/her own initiative. Only the personal data identifying the applicant can be requested in the application. A citizen will also have the

[26] Section 6, para. 1, of the National Council of the Slovak Republic Law No. 300/1993, Coll., on name and surname, as amended.

right to apply for an extract from the Criminal Register by means of an authorized person.

Because of its importance – and given the difference that a 'non-convicted' mark can make on an individual's chances for certain types of employment – the record should have the nature of an official document and, as such, it should be legally protected in accordance with the definition of the criminal offence of forgery and fraudulent alteration of an official document, official enclosure and official mark as stipulated in Section 352 of the Criminal Code.

The bill regulates differently the procedure for verifying the validity of data stated in the application for an extract from the criminal records where such an application is made by a Slovak national and where it is made by a foreigner. In the procedure for issuing an extract from the criminal records, only original documents may be used. Only the employees of the Public Prosecution Service are allowed to verify data, i.e. persons who are allocated to the criminal record register within the organisational structure of the Public Prosecution Service as well as employees of the district, regional and Military prosecution offices and the General Prosecutor's Office. This way, the number of persons who are authorised to receive and verify the applications within the whole Public Prosecution Service is limited. If an application is submitted to the register of births, marriages and deaths or in the Slovak Embassy in a foreign country then the verification of the data included falls within the responsibility of those institutions.

The electronic scanning of an identification document may be used within the regime of the prosecution bodies while verifying the data or finding the applicant's file. If applications for an extract from the criminal register are transmitted electronically from other prosecution units, they shall be kept in the special files of that unit where the application was submitted; after the expiration of three years from the date of application they shall be withdrawn from the files. The extract from the criminal records shall contain any conviction that has not been erased including information on the length of the sentences imposed, protective measures and appropriate restrictions, unless the perpetrator is considered as not convicted upon the court's decision or pursuant to a law.

The extract from the Criminal Register may also be issued upon a request by a court or the prosecution service for a purpose other than penal proceedings, e.g. for the needs of court proceedings in civil, commercial or administrative matters and it may also be issued upon a request from a public authority for the purpose of a proceeding on administrative delicts. The extract from the Criminal Register may also be issued in other cases, e.g. for the needs of administrative proceedings if a special law so provides. In such a case, the precise name of the requesting authority and the purpose of the request must be stated in the application. On the basis of a Regulation of the European Parliament together with the Council on Services in the Internal Market, an administrative authority should arrange for all necessary procedures and formalities including an extract from the Criminal Register when issuing a business licence. This Regulation has been elaborated by means of Government Resolution (no. 324 of 19 April 2006) and the bill allows for its implementation. Within the tabled regulation, both personal data protection and prevention to causing unnecessary difficulties to the citizens are guaranteed.

Whilst the extract from the criminal records will include any conviction that has not been executed nor expunged, the copy of the criminal record will contain all significant information irrespective of whether it has or has not been expunged. In addition to the decisions on guilt and sentencing, or on approval of agreement on guilt and sentencing, and on related data, the Register will contain data of convictions on a court's or prosecutor's final judgment, on conditional discontinuance of criminal prosecution, on conditional discontinuance of criminal prosecution of an accused who assists the process of justice, on the final decision of a court or prosecutor to approve conciliation, and on discontinuance of criminal prosecution. The Register will also contain data that have been issued by a foreign court, whose decision has been recognised by a Slovak court, on final convictions of Slovak nationals or of individuals permanently residing in Slovakia.

Information resulting from data sent by competent authorities of other Member States shall only be entered in the copy of the criminal record if it has the nature of data resulting from penal information sent by foreign courts whose decisions have been recognised by a Slovak court. No other information shall be stated in the copy of the criminal record other than that one permitted by law.

Individual citizens may request copies of their own records. It has been proposed that such authorisation should be granted only to legally designated authorities and for a purpose defined by law. The bill includes an exhaustive list of formalities to be complied with while applying for copy of the criminal record. A legally authorised body shall be obliged to inform in writing the Register of criminal convictions about the name and surname of the person that it has designated to apply for and receive the copy of the criminal record. This person shall be responsible for the verification of the data included in the application. An authorised employee of the Register will verify the authorisation of the application and the legality of the purpose for which the application was made. No purpose need be stated where the police, the National Security Agency and the Slovak Intelligence Service or Military Defence Intelligence Agency apply for a copy of the criminal record with the purpose of fulfilling tasks related to the protection of state security. There are several purposes for which an application for a copy of the criminal record might be submitted: criminal proceedings, protection of state security pursuant to special rules, as well as personnel affairs if so provided under separate law.

The Code of Criminal Procedure represents basic legal rules imposing directives and competencies of the prosecuting and judicial bodies. In addition, further state authorities as well as constitutional officials are so empowered within the scope of criminal proceedings. Pursuant to Article 103, para. 1(j) of the Constitution, the President of the Republic may grant pardons or reduce penalties imposed by the courts in criminal proceedings. The President is also empowered to expunge a sentence by means of an individual pardon or amnesty. The Minister of Justice has the power to file for an appellate review, to take a position with respect to an application for a decision on amnesty or pardon, to decide on the release of an offender from serving his/her term or its remainder if he/she is expected to be extradited or expelled, to decide on the extradition of an individual as well as on a motion to recognise and execute a foreign court's decision. There are also specific obligations and powers resulting from international treaties.

The Office of the President of the Republic discharges the powers of the President of the Slovak Republic. The tasks of the Minister of Justice are carried out by the respective departments of the Ministry. They are therefore authorised to apply to copies of criminal records for these purposes.

In order to enhance the fight against serious criminal activities the EU has established a special unit: Eurojust. The representative of the Slovak Republic at Eurojust (or his/her deputy acting on his/her behalf) is empowered to apply for a copy of the criminal record.[27]

A number of state authorities carry out their tasks under special rules while protecting state security and they perform their duties under

[27] Rules of procedure on the processing and protection of personal data at Eurojust. Text adopted unanimously by the College of Eurojust during the meeting of 21 October 2004 and approved by the Council on 24 February 2005, OJ C 68, 19 March 2005.

special regulations and by means of special forms and methods. Police units have special powers, e.g. in matters of immigration, in checking the reliability of holders of firearms or in providing services in the area of private security. The National Security Authority and the Military Defence Intelligence discharge duties within the area of state security protection and for that reason provision of information from the criminal records Register is deemed justified. Provision of copies of criminal records for official purposes to these state authorities represents only one of many means at their disposal for the effective discharge of responsibilities.

It is in the interest of the state and society in general that some functions defined by law are carried out only by individuals who have no criminal record. The principle of so-called zero tolerance results from separate laws and applies to the Slovak Constitutional Court's judges, judges of general courts, trainee prosecutors, prosecutors, persons discharging functions within state services, members of the police, the Slovak Intelligence Agency, judicial police and prison guards, railway police, professional troops of the Slovak armed forces, customs officials, notaries, officials carrying out execution proceedings or judicial executors, and advocates. Creation of a separate law regulating the status of a specific function is a basic precondition for the provision of a criminal record copy.

The bill is concerned with this legal status. It also allows the issue of a criminal record copy for the purpose of appointing a member of the Slovak Judicial Council when requested by the authorities that submit a list of candidates to the Slovak President, the Slovak National Council and the Slovak Government. Legal regulations that apply to the competitive appointment procedures and to withdrawal/removal procedures vary. For that reason it has been suggested that the authorities responsible for competitive appointment and removal procedures should be allowed to apply for copies of the criminal record.

A citizen shall not be denied his/her right to be informed about the contents of his/her own criminal record. The extract from the criminal register should primarily be issued for official purposes. Therefore, it has been suggested that citizens be given the right to inspect their own files. upon a written application and the payment of a relevant fee. The Register of criminal records may not refuse a citizen the ability to inspect his/her own files; it shall inform the applicant about the time and place of the inspection and an employee of the Criminal Register shall make a note in the application that the inspection of files was carried out.

The mutual exchange of information on convictions between Member States is regulated in the sections within the meaning of the Council Decision 2005/876/SVV of 21 November 2005 on exchange of the information extracted from the criminal record. The Register of criminal convictions of the General Prosecutor's Office of the Slovak Republic is the central authority to implement this Decision – and it is a partner for central authorities of other Member States. The Register of criminal convictions provides information on its own initiative to central authorities of other Member States about citizens finally convicted by Slovakian courts within criminal proceedings. In the event that a convict is a national of several Member States the Criminal Register shall send the information to all of them. Information is sent in an official form, immediately after entry into the Register and in the Slovak language (unless agreed otherwise).

Upon written request, the Register is empowered to provide the information mentioned to the central authority of other Member States. Information is transmitted for the purposes of criminal proceedings and for other proceedings to a judicial authority, to an administrative authority as well as to the individual concerned, who has or had permanent residence in Slovakia or in the territory of the requesting state or who is or was a national of that state. Information is transmitted via central authorities not by means of direct contact. The proposed procedures are in line with the requirements of Council Decision no. 2005/876/SVV of 21 November 2005 on the exchange of the information extracted from the criminal record.

The Criminal Register shall request a central authority of another Member State for information on conviction upon a written request by a Slovak national or by an individual who has permanent residence in Slovakia under the following conditions: that the information concerns the applicant or court or prosecution service or it concerns proceedings other than criminal or public administration or administrative proceedings or proceedings by an authorised body for the purposes of criminal proceedings or for the needs of state security or for the purposes of employment. In this way the reciprocity principle is realised.

The bill transposes the legal instruments of the European Communities and European Union, i.e. the European Convention on Mutual Assistance in Criminal Matters, the Additional Protocol to the European Convention on Mutual Assistance in Criminal Matters, the Convention on Mutual Assistance in Criminal Matters between the Member States, the Convention for the Protection of Individuals with regard to Automatic Processing of Personal Data, the Council Decision establishing Eurojust for the purposes of the fight against extremely serious crimes and the Council Decision on the exchange of information extracted from the criminal register.[28]

The Register of criminal convictions, contains information that has been collected since the creation of Slovakia as an independent nation state. After the establishment of the Slovak Republic, information that had been kept in the Czech Criminal Register has been also included. This information concerns Slovak nationals convicted by Czech courts and a legal framework was created to transmit information on such convictions. Objectively, the Register of criminal convictions is not expected to be able to handle each application by the date of entry into force of the new law pursuant to the current regulation. For that reason, it has been provided that applications made before the date of entry into force of the new law shall be handled within the new law's regime.

It has been proposed that the fee for issuing data from the Criminal Register should be modified. A fee must be paid by any person submitting an application to the register of births, marriages and deaths or to the Slovak Embassy. A special fee has been proposed for the inspection of a copy of the criminal record, the issue of an extract from criminal records, for providing data from archives and for issuing a copy of the criminal record to authorities not owned by a state, i.e. to the Notary Association, the Association of Judicial Executors and the Slovak Bar Chamber. State authorities of the Slovak Republic shall be exempt from fees when applying for a copy of the minimal record or for data from archives. Judicial authorities of foreign countries and central authorities of the Member States shall also be exempt from fees. Exchange of the information extracted from the Criminal Register is carried out on the reciprocity basis resulting from international treaties by which the Slovak Republic is bound or from the decisions of the competent EU authorities.

[28] European Convention on Mutual Assistance in Criminal Matters, publication SK OJ, no. 550/1992, Coll.; Additional Protocol to the European Convention on Mutual Assistance in Criminal Matters of 20 April 1959 publication SK OJ, no. 12/1997, Coll.; Convention of 29 May 2000 on Mutual Assistance in Criminal Matters between the Member States, OJ C 197, 12 July 2000; Convention for the Protection of Individuals with regard to Automatic Processing of Personal Data publication SK OJ, no. 49/2001, Coll; Council Decision 2002/187/SVV of 28 February 2002 establishing Eurojust for the purposes of the fight against extremely serious crimes; Council Decision no. 2003/659/SVV of 18 June, 2003 OJ EU L 245, 23 September 2003; Council Decision 2005/876/SV of 21 November 2005 on the exchange of the information extracted from the criminal register OJ L 322, 9 December 2005.

The bill also addresses the use of the information and communication technologies between the Register of criminal convictions and competent authorities of the Slovak Republic or competent foreign authorities. The bill imposes an obligation on the General Prosecutor's Office to arrange for the use of uniform forms for the applications and for transmission of data.

The proposed alteration to be made to the Slovak National Council's Act on Judicial Fees and Fee for Extract from the Criminal Register as amended[29] is a response to the newly introduced rule for inspection of the copy of criminal register by the person concerned and in response to the introduction of provision of data from archives. Regulation still has not been made with regard to the latter, although similar requests have already been handled. Primarily, such data have been necessary for the rehabilitation of offenders. It is expected that such data could be requested in the future as well.

It has been proposed that the new legislation should enter into force in such a way that adequate *vacantia legis* is allowed in order for its provisions to become familiar. It is expected that the new Act will enter into force at the end of 2007.

[29] Law No. 71/1992, Coll., on judicial fees and fee for extract from Criminal Register as amended.

14

The European Criminal Record in Spain

FRANCISCO JAVIER GARCÍA FERNÁNDEZ[1]

1. Introduction

Re-education and social rehabilitation of offenders are constitutional principles in Spain. The law also states that criminal records can never justify legal or social discrimination. In Spain criminal records mainly serve to determine penalties: their existence may aggravate penalties imposed on recidivists. They also serve to classify offenders, in access to some forms of employment, or in obtaining some authorisations, such as the right to carry guns. Criminal records that entail a criminal responsibility are included in the national criminal record and cancelled after a short period, compared to other jurisdictions, once the criminal liability has ended. Only judges have access to cancelled criminal records but those have no legal effect whatsoever.

Criminal records are not public. The law states that only the person concerned or his/her representatives and the judiciary can access criminal records in Spain. The constitutional court has also proclaimed this doctrine. No other person or institution has access to them. The current Spanish legal system and doctrine could accept the creation of a European register of criminal records only if the principles established to rule it were compatible with those governing the Spanish one, namely a register with a judicial character, with access limited to the judiciary and those concerned and cancellation of records after a reasonable period of time to facilitate and guarantee social rehabilitation of ex-offenders.

The creation of a European central register would ease and speed up judicial investigations in Europe enhancing security. It would also help

[1] The author is deeply indebted to the following persons for their invaluable cooperation to complete this chapter: Isabel Vevia (Deputy Director of International Judicial Cooperation at the Ministry of Justice), Eduardo de Urbano (magistrate at the Spanish *Tribunal Supremo*), Rubén Jiménez (Spanish judge at Eurojust), Pedro Romero (Head of the Spanish Register of criminal records) and Colonel Manuel Mingoranze.

to create a European 'judicial space' and finally have a positive impact on European integration. If the previous guarantees and aims were respected and a public information campaign to show its advantages was undertaken, then Spanish citizens and human rights activists might accept a European register with no major controversy.

2. Criminal records in Spain: the legal framework

In Spain, cancellation of criminal records is linked to the concept of rehabilitation. And rehabilitation is a constitutional mandate. Article 25(2) of the 1978 Constitution states that: 'all imprisonment sentences and all safety measures will be orientated to the re-education and social rehabilitation of offenders ... All offenders will fully enjoy the fundamental rights of this Chapter except those which are expressly limited by the sentence, the kind of penalty or the penal law.' Article 10 (2) declares that: 'the norms related to fundamental rights and constitutional freedoms will be construed in accordance with the Universal Declaration of Human Rights and other human rights treaties ratified by Spain.'

Without analysing the different conceptions applied to the purposes of penal sanctions, these precepts deal with two important issues: 'the goals of imprisonment and other security measures and the deprivation of rights that all penalties entail'.[2] Although there are several interpretations on Article 25(2),[3] commentators widely accept that this article establishes the orientation that penalties must follow in the Spanish criminal system: the re-education and social rehabilitation of offenders.

Article 73(2) of the general penal law[4] applies the constitutional principles and declares that 'criminal records can never justify legal or social discrimination'. This unequivocal statement can be debated as in Spain the end of penal responsibility does not do away with all the consequences of a crime[5] since criminal records are not cancelled once the penal liability ends. Indeed, some academics consider that some

[2] J. M. Serrano Alberca, *Comentarios a la Constitución*, 3rd edn (dir. Fernando Garrido Falla, Madrid: Civitas Ediciones, 2001), p. 601.

[3] Ibid., pp. 602–603; see also, M. Cobo del Rosal and M. Quintanar Diez, *Comentarios a la Constitución Española de 1978* (Vol. III, Edersa, Madrid, 1996–1997), p. 140 and following.

[4] *Ley Orgánica General Penitenciaria de 26 de septiembre de 1979.*

[5] See for instance Aránguez Sánchez who shares this criticism, in C. Aránguez Sánchez, *Comentarios al Código Penal* [headed by M. Cobo del Rosal] (Vol. IV, Granada: Edersa, 2000), p. 1183.

restrictions that criminal records provoke, especially those which are regulated by pre-constitutional norms, may be against Article 25(2) of the 1978 Constitution.[6]

In Spain there are many legal references to criminal records, among others the 1995 new Penal Code[7] and the Royal Decree of 23 July 1983 that regulates the central Register of criminal records.[8] Article 3 of the law for the protection of personal data 15/1999 of 13 December 1999, declares that a number of registers, among others the central Register of criminal convictions and persons in contempt (Register of criminal records) will follow their own regulations. In those cases, the law of personal data will apply to those aspects which are not covered by the criminal records rules. That means that the level of protection guaranteed by the Register of criminal records is considered as adequate.

Article 136 of the 1995 Penal Code establishes the following conditions for the cancellation of criminal records:

(a) Termination of the penal responsibility related to the aim of the penalty, clemency or pardon by official authority or by the injured party, or expiry of the sentence.[9]

[6] M. Cobo del Rosal and T. Vives Antón, *Derecho Penal. Parte general* (Valencia: Tirant lo Blanch, 1996), p. 873, ibid. p. 1184. Aránguez himself also shares this opinion, ibid. p. 1185.

[7] The Penal Code was reformed by law 15/2003 of 25 November 2003, as published in the *Official Journal* on 26 November 2003.

[8] In addition to this register there are several more, namely the register of drivers and driving offenders, those of security forces and the penitentiary ones. The existence of records of suspension of the driving licence is important for various reasons, among others the ability to obtain the especial authorisation to drive school coaches (Art. 32, RD 772/1997, of 30 May). Records kept by security forces are submitted to the law of protection of personal data. Regarding penitentiary registers (the so-called *Ficheros de Internos de Especial Seguimiento*) they are regulated by the Instruction of the General Office of Penitentiary Institutions 8/1995 of 28 February. It divides offenders into five categories: (1) Dangerous and violent offenders; (2) drug dealers; (3) terrorists; (4) former members of the security forces; and (5) various (others). Theoretically, it serves to prevent problems but Aránguez questions the lack of control about the correctness and utility of these registered data. This register is also subject to the law of protection of personal data, in Aránguez Sánchez, *Comentarios al Código Penal*, pp. 1177–1178.

[9] Article 130 of the Penal Code adds others, namely the death of the offender, the lapsing of the period during which prosecution may be brought and *res judicata*, but none is relevant to the cancellation of criminal records.

(b) The satisfaction of civil responsibilities, the guarantee to pay any sum due by instalments, or a judicial declaration that recognises the impossibility of such payment.[10]

(c) The expiry of different periods of time, depending on the seriousness of the crime, without any further offence having been committed since the expiry of the sentence or the termination of penal responsibility in cases of pardon, clemency or expiry of the sentence.[11]

(d) The obtaining of a previous report from the judge or tribunal that imposed the sentence in the case. Article 136 also declares that criminal records are not public. Finally, it states that criminal records, even those cancelled, will in any case be sent to judges and magistrates, emphasising the idea that in Spain criminal records mainly serve the judiciary.

Although the Registrer of criminal records is regulated by the Royal Decree of 1983[12] the registration of criminal records was set up in 1878. Before that, there were local registers which were not centralised. Currently, the Register depends on the Ministry of Justice and has two sections. The first section deals with entries in the criminal records of Spaniards and foreigners and periodically, following international agreements, receives information from foreign courts regarding convictions of Spanish nationals. The second section registers cancellations and extinctive prescriptions.[13] The Register has some other functions[14] which include the register of military crimes.[15]

Criminal records have several functions in Spain. The informative function is performed through certification on the existence or non-existence

[10] Rightly, Serrano Butragueño observes that once again civil responsibilities are used as an instrument of criminal policies although in practice attention is not given to this issue, in I. Serrano Butragueño, *Código Penal, Comentarios y Jurisprudencia* Vol. I, 3rd edn (Granada: ed. Comares, 2002), p. 1286.

[11] Ibid., pp. 1286–1287.

[12] *Registro Central de Penados y Rebeldes*, here after 'the Register'.

[13] Butragueño, *Código Penal, Comentarios y Jurisprudencia*, p. 1284.

[14] The Register also collaborates with the office responsible for the register of electors to correctly apply the penalty of disqualification from holding a voting right (RD 435/1992 of 30 April. BOE of 30 October), see Aránguez Sánchez, *Comentarios al Código Penal*, pp. 1176–1177 (footnote 19).

[15] Article 341 of the law of military procedure (*ley orgánica procesal militar*) 2/1989, of 13 April.

of criminal records.[16] Criminal records also affect recidivists as the existence of a criminal record may aggravate penalties.[17] Criminal records are relevant to the penal law in order to classify offenders,[18] achieve a conditional release[19] or bring to Spain offenders who are serving their convictions abroad.[20] Furthermore, criminal records must be available in criminal proceedings[21] and are important in determining penalties. Finally, criminal records are relevant to rehabilitate ex-offenders as a negative criminal record is necessary in order to have access to certain professional associations, e.g. the Spanish Bar and other positions, and to obtain certain legal authorisations, such as the right to carry guns.[22] In these cases, it is the subject of the record who may access the register and receive the certificate so that he/she can submit it to the relevant body or professional association.

Concerning minors, the organic law 5/2000[23] that regulates the penal responsibility of minors states that the Ministry of Justice will keep a register of final judgments whose data will only be used by judges of minors and public prosecutors. The law also pronounces that regarding minors the guarantees established in the law of protection of personal data will have to be respected.

[16] Butragueño has suggested that the register should also carry out statistics on criminality; see Butragueño *Código Penal, Comentarios y Jurisprudencia*, p. 1284.

[17] For instance, Article 22(8) of the Penal Code states that cancelled criminal records or those that should have been cancelled will not be considered to aggravate penalties. Similarly, Article 81(1) requires, among other things, the cancellation of criminal records or the existence of criminal records 'that should have been cancelled in accordance with Article 136'. Article 94 establishes that three or more convictions for crimes of the same Chapter of the penal code are necessary to declare someone as 'an habitual criminal'. Art. 81 states that they are also relevant to concede or deny the suspension of the penalty. By contrast, the Supreme Court does not consider the absence of criminal records as an alleviating circumstance (STS of 10 June of 1994 (RJ 4940)).

[18] Article 102 of the Penal Rules *(reglamento penitenciario)*. [19] Article 195 ibid.

[20] See, for instance, Art. 3(3) of the international agreement between Spain and El Salvador of 14 February of 1995 (*Tratado sobre el traslado de Personas Condenadas*). Also, Art. V.5 of the agreement between Spain and Ecuador for the accomplishment of criminal condemnations (*Convenio para el cumplimiento de condenas penales*) of 25 August 1995, both in Aránguez Sánchez, *Comentarios al Código Penal*, footnote 56, p. 1187.

[21] Article 379 of the *Ley de Enjuiciamiento Criminal (LECrim.)* obliges criminal records to be available in criminal proceedings.

[22] See Butragueño, *Código Penal, Comentarios y Jurisprudencia*, pp. 1284–1285.

[23] *Disposición Adicional Tercera, Ley Orgánica 5/2000, entrada en vigor el 13/01/2001*, ibid., pp. 1285–1286.

2.1 Entries to the Spanish criminal record and erasure

In Spain, all crimes that entail a criminal responsibility are included in the national criminal record. Spanish judges and tribunals must send without delay notification of all their final judgments to the registry. Petty crimes,[24] less serious penalties (*penas menos graves*) that include those penalties imposed in virtue of any statutory offence arising out of negligence, and serious offences (*penas graves*) are part of criminal records and are included in the national register of criminal records. According to Article 136 of the Penal Code,[25] criminal records are cancelled[26] if the following requirements are fulfilled:

(1) Those offenders who have satisfied their criminal liability have the right, *ex officio* or *ex parte*, to obtain from the Ministry of Justice the cancellation of their criminal records.[27] To do that, a previous report of the judge or tribunal that sentenced the case will have to be obtained.

(2) For the cancellation of criminal records it is necessary for any civil liability[28] arising from the crime to have been discharged, except in

[24] *Penas leves.* Those do not include misdemeanours (*faltas*). See Art. 1(b) of the Royal Decree of 28 July 1983, n. 201283. Also, most academics construe it in that way: see, for instance, Aránguez Sánchez, *Comentarios al Código Penal*, p. 1199. This classification of crimes, according to the seriousness of the offence committed, has remained although affected by the reform of 25 November 2003 (organic law 15/2003).

[25] Article 136, among others, was affected by a reform in 2003. See organic law 15/2003 of 25 November 2003 as published in the Official Journal, *Boletín Oficial del Estado*, of 26 November 2003, no. 283/2003.

[26] Instead of referring to 'rehabilitation' as Article 118 of the former penal code did, Article 136 focuses on the suppression of criminal records as a limited contribution to attain the final goal of social rehabilitation: G. Guinarte Cabada, 'Comentarios al Código Penal de 1995' in T. S. Vives Anton et al., Vol. I (Valencia: Tirant lo Blanch, 1996), p. 693. In the text of the law the term used for erasure of criminal record entries is 'cancellation'.

[27] It is remarkable that the 1995 Penal Code has preferred the expression 'cancellation of criminal records' to 'rehabilitation' that had been used in the reform of the Penal Code carried out in 1983. In any case, this reform remains loyal to the goal pursued in 1983: to avoid criminal records being an obstacle to rehabilitation as the Constitution orders in Article 25. See J. M. Tamarit Sumalla, 'Comentarios al Nuevo Código Penal', (dir. G. Quintero Olivares, coord. F. Morales Prats et al.) 2nd edn (Elcano: Aranzadi Editorial, 2001), p. 663.

[28] 'The civil liabilities' are those of Articles 109 and following, namely, restitution, reparation of damages and compensation of moral and material damages. Those do not include court costs, compensations to the state or fines. Consequently, the previous payment of all pecuniary responsibilities of Article 126 is not required. See J. L. Manzanares Samaniego, *Código Penal, Doctrina y Jurisprudencia* (director C. Conde-Pumpido Ferreiro) Vol. I (Madrid: Ed. Trivium, 1997), p. 1657.

> those cases when either the judge or the tribunal in charge made an order for the insolvency of the offender.[29] Nevertheless, if the offender has sufficient means to meet the civil liability arising from the crime, he/she shall pay the sum due in order to have his/her criminal record cancelled.

According to Article 125 of the Penal Code, the civil liability, subject to the offender's means, may be paid in instalments if the court so ordered. In this case the criminal record entry can be cancelled if the offender is up to date with his payment instalments ordered by the court and if he can guarantee the payment of the remaining debt to the court. According to Article 136(2)(3) of the Penal Code the conditions for cancellation are:

(a) Six months for minor offences.
(b) Two years for those penalties that do not exceed twelve months[30] and those sentenced by virtue of any statutory offence arising out of negligence.
(c) Three years for the remainder of the 'less serious offences'.
(d) Five years for those qualified as 'serious offences'.

Article 136(4) of the Penal Code states that 'criminal records are not public'. During their validity, criminal records will be only accessible to those concerned and for those cases authorised by the law. In any case, certificates will be delivered to judges and tribunals if they ask for them – including the certificates referring to a cancellation. In that case, the Register will expressly place on record such circumstance.

Considering that judges and tribunals have access to cancelled criminal records' entries, cancellation of criminal records may be defined 'as

[29] 'This is a novelty that was introduced in the penal reform of 1983 as, for instance, the regulation of 1928 did not contemplate it and, consequently, supposed an additional load on the offender', see Tamarit Sumalla, 'Comentarios al Nuevo Código Penal', p. 665.

[30] As these penalties include not only imprisonment but also fine-days (*días multa*), weekend arrests (which the 2003 reform has suppressed), deprivation of driving licences, etc., there is a problem in calculating the 12 months mentioned. Regarding fine-days two criteria may be used: the duration of the penalty or the duration of the explicit penal liability which is one day out of two days of fine-days – according to Article 53(1) of the Penal Code. Aránguez thinks that the last solution is the right one. He also argues that, following Article 37(1) of the Penal Code, this criterion is adequate for weekend arrests. Without going further into these issues, it can be concluded that the legislature has failed to establish a system that makes clear how to calculate terms in order to cancel criminal records and to do so in a manner that will consistently favour ex-offenders. The principle *in dubio pro reo* should always be considered, especially so in those situations that affect rehabilitation. See, Aránguez Sánchez, *Comentarios al Código Penal*, pp. 1199–1202.

the right to have recognised that all the legal effects provoked by a penal sentence have ceased, even if the essential data related to sentences are conserved'.[31] Consequently, 'cancellation' of criminal records does not amount to 'erasure' of criminal records in Spanish law. The Supreme Court stated in a judgment on 5 November 1991 that:

> the cancellation [of criminal records] is a rule that in law erases all the consequences arising from former criminal sentences. Any judicial body must recognise and *ergo* apply those effects ... It is not only the accused who must bring to the lawsuit the cancelled criminal records and declare those facts, but also the public prosecutor and ... lastly the judicial body that judges the case.[32]

As a result, the judge or tribunal will have to ask for the criminal records of the accused from the central register of criminal records.

Article 136(5) declares that judges and tribunals will order the cancellation of those criminal records that should already have been cancelled either *ex parte*[33] or *ex officio* by the Ministry of Justice. That will be done if all the legal requisites for cancellation them are fulfilled. Moreover, Article 136(5) states that the judge or tribunal will not take those records into consideration.[34]

Article 137 states that 'entries of disciplinary or safety measures will be cancelled once they are redeemed or the period during which prosecution may be brought has lapsed. Meanwhile, the above measures will only be delivered by the Register to judges, tribunals or those authorities[35] determined by the law.'

[31] Ibid., p. 1169.

[32] Similarly, the Supreme Court's final judgment of 3 November 1992 declared that 'it cannot be admitted that the *onus probandi* may correspond to the one that pleads for the hypothetical cancellation of criminal records'.

[33] RD 1879/1994, of 16 September 1994 establishes, in Article 3, that the petitions for cancellation of criminal records performed *ex parte* will have to be responded to within three months. If there is no answer, the criminal records concerned will have to be considered as cancelled.

[34] Regarding jurisprudence on cancellation of criminal records, 'Following a sentence of the Supreme Court, 2ª 14 June 1986, the cancellation of criminal records can be carried out through three different ways: (a) *ex officio* by the Ministry of Justice (Art. 136 (1)(5) of the Penal Code); (b) at the request of the person concerned (Art. 136(1)(5) of the Penal Code); and (c) by order of the court that sentenced the case (Penal Code Art. 136(5)). In the last case other judges or courts may *ex officio* not consider them even if they have not been formally cancelled considering that all the prerequisites are met, see Butragueño, *Código Penal, Comentarios y Jurisprudencia*, p. 1287.

[35] *Autoridades Administrativas.*

Article 1 of Royal Decree of 28 July 1983, no. 2012/83, on criminal records states that without any special previous declaration the central Register of offenders and persons in contempt will cancel criminal records, according to Article 136 of the 1995 new Penal Code, when judges and tribunals prescribe their cancellation. Criminal records referring to misdemeanours,[36] cited by Articles 587, 593 and 596 of the old Penal Code and Article 43 of Statute 1/1970 of 4 April 1970, will not be recorded anymore.

Article 2 states that the Agency for Penal Matters will propose the cancellation of criminal records upon expiry of the time limit established by Articles 113 and 115 of the Penal Code.[37] These terms will respectively start running either from the date of the declaration of contempt or from the date of the final judgment unless the Register has no record that could entail expiry of a period during which prosecution may be brought.[38] The cancellations cited above in Article 1(2) and Article 2 will imply the definitive suppression of all safety and disciplinary measures.

Article 3(1) states that every month the Register will set out a list of the criminal records that must be cancelled *ex officio* in accordance with the Penal Code due to non-commission of any crime during the terms determined by Article 118 (now Article 136). Those terms will be calculated as established in the previous Article. This list will be sent to the Agency for Penal Matters. According to Article (3)(2) the Agency for Penal Matters will cancel criminal records if all the conditions stipulated by Article 118 of the Penal Code (now Article 136) are fulfilled. If the Agency deems that they are not, it will send the list of criminal records to those judges and tribunals concerned who should within 30 days inform the Agency on the completion or non-completion of all requirements necessary for cancellation. If the judges do not issue their opinion on the fulfilment of all the necessary requirements within 30 days then the Agency will consider that all the legal preconditions are met and subsequently cancel *ex officio* the records concerned.[39]

[36] *Faltas*. Equally, Article 252 of the law of criminal procedure (*ley de enjuiciamiento criminal*) states that 'judicial bodies will only send to the register those final judgments that impose penalties because of crimes and those that declare offenders as being in contempt of court'.

[37] The articles mentioned have been superseded by Article 136 of the new penal code.

[38] Referring to this issue, see note 29.

[39] In any case, the petition of a report from a judge or court is compulsory but not binding, see Aránguez Sánchez, *Comentarios al Código Penal*, p. 1213.

Article 4 determines that the person concerned may apply to the Register for the cancellation of his criminal records. He/she will have to present a document that fully identifies him/her. Within fifteen days the Register will examine if all the legal demands are fulfilled; if they are not fulfilled it will notify the person concerned. If the Register finds that those prerequisites are met but there is no certification from the judge or tribunal that passed sentence then the Register within 15 days will send the file to the judge or tribunal that sentenced the case. That judge or tribunal should within 20 days inform the Register on the accuracy of the petition. If the Registry does not obtain a reply, after 10 additional days, it will consider that all the legal specifications are satisfied and will proceed to the cancellation. In that case, the Register will inform the tribunal about it. If the same file must be sent to different tribunals, the Register will send the original one to the tribunal that had passed the final sentence and authorised copies to the rest of them in order to simultaneously carry out the necessary procedure.

Article 5 states that cancellations of criminal records will be notified to the person concerned, the judge or tribunal that sentenced the case, the judge that had initiated proceedings and the district court of the ex-offender if it had so demanded. Finally Article 6 stipulates that the Register will never certify those records that have been cancelled except to judges or tribunals that have asked for them. If that happens, the Register shall expressly mention that those records have been cancelled.

2.2 Access to the Spanish criminal Register

As described above, Article 136(2)(4) of the Penal Code states that 'criminal records are not public'. During their validity, criminal records will be accessible only to those concerned and in those cases authorised by the law. In any case, certificates will be delivered to judges and tribunals that ask for them even if referring to a cancelled entry. In that case, the Register will expressly place on record such a circumstance.[40] Article 136(5) complements the previous paragraph and, to avoid contradictions, states that judges and tribunals will not take in consideration cancelled criminal records or those that should have been cancelled.

[40] Rightly, Serrano Butragueño criticises the fact that cancelled criminal records may be sent to judges. He thinks that they should be definitively erased instead of cancelled, in Butragueño, *Código Penal, Comentarios y Jurisprudencia*, p. 1286.

As Manzanares indicates[41] 'the Register cannot be an office that provides free information on criminal records as that would infringe Article 18(1) of the constitution that guarantees the right to privacy'. Under various pieces of legislation, the following people have access to criminal records:

(a) Judges and tribunals (CP Art. 136(4)).
(b) The person concerned.[42]
(c) The following legal representatives of the person concerned:[43]
  (1) lawyers;
  (2) *procuradores* – those who represent either the plaintiff or the defendant before a judge or tribunal;
  (3) *graduados* and *Diplomados Sociales* – graduates whose work is mostly related to labour law;
  (4) *gestores Administrativos*[44] – agents for administrative matters who advise their clients on how to deal with the administration. They may act personally or through their professional associations.

  In any of these cases, representatives must submit: (a) an original and express authorisation signed by the person concerned, (b) their identity card, and (c) the identity card of the person concerned or a due legalised copy of it.
(d) The following legal representatives of the person concerned:[45]
  (1) the parents, brothers and sisters, daughters and sons of the person concerned if they certify their relationship. In any of these cases, the dependent who asks for the criminal record must present, in addition to the requirements cited above, the Book of Family (*libro de familia*) which is a sort of identity card for families having various functions;

[41] Samaniego, *Código Penal, Doctrina y Jurisprudencia*, p. 1666.

[42] *Reales Ordenanzas* 1 April 1896 and 9 January 1914 establish that individuals may ask for negative certification of criminal records: Aránguez Sánchez, *Comentarios al Código Penal*, p. 1179. 'Art. 4 of the *Real Orden* of 30 November 1910 declares that positive certificates of criminal records will only be given to the person concerned or to those that have been correctly authorised by him': M. Grosso Galván, *Los antecedentes penales: rehabilitación y control social* (Barcelona: Ed. Bosch, 1983), p. 166.

[43] Rules 3 and 4 of the Royal Order (*Real Orden*) of 1 April 1896, ibid., p. 161.

[44] The authorisation to them was approved by Resolution of 27 August 1942. Grosso criticises the fact that this authorisation covered an economic interest as most petitions carried out by them involved an enormous amount of money, in Grosso Galván, *Los antecedentes penales*, pp. 170 and following.

[45] Ibid., p. 161.

(2) anyone to whom the person concerned has conceded a power of attorney (*poder notarial*) that allows him to act in matters concerning the public administration of the state.

Certificates of criminal records may also be demanded by post. In this case, those mentioned earlier will be authorised to demand them. They will have to fulfil all the legal requirements described above and send legalised copies of all the documents required.[46] The Constitutional Court affirmed in its ruling 144/1999 of 22 July 1999,[47] that criminal records are not public and will only be delivered in legally authorised cases. It dictated that certificates of criminal records can only be obtained in accordance with the law and, in any case, be given to judges and tribunals. Consequently, 'only the person concerned, the judiciary and those public institutions that have been legally authorised may ask for criminal records'. It stated that 'out of those cases established by the law, certificates of criminal records cannot be given to anyone else. If that happens, it will infringe the right to privacy guaranteed by the constitution'. The Constitutional Court also affirmed that Article 118 of the previous Penal Code (now Article 136 of the new Penal Code) and the laws cited by it establish the limits regarding criminal records. It declared that the right to privacy aims to guarantee the individual 'an area of privacy in his life that is not open to others whether they be public authorities or fellow citizens'. 'That right is linked to the respect for dignity'.[48] 'The right to privacy gives the individual the right to keep that reserved area private and safeguarded from any unwanted publicity'. 'Some data can be excluded from privacy: in those cases public authorities must be precise about the information that can be released, establish those that can have access to it and guarantee that those who are not authorised to obtain

[46] The first legislation that contemplated that option was the *Real Orden* of 30 November 1910. For practical reasons related to the impossibility to collect money to pay for certificates, that was forgotten until 1961. That did not work either due to vested interests of agents for administrative matters. Just to get an idea about the business in 1974, 12,000 petitions for criminal records were on average received every day. As each one of them cost at that time around £2.50, it is easy to understand why the association of agents for administrative matters who in practice controlled the system wanted to keep the business for themselves. The system was finally implemented by an order (*Orden*) of 20 March of 1981. That order permitted that printed forms of criminal records could be bought in tobacco shops throughout the country, in Grosso Galván, *Los antecedentes penales*, p. 175 and following.

[47] STC 144/1999, 22 July (RTC 1999, 144). RAC. Sala 2.

[48] See, SSTC 73/1982 [RTC 1982, 73], 110/1984 [RTC 1984, 110], 170/1987 [RTC 1987, 170], 231/1988 [RTC 1988, 231], 197/1991 [RTC 1991, 197], 143/1994 [RTC 1994, 143], and 151/1997 [RTC 1997, 151].

the information do not acquire it'. Finally, the constitutional court expressed that the Register of criminal records must respect the right to privacy concerning its registered information even if that Register is excluded from the law of personal data. Consequently, the legal norms that regulate the treatment and release of the information related to criminal records 'must be construed in a rigorous and restrict manner'.

2.3 Use of criminal record in Spanish law

In Spain, criminal records are mainly used in criminal cases to demonstrate the existence or non-existence of the criminal record of those accused. The existence of criminal records may aggravate penalties. The Supreme Court requires the absence of any doubt on the cancellation of criminal records if the recurrence of offence (*Reincidencia*) as an aggravating circumstance is to be considered. It demands that sentences which consider the recurrence of offence as an aggravating fact must include in the *factum* all necessary elements. These are the following: date of the final judgment, date when a previous sentence was completed, date when the facts as found by a court occurred, date of any preventive custody and its duration, remission obtained because of work performed in prison, and date if any of conditional remission and period of suspension.[49]

Other functions of criminal records are connected to access to public posts related to the judiciary,[50] the Bar,[51] public prosecutors,[52]

[49] The Supreme Court (*Tribunal Supremo*) has on many occasions declared that recurrence of infringement will not be an aggravating circumstance if there are doubts about the cancellation of criminal records. See, for instance, STS, 2ª, 225/1998, of 30 January, STS of 25 March 1995 and STS of 29 February 1996 among many others. If not, the principle *in dubio pro reo* must be applied (see, for instance, STS of 23 January 1998 (R.J.51), STS of 29 February 1996 (R.J. 1338), STS of 6 July 1994 (R.J.6251), STS of 10 November 1993 (R.J.8493) among many others. There are other decision quashing judgments that had considered as aggravating circumstances non-cancelled criminal records that should have been cancelled. See, for instance: STS 16 June 2000, STS 23 January 1998 (R.J.49), STS 4 November 1997 (R.J.7950), STS of 18 February 1994 (R.J. 939), etc. It is interesting that the adoption of the principle *in dubio pro reo* to recidivists prevents the Supreme Court from ordering the cancellation of criminal records in cases when all the legally demanded conditions for rehabilitation are not certified as Arts. 22(8) and 136(5) require. See, for instance, the following sentences: STS, 2ª, 885/1998, of 29 June; STS, 2ª, 311/1998, of 2 March, among others.

[50] Articles 302, 303 and 457 of the law of the judicial power, *Ley del Poder Judicial*. See also Articles 14, 24, 27 and 91 of the court officers' regulations and Article 7 of Royal Decree 2046/1982 of 30 July related to *procuradores*.

[51] Articles 15, 16, 25 of lawyers' professional regulations, *Estatuto General de la Abogacía*.

[52] Articles 44 and 46 of the public prosecutor's regulations.

notaries,[53] certified accountants,[54] the ombudsman,[55] the public administration, security forces, police forces or the army.[56] Without going into details for each one of them, those whose criminal records have not been cancelled cannot have access to such posts and can be expelled if a sentence disqualifies them for the post. There are various other uses related to criminal records concerning the concession of permits of residence and work,[57] emigration,[58] to open a gambling or bingo business, to obtain a licence to carry guns[59] or hunt,[60] or to be a director of a private security company.[61] The absence of criminal records is also relevant to conclude contracts with the public administration,[62] to be a director of a credit institution,[63] a member of a jury,[64] a forensic surgeon,[65] or to acquire Spanish nationality.[66] Finally, some crimes provoke specific disabilities.

[53] Article 7(2) Royal Decree 2 June 1994. [54] Article 7, law 19/1988, 12 July 1988.

[55] Art. 5(1) of law 3/1981, of 6 April (*ley orgánica 3/1981, de 6 de abril sobre el defensor del pueblo)*.

[56] Orden of 6 March 1937.

[57] See Art. 29(4) of the law 4/2000, of 11 January, on rights and freedoms of foreigners in Spain (*ley orgánica sobre derechos y libertades de los extranjeros en España and their social integration)*; Arts. 27, 56 and 85 of the Royal Decree 155/1996, of 2 February; 3(5) of the resolution of the sub-secretary of the Ministry of the Presidency of 15 April 1996; Art. 11 of the *Orden* of the Ministry of the Presidency of 8 May 1997 (*BOE n. 114, of 13 May*), in Aránguez Sánchez, *Comentarios al Código Penal*, footnote (75), p. 1190.

[58] Article 10 of the rule of emigration (*Reglamento de Emigración*) of 20 December 1924 and Article 29 of the law of organisation of emigration of 15 May 1962 (*Ley de Ordenación de la Emigración*). Once again, those are pre-constitutional norms difficult to understand under the current Constitution and legal system. The absence of a criminal record used to be necessary to obtain the permit of work required to obtain the right to emigrate. The consequence of those petitions, in addition to the absence of a criminal record to obtain a passport, was to make more difficult the rehabilitation of ex-offenders and increase control over them.

[59] Art. 82 of the Royal Decree 2179/1981, of 24 July, in Aránguez Sánchez, *Comentarios al Código Penal*, p. 1190.

[60] Art. 34 of the law on hunting (*ley de caza*) of 4 April 1970, ibid., p. 1190.

[61] Art. 8(b) of the law 23/1992, of 30 July, of private security companies, in Aránguez Sánchez, *Comentarios al Código Penal*, p. 1190.

[62] Article 4 of the law of public procurement (*ley de contratos del Estado*) of 8 April 1965, in Grosso Galván, *Los antecedentes penales*, pp. 162–163. It is remarkable that criminal records are not relevant any more to the obtaining of a driving licence (*Decreto* 1 October 1976, Art. 264 only demands not to be disqualified), ibid., p. 162.

[63] Art. 5 of the Royal Decree 692/1996, of 26 April *(BOE n.126, de 24 de mayo)*, in Aránguez Sánchez, *Comentarios al Código Penal*, p. 1189.

[64] Art. 9 of the law 5/1995, of 22 May, that created the institution of the jury, ibid., p. 1188.

[65] Art. 71 of the Royal Decree 296/1996, of 23 February (*BOE no. 53*, of 1 March), ibid., p. 1188.

[66] Butragueño, *Código Penal, Comentarios y Jurisprudencia*, p. 1285.

For instance, the person condemned as perpetrator or accomplice of a murder or malicious homicide cannot marry the widow of the victim.[67] Those that have criminal records for malicious falsehood, disclosure of information to be kept secret, tax crimes or crimes against property cannot be directors of insurance companies.[68] Those that have been condemned during the previous five years for invasion of privacy, violating of the secrecy of communications or any other fundamental right cannot be engaged in the business of private security companies.[69]

There are problems in correctly identifying those cases that make necessary the absence of positive criminal records as there is no unified legislation on criminal records. Moreover, some pieces of legislation that directly or indirectly have an impact on criminal records and rehabilitation are pre-constitutional norms and present problems of adaptation to the constitution of 1978 and subsequent legislation. In non-penal fields there are situations where cancelled criminal records still maintain negative effects for the individuals concerned. For instance, fraudulent bankrupts suffer a 'perpetual' disqualification to rehabilitate. It is paradoxical that in those cases the penal law legally *stops* its negative impact vis-à-vis the one concerned whereas that negative effect for the individual is maintained in non-penal fields.[70] That in fact prevents full rehabilitation and consequently ignores the constitutional mandate of Article 25 and connected legislation. Indeed, 'non-penal norms should be checked to avoid the extension of the effects of criminal penalties'.[71]

Finally, according to this author's research at the central Register, some companies demand the criminal records of their prospective employees but this is an unusual and non-legal requirement. Although that was a common practice years ago, such a request would currently pose legal problems in relation to Articles 14 and 25 of the Spanish Constitution. The Constitution clearly designs a criminal system orientated to the rehabilitation of offenders. Consequently, once the criminal

[67] Art. 47 of the Civil Code, although that can be dispensed with by the Ministry of Justice, in Aránguez Sánchez, *Comentarios al Código Penal*, p. 1189.

[68] Art. 15 of law 30/1995, of 8 November, on private insurance companies (*Ley de ordenación y supervisión de los seguros privados*), in ibid., p. 1189.

[69] Art. 10 of law 23/1992, of 30 July, of private security companies (*ley de seguridad privada*), ibid., pp. 1189–1190.

[70] Article 920 of the Code of Commerce, ibid., p. 1191.

[71] Ibid., p. 1191.

record has been cancelled no discrimination based on a former conviction may be practised.

2.4 Collaboration with foreign authorities for the acquisition of criminal records of foreign individuals

The Spanish Register of criminal records[72] keeps records on crimes committed by foreigners in Spain and crimes committed by Spaniards abroad and, in general, those related to Spanish justice. Collaboration with other countries to transmit information is fluid and regular.[73] It is carried out as Spain belongs to several international agreements on judicial assistance on criminal matters, the most important of which being the European Convention on Judicial Assistancc on Criminal Matters, concluded in Strasbourg on 20 April 1959. Spain became part of this treaty in 1982[74] and has also incorporated its Protocol of 1978.[75]

Spain has also concluded several bilateral or multilateral agreements with some other countries which are related to the issues cited above, e.g. the one concluded with Portugal and the ones with most of the countries in Central and South America.[76]

According to Pedro Romero, head of the Spanish central Register of offenders, the system works reasonably well and every six months information is sent to other countries and received from them. Also, information can be transmitted in relation to individual cases. According to Romero the volume of the information transmitted every year is equivalent to 10,000–12,000 convictions. In spite of this optimistic description some academics criticise the Register's lack of means, such as the absence of translators or ability to analyse the information

[72] That had been regulated by an order (*Orden*) as far back as 18 November 1926, in Grosso Galván, *Los antecedentes penales*, p. 121.

[73] Aránguez criticises the fact that the recording of foreign convictions does not include essential data such as the expiration date of the final judgment, in Aránguez Sánchez, *Comentarios al Código Penal*, p. 1181.

[74] BOE 1982, 17 September, no. 223, p. 25166

[75] 17 March, BOE 27 May 1991 (RCL 1991/1966).

[76] The Royal Decree 1176/1992, of 2 October (BOE of 3 October 1992) aims to make more effective the registration of foreign criminal sentences. It regulates the register of final judgments related to drugs trafficking that applied what was signed in the agreement concluded with most of the American countries (*Convenio de la Conferencia de Ministros hispano-luso-americanos sobre comunicación de antecedentes penales y de información sobre condenas judiciales por tráfico de estupefacientes y sustancias psicotrópicas, hecho en Lisboa el 12 de octubre de 1984, y ratificado por España el 18 de abril de 1989*), in Aránguez Sánchez, *Comentarios al Código Penal*, p. 1181.

received, that renders almost useless such cooperation.[77] Effectively, Spain periodically transmits via the Ministry of Justice the information related to those foreigners that have been condemned in Spain. Moreover, judges and tribunals may ask the Spanish central Register, either directly or occasionally via Interpol, for information that may be necessary in court proceedings. In line with the treaty cited above, Spanish tribunals also may ask other central registers and foreign tribunals for information about convictions.

After the Office for International Judicial Cooperation of the Ministry of Justice only judges and tribunals are considered as legitimised authorities for the transmission of the information referred to above. Nevertheless, there are some exceptions to the general rule, as in the case of Switzerland where the Federal Office of the Police is considered as a legitimate authority and, consequently, may ask the Spanish central Register for information.

It has to be noted that, in addition to the treaties referred to above, Spain collaborates with Interpol and Europol. Indeed, Pedro Romero, head of the central Register, has confirmed to this author that in a very few urgent cases information is directly released to Interpol in order to be transmitted to other countries. This author questions whether this practice follows the doctrine that the highest Spanish court, the Constitutional Court, affirmed in its ruling 144/1999, of 22 July,[78] namely that criminal records are not public and will only be delivered in legally determined cases. It declared that certifications of criminal records can only be obtained in accordance with the law and, in any case, be given to judges and tribunals. Consequently, 'only the person concerned, the judiciary and those public institutions that have been legally authorised may ask for criminal records'. It stated that 'apart from those cases established by the law, certifications of criminal records cannot be given to anyone else. If that happens, it will infringe the right to privacy guaranteed by the constitution.' This doctrine reflects the fact that the protection of access to criminal records is, or should be, in Spain, tightly

[77] Grosso says that many sentences are not translated. That happens because the office of translators of the Ministry of Foreign Affairs lacks the personnel. Consequently, most foreign convictions are stored without being translated. Finally, they are destroyed when a period of time has elapsed and no more room is available to store them, in Grosso Galván, *Los antecedentes penales*, pp. 121–122. This author points out that it has not been possible to check at the registry to see whether the situation described by Grosso in 1983 still remains in 2003.

[78] STC 144/1999, of 22 July (RTC 1999, 144). RAC. Sala 2.

controlled and rigorously limited to the judiciary, the person concerned or that person's representatives, who are strictly determined by law.

2.5 *The effectiveness of the Spanish system: a critique*

The Spanish Constitution proclaims social rehabilitation as the goal to achieve through any criminal policy. Moreover, Article 73(2) of the penal law establishes that criminal records can never justify legal or social discrimination. Is that effectively applied when, for instance, the state does not permit an ex-offender whose penal liability is extinguished to sit an examination to become a civil servant, among the many others impediments analysed above?[79] No, it is not. This example is just one of the contradictions that the permanence of a register of criminal records creates in relation to the constitutionally proclaimed goal of rehabilitation. There are others.

Criminal records are a stigma for ex-offenders as they last longer than their penal liabilities. Criminal records conflict with ex-offenders' right to rehabilitation. They are as effective today to keep a record of ex-offenders' criminal backgrounds as they were in the past. This impression is confirmed by the fact that criminal records are not erased in Spain when legally established sentences have elapsed: they are simply 'cancelled' and may still be sent to judges although their cancellation will be expressly mentioned. Why keep those souvenirs? Why deliver them to judges and magistrates if by law cancelled criminal records cannot have any legal effect? The only answer is this: the state does not want to abandon the power that information on individuals provides.[80]

[79] See pp. 13 and following on 'use of criminal records'.

[80] The Supreme Court produced a surprising final judgment on its sentence 811/1988 of 8 July 1988. Its conclusions are more related to the spirit of previous regulations of criminal records than to the current conception under the 1978 constitution. The facts were related to an ex-offender who had been twice convicted for 'outrage against decency' and was considered as a 'sexual maniac'. However, those criminal records had been cancelled when that man was accused of 'indecent assault' on a minor that had allegedly occurred in a lift. The district court of appeal sentenced him to prison and that decision was appealed before the Supreme Court on the grounds of of infringement of his constitutional presumption of innocence. The Supreme Court dismissed it because the minor had no doubts in recognising him as the author of the crime during the previous trial. The Supreme Court added that 'the past of sexual assault of the one accused ... his consideration as a sexual maniac ... in a way strengthen and reinforce the declaration of the victim ... as that past is related to the currently analysed deeds'. The Supreme Court declared that 'those facts would be criminally irrelevant if they were not interconnected and not related to the alleged events'. In summing up, the Supreme

Information is power. Information on ex-offenders is a way of exercising power over those that once violated established values. Grosso Galván considers that the real objectives of criminal records are 'firstly, to inform the judiciary [. . .] about prison sentences, and secondly to use that information as a mean of control and stigmatisation [of those condemned]'.[81] He adds that 'the most evident practical consequences of that control and stigmatisation are the perpetuation of the penal stigma through the extension of the effects of convictions even if penalties have been served, and an added difficulty for ex-offenders to reintegrate in society'.[82] He considers this as being in plain contradiction to the Spanish Constitution and other norms such as the general penal law.[83] On the other hand, he concedes that the endurance of criminal records responds to the goal of general prevention of criminality even if it is known that criminal records favour the creation of criminality.[84]

The treatment and use of criminal records, since their creation, have nevertheless positively evolved in Spain. The Register is not public as it used to be. Only those legally authorised may ask for criminal records and a tight right to privacy is established by the law, so long as practices such as the direct sending of information to police-oriented agencies are controlled, and guaranteed by the Constitutional Court.[85] Criminal records *mainly* serve to aggravate penalties imposed on recidivists and cancelled criminal records are not criminally relevant. Cancellation of criminal records must automatically be carried out if the legal requirements are fulfilled. Cancellation is legally determined and the periods after which records are cancelled are short compared to other jurisdictions. In a way, it is surprising how within fifty years the system has evolved from one that only permitted the cancellation of criminal records of non-recidivists[86] to the present that cancels the records of *all* ex-offenders once the legal requirements have been met. Maybe the time has come to have legislation to do away with the whole institution

Court did not concede penal relevance to cancelled criminal records but it considered that they reinforced the declaration of the victim and, consequently, constituted a sort of evidence to be considered. That conclusion responded more to the traditional function of criminal records rather than following the principles derived from the Constitution and subsequent legislation. In a way, it shows how ancient prejudices and criminal policies, connected to distrust regarding ex-offenders and not to social rehabilitation, are deeply rooted in institutions, and how they are opposed to the spirit if not the letter of the law.

[81] See Grosso Galván, *Los antecedentes penales*, p. 393. [82] Ibid. [83] Ibid.

[84] Ibid., pp. 393–396. [85] See note 79 above.

[86] Grosso Galván, *Los antecedentes penales*, p. 269.

or, if not, to erase criminal records when the penal responsibility is extinguished. The result would be a legal system much closer to the sort of values proclaimed in the Constitution.

Other problems are intimately linked to the historic development such as the lack of a unified legal framework in order to suppress all pre-constitutional norms that affect criminal records, make them respond to constitutional principles and follow the same homogeneous basis. Consequently, penal and extra-penal norms should be analysed to avoid the extension of the effects of criminal convictions[87] that may contradict social rehabilitation.

It is necessary to strictly control police records to avoid that their keeping information on citizens that may infringe their right to privacy and other basic civil liberties. Modern techniques and devices provide an unlimited power to obtain, process, and store personal data that must be legally controlled. Finally, the enhancement of international cooperation should proceed but in a way that respects the guarantees nationally observed. The national Register of criminal records should be given enough means to carry out that cooperation and process the information received. The fight against the new international threats, namely sophisticated international crime and terrorism, should not destroy the sort of values that those protective measures proclaim to defend.

3. Contents of a European Criminal Record

Considering the current Spanish system, there are several approaches which could be workable. All of them should respect the core idea that a European Criminal Record (ECR) should mainly serve the judiciary and be kept under judicial control. Isabel Vevia, Deputy Director of International Judicial Cooperation, also considers that this register should principally have a judicial character. Her views coincides with those of Eduardo de Urbano,[88] Judge of the Supreme Court[89] in Spain, and those of this author that the necessity to place criminal records under judicial

87 See notes 72 and 73 above.

88 Invaluable collaborations and views that helped to complete this work, for which this author is deeply grateful, were obtained during the research performed for the Grotius project carried out in 2000 and 2001 by the IALS. Their opinions, alongside and coincident with this author's, will be used to develop the questions raised in sections 3, 4, 5 and 6.

89 That is the equivalent to the Cour de Cassation in France.

control eliminates the possibility that either Europol or Interpol could control it.

With Judge Eduardo de Urbano, this author considers that there are several concepts which might be applied. One would be to initially include a number of relevant crimes and, later, integrate all sort of crimes as national criminal records do. The crimes to be considered, at the start, might be drug-related crimes, homicide in all its forms, torture, 'crimes against sexual freedom' (sex related crimes), crimes against the constitution, and crimes against the international community and human rights. Mrs Vevia adds terrorism, human trafficking and money laundering. Another way would be to include all crimes from the srart, although the list of crimes would probably be more difficult to agree on.

4. Access to the ECR

The charter of the ECR should declare its purposes and users. Judge Eduardo de Urbano, Isabel Vevia and this author believe that it should establish a closed list of authorities to access the register. These authorities should certainly be judicial authorities and appointed public prosecutors. Individuals affected, and their fully identified representatives, should also be admitted access. Additionally, an agreement might be reached to allow access to the national heads of the different agencies for data protection, and to some designated authorities belonging to the Ministries of Justice and Internal Affairs of the signing countries. In the last two cases, the diverse scenarios to access the ECR should be previously and carefully determined and, maybe, could affect situations such as immigration, nationality, or others specifically agreed on although this authorisation would probably require a modification of the current Spanish legislation on criminal records.

Banking institutions should not be allowed to access the ECR. Similarly, direct access to tendering authorities or professional associations would again demand a prior, and deep, modification of the Spanish laws and jurisprudence relating to criminal records and privacy. As an example there is the Constitutional Court's ruling 144/1999, of 22 July,[90] referred to above.

[90] STC 144/1999, of 22 July (RTC 1999, 144). RAC, Sala 2.

5. Use of the ECR

Without previous changes in the Spanish system, an ECR should be loyal to the principles which inform the Spanish Register. It should serve the judiciary and be kept under judicial supervision with a tight control over data and their release. It should aim at rehabilitation of ex-offenders as a desirable goal and, therefore, consider cancellation and erasure of data after reasonable periods of time once sentences have been served. The information to be released to bodies not belonging to the judiciary, if at all, especially to police-oriented agencies, should be strictly regulated and rights safeguarded.

An ECR would help to speed up internal, not only judicial, cooperation among EU Member States and contribute to the building up of a European 'judicial space'. Its immediate effect would be a faster transmission of data among EU judges and courts relating to the existence or non-existence of criminal records, so increasing security and a faster response to criminality. Also, it would provide information that would enable offenders and minors to be classified and also allow conditional releases. Other effects would depend on the type of crimes to be included and the authorities that could access the ECR. Access to professional positions, as in the case of lawyers or qualified accountants, or the right to carry guns, for example, could be better controlled although, to be in accordance with Spanish law, only the persons interested should be allowed access to the register to subsequently present the certification to the body concerned.

6. Critical evaluation

The idea of an ECR is a high-calibre initiative which goes further than strict criminal and juridical fields to have an impact on European integration and improved of public security across Europe. It would contribute to build up a European 'judicial space' and help to make it more efficient as there would be speedier judicial access to key information. As indicated, the ECR should serve the judiciary and keep a judicial character and protection. But, first, we should question the concept of criminal records, what they mean as legal and social institutions. Are national criminal records useful and useful for what? Does their existence facilitate the social rehabilitation of offenders?

An ECR should establish clear principles related to the pursued aims. It should balance principles that will sometimes be in conflict, such as the promotion of security, the right to privacy and the rehabilitation of ex-offenders. Criminal records help authorities to fight criminality but also serve to trace people's past. A longer time before criminal records are cancelled means more difficulties for ex-offenders to reintegrate in society. Total erasure of criminal records helps them in that regard. Finally, it is important to regulate how data is maintained, privacy protected, who controls data and who can access the information.

The SIS system to exchange information among Schengen countries has proven a positive step in the fight against organised crime. The creation of a ECR would reinforce, at EU level, this fight and, ultimately, promote European integration and security. But this improvement should be linked, if the current system in Spain is to be maintained, to judicial investigations of crimes, instead of police-oriented investigations of crimes. A lesson from the past, additional to legal works, among others dramatically transmitted respectively by Victor Hugo and Alexandre Dumas in *Les Miserables* and *Le comte de Monte-Christo*, is that the existence of criminal records does not help to rehabilitate ex-offenders and, finally, reduce criminality. That lesson should not be forgotten, especially when modern technology permits an unparalleled ability to collect and store data on people's actions.

I have discussed some of the positive consequences of a EU Criminal Record. Attention should also be paid to possible negative aspects. Guarantees to protect data should be established, firstly to respect our legally established values and, secondly, to make the cession of sovereignty accepted by people and human rights defenders across Europe: privacy must be respected. National authorities in charge of coordination and transmission of data should be clearly determined. This author, in coincidence with Judge Eduardo de Urbano and Pedro Romero,[91] head of the Spanish criminal Register, considers that the persons responsible for the different national records, or others appointed for it at Ministries of Justice, could perform this task.

Adequate political 'marketing' and informative campaigns should be carried out to show how better security and judicial cooperation in the EU, through the creation of such a register, would immediately produce advantages for European citizens. An ECR is not an unnecessary intrusion into national law but a necessity which emanates from a modern Europe, and world, where criminal bands are internationally organised

[91] Pedro Romero, head of the Spanish Register of criminal records, collaborated with this author in relation to the Grotius Project carried out in 2001/2002 for the IALS. The author deeply thanks him for that.

and have international influence. And this unequal combat needs faster responses, especially in a free Europe without internal borders.

If the creation of a European Criminal Record appears to be too ambitious, and it should not, a better coordination among the different national registers to make collaboration faster could be explored. This could work too, as it does now, albeit imperfectly due to the lack of means. Thus, according to Pedro Romero, more than 10,000 convictions are transmitted per year applying the European Convention on judicial assistance on criminal matters.[92] Nevertheless, this better coordination would not have the same impact as the creation of a European Criminal Record would certainly have on security and European integration. And practically, it will be more difficult to guarantee enough means to develop a more efficient collaboration between a number of national registers than doing the same for a unique central register at the EU level.

[92] It was concluded in Strasbourg on 20 April 1959. Spain became part of it in 1982 (BOE 1982, of 17 September, no. 223, p. 25166) and also incorporated its Protocol of 17 March 1978, 27 May 1991 (RCL 1991/1996).

15

The European Criminal Record in England and Wales

LISA WEBLEY

1. Introduction

The research that underpins this chapter was originally conducted for two European Commission funded projects to provide baseline data for all EU jurisdictions and is thus broadly descriptive of law and policy.[1] The research sought views on the proposals for a European Criminal Record (ECR) from key agencies and organisations. This has been supplemented by consideration of the House of Commons European Scrutiny Committee's first, twenty-first and twenty-eighth reports[2] and the minutes of evidence from the House of Lords Select Committee on European Union and its twenty-third report, all of which examined this issue. This chapter considers the existing legal framework for criminal records and any amendments that would be required to accommodate some of the proposals made in respect of the ECR. It addresses the content of domestic criminal records and policy views on the appropriate content of an ECR. It considers those categories of people who are permitted to access domestic criminal records and the policy debates in respect of the ECR, as well as the use to which criminal records may be put both domestically and across Europe. Finally it evaluates that debate on the proposed ECR from the England and Wales' perspective.[3]

[1] Grotius Project JHA/199/FAL/197 and Falcone Project 2000/FAL/168 both directed by Dr H. Xanthaki and Dr C. Stefanou.

[2] *The Select Committee on European Scrutiny Twenty-Eighth Report* (July 2004) and in particular Part V Civil and Criminal Justice paragraphs 30–42.

[3] The research which forms the basis of this chapter pertained to the jurisdiction of England and Wales although many of the same issues are pertinent to the UK.

2. The existing legal framework[4]

In England and Wales criminal convictions are recorded at both a national and local level. Criminal convictions are defined as findings of fact and law made by the courts and an official record of convictions is defined as:

> a record kept for the purposes of its functions by any court, police force, Government department, local or other public authority in Great Britain, or a record kept, in Great Britain, or elsewhere, for the purposes of any of Her Majesty's forces, being in either case a record containing information about persons convicted of offences.[5]

Information is stored on all recordable offences; the Rehabilitation of Offenders Act 1974 (ROA 1974) regulates the area of law relating to criminal convictions and how they are recorded.[6] The Act sets out which types of convictions are to be held on record, which are to be held indefinitely and which can be removed and under what circumstances. The framework in respect of the record of criminal convictions is consequently controlled through primary legislation rather than by the judiciary as is the case in some jurisdictions.

The police maintain the record of criminal convictions, which is held on the Police National Computer in the Phoenix application.[7] The Criminal Records Office for England and Wales, based at New Scotland Yard, maintains the centralised record of criminal convictions,[8] although local police forces are currently responsible for inputting details of offenders onto this central database. Older offences may have been entered on to the database from information stored on the Criminal Records Office/National Identification Service microfiche collection, which holds the national microfiche collection of older

[4] Some of the material is this section appeared in the earlier publication L. Webley, 'Criminal Records and Organised Crime in England and Wales', in H. Xanthaki and C. Stefanou (eds.), *Financial Crime in the EU* (The Hague: Kluwer Law International, 2005), pp. 133–148.

[5] Section 9(1) of the Rehabilitation of Offenders Act 1974.

[6] See *A Review of the Rehabilitation of Offenders Act 1974*, The ROA Review Team/Action Against Crime and Disorder Unit, The Home Office July 2001. This may be accessed at www.homeoffice.gov.uk/roareview/roapncnis.htm. The Act is still under review.

[7] Concern has been expressed about the quality and reliability of data held on criminal convictions. See T. Terry, 'The National Collection of Criminal Records: A Question of Data Quality' (2001) *Criminal Law Review* 886–896 at 890.

[8] For an interesting account on the history of criminal records in England and Wales see ibid.

offences.[9] The Criminal Records Bureau (CRB) draws upon the data held by the Criminal Records Office in order to provide the new criminal record 'disclosure' system, which is made available to individuals themselves and to third parties under certain statutorily defined circumstances.[10] Consequently there is a national criminal record in England and Wales held on an electronic database, which may be searched in order to retrieve court convictions relating to an individual. Older offences are gradually being added to the database, but over time the database should become a complete record of criminal convictions. There is a mechanism in place for individuals to check the details held about them on the database and also a mechanism for challenging the accuracy of the record and requesting that the record be rectified in the event that errors are found. This would meet the basic requirements of the ECR proposals in respect of convictions data.

Criminal records have three primary functions: as an aid to appropriate sentencing for the judiciary once defendants have been convicted; to assist others in making judgements about the suitability of others for employment in certain sectors, and as criminal intelligence for the police. However, the police may wish to access a wider source of criminal intelligence material that goes beyond criminal conviction data. The police have a record of operational data on the Police National Computer, which they use for investigative purposes. The National Criminal Intelligence Service (NCIS) collects and stores criminal intelligence as required under section 2(2) of the Police Act 1997.[11] These records are not a record of criminal convictions but of information that may be of use in future criminal investigations. There is thus a distinction between criminal convictions and other findings of fact, and information that is stored for operational and investigative purposes. This foreshadows an ongoing debate in the context of the proposals for an ECR, in which Member States have

[9] The older records (those up to 23 May 1995) are gradually being added to the Police National Computer, but only when the individual's record comes to the police's attention. The older records are likely to be computerised at an increased rate over time as checks are made through the operation of the Criminal Records Bureau. I am grateful to Mr. Snelham, the International Dimension Project Manager of the Criminal Records Bureau for explaining the way in which criminal record information is stored.

[10] This operates as part of the Passport Agency under Part V of the Police Act 1997.

[11] The National Criminal Intelligence Service was formed in 1992, although since the enactment of the Police Act 1997 it became independent of central government from 1 April 1998. It is charged with gathering, storing and analysing information to provide criminal intelligence and to provide this to other law enforcement agencies. Further information about NCIS can be found at www.ncis.co.uk/.

differing views on the need for a distinction to be drawn between conviction and investigation records. The implications of this divide will be considered in more detail in the subsequent sections. The content of the criminal record and criminal intelligence may be disclosed under certain circumstance to foreign authorities, and so few legislative changes would be required in respect of the recording of convictions and intelligence data and the disclosure of this data, subject to the caveat that the detail of the ECR is not clear at this stage and this detail may result in the need for further legislative change.

3. Contents of the ECR

3.1 The domestic criminal record

All recordable criminal convictions are placed on the criminal record, which includes all those offences that may result in a prison sentence being imposed as well as certain other specified offences. The list of recordable offences is contained within statutory instruments (secondary legislation), the National Police Records (Recordable Offences) Regulations 2000 and the National Police Records (Recordable Offences) (Amendment) Regulations 2003.[12] However, not all convictions remain on the record indefinitely. The ROA 1974 sets out those convictions that will remain on the record and those which may be removed after a certain period of time has elapsed. The purpose behind this is to assist offenders to reintegrate into society after they have served their sentence and have returned to the community.[13]

Criminal convictions that have resulted in a jail sentence of less than thirty months will become 'spent' after a specified period.[14] The system for spent convictions applies to all court convictions incurred by an individual, whether they are convictions passed by a court in this country or abroad.[15] The convicted person is then considered to be rehabilitated for the purposes of the Act. In practice this means that

[12] SI 1139 and SI 2823.

[13] For a discussion see The Home Office, *The Rehabilitation of Offenders Act 1974 and Cautions, Reprimands and Final Warnings A Consultation Paper*, August 1999, p. 2.

[14] The period of time that must elapse before the conviction becomes 'spent' varies depending on the length of the sentence imposed and also the number of convictions imposed at the time, and whether the offender commits a further offence during the rehabilitation period.

[15] Further detail on rehabilitation and spent convictions is provided in section 6 of the Rehabilitation of Offences Act 1974.

the rehabilitated offender is treated as if he or she had not committed the offence as regards the need to disclose a previous conviction in judicial proceedings and the requirement to answer questions about one's past that cannot be answered without referring to a spent conviction. The person is also not required to disclose the existence of a spent conviction to another person and cannot be legally accountable for non-disclosure, if the conviction is spent. Disclosure may, however, be ordered by a court if, after looking at the evidence, justice cannot be served without admitting or requiring evidence relating to a person's previous convictions (or circumstances that are ancillary to them from being disclosed).[16] Disclosure may also be required as a result of an exceptions order by the Secretary of State, which has the effect of limiting the immunity afforded to the rehabilitated person.[17] Therefore, questions can be asked in relation to the spent offence and employment may be refused or terminated on the basis of the spent conviction.

Other sentences are excluded from rehabilitation as a result of section 5(1) of the ROA 1974 and therefore the duty to disclose cannot be side-stepped by the offender. These include those that result in a sentence of life imprisonment and a sentence of imprisonment exceeding thirty months. As the CRB argue:

> there is a distinction to be made between 'removing' convictions from a record and being able to 'deny' the existence of 'spent' convictions. When a conviction becomes 'spent', the conviction is not actually removed from the Police National Computer (or from the microfiche files if the conviction is still held in that format)... Convictions are only physically removed from the records according to the Association of Chief Police Officers (ACPO) Weeding Rules, which are not directly related to the provisions of the ROA.[18]

The offence is thus not expunged from the record, but instead remains dormant on the file unless and until this data is required for specified purposes. The extent to which convictions remain on the record will vary from Member State to Member State and any move

[16] See section 7 of the Rehabilitation of Offenders Act 1974 for further information.

[17] At present, exceptions orders are in force in relation to people working on matters in the area of national security, with children, young and vulnerable people, in the field of the administration of justice and occupations relation to 'financial probity'.

[18] My thanks to Mr Snelham, International Dimension Project Manager at the Criminal Records Bureau, for his clarification of the way in which convictions are recorded and kept by the organisations responsible for holding this information.

towards an ECR will need to address such differences in order for the data to be used reliably by foreign authorities and nationals.

3.2 Foreign convictions data on the domestic record

The research considered the extent to which the foreign criminal convictions of British nationals and foreign nationals resident in the UK are held and should be held on the UK centralised database. NCIS confirmed at the time of the research that foreign criminal convictions of British nationals and foreign nationals were not held on the centralised database.[19] Since this interview there has been a greater exchange of foreign criminal convictions data between Member States, although it is still argued that some of the data is of low quality and requires further checking before it can be entered onto the central database. The extent to which the UK is routinely notified of the criminal convictions of UK citizens abroad is unclear – a recent statement by the Association of Chief Police Officers noted that 27,259 foreign criminal convictions were in Home Office paper files but had yet to be entered onto the Police National Computer.[20] Although data has not in the past been routinely available in the UK on crimes committed abroad, there was a mechanism that permitted a procedural request to be made via NCIS and then via either Interpol or Europol to the local force to provide details of their criminal records. This has since been standardised to provide a central registry to receive and submit criminal records data from and to other Member States. The CRB indicated that it would be of benefit to have increased access to data sources on convictions, their

[19] A representative from the International Services Division's Policy Unit at NCIS kindly answered questions on the Falcone project JHA/199/FAL/197 on behalf of NCIS.

[20] During questioning by the Home Affairs Select Committee in January 2007, it became clear that foreign criminal convictions data were now being made available to the UK authorities in greater quantities than before 2005, as a result of a European decision that required each Member State to have a mechanism for receiving and submitting such data. Data were made available via the Home Office, although this responsibility has since been transferred to the Association of Chief Police Officers. It became apparent that information relating to foreign criminal convictions of UK citizens for offences including rape and murder had not been entered onto the Police National Computer. The Home Secretary John Reid reported that there would be an internal inquiry into the findings, the Association of Chief Police Officers called for greater funding to assist in the data entry effort, and the Criminal Records Bureau announced that it would check whether criminal record disclosures to employers needed to be updated in the light of the new information on convictions abroad. A senior civil servant was suspended pending the internal inquiry findings.

representative stating that the more information it has to draw upon, the greater the protection that can be afforded to children and vulnerable adults. At present the CRB is only able to access data sources within the UK.[21] The CRB did, however, identify a number of issues with access to an ECR including that employers in the UK would have access to this information unless legislative changes were made here to the UK system of disclosure, and there may be objections among some of the EU police forces at this information being so readily available. In addition, there are questions of principle that would need to be decided such as what type of data should be stored on the criminal record, whether that is a separate European database, or whether that is a series of linked national databases. There are also concerns about the integrity of data received from other jurisdictions and also the extent to which convictions reached in other countries would meet the procedural justice standards expected in the UK. This will be discussed in more detail below.

3.3 *Issues raised by the ECR*

The proposals for an ECR also raise profound questions about the nature of each Member State's criminal records – whether the types and range of offences to be recorded should be harmonised along with the time period prior to them becoming spent. Both parliamentary select committees considered it important to put on record that the content and composition of the ECR is a matter for Member States rather than the EU as it related directly to the rights of the individual.[22] The Law Society sought clarification as to which offences would be included on the ECR and how this related to the *Corpus Juris*. It was noted that there could be great disparities between the types of offences that were eligible to be recorded within Member States and therefore citizens from different countries may not be treated similarly. Other factors require some consideration. The National Association of Youth Justice (NAYJ) is particularly concerned with the potential injustices that could flow from an ECR in respect of children's rights in the UK.[23]

[21] This includes access to the PNC centralised data base, to local police force data from England, Scotland and Wales and to Department of Health and the Department for Education and Skills data.

[22] See the House of Commons Select Committee on European Scrutiny twenty-first report paragraph 7.20.

[23] The NAYJ referred to Article 40(3)(a) of the United Nations Convention on the Rights of the Child and to Article 4.1 of the United Nations Standard Minimum Rules for the

The criminal age of responsibility for children in England and Wales is 10 years old, in Northern Ireland it is also 10 years old and it is lower at only 8 years old in Scotland. This is at odds with the higher ages of criminal responsibility in many other European countries.[24] The NAYJ is concerned that any ECR has the potential, even if designed to prevent organised crime, to include the names and details of children and young people from the UK who would not otherwise be included if they had been convicted within other European countries who have a higher age of criminal responsibility. Therefore, if an ECR is to be introduced, albeit it with the intention of reducing organised crime, the NAYJ feel that is it important to consider at what age a child or young person's criminal record would be included on a database that would be even more widely available than current criminal records are within England and Wales at present.

The House of Commons European Scrutiny Committee, the parliamentary committee responsible for overseeing proposals of European law and policy, has reviewed the proposals for the ECR, drawing upon expertise from legal academia and the legal profession. Its makes a number of conclusions about the content of the proposed record. In the first instance the Committee concluded that it would be preferable, if the content of individual Member State's records were to be retained in their present format, but that information exchange mechanisms were to be improved if that were to be the obstacle. If a centralised database were to be established then the Committee concluded that the House of Lords Select Committee on European Union twenty-third report took evidence from, amongst others, Dr Xanthaki and Dr Stefanou in respect of the proposals for an ECR. They noted the safeguards that Xanthaki and Stefanou suggested: that the ECR should contain data only on convictions, data on purely transnational offences, and that only judicial authorities be allowed to access it and make use of it.[25] The House of Lords committee was not of the opinion that there was no necessity to establish an ECR contained within a central database.[26] However, if a

Administration of Juvenile Justice (the 'Beijing Rules') in its submission. The UN Committee on the Rights of the Child observes that it is desirable to set the highest possible minimum age of criminal responsibility and has criticised countries where the age has been set at 10 years old or below.

[24] NAYJ noted the following ages in their response: in Greece and the Netherlands it is 12; in France 13; in Austria, Germany and Italy 14; in Denmark, Finland and Sweden 15; in Portugal and Spain 16 and in Belgium and Luxembourg 18.

[25] See paragraph 100 and 101 of the twenty-third report.

[26] See paragraph 102 of the twenty-third report.

central database were to be created, it should be established with the safeguards referred to by Xanthaki and Stefanou and be limited in scope to convictions data in respect of transnational offences.

4. Access to the ECR

4.1 Access to the domestic record by British residents

In England and Wales, the criminal record is not a public document and consequently access to the information is not routinely available. The CRB may issue three types of certificates relating to criminal records[27] resulting from three different levels of check. These checks permit individuals to provide details about their criminal record status to interested parties, and also provide interested parties with the opportunity to criminal record check others.[28] Investigative data is not included in any of these criminal record certificates. The integrity and reliability of this type of data has not been tested in court and the subject has not had the opportunity to counter any data on the database. It cannot be considered as 'fact' for the purposes of decision-making, even if it is of use in the conduct of future police investigations. This form of operational data is available to the police but not to the judiciary nor to other organisations or individuals. This distinction is considered to be an essential feature of the separation of powers, and that any erosion of the distinction would be unacceptable within the UK.

Strict controls are placed on those who may apply for information about others' criminal record status and stringent restrictions placed on the disclosure of and the use to which that information may be put in respect of criminal convictions. It is both a civil wrong and a criminal offence[29] to publicise information in relation to a person's spent

[27] Part V of the Police Act 1997 makes provision for these certificates.

[28] A *Criminal Conviction Certificate* includes non-spent convictions that are still on the record, recorded at a national level. A *Criminal Record Certificate* is issued for those individuals who work or apply for positions exempted under the ROA 1974. This certificate includes spent convictions and cautions, reprimands and warnings held nationally. An *Enhanced Criminal Record Certificate* is issued for those who have sole charge or who are regularly caring for, training or supervising under 18s, vulnerable adults or those who are being considered for judicial appointments. This includes, in addition to the above, non-convictions information and information from local police records and checks on the Department for Education and Skills and the Department of Health lists in respect of those who work or will work with children or the vulnerable.

[29] Section 9 The Rehabilitation of Offenders Act 1974.

convictions unless disclosure is made within the course of an official duty. It is an offence for a member, an officer or an employee of a registered body to disclose information provided as a result of an application unless the disclosure falls within the terms of section 124 of the Police Act 1997,[30] and disclosure will only be made to the subject of the criminal record or to an individual or body registered with the Secretary of State.[31] The circle of people who may obtain information about an individual's criminal record is actually very limited and by asking for such information, the individual or employer places the applicant on notice of their identity and why they are asking for the information – such a search cannot be done secretively.

4.2 Access to the domestic record by external residents and sources

In addition to domestic request for certain types of criminal conviction information, external requests may also be accepted. There is judicial authority for the proposition that criminal records can be disclosed, even for spent offences, to foreign police authorities.[32] While there is no legal bar to information being shared with other European countries in relation to criminal records, individual requests have to be made via Interpol and Europol to NCIS.[33] Equally, local forces within England

[30] The Police Act 1997, Part V, section 124(1): 'he discloses it, in the course of his duties, – (a) to another member, officer or employee of the registered body, (b) to a member, officer or employee of a body at the request of which the registered body countersigned the application, or (c) to an individual at whose request the registered body countersigned the relevant application.' Disclosure offences do not apply if the subject provides written consent to the disclosure.

[31] M. Colvin, M. Spencer and P. Noorlander, *The Schengen Information System, A Human Rights Audit: A Justice Report* (London: JUSTICE, 2000); M. Colvin, M. Spencer and P. Noorlander, *The Schengen Information System, A Human Rights Audit: A Justice Report* (London: JUSTICE, 2000).

[32] *X* v. *Commissioner of Police of the Metropolis* [1985] 1 WLR 420 per Whitford J. It was argued that disclosure to the Paris Office of Interpol was unlawful under section 9 ROA 1974 as the disclosure had been to a foreign police force, however, the court held that the disclosure was made in the course of the police officer's official duty and no offence had been committed under section 9(2) of the Act. The reasoning given for the decision was that it has long been accepted that there is an obligation to provide such information to foreign police forces in order to suppress international crime.

[33] Requests for legal assistance in criminal matters must be sent to the Home Office. Requests for details about previous convictions and for intelligence information (as long as this is not requested for use in proceedings) are sent to the UK National Criminal Bureau of Interpol at the National Criminal Intelligence Service. See *Seeking Assistance in Criminal Matters for the UK, Guidelines for Judicial and Prosecuting*

and Wales may also request information from other jurisdictions but must do so via Europol who make contact with the relevant authority in the given country. Consequently there is already a certain degree of data lawfully passed between European countries, and it is this system of data exchange that is preferred by the House of Lords Select Committee on European Union and the House of Commons Select Committee on European Scrutiny.

4.3 Issues raised by the proposals for an ECR

The Commission's proposition is to set up a European-wide database of criminal records that all Member States may access without the need to make individual requests, although whether this would be a database of all criminal convictions plus operational intelligence or whether it would be an index of offenders who are not EU Member State nationals is unclear at this stage. Data from the database may be used to alert investigatory authorities to the criminal history of individuals who may be working, residing or travelling through their jurisdictions. However, criminal records are not only used for this purpose. Such data may also provide the prosecuting authorities with information that they can use when prosecuting defendants, and it could even be taken into account in the judicial process, and once again it is this aspect that causes concern within the UK. The multifaceted nature of any such database may be of great benefit to law enforcement agencies and to the public more generally if it leads to greater security and freedom from crime. However, it also gives cause for concern to the organisation JUSTICE and others because it is not clear what the information will be used for and therefore what data protection safeguards will need to be introduced.[34] For others, it is the separation of powers and the distinction between prosecuting and judicial authorities that causes the greatest concern and this will be considered in the next section.

Authorities, 2nd edn, published by the Judicial Co-operation Unit, Organised and International Crime Directorate.

[34] See *EU Cooperation in Criminal Matters Response to Specific Proposals* (London: JUSTICE, 2001) for JUSTICE's response to the European Commission's Paper on mutual recognition of final decisions in criminal matters and the Council's paper on the programme of measures to implement the principle of mutual recognition in criminal matters. The response builds on JUSTICE's paper *EU Cooperation in Criminal Matters: A Human Rights Agenda* (London: JUSTICE, 2000), considering the implications of the Tampere agenda on criminal matters.

NCIS is the agency charged with the duty to fight serious and organised crime and to work with law enforcement agencies, governments and other relevant bodies around the world, including Europol.[35] There is certainly a mechanism to allow an exchange of criminal intelligence and also a legal power to provide such information. NCIS has cooperated and worked in numerous tripartite and multipartite investigations and has provided analysed (summary) investigative data to foreign authorities rather than raw intelligence data. This was NCIS's preference for subsequent investigations, even though it believed that Europol would like greater access to the information that NCIS had at its disposal, because NCIS holds information from a number of different agencies and was not the owner or originator of some of the data to which it had access. Consequently, issues of data ownership, data control and data integrity need to be considered in detail before investigations data is to be made accessible to foreign authorities via an ECR. Such data has not been tested in court, is not easily open to challenge by the subject and could be quite incorrect, and in addition may be sensitive to the point that ongoing investigations may be prejudiced if raw data were to be revealed.[36]

5. Use of the ECR

The use to which criminal convictions data should be put depends in part on the data that is collected and who has access to that data, however there are some fundamental issues of principle that must be considered regardless of whether the data would be useful to foreign authorities. The general rule in England and Wales, subject to some exceptions is that a defendant's previous convictions for similar or different types of offences from the one being tried in court, will not be revealed in court until after the defendant has been convicted.[37] Previous convictions go to the duration of sentence that will be handed down by the judge on conviction; however, previous convictions are not generally revealed in the process of trying to reach a verdict.[38] The

[35] Under the terms of section 2(2) of the Police Act 1997.

[36] There are a number of reasons why it may be undesirable for investigations data to be included within a European criminal record, not least that it may be unconstitutional within some Member States to provide this data. See for a discussion question 264 of the 'Minutes of Evidence' to the House of Lords Select Committee on European Union.

[37] See further Webley (2005).

[38] There are exceptions to this. For a description of some of these see Webley (2005).

rationale for this is that if a person is considered to be innocent until proven guilty and revelation of previous convictions may prejudice the jury against the defendant. The fact that an individual has committed similar offences in the past to the one he or she is charged with does not necessarily mean guilt in this instance. As long as the existence of an ECR did not weaken this principle then the fact that data was held on British nationals' foreign convictions, or that Member States made use of UK criminal convictions in a different way in their own legal system is unlikely to be a significant problem. However, this is predicated on the assumption that such data was reliable and was the result of a free and fair trial process in both the UK and in other Member States.

A number of groups and organisations are challenging the current balance between society's need to know about the past convictions of ex-offenders and the needs of ex-offenders to be rehabilitated into society and putting their past offending behind them. One such organisation that is running a campaign on this issue at present is UNLOCK, the National Association of Ex-Offenders. It has called for a Criminal Records Tribunal to be set up to allow ex-offenders (other than ex-sex offenders) who have been free of criminal convictions for serious (recordable offences) for at least seven years to be suspended from their obligation to disclose their criminal record, as long as they have remained free of further convictions for an indictable offence.[39] A review of the ROA 1974 has led to Government proposals for primary legislation on these points, however, a Bill has yet to be brought before parliament.[40] This has profound implications in respect of an ECR. Concerns have been expressed that the 'spent' convictions provisions that apply to UK criminal records may not apply in other jurisdictions and similarly that non-UK residents who have been convicted of offences abroad may also not benefit from these provisions. This may mean that offenders are unfairly prejudiced depending on the Member State within which they have been convicted.

An additional concern relating to an EU criminal record rests with issues of dual criminality, whereby only offences recognised by all Member States should be included on the database. JUSTICE believes

[39] For further information visit UNLOCK's web site on www.tphbook.dircon.co.uk/unlock.htm.

[40] A summary of Government thinking can be found in *Breaking the Circle: A Summary of the Views of Consultees and the Government Response to the Report of the Review of the Rehabilitation of Offenders Act 1974*, although a consultation process and an enquiry are currently in progress subsequent to this document.

as a matter of principle that Member States should not be entitled to take account of offences that would not be considered to be offence in their own jurisdiction. Even if such recognition is prohibited, the interests of an individual may be prejudiced by virtue of the information being available on the database for consideration. JUSTICE points to contentious and sensitive areas of law, for example as regards soft drugs offences, abortion and euthanasia, for which there is no consensus between Member States. Once again, decisions reached on issues of detail will have a profound impact on the extent to which an ECR is considered to be desirable and feasible.

Finally, there are serious concerns about whether an ECR would hold information other than criminal convictions on file. If the record were to be used as a tool to alert investigatory authorities within Member States to pending investigations, rather than as merely a record of criminal convictions, it would be important to determine how Eurojust's relationship with other bodies such as Europol and SIS would function in order to determine whether an expanded database set up for the purpose of targeting serious crime would be more suitable rather than the ECR. Indeed, the CRB noted that the biggest obstacle would be gaining the acceptance for the ECR being used for non-criminal justice purposes (operational purposes) rather than for the more traditional and more widely accepted criminal justice ones. In this respect, investigations data is more problematic due to the lack of verification of its accuracy, including the fact that it may be the product of information provided by disgruntled or malicious individuals who wish to cause problems for other individuals with law enforcement agencies or gain a professional or personal advantage over them. While this is a difficulty inherent in intelligence information stored and used at a domestic level, these problems are greatly magnified at EU level, with differences in law enforcement legal frameworks and strategies, informant policies as well as translation issues. The inclusion of raw investigations data would prove controversial and according to the views expressed by NCIS, undesirable in a UK context.

6. Critical evaluation

The issues raised in respect of the ECR relate firstly to the mechanism through which the data is collected and provided to other Member States, secondly to the integrity of the data and thirdly the uses to which the data will be put. In relation to the first of these, Europol currently acts as an intermediary between Member States for the exchange of data, although it has been suggested that Eurojust perform this function. NCIS mooted support for Eurojust's role, but felt that this may not be universally supported due to Eurojust's objectives. NCIS considered that Europol would be able to take on the role of transferring data from Member States to an EU database situated within Eurojust, and advised it was entirely feasible that the proposed EU database could be housed within Europol. There are data protection safeguards within the Europol convention as an 'operative force'.[41] However, these do not apply to Eurojust which is a coordinating body. Eurojust has a data protection regime, but its legal powers have not been drafted with the task of holding the central ECR in mind.[42] Consequently this poses some difficulties. The Council Decision that established Eurojust details a comprehensive raft of control mechanisms associated with Eurojust handling, storing and processing Member States' data and information.[43] This Council Decision does not, however, delegate Eurojust any legal powers to take on the task of holding the proposed central ECR. Were this task to be delegated by Ministers to Europol, then as a result of Article 4(2) of the Convention, only NCIS would be legally entitled to undertake the task of transferring data/information held in England and Wales to Europol. Concerns have been expressed during the research about Eurojust's lack of accountability, its ill-defined role and the lack of mandatory rigorous data protection standards that could be applied to the proposed criminal record.[44] However, these concerns appear to have been met, at least in part, by the entry into force of the Council Decision earlier this year.

JUSTICE's response is focused on the civil liberties' consequences associated with the implementation of the principle of mutual recognition and it has serious concerns about criminal records in Member States being networked, or being compiled as one database. It points to its research findings in relation to the Schengen Information System, and feel that it is unlikely, especially in the light of Article 8 of the ECHR, that the risks inherent in large databases of this kind (concerns about

[41] Convention on the Establishment of a European Police Office, OJ C 316, 27 November 1995.

[42] My thanks to Mr Pyne of the Judicial Cooperation Unit for its comments on this section in an early draft of the England and Wales Falcone report to the European Commission.

[43] Council Decision: Eurojust 1/5358/02, which came in to force on 28 February 2002.

[44] See for example JUSTICE's *Submission on the Proposals for the Establishment of EUROJUST* (London: JUSTICE, 2000), at p. 6.

inaccuracy and the lack of safeguards for individuals), will outweigh the potential benefits of such a system.[45] JUSTICE's recommendations resonate with concerns expressed by other respondents to this study on the accuracy of information to be contained on an ECR and the availability of that information across Europe. It proposes that Member States be made legally responsible for the accuracy of data input onto any national system that may provide the data to a central record or via a networked system, and that this data be overseen by a national independent data protection authority that oversees the accuracy of the data and the data protection provisions. It considers too that any EU criminal record should be clearly overseen by judicial authorities and that effective remedies should be introduced for individuals so that they may have access to their information and to have any of their information corrected. Other respondents also had concerns about the operation of the ECR and the effect on civil liberties. The Law Society did not object to the establishment of an ECR, but that this would depend upon their being adequate safeguards in place to protect individuals who may be included on the criminal record.[46] The concerns primarily relate to safeguards to protect individuals' civil liberties as a result of the proposals rather than concerns about disclosure of criminal record information as a matter of principle.

7. Conclusions

Views are mixed on the feasibility and desirability of an ECR, in part as the conditions under which data is recorded, accessed, its use and the responsibility for its integrity including data protection safeguards are relatively under-developed at this stage. Few of those that took part in the original research felt confident about giving a definite conclusion to the proposition, most as a result of the lack of detail accompanying the general proposition. Even the House of Commons and the House of Lords Select Committees have been relatively reserved in their conclusions in respect of the proposals for similar reasons as has the UK Government.[47]

[45] See Colvin, Spencer and Noorlander (2000).

[46] The Policy Adviser for criminal law at the Law Society provided an oral report to the Falcone project in respect of the proposals for a European criminal record.

[47] As reported in the House of Commons Select Committee on European Scrutiny twenty-first report at paragraph 7.12: 'In her Explanatory Memorandum of 5 May 2004 the

There was cautious support from some quarters, tempered with real concerns. Concerns have been expressed about the extent to which individuals' human rights would be safeguarded. Some raised broad data protection issues, others went further to say that large databases of the type envisaged had the potential to include inaccurate information that could have a profound impact on people's lives, were difficult to maintain and to guarantee and individuals would find it very difficult to seek an effective remedy if such problems were to arise in practice. There were also concerns expressed about the use to which the data would be put and the extent to which offenders would be able to reintegrate into society after serving their sentences. The distinction between operational data and court proven criminal conviction data remains an extremely important issue, as is the operation of the separation of powers within Member States in respect of the data that judicial authorities have in front of them when deciding cases. For others, issues related to the operation of the separation of powers were expressed as fair trial guarantees in all Member States.

On the other hand, some provided broad support for the proposal. NCIS felt that it would be a useful proposition and indeed a necessary one, which in view of current intelligence and police cooperation was in many ways a formalisation and systematisation of current bilateral practices. Readily accessible reliable data was considered to be 'the jewel in the crown' of law enforcement and without it individual freedom and rights could not be ensured in the face of organised crime. The general feeling from the non-governmental organisations that took part in the research was that much more needed to be considered before they felt they could comment effectively on the proposal, although they would welcome the opportunity to comment at a later date on more detailed proposals. The devil, as they say, may well lie in the detail.

Parliamentary Under-Secretary of State at the Home Office ... explains that it is not possible to assess the impact on UK law of the measures outlined in the Communication until these have been developed into firm proposals.' Further at 7.16: 'On the proposal for a European criminal record, the Minister comments as follows: The UK is doubtful whether the benefits of a central EU criminal register of records relative to those offered by simply improving access to national criminal records would justify the cost and complexity of overcoming the considerable differences in the formats in which criminal records are stored across Europe.'

PART III

16

Databases in the area of freedom, security and justice: Lessons for the centralisation of records and their maximum exchange

VALSAMIS MITSILEGAS

1. Introduction

A key element in the development of EU action in Justice and Home Affairs in recent years has been the creation of legal and technical mechanisms aiming to facilitate the collection, exchange and analysis of personal data. Steps in this direction have taken the form of initiatives aiming both at eliminating obstacles to the exchange of personal data between national authorities and at creating EU-wide structures and databases.

The emphasis on developing EU-wide databases can be witnessed in both the immigration and asylum field (with the establishment of the EURODAC and Schengen Information System (SIS) databases and proposals to establish a Visa Information System (VIS) in the pipeline) and the criminal law/policing field (the Europol database and part of the SIS database being prime examples). Political reactions to terrorist attacks this decade have led to calls for increasingly linking these databases (notwithstanding their different purpose) and increasing their 'interoperability' – a strategy clearly visible in the 2004 Hague Programme, a five-year renewal of the EU Justice and Home Affairs strategy. The Hague Programme also calls for the further facilitation of bilateral information exchanges in the police field under the so-called 'principle of availability' and for the 'deepening' of surveillance by the use of biometrics in the various databases. In this climate, one of the main features of the development of the EU Justice and Home Affairs legislative agenda in the past three years have been proposals – within but also outside the EU framework – to develop further existing databases, create new ones and enhance their interoperability, as well as boosting bilateral information exchange. These proposals raise a number of important issues touching upon the protection of fundamental rights and may have a huge potential to redefine the relationship between the individual and the state. Although they cover a very specific area of judicial cooperation in criminal matters (and potentially police cooperation), proposals to enhance the exchange and use of criminal records (and ultimately proposals to create a European Criminal Record) can be seen as falling within the same climate of achieving maximum centralisation and/or exchange of personal data for security purposes.

In this context, this chapter will examine existing and developing databases in EU Justice and Home Affairs, as well as initiatives aimed at boosting information exchange, with the aim of drawing a number of lessons for proposals to facilitate the exchange of criminal records across the EU. The analysis of issues surrounding the development of the various EU initiatives and databases will be followed by an attempt to test these issues in the context of criminal records and to examine the implications of making criminal records databases 'interoperable' with other EU databases.

2. Europol

Europol is the prime example of EU centralisation in the field of police cooperation and (along with Eurojust) in the field of cooperation in criminal matters in general.[1] While the Convention establishing Europol was signed in 1995,[2] the organisation started work in 1999, with the Europol Information System being only established in 2005.[3] As the collection and analysis of information is central to Europol's mandate, the Europol Convention contains a number of provisions on the Information System and the Analysis Files that can be opened by Europol for specific cases. The Europol Information System contains information on persons who have been convicted for one of the offences

[1] For a look behind the scenes to Europol's establishment and the Member States pushing for centralisation at the time, see C. J. F. Fijnaut, 'The "Communitization" of Police Cooperation in Western Europe', in H. G. Schermers (ed.), *Free Movement of Persons in Europe. Legal Problems and Experiences* (Dordrecht/Boston/London: Kluwer Academic Publishers, 1993), pp. 75–92.

[2] OJ C316, 27 November 1995.

[3] See S. Peers, *EU Justice and Home Affairs Law*, 2nd edn (Oxford: Oxford University Press, 2006), p. 551; see also R. Genson and P. Zanders, 'Le développement de la coopération policière dans l'Union Européenne. Quel avenir pour Europol?' (2007) 504 *Revue du Marché Commun et de l'Union Européenne* 8. The authors note that the first instances of work by the system were organised by the Belgian presidency in 2001, but that the final decision as to the technical components of the system was taken in 2005.

which fall within Europol's mandate;[4] it may also contain information on persons who are suspected of having committed or having taken part in one of these offences, but also information on persons for whom there are serious grounds under national law for believing that they will commit such offences.[5] This broad list may become even more extended in cases where Europol opens Analysis Work Files (AWF): the latter may also include a wide range of information on witnesses (actual or potential), victims, contacts and associates and informers.[6] Along with the information it receives by and exchanges with EU Member States, Europol has legal personality,[7] and the power to conclude agreements regarding the exchange of personal data with other EU bodies (such as Eurojust), but also with third bodies (such as Interpol) and States.[8] A prime example of cooperation with third countries has been the Agreement on the exchange of personal data concluded between the Director of Europol and the USA.[9] The broad categories of collected personal data and their potential use for analysis and exchange purposes[10] pose prominently the question of whether Europol's work is covered by adequate standards for the protection of personal data and privacy. The Europol Convention itself contains a number of provisions on data protection and provides the legal basis for the establishment of a Joint Supervisory Body for data protection.[11] However, there is as yet no clear general data protection/privacy legal framework in the third pillar along with the specific Europol data protection rules and the powers of the Europol Joint Supervisory Body are limited.[12]

[4] On the offences falling within the mandate of Europol, see Article 2 of the Convention and annex attached therein, as well as the Protocols amending the Convention.

[5] Article 8(1) of the Europol Convention.

[6] Article 10 of Europol Convention and Europol rules on analysis files – for details see Peers, *EU Justice and Home Affairs Law*, pp. 551–552. An index system for analysis work files is also created (Article 11).

[7] Article 26 of the Europol Convention.

[8] See Article 18 of the Europol Convention. See the Europol website for texts of such agreements.

[9] For details, of the Europol–USA Agreement, see V. Mitsilegas, 'The New EU–US Co-operation on Extradition, Mutual Legal Assistance and the Exchange of Police Data' (2003) 8 *European Foreign Affairs Review* 515–536.

[10] On 18 December 2006 the Information System contained 4,311 'offences': *Europol Annual Report 2006*, The Hague, 21 March 2007, File no. 1423-45r1, Council doc. 7950/07, p. 20.

[11] Article 24 of the Europol Convention.

[12] This is in particular the case when Europol concludes agreements with third states or bodies – the Joint Supervisory Body has the mandate to give an Opinion on the

Since the entry into force of the Europol Convention in 1999, there have been constant talks regarding the necessity of amending the Convention with the aim to broaden the mandate and role of Europol. Changes – most notably broadening the scope of offences covered by Europol and broadening access to the Europol databases – have been brought about by way of amending Acts/Protocols amending the Europol Convention.[13] With the legal form of a Convention (and its amendments by Protocols) delaying the entry into force of the instruments (at least in comparison to the period required for the entry into force of more 'orthodox' EU instruments such as Framework Decisions or Decisions), a number of the amending Protocols entered into force only in the Spring of 2007.[14] However, the completion of the amendments to the Europol Convention has not stopped the general discussion on the future general direction and mandate of Europol (which was also prominent in the negotiations leading to the EU Constitutional Treaty).[15] Discussions continued notwithstanding the 'freezing' of the Constitutional Treaty, focusing on two main issues: the change in the legal basis of Europol (with the instrument of the Convention deemed too cumbersome) and the change in Europol's mandate and powers (in particular the question of whether Europol should become more 'operational'). The 2006 Austrian EU Presidency prioritised the issue by organising a High Level Conference on the Future of Europol and by commissioning a 'Friends of the Presidency' Working Group to discuss the issue. Both initiatives proposed sweeping changes to the current Europol framework: the High Level Conference called for making Europol 'operational' and for ways to be found 'to enable Europol to exchange information also with countries that do not have the same data protection standards as those that are applicable within the European Union'.[16] The 'Friends of the Presidency' Report went further, in particular as regards the issue of information collection and exchange. Introducing

adequacy of data protection in the third state/organisation involved, but does not have the power to block the agreement from going ahead.

13 These include legislation to extend Europol's mandate to protect the euro (OJ L185, 16 July 2005), to combat serious organised crime (OJ C362, 18 December 2001), and to combat money laundering (OJ C358, 13 December 2000) and to extend its powers and access (OJ C2, 6 January 2004). For a full list see the Europol website.

14 See note by Steve Peers, *Europol: The Final Step in the Creation of an 'Investigative and Operational' European Police Force*, on www.statewatch.org.

15 See the Final Report of Working Group X on 'Freedom, Security and Justice', CONV 426/02, WG X 14, Brussels, 2 December 2002, p. 18; see also Constitutional Treaty, Article III-276.

16 Chairman's Summary of the High Level Conference on the Future of Europol (23 and 24 February 2006), Council doc. 7868/06, Brussels 29 March 2006, p. 3.

far-reaching proposals which would change both the mandate and the nature of Europol, the Report called for Europol to, inter alia:

- act as a service provider for EU information systems within the area of internal security but *outside* its current competence (for example a DNA or PNR database);
- be allowed to cooperate with *private* entities, such as universities and credit card companies; be given access to other EU databases (and access to be given to Europol national units to all information on the Europol database in order to introduce an automated cross-check mechanism in various Europol systems);
- be given access to *national* IT systems on the basis of the principle of availability (to be examined further in the chapter).[17]

Taking note of the 'Friends of the Presidency' Report, the Justice and Home Affairs Council at the end of the Austrian EU Presidency adopted a series of conclusions sketching a number of options on the future of Europol.[18] These were followed by further conclusions at the end of 2006, whereby the Council agreed that the Europol Convention should be replaced by a Council Decision.[19] A few days later, the Commission tabled such a draft Decision.[20] Along with the change in the legal basis of Europol, the proposal introduced a number of changes in the organisation's mandate and powers. With regard to Europol's tasks regarding databases and information collection, analysis and exchange, the proposal largely follows the 'Friends of the Presidency' proposals by extending the reach of Europol to information and intelligence forwarded by third countries 'or other public or private entities'.[21] The potential extension of Europol's role with regard to personal data is also evident in Article 10 of the Commission's draft, which mentions the possibility of the establishment by Europol of a system for the processing of personal data other than its current Information System.[22] The same

[17] Austrian Presidency of the European Union, *Future of Europol. Options Paper reflecting the Outcome of the Discussion on the Future of Europol held during the Austrian Presidency*, May 2006, (Council doc. 9184/1/06 REV 1, Brussels 19 May 2006), pp. 6, 8 and 9 respectively. Emphasis added.

[18] Justice and Home Affairs Council of 1–2 June 2006, doc. 9409/06 (Presse 144), pp. 22–23.

[19] Justice and Home Affairs Council of 4–5 December 2006, doc. 15801/06 (Presse 341), pp. 20–21.

[20] Proposal for a Council Decision establishing the European Police Office (EUROPOL), COM (2006) 817 final, 20 December 2006.

[21] Article 5(1)(a). [22] Article 10(3).

provision expressly calls upon Europol to ensure the interoperability of its data processing systems with the data processing systems in the Member States and in particular with the processing systems of EC or EU bodies such as the European Borders Agency (Frontex), the European Central bank, the European Monitoring Centre for Drugs and Drug Addiction (EMCDDA), the European Anti-Fraud Office (OLAF), Eurojust and the European Police College (CEPOL).[23] Moreover, access to the Europol Information System will no longer be limited to national units but will be extended to other authorities designated as such by Member States (however only on a hit/no hit basis).[24] The mandate of Europol will include 'serious crime', including terrorism.[25]

If adopted, the proposals – which, as the Commission admits, were not subject to detailed consultation from its part as consultations took place only by the Austrian Presidency and extended to the level of governments and technical experts[26] – will introduce significant changes in the mandate of Europol with regard to its handling of personal data. These changes become more significant when viewed in the light of parallel proposals to grant Europol access to non-police databases such as the Visa Information System (VIS). The Commission proposal signifies the end to the basic principle underlying the work of Europol, namely that the main channel of cooperation is between Europol and central national police units – according to the proposals other national authorities could have access to Europol databases while Europol can also work with the private sector. At the same time, the exchange of data between Europol and other EC/EU bodies is boosted by the express reference of the proposal to 'interoperability' of their databases. These developments – indicative of the trend towards maximising the exchange of personal data in the EU – have been criticised by EU data protection authorities. The European Data Protection Supervisor (EDPS) noted that the principle of interoperability reverses the current approach of the Europol Convention, which in Article 6(2) strictly prohibits the linking between the Europol Information System and other automated processing systems and opposes the view that

[23] Articles 10(5) and 22. [24] Article 13(6).

[25] Articles 3 and 4 of the proposal, which seem to distinguish between the objective and the competence of Europol.

[26] COM (2006) 817 final, 20 December 2006, p. 4.

interoperability should be treated merely as a technical concept.[27] This view is shared by the Europol Joint Supervisory Body (JSB), which notes that technical interoperability does not mean that data may actually be exchanged without legal provisions in place.[28] The JSB also expresses concerns regarding the extension of the scope of Europol in the context of the emerging distinction between objectives and competences of Europol.[29] Finally, the JSB puts forward the view that, by dispensing with the limitation of access to national units, a concept of availability is introduced and is critical of the extension of Europol's mandate in Article 5 (which includes receiving data from private sector authorities).[30]

3. The Schengen Information System

Another important EU database in the field of Justice and Home Affairs is the SIS. Established by the Schengen Implementing Convention, which was incorporated in EC/EU law by the Amsterdam Treaty, the SIS contains data categorised in the form of various 'alerts': these alerts concern both immigration data (alerts on third country nationals who should be denied entry into the Schengen territory) and data related to police and judicial cooperation in criminal matters (alerts on persons wanted for extradition to a Schengen State, on missing persons, on persons wanted as witnesses or for the purposes of prosecution or the enforcement of sentences, on persons or vehicles to be placed under surveillance or subjected to specific checks, and on objects sought for the purpose of seizure or use in criminal proceedings).[31] The system works on a hit/no hit basis and Member States

[27] Opinion of the European Data Protection Supervisor on the proposal for a Council Decision establishing the European Police Office, 16 February 2007, points 21 and 22 respectively.

[28] *Opinion of the Joint Supervisory Body of Europol with respect to the Proposal for a Council Decision establishing the European Police Office*, Opinion 07/07, 5 March 2007, p. 11.

[29] Ibid., p. 3. This could arguably lead to very broad objectives and thus to the extension of Europol's scope of action. Concerns regarding the potential extension of Europol's mandate have also been expressed by the House of Commons European Scrutiny Committee (see 9th Report, session 2006–07, p. 30).

[30] Ibid., pp. 5, 6. These concerns are also reflected in Council doc. 7539/07, 19 March 2007.

[31] Articles 95–100 of the Schengen Implementing Convention, OJ L19, 22 September 2000, pp. 42–45. For further details, see House of Lords European Union Committee, *Schengen Information System II (SIS II)*, 9th Report, session 2006–07, HL Paper 49; for overviews see also Peers, *EU Justice and Home Affairs Law*, pp. 547–549; and C. Stefanou, 'Organised Crime and the Use of EU-wide Databases', in I. Bantekas and G. Keramidas (eds.), *International and European Financial Law* (Lexis Nexis Butterworths, 2006), pp. 224–225.

determine which of its law enforcement or immigration authorities have access to the respective part of the SIS.[32] The System became operational in 1995 for an initial group of seven Member States and by 2001 it applied fully to thirteen out of the fifteen 'old' Member States (excluding the UK and Ireland).[33] Meeting the SIS requirements by candidate countries was a central requirement of the EU in accession negotiations for the 2004 and 2007 enlargements[34] – currently the new Member States are not full Schengen members but it is expected that the majority will be able to participate in the next few months.[35]

The challenge of adaptation of candidate countries to SIS standards (and their participation in the System after their accession to the EU) was particularly complex in the light of efforts by the Schengen Members to develop further the SIS so that they can respond to both events such as terrorist attacks and to technological advancement. Specific aims of proposals to develop the SIS have been to extend the data included in the database and to broaden the categories of national authorities having access to Schengen data. A significant step towards the achievement of the latter goal has been made on the basis of counter-terrorism considerations: in 2004, the Council adopted a first pillar Regulation and a third pillar Decision concerning the introduction 'of some new functions for the Schengen Information System, including in the fight against terrorism.'[36] The Regulation extended access to SIS data to national judicial authorities and access to immigration data specifically to authorities responsible for issuing visas and residence permits and examining visa applications. The Decision extended access to certain categories of 'criminal law' SIS data to Europol and Eurojust.

32 For further details see House of Lords, *Schengen Information System II (SIS II)*.

33 Ibid.

34 See V. Mitsilegas, J. Monar and W. Rees, *The European Union and Internal Security* (Palgrave, 2003) chapter 5; see also J. Monar, *Enlargement-related Diversity in EU Justice and Home Affairs: Challenges, Dimensions and Management Instruments*, WRR (Netherlands Scientific Council for Government Policy) Working Document 112, The Hague December 2000.

35 See the Conclusions of the Justice and Home Affairs Council of 4–5 December 2006, doc. 15801/06 (Presse 341), pp. 20–22. In the light of delays in the development of the second generation Schengen Information System (which will be discussed in the next paragraphs), it was decided that new Member States will at the first stage be integrated in a developed version of the original Schengen Information System (SIS1+), a proposal called 'SISone 4all'. The Council called for the integration of new Member States to SIS1+ by end-June 2007.

36 Reg 871/2004, [2004] OJ L162, 30 April 2004, p. 29; Decision 2005/211/JHA, [2005] OJ L68, 15 March 2005, p. 44.

A broader debate on the nature and development of the SIS has been taking place in the context of discussions on the establishment of a so-called 'second generation' System, or SIS II. In May 2005, the Commission tabled three draft legislative proposals (two first pillar Regulations and one third pillar Decision – reflecting the fact that the SIS covers both immigration and criminal law data), which would constitute the legal basis for the establishment of a SIS II.[37] At the time of writing, the two Regulations had been adopted,[38] while the third pillar Decision was in the process of being formally adopted.[39] The provisions of the general SIS II Regulation are largely mirrored in the third pillar Decision. The main changes involve the nature and use of personal data included in the System. Both the Regulation and the Decision provide the legal basis for the inclusion in the SIS of biometrics, in the form of photographs and fingerprints.[40] The provisions on the use of biometrics are extremely significant in this context. In the first stage, biometrics will be used only for 'one-to-one' searches – seeking to confirm someone's identity by comparing the biometric identifiers of the person only with those existing in the SIS under this person's name; however, in the future (following the presentation by the Commission of a Report on the availability and readiness of the required technology), biometrics will also be used for 'one-to-many' searches, where biometric data of one person will be compared with the whole SIS database.[41] This development may have substantial implications for privacy, but also for the nature of the SIS, which is increasingly

[37] Proposal for a Council Decision on the establishment, operation and use of the second generation Schengen Information System, COM (2005) 230 final; Proposal for a Regulation on the establishment, operation and use of the second generation Schengen Information System, COM (2005) 236 final; and Proposal for a Regulation regarding the access to SIS II by the services in Member States responsible for issuing vehicle registration certificates, COM (2005) 237 final.

[38] Regulation 1987/2006 on the establishment, operation and use of the second generation Schengen Information System (SIS II), OJ L381, 28 December 2006, p. 4; Regulation 1986/2006 regarding access to the second generation Schengen Information System (SIS II) by the services in the Member States responsible for issuing vehicle registration certificates, OJ L381, 28 December 2006, p. 1.

[39] Draft Council Decision on the establishment, operation and use of the second generation Schengen Information System (SIS II), latest publicly available draft at the time of writing Council doc. 14914/06, Brussels, 12 December 2006.

[40] Article 20(3)(e) and (f) of the Regulation and the draft Decision. See also their Preamble (recital 14 in the Regulation and recital 12 in the draft Decision).

[41] Article 22 of Regulation and draft Decision. For further explanation of these searches, see House of Lords Report, paragraphs 57–60.

developing from a hit/no hit database to a general intelligence database. The fact that such an important decision to instigate one-to-many searches is essentially deemed as a technical issue and will be taken with little debate (the European Parliament being merely consulted), has raised serious concerns of transparency and democratic scrutiny.

Another sign of the development of SIS into a general intelligence/investigative database is the provision, in both the Regulation and the draft Decision, allowing the interlinking of alerts.[42] Such interlinking is allowed only if there is a 'clear operational need'[43] but is subject to the national law of the Member State which decides to use this option[44] – thus rendering possible the creation of significantly different systems across the EU. Interlinking of alerts is a major departure from the limited hit/no hit character of the current SIS and its potential for profiling is significant. As the European Data Protection Supervisor has noted in his Opinion on the SIS II proposals 'the person is no longer "assessed" on the basis of data relating only to him/her, but on the basis of his/her possible association with other persons', which may lead to their treatment with greater suspicion if they are deemed to be associated with criminals or wanted persons;[45] moreover, the Supervisor notes, interlinking extends investigative powers because it makes possible the registration of alleged gangs or networks (e.g. data of illegal immigrants and data on traffickers).[46] The Supervisor noted that authorities with no right of access to certain categories of data should not even be aware of the existence of these links.[47] The Regulation and draft Decision seem to have taken to some extent this view on board, by stating that authorities with no right of access to certain categories of alert will no be able to *see* the link to an alert to which they do not have access.[48] However, this may not necessarily mean that these authorities will be unaware of the *existence* of a link.

A further extension to SIS I standards is the provision – in the third pillar Decision only and with regard to the criminal law part of the System – that processing of such data may take place for other purposes

[42] Article 52 of Regulation and 37 of the draft Decision (see also preamble, recitals 17 and 13 respectively).
[43] Article 37(4) of the Regulation and Article 52(4) of the draft Decision.
[44] Article 37(5) of the Regulation and Article 52(5) of the draft Decision.
[45] European Data Protection Supervisor, Opinion of 19 October 2005, [2006] OJ C 91/38. Also available at www.edps.eu.int. p. 13.
[46] Ibid. [47] Ibid.
[48] Article 37(3) of the Regulation and Article 52(3) of the draft Decision. Emphasis added.

than those expressly mentioned in the draft Decision. For this to be allowed processing must be linked with a specific case and justified by the need 'to prevent an imminent serious threat to public policy and public security, on serious grounds of national security or for the purposes of preventing a serious criminal offence'.[49] This provision (which does not exist in the Schengen Implementing Convention)[50] challenges the purpose limitation principle and may lead to a considerable extension of the use of Schengen data. On the other hand, in a departure from the Commission's original proposals, the rules on access to SIS data have not changed drastically.[51] Some changes have been introduced in the context of access to SIS II data by Eurojust – along with access to extradition and missing persons data, Eurojust will also have access to alerts concerning wanted persons and objects.[52] However, the more general question has been raised about what happens to SIS data which are accessed by other EU bodies and whether the limits to access of such data set out by the SIS legislation can be circumvented by the relevant rules governing these bodies. The question has been raised in particular with regard to whether Europol can treat SIS data as its own data (considered as Member States contribution to Europol). If SIS data become Europol data in this process, the express prohibition in the SIS II legislation of transferring such data to third countries may be circumvented.[53]

4. Interoperability and access to immigration databases

In efforts to enhance the exchange of personal data, great emphasis has been placed in the recent past on enabling the flow of data between the various EU databases and/or EU agencies and bodies. Examples of developing legal bases to enable access by EU bodies to databases for the purposes of police cooperation and judicial cooperation in criminal matters have been examined above in the context of access by Europol

[49] Article 46(5) of the draft Decision.

[50] See Articles 101 and 102 of the Schengen Implementing Convention-House of Lords Report, paragraph 92.

[51] See House of Lords Report. In particular, see the express prohibition of transferring or making available SIS II data to third countries or international organisations (Article 39 of Regulation and 54 of draft Decision).

[52] Article 42 of draft Decision; see also House of Lords Report, paragraph 45. This extension reflects related calls by Eurojust: see Eurojust's Contribution to the Discussion on the SIS II, Council doc. 11102/06, Brussels, 30 June 2006.

[53] House of Lords Report, paragraph 108.

and Eurojust to the Schengen Information System. These efforts have been coupled by initiatives such as agreements enabling the exchange of personal data between EU bodies, with the agreement between Europol and Eurojust being a prime example.[54] However, largely justified on the basis of the 'war on terror', efforts for greater synergies in data sharing have been proliferating in the recent past under the guise of two main initiatives: to enhance the 'interoperability' between EU databases; and to allow access by law enforcement authorities to immigration databases, in spite of the undoubtedly different purposes of managing migration and fighting crime – the justification put forward being that access by police authorities to immigration data is necessary for security reasons.[55] These trends were clearly visible already in 2004 when the European Council, in the Declaration on combating terrorism, linked the monitoring of the movement of people with the 'war on terror' by stressing that 'improved border controls and document security play an important role in combating terrorism.'[56] The European Council stressed the need to enhance the interoperability between EU databases and the creation of 'synergies' between existing and future information systems (such as SIS II, VIS and EURODAC) 'in order to exploit their added value within their respective legal and technical frameworks in the prevention and fight against terrorism'.[57]

Justifying the observation that immigration and security are increasingly linked in EU JHA discourse and policy making, thus creating an (in)security continuum,[58] the Hague Programme – adopted by the European Council later in 2004 – articulated more clearly the perceived link between movement, migration and terrorism, stating that:

> the management of migration flows, including the fight against illegal immigration should be strengthened by establishing *a continuum of security measures* that effectively links visa application procedures and entry and exit procedures at external border crossings. Such measures are

[54] For more details on these agreements, see House of Lords European Union Committee, *Judicial Co-operation in the EU: The Role of Eurojust*, 23rd Report, session 2003–04, HL Paper 138.

[55] See V. Mitsilegas, 'Contrôle des étrangers, des passagers, des citoyens: Surveillance et anti-terrorisme' (2005) 58 *Cultures et Conflits* 155–182.

[56] Ibid., pt 6, p. 7.

[57] Ibid., pt 5, p. 7. Text to be found at www.consilium.europa.eu under 'European Council Conclusions'.

[58] See in this context the seminal work of D. Bigo, in particular *Polices en réseaux – l'éxperience européenne* (Paris: Presses Sciences Po, 1996).

> also of importance for the prevention and control of crime, in particular terrorism. In order to achieve this, a coherent approach and harmonised solutions in the EU on biometric identifiers and data are necessary.[59]

The Hague Programme also mentions interoperability both in the context of strengthening security (calling for interoperability of national databases or direct online access including for Europol to existing central EU databases),[60] and in the context of migration management – where the European Council called on the Council to examine 'how to maximise the effectiveness and interoperability of EU information systems' and invited the Commission to present a Communication on the interoperability between the SIS the VIS, and EURODAC.[61] The Commission presented its Communication a year later, in November 2005.[62] The purpose of the Communication was to highlight how, beyond their present purposes, databases 'can more effectively support the policies linked to the free movement of persons and serve the objective of combating terrorism and serious crime'.[63] On the basis of this approach, the Commission argued strongly in favour of access of authorities responsible for internal security to immigration databases such as SIS, VIS and EURODAC.[64] The Communication provided a definition of 'interoperability', which is the 'ability of IT systems and of the business processes they support to exchange data and to enable the sharing of information and knowledge'.[65]

According to the Commission, interoperability is a technical rather than a legal/political concept.[66] The attempt to treat interoperability as a merely technical concept, while at the same time using the concept to enable maximum access to databases containing a wide range of

[59] Paragraph 1.7.2. Emphasis added.

[60] Paragraph 2.1. It is important to note in this context that the European Council expressly states that new centralised European databases should only be created on the basis of studies that have shown their added value.

[61] Paragraph 1.7.2.

[62] Communication on Improved Effectiveness, Enhanced Interoperability and Synergies among European Databases in the Area of Justice and Home Affairs, COM (2005) 597 final, 24 November 2005.

[63] Ibid., p. 2.

[64] Ibid., p. 8. The Commission also took the opportunity to float proposals for longer-term developments, including the creation of a European Criminal Automated Fingerprints Identification System, the creation of an entry-exit system and introduction of a border crossing facilitation scheme for frequent border crossers, and European registers for travel documents and identity cards (pp. 8–9).

[65] Ibid., p. 3.

[66] Ibid.

personal data (which become even more sensitive with the sustained emphasis on biometrics) is striking.[67] It can be seen as an attempt to depoliticise an issue which may have major repercussions for the protection of fundamental rights and civil liberties, and which has the potential to shield far-reaching developments (including the blurring of the boundaries between databases established for different purposes and containing different categories of data for the benefit of law enforcement agencies) from effective scrutiny and democratic control.[68] The emphasis on interoperability may lead to the justification of the development of important initiatives in this context at the operational level, with the adoption of negotiated legislative standards underpinning the evolving databases (or their capacities) potentially deemed unnecessary.[69]

While the Commission's far-reaching proposals for access by internal security agencies to the second generation SIS have not been accepted, the situation may not prove to be the same with regard to the VIS.[70] The development of the VIS is a clear example of the trend to blur the boundary between immigration and police databases.[71] The Justice and Home Affairs Council adopted detailed conclusions on the development of VIS in February 2004, stating clearly that one of the purposes

[67] See also the criticism by the European Data Protection Supervisor in his Opinion on the Communication (10 March 2006), www.edps.eu.int. The Supervisor highlighted the potential over-reach of those having access to databases under interoperability, noting that the latter 'should never lead to a situation where an authority, not entitled to access or use certain data, can obtain this access via another information system'.

[68] On the trend towards de-politicisation in the context of border security in the EU, see V. Mitsilegas, 'Border Security in the European Union. Towards Centralised Controls and Maximum Surveillance', in E. Guild, H. Toner and A. Baldaccini, *Whose Freedom, Security and Justice? EU Immigration and Asylum Law and Policy* (Oxford: Hart Publishing, 2007).

[69] A similar trend can also be discerned in the negotiation of legislative instruments on databases, where a number of issues perceived as 'technical' are left to be decided by comitology. See for example the development of 'technical rules for linking alerts' in the SIS II Regulation, Article 37(2).

[70] The Visa Information System would contain data (including biometrics) on visa applicants, but also a series of data on the visa application, including details of sponsors (see Articles 3 and 6 of the draft VIS Regulation). For further details, see Peers, pp. 165–167.

[71] The latter tendency is also discernible in proposals to allow access to the EURODAC database (containing fingerprints of asylum seekers) by internal security authorities – see the Commission interoperability Communication, but also the German Presidency Programme on Police and Judicial Cooperation (Council doc. 17102/06, Brussels, 22 December 2006). However, at the time of writing, it appears that such proposals are not going forward.

of the system would be to 'contribute towards improving the administration of the common visa policy and towards internal security and combating terrorism'.[72] It also called for access to VIS to be granted to border guards and 'other national authorities to be authorised by each Member State such as police departments, immigration departments and services responsible for internal security'.[73] In June 2004, the Council adopted a Decision forming the legal basis for the establishment of VIS[74] and negotiations began to define its purpose and functions and formulate rules on access and exchange of data. The Commission subsequently tabled a draft Regulation aiming to take VIS further by defining its aims and rules on data access and exchange.[75] The Justice and Home Affairs Council of 24 February 2005 called for access to VIS to be given to national authorities responsible for 'internal security', when exercising their powers in investigating, preventing and detecting criminal offences, including terrorist acts or threats and invited the Commission to present a separate, third pillar proposal to this end.[76] The Commission tabled such a proposal in November 2005.[77]

The two texts are currently being negotiated in parallel.[78] Reflecting the Conclusions of the JHA Council, the draft Regulation accepts that one of the purposes of the VIS is to contribute to the prevention of threats to internal security of the Member States.[79] However, the precise conditions of access to internal security authorities to VIS are still under negotiation between the Council and the European Parliament (which is now a co-legislator in the field), with a number of differences emerging.[80] The latest draft of the Regulation contains a bridging clause to the third pillar Decision allowing access to national internal security

[72] Doc 5831/04 (Presse 37). The Council called for the inclusion in VIS of biometric data on visa applicants.

[73] Ibid.

[74] Council Decision of 8 June 2004 establishing the Visa Information System (VIS), [2004] OJ L 213/5, 15 June 2004.

[75] Proposal for a Regulation of the European Parliament and of the Council concerning the VIS and the exchange of data between Member States on short-stay visas, COM (2004) 835 final, 28 December 2004.

[76] Doc. 6228.05 (Presse 28), pp. 15–16.

[77] COM (2005) 600 final, 24 November 2005.

[78] Latest drafts at the time of writing: Council doc. 8198/07 (2 April 2007) (draft Regulation); and Council doc. 81711/07 (23 April 2007) (draft third pillar Decision).

[79] Article 1A(g).

[80] A fundamental difference involves the transfer of VIS data to third countries and international organisations. Such transfer (prohibited by the SIS II legislation) is allowed under the draft VIS Regulation (see Article 25B), but the European Parliament is opposed (see Council doc. 8185/07).

authorities 'if there are reasonable grounds to consider that consultation of VIS data in a specific case will substantially contribute' to the prevention, detection or investigation of a number of criminal offences.[81] The wording of this clause has been subject to extensive debate, with the view being put forward that a higher threshold is necessary for allowing access, requiring also the existence of factual indications as the basis for the reasonable grounds mentioned above.[82] The latest draft of the third pillar Decision differs from the Regulation as it includes a reference not to factual, but to 'substantive' indications as the basis for reasonable grounds.[83] The draft Decision also raises the threshold for access to the VIS by national internal security authorities by requiring such access to be necessary in a specific case, and by indicating what would constitute a specific case.[84] The VIS legislative instruments also grant – along with national authorities – access to the VIS to Europol. According to the draft Decision, Europol has access to VIS on the basis of more general conditions – if this is necessary for the performance of its tasks.[85]

5. Exchange of data between national police authorities: The principle of availability

Along with the proliferation and development of EU databases and attempts to enhance their synergies and interoperability, another central element to the development of law enforcement cooperation in the EU has been the promotion of cooperation between national authorities. In recent years, in particular since the adoption of the Hague Programme, the main means of achieving this goal is the application of the so-called principle of availability in the police field. According to the Hague Programme, this means that 'throughout the Union, a law enforcement officer in one Member State who needs information in order to perform his duties can obtain this from another Member State and that the law enforcement agency in the other Member State which holds this

[81] Article 1B. The Article also refers to Europol's access to VIS.

[82] See Council doc. 5456/1/07 REV 1, Brussels, 20 February 2007.

[83] Article 5(1)(d).

[84] Article 5(1)(c). The earlier draft merely required that access must be linked to a specific case. The European Parliament seems to have succeeded in allowing access by national authorities to the VIS only via national central access points and not directly (Article 4a – see also Council doc. 8540/07, Brussels, 18 April 2007).

[85] Article 7 of draft Decision. The wording was criticised by the Europol Joint Supervisory Body for being too general – see Opinion 06/22, Council doc. 5049/07, Brussels, 4 January 2007.

information will make it available for the stated purpose, taking into account the requirement for ongoing investigations in that State'.[86] The Commission tabled in 2005 a proposal for a third pillar legal instrument in the field.[87] The general principle of availability is established in Article 6 of the draft, according to which Member States must ensure that 'information shall be provided to *equivalent* competent authorities of other Member States and Europol . . . *in so far as these authorities need* this information to fulfil their lawful tasks for the prevention, detection or investigation of criminal offences'.[88]

The principle of availability, as outlined in the Commission's proposal, is based on a maximal version of mutual recognition and may have far-reaching implications for both the protection of human rights and for the legitimacy of EU action in the police field.[89] It calls for the provision of information to 'equivalent' authorities of other Member States almost exclusively on a 'need to know basis', with exchange of information taking place on the basis of standard, pro-forma documents, and with very few grounds for refusal available to the requested authorities.[90] Thus, information exchange becomes almost automatic. This form of cooperation may have substantial implications for the protection of fundamental rights, in particular the right to privacy. As conceived by the Commission, the principle would apply without any harmonisation in Member States' systems. Competent authorities potentially covered by the principle would be national authorities responsible for police and judicial cooperation in criminal matters, but also Europol.[91] However, there are differences between the powers and mandate of national police and judicial authorities across the EU. The Commission's proposal does require a level of equivalence between such authorities but equivalence is to be defined by a comitology

[86] Point 2.1, p. 27. The Hague Programme calls for the principle of availability to be applied from 1 January 2008.

[87] Proposal for a Council Framework Decision on the exchange of information under the principle of availability, COM (2005) 490 final, 12 October 2005.

[88] My emphasis.

[89] See V. Mitsilegas, written evidence to the House of Commons Home Affairs Committee, inquiry on EU Justice and Home Affairs.

[90] See Article 14 of the Commission draft. It must be noted however that, unlike the Framework Decision on the European Arrest Warrant, the draft Framework Decision would allow for refusal on human rights grounds.

[91] Article 3(b) of draft Framework Decision, which refers to authorities covered by the first hyphen of Article 29 TEU.

procedure, thus evading full parliamentary scrutiny.[92] National authorities (and Europol) are to be given, inter alia, online access to databases of their counterparts in other Member States,[93] and are obliged to provide information to their counterparts for the very broad purpose of preventing, detecting or investigating criminal offences.[94] This framework enables a very extensive access to national data and raises not only human rights but also important constitutional questions: can a national authority obtain, under the principle of availability, information that it would not be allowed to obtain under its national law?[95] Can the requested authority be obliged to collect information on behalf of the requesting authority, even by using coercive measures?[96] A number of questions also arise from the application of the principle to Europol, which seems to be treated in the same way as a national police authority. However, such a move seems to disregard both the nature of Europol (which currently is rather an intelligence organisation in principle without coercive powers in Member States' territories) and its strictly delineated relationship with national police authorities.[97]

The Commission's legislative proposal introducing the principle of availability gave a flavour of the direction of police cooperation in the EU but, although tabled in 2005, negotiations have not proceeded very far. The reason for this has been the parallel emphasis of a number of Member States on enhancing police cooperation between them outside the EU framework. This has led to the signing, in May 2005, by seven Member States,[98] of a Convention on the 'stepping up of cross-border

[92] Article 5. Moreover, measures adopted under this procedure will be classified as 'confidential'.

[93] See Article 9, access will be given to databases to which the corresponding competent authorities have online access.

[94] The proposal also contains a provision on purpose limitation (Article 7) – information can be used for the prevention, detection or investigation of the criminal offence for which the information is provided.

[95] Similar questions have arisen in the context of mutual recognition in judicial cooperation in criminal matters with regard to the European Evidence Warrant.

[96] According to Article 2(2) of the proposal, requesting police authorities and Europol cannot ask for information to be obtained – with or without coercive measures – by the requested authority solely for the purposes of cooperation; but information already lawfully collected by the requested authority by coercive measures may be provided (even though these measures may not be lawful in the requesting State – something that would potentially infringe national constitutional provisions through the 'back door').

[97] Although as seen above these limits are currently subject to revision in the proposal amending the Europol Convention.

[98] Belgium, Germany, Spain, France, Luxembourg, the Netherlands and Austria.

cooperation, particularly in combating terrorism, cross-border crime and illegal immigration' – the Prüm Convention.[99] Like Schengen, the Prüm Convention was named after the town where it was signed. Like Schengen, it is a pioneering document, where a number of Member States decide to push ahead on an intergovernmental basis and forge closer cooperation in home affairs matters – presumably in an effort to address obstacles in cooperation resulting from the lack of trust in a Europe of twenty-five and legislative paralysis in the light of the EU's 'frozen' Constitution.[100] The Convention contains far-reaching proposals which may have significant consequences for the protection of civil liberties and fundamental rights. In the context of exchange of information, these include the establishment of national DNA analysis files and the automated search and comparison of DNA profiles and fingerprinting data.[101]

From the very outset, Prüm members stated that participation to their group is open to all Member States and that a proposal would be tabled in three years from the entry into force of the Convention leading to its incorporation into the legal framework of the EU.[102] Such an initiative happened in fact much earlier, due to the fact that the incorporation of the Treaty of Prüm into the EC/EU legal order has been one of the top priorities of the 2007 German EU Presidency. In February 2007, the Justice and Home Affairs Council agreed to integrate into the EU legal framework the majority of the parts of the Prüm Treaty relating to police and judicial cooperation in criminal matters.[103] Evoking the perceived operational success of automatic information exchange brought about by the Prüm Treaty in the context of DNA data exchange between Germany and Austria, the Council noted that:

> the special value of the [Prüm] Treaty lies in the substantially improved and efficiently organised procedures for the exchange of information. The states involved may now give one another automatic access to specific

[99] Council document 10900/05, Brussels, 7 July 2005.

[100] See V. Mitsilegas, *What are the Main Obstacles to Police Cooperation in the EU?*, Briefing Paper for European Parliament LIBE Committee, IP/C/LIBE/FWC/2005-24, 14 February 2006.

[101] For an early analysis, see T. Balzacq, D. Bigo, S. Carrera and E. Guild, *Security and the Two-Level Game: The Treaty of Prüm, the EU and the Management of Threats*, CEPS Working Document no 234, January 2006, www.ceps.be.

[102] Mitsilegas, *What are the Main Obstacles to Police Cooperation in the EU?*

[103] Justice and Home Affairs Council of 15 February 2007, doc. 5922/07 (Presse 16), p. 7.

> national databases. This amounts to a quantum leap in the cross-border sharing of information.[104]

No less than fifteen Member States tabled a proposal for a third pillar Decision incorporating the police cooperation aspects of Prüm into the EU legal framework.[105] The Preamble of the draft Decision makes express reference to the principle of availability and refers to the need to introduce procedures for promoting fast, efficient and inexpensive means of data exchange.[106] The text of the proposal effectively mirrors the provisions of the Prüm Treaty. On data gathering and exchange, the proposal obliges Member States to establish national DNA analysis files for the investigation of criminal offences.[107] Member States must ensure the availability of DNA profiles from their national DNA files[108] and allow automated searches in these databases by other Member States' national contact points.[109] Cellular material may also be collected and become available.[110] Moreover, Member States must ensure 'the availability of reference data from the file for the national automated fingerprint identification systems established for the prevention and investigation of criminal offences'.[111] It is not clear whether this wording assumes that such databases have already been established in all Member States. Similarly to the DNA databases, automated searching and comparison of fingerprint data is allowed.[112] Automated searching of vehicle registration data is also allowed.[113]

The potential impact of these proposals on privacy and the relationship between the individual and the State is significant. The proposal effectively obliges Member States to establish DNA databases in the first place. Moreover, it calls for availability of sensitive data if a hit is found and automated searches of national databases containing sensitive data by authorities of other Member States. The proposal contains a number

[104] Ibid., p. 8.

[105] Initiative of the Kingdom of Belgium, the Republic of Bulgaria, the Federal Republic of Germany, the Kingdom of Spain, the French Republic, the Grand Duchy of Luxembourg, the Kingdom of the Netherlands, the Republic of Austria, the Republic of Slovenia, the Slovak Republic, the Italian Republic, the Republic of Finland, the Portuguese Republic, Romania and the Kingdom of Sweden, with a view to adopting a Council Decision on the stepping up of cross-border cooperation, particularly in combating terrorism and cross-border crime, latest draft at the time of writing Council doc. 7273/1/07 REV 1, Brussels 17 April 2007.

[106] Recitals 5 and 9 respectively. [107] Article 2(1). [108] Article 2(2).

[109] Article 3(1) – the latter can thus compare DNA profiles. Comparisons of unidentified DNA profiles with all DNA profiles are also allowed – see Article 4.

[110] Article 7. [111] Article 8. [112] Article 9. [113] Article 12.

of data protection provisions,[114] but beyond this the mechanism of cooperation it would introduce would operate in an environment with rules that are far from clear and based largely on national legislation. The proposal does not specify what kind of data could be included in DNA or fingerprint databases. This may lead to substantial discrepancies in national approaches, with some Member States including data only of persons convicted of serious crimes, and others including data on a wide range of individuals, including suspects or persons subject to disqualifications.[115] There may also be substantial differences on the reasons for collecting DNA data or fingerprints between national systems. A number of questions arise in this context, including whether this will lead to Member States extending the collection of personal sensitive data[116] and whether cooperation on that basis would lead to the requesting Member State gathering sensitive data from databases in other countries, which it would not be allowed to gather under its national law.[117] Notwithstanding these very important issues, and the changes that the proposal may bring about, scrutiny and debate on the issues concerned remains limited. In the first place, the Prüm Convention was negotiated largely in secret as an international Treaty prior to it being submitted to national parliaments for ratification. Thereafter, it has been presented as almost a fait accompli to the Member States and is being negotiated under the third pillar (with a limited role for the European Parliament) and, in a manner reminiscent of the adoption of the European Arrest Warrant, under very tight deadlines[118] and with a rush that has not been justified.[119]

[114] Articles 25–32.

[115] See also the Opinion of the European Data Protection Supervisor, paragraph 37.

[116] The European Data Protection Supervisor reads the proposal as requiring from the Member States to collect and store information, even if it is not available yet in the national jurisdiction: see paragraph 4 of his Opinion on www.edps.europa.eu In an attempt to alleviate concerns in this context Jonathan Faull, Director, Commission Directorate for Freedom, Security and Justice, stated in his evidence in the House of Lords EU Committee in their inquiry on the Prüm Convention: 'We are not obliging Member States to build up DNA databases of innocent people just in case one day somebody else in another Member State might be interested in knowing about them.' Q98. Evidence session of 22 March 2007. Uncorrected evidence.

[117] Articles 3(1), 9(1) and 12(1) of the draft Decision contain a safeguard by stipulating that automated searches may be conducted only in individual cases and in compliance with the requesting Member States' national law.

[118] With Germany aiming to achieve agreement on the proposal within its Presidency.

[119] The transfer of the Prüm Treaty to the EU framework seems to weaken national parliaments of Member States, which would have to ratify the Convention if it remained outside the EU framework and their Member States wished to accede to it.

6. Conclusion: Lessons for facilitating the exchange of records in criminal matters

The development of EU law and policy on Justice and Home Affairs has increasingly been marked by an emphasis on the creation, development and interlinking of centralised EU databases. New databases are in the process of being established (such as the VIS), existing databases are being developed in order to include expanded types of data (in particular biometrics – see SIS II) and changes are being introduced to expand access to existing systems (for instance the rules on SIS II and the Europol information systems). Moreover, a number of efforts are being made to ensure the interlinking not only of information within a specific database (see the interlinking of alerts in the SIS) but also to link various databases together. On the one hand, the concept of interoperability is used to make possible the linking of diverse and wide-ranging databases by presenting the endeavour as a technical issue; on the other hand, legislation developing or creating EU databases aims at ensuring maximum access by law enforcement authorities, even in cases where the databases involve sensitive personal information collected for purposes other than fighting crime and covering individuals engaging in perfectly legitimate activities (such as applying for a visa) or deemed a threat (under an alert on the SIS). This attempt to link databases established for different purposes under the banner of 'internal security' maximises data exchange, blurs the boundaries of data collection and processing, expands the reach of the law enforcement authorities and treats individuals increasingly as suspects – thus shifting gradually the boundaries of the relationship between the individual and the state.

Attempts at centralisation of EU databases and their interlinking do not come at the expense of the enhancement of bilateral cooperation between national law enforcement authorities in Member States – they rather go hand in hand. Cooperation between national police authorities is boosted by the adoption of the principle of availability and the attempts to incorporate the Prüm Treaty into the Union's legal order. As with centralisation, these developments have the potential to maximise the exchange of information, which is increasingly becoming more sensitive (see fingerprints and DNA data). This expansion is happening without any harmonisation at the national level on what kind of data are included in national databases, by whom and for what purpose. Cooperation without harmonisation in this context may lead to an implicit push to Member States to allow the collection of an increasing amount of personal data and might lead – if safeguards are not included and monitored – to police authorities in one Member State obtaining information by their counterparts elsewhere which they would not normally obtain in a purely domestic law situation.

Further challenges arise from the fact that both the centralisation of EU databases and the enhancement of bilateral cooperation between law enforcement increasingly proceed with limited debate and democratic scrutiny. The framing of interoperability as a technical issue serves to depoliticise the significant civil liberties repercussions of its application, viewing the interlinking of extensive and diverse centralised databases as merely a technical issue to be resolved by experts. This tendency is also visible in legislation establishing databases, which in many instances allows recourse to the comitology procedure for future elements of information systems to be developed. Yet, the principle of availability – much like the application of mutual recognition in criminal matters – does not involve the negotiation of commonly accepted substantive standards across the EU, but rather involves agreement on the *procedural* matter of allowing national police authorities access to databases of their counterparts in other Member States. There is little control on what this access will entail in terms of information included in national databases and their subsequent use in the requesting Member State. Moreover, as seen above, transparency and democratic scrutiny have been seriously undermined by the method under which the Prüm provisions are imposed into EU law.

The challenges of these developments to the protection of privacy are manifold. The examination of the complex issue of privacy and data protection in the context of police cooperation in the EU falls outside the scope of this chapter, but it is important at this point to refer to some of the current limitations of the EU's legal framework. The proliferation of EU databases goes hand in hand with the proliferation – and at the same time fragmentation – of data protection regimes. Each system (SIS, VIS, Europol information system, the Prüm Treaty) has its own rules of data protection and supervision. There is no general data protection framework in the third pillar, with a relevant Framework Decision being currently negotiated and most EU proposals making references to Council of Europe instruments. While a horizontal EU data protection regime for the third pillar would be an important step forward, a main challenge for data protection and privacy law is to provide comprehensive safeguards vis-à-vis the increasing interlinking of databases. Data protection and privacy law may further need to be reconsidered in the light of the deepening of surveillance by the inclusion in databases of sensitive personal data such as biometrics.

All of the above points are relevant in the specific context of the development of cooperation in the EU on the exchange of criminal records. At present, there seems to be a tension between establishing cooperation on the basis of bilateral exchanges between national criminal record databases and cooperation on the basis of a centralised European criminal record. At the national level, the issues arising in the context of the application of the principle of availability are relevant. Most notably, potential discrepancies in the content of national criminal records in a climate of maximum information exchange between national databases (What information is included? For which offences?[120] For what purpose?[121] For what use?[122] Of what kind?[123]) may lead to challenges for legal certainty and the protection of fundamental rights, in particular privacy. The potential application of the principle of availability in this context needs to be monitored, in particular since the bilateral exchange of criminal records is envisaged to happen under a great degree of automaticity, on the basis of pro-forma forms. At the level of a potential centralised EU database (which, on the basis of the wording of the Hague Programme, that largely discourages the creation of new EU databases, must be justified comprehensively), issues arising concern not only the content of this database but also, in the light of the preceding discussion, access to the database and its interlinking with other EU databases. The potential for profiling and its consequences for private life arising from the interlinking of databases (in particular if European Criminal Record databases include data

[120] The latest draft of a Framework Decision on the organisation and content of the exchange of information extracted from criminal records between Member States (Council doc. 6372/07, Brussels, 16 February 2007), seems to include only convictions for criminal offences (Article 2(a)). There is a debate on whether to also include administrative offences on the list. However, it is noteworthy that even if the scope is limited to 'criminal law' convictions, the scope may still vary between Member States, especially if the scope of the proposal is not limited to specific crimes.

[121] The latest draft seems to include a very broad purpose – according to Article 6, criminal records are requested 'for the purpose of criminal proceedings against a person or for any other purpose than that of criminal proceedings'. The compatibility of the wording with the purpose limitation principle of data protection law is questionable.

[122] The latest draft allows the broad use of criminal record data 'for preventing an immediate and serious threat to public security' – Article 9(2).

[123] The request form for the criminal record allows Member States to ask for fingerprints (see annex).

extending beyond criminal convictions – such as disqualifications, and if such database is linked with non-criminal law databases[124]) are considerable. Whether on a bilateral or on a centralised basis, the need for the proliferation of information exchange of criminal records must be subject to a rigorous, open and transparent debate and, given its potential impact on the relationship between the individual and the state, fully justified.

[124] It is interesting to note that in the context of the criminal records debate, the Commission – in a Working Document – has floated the idea of an index of third-country nationals convicted in the EU (one of the options proposed is an index containing biometric data for third country nationals), COM (2006) 359 final, 4 July 2006. It is not unlikely that the creation of such an index will be followed by calls to link it with databases such as the Visa Information System or the immigration part of the Schengen Information System.

17

A European criminal records database: An integrated model*

ELS DE BUSSER

1. Introduction

The growth of cross-border crime and the progress in the ability to fight the phenomenon has made the exchange of information between judicial and enforcement authorities of Member States increase in importance during the past decade. The term 'exchange of information' is used here in its widest sense, referring to the events happening before, during and after sentencing a person who committed a criminal offence. Broadly speaking, the exchange of information becomes evident in four stages.

Firstly, before passing judgment, exchanging information is very important in the context of tracing and arresting an individual suspected of committing a criminal offence. Predominantly law enforcement authorities will be involved in the trading of data necessary in order to locate, and subsequently arrest the required person. Secondly, the extradition of the person concerned, with a view to prosecuting him, will entail the sending and receiving of information between, mainly, judicial and to a lesser extent law enforcement authorities of the states involved. The actual prosecution of the offender in a specific state can, as a third possible moment of exchanging information between states' authorities, cause the need for receiving data from foreign – primarily judicial – authorities in the context of international recidivism and the individualisation of sanctions. Fourthly, after judgment has been passed

* This article is based on the published report of the project done by the Institute of International Research on Criminal Policy of Ghent University for the European Commission in 2001: G. Vermeulen, T. Vander Beken, E. De Busser and A. Dormaels, *Blueprint of an EU Criminal Records Database. Legal, Politico-institutional and Practical Feasibility* (Maklu: Antwerp-Apeldoorn, 2002), p. 91.

in a specific case, the possibility of international recidivism by the convicted offender can again require the exchange of information on previous convictions by predominantly judicial authorities.

The smooth functioning of the exchange of information in these four stages would therefore significantly improve the course of the process of bringing offenders to justice on an international level and consequently the fight against cross-border crime. The recommended model of an EU criminal records database attempts to integrate both an efficiently working and supervised system of information exchange and the interests of the Member States to record their criminal records data on a national level.

2. The project aims

The project carried out by Ghent University for the European Commission in 2002 has developed a model for the organisation of an EU criminal records database including recommendations concerning contents, access and use. Developing the model, the project reflected on the policy documents in which the Commission and the Council of the EU expressed the options that are open. The prospect of creating an EU criminal records database has been mentioned and developed in several policy documents and proposals and was last reiterated in the Hague Programme of 2004.[1]

Three motives for building a database that fulfils the needs listed in these instruments, were presented by the 2000 Mutual Recognition Plan[2] of which the second and third motive – individualisation of sanctions and the creation of a register of disqualifications – were taken into account in the development of the recommended model. Avoiding double prosecution (*ne bis in idem* principle) was not

[1] Point 49 of the Vienna Action Plan stressed the substance of performing a feasibility study of formalising the exchange of criminal records data towards a genuine central database for the EU for the first time. See: Action Plan of the Council and the Commission on how best to implement the provisions of the Treaty of Amsterdam on an area of freedom, security and justice, OJ C 19, 23 January 1999. More recently the system was developed in: European Council Declaration on Combating Terrorism, 25 March 2004, and in the Hague Programme, Strengthening Freedom, Security and Justice in the European Union, 16054/04 JAI 559, 13 December 2004; Council and Commission Action Plan implementing the Hague Programme on strengthening freedom, security and justice in the European Union, OJ C 198, 12 August 2005.

[2] Council of the European Union, Programme of measures to implement the principle of mutual recognition of decision in criminal matters, OJ C 12, 15 January 2001.

considered. Due to the specific nature of these decisions, which entail a different structure and a different set of rules governing the database as compared to final judicial decisions, the model database does not include decisions regarding prosecution. Disqualifications are included in the scope of the recommended criminal records database for reasons of efficiency as only the disqualifications that are incorporated in criminal judgments are included in criminal records. Individualisation of sanctions is, finally, the established consequence of the 'interconnecting' of Member States' criminal registers as international recidivism is then a genuine possibility.

3. The recommended model

Essentially, two options are open to organise the exchange of information between the (judicial and law enforcement) authorities of the Member States: the intergovernmental approach and the supranational approach. The Mutual Recognition Plan presents three possibilities: a facilitated bilateral exchange of information,[3] a network between national criminal records registers and a central EU office of criminal records. The first two options are two intergovernmental structures, while the possibility of establishing an EU office in which all Member States' criminal records registers are centralised is evidently a supranational procedure.

The two intergovernmental methods are relatively effortless to organise since the adjustments they require are located on a national level and do not impose the granting of sovereignty from the Member States onto a supranational authority. In addition to an EU instrument calling for the facilitation of the sending and receiving of information between Member States' authorities or introducing a network between the national criminal records registers, no essential changes are to be made within the Member States' criminal justice systems. A significant disadvantage of both intergovernmental systems is the lack of (EU) supervision. Even if a supervising EU authority was installed, Member States' authorities can be encouraged to exchange information bilaterally but this procedure cannot be enforced by means of sanctioning the

[3] The spontaneous trading of information – on a yearly basis – was already included in Article 22 of the Council of Europe Convention on Mutual Assistance in Criminal Matters of 1959. Currently, the facilitating of information exchange is provided in a Council Decision: Council of the European Union, Council Decision of 21 November 2005 on the exchange of information extracted from criminal record, OJ L 322, 9 December 2005.

non-cooperative states. Creating a link between all national criminal records registers only ensures a regular exchange of data when the network determines a permanent link between the computerised national registers or in the case where Member States are required to insert data on criminal convictions in the network on a regular basis, for example every 24 hours. Nevertheless, the smooth functioning of this system depends on the goodwill of the Member States to act in accordance with the procedure. Evidently, this is the most essential advantage of the supranational option.

A combination of both the intergovernmental procedures of a network between national criminal records registers and the supranational system of a central EU office for criminal records will therefore be the most efficient way of working, combining the advantages and avoiding the disadvantages of the two options in an integrated model. The merging of the two structures consists of a decentralisation of the information within the national criminal records registers and a centralised index of 'labels' attached to the criminal records information. Utilising one of the existing EU infrastructures – such as the Europol structure – can make this system work without introducing new and complicated regulations or *modi operandi*. Data protection can be assured by establishing a monitoring body based on the model used for the Europol joint supervisory data protection body. More specifically, an electronic link is installed between the existing national criminal records databases providing Member States' authorities with the opportunity to look for criminal records information in other Member States. The search method is centralised by means of an EU index system of labels that will indicate the specific characteristics of related crimes. The problem of diverse qualifications for the same criminal acts within the Member States' criminal justice systems will be avoided by using this labelling technique.

3.1 The labelling technique

Every final judicial decision related to a criminal act can receive a specific label linked to the aspects of that particular offence.[4] By means of a Council Decision, a limited list of labels in all official languages of the Member

[4] The proposal for a Council Framework Decision regarding this system only requires the convicted person's nationality to be attached to the convictions included in his/her national criminal records registers. See: Council of the European Union, 6372/07 Limite Copen 20, Proposal for a Council Framework Decision on the organisation and content of the exchange of information extracted from criminal records between Member States, 16 February 2007.

States can be given to every judge who is competent to make decisions related to one or more criminal acts, together with the duty to attach one or more labels to such verdicts. No additional labels should be created on a national level. The labelling technique is not intended to establish an EU categorisation of offences but is focused on facilitating searching the system through the introduction of the mentioned indicators.

Although the duty for these judges to connect certain labels to their decisions is also a non-enforceable responsibility and, therefore, a matter of goodwill, the labelling technique requires minimal effort for them. As the judge ruling on a particular criminal case is the most appropriate person to decide on the detailed characteristics of the case, he/she needs to indicate these qualities within the restricted list of labels that have been imposed. The Council Decision introducing this requirement should call upon the responsibility of judges to make an adequate choice of labels in order to rule out every possible doubt regarding the type of the case indicated by means of its label(s).

The construction of a list of labels should be done in a very accurate manner, listing all necessary labels and avoiding any overlap. The list should be developed in such a style that no two labels can stand for exactly the same type of case or offence. At the same time, any possible doubt should be removed regarding the exact meaning of a specific label. Even though the intention is to mark particular criminal cases or offences, the list of labels should not be too extensive in order to make it effective as an instrument in the individualisation of sanctions as well as making this an uncomplicated task for the national judges to perform. Identifying all possible labels can be done by using a threefold branch structure with the larger categories of criminal acts, mandated areas and framework decisions as guidelines.

3.1.1 Larger categories of criminal acts

The first branch will include groups of criminal acts that are interrelated regardless of their potentially unrelated or even divergent qualifications[5] in the Member States. Introducing this type of labels and making them work as efficiently as possible means they have to be sufficiently wide to encompass a specific range of criminal behaviour. However, the labels

[5] For example Belgium and The Netherlands use a different qualification of the offence of 'stalking'. The Belgian Criminal Code requires only the disturbance of a person's peace by the offender's behaviour, while the Dutch Criminal Code demands the systematic violating of a person's life with the intention of forcing this person to do something, not to do something, to tolerate something or to intimidate this person, in order to justify prosecution for stalking.

should be restricted to an adequate extent in order to cover only those offences that have an identifiable common feature and to make the system work in a functional manner.

Common characteristics can include of a variety of factors. Firstly, the *modus operandi* of the criminal act(s) is an important individualising element.[6] Secondly, the sector in which the criminal acts are situated can establish a common aspect, such as the IT sector (e.g. illegal software copying), industrial sector (e.g. producing forged fashion goods) or the financial sector (e.g. fraud and counterfeiting). Thirdly, the goods that are the object of the criminal behaviour are a distinctive element, such as drugs, food, software, etc. Fourthly, the specific human rights violated by the offence(s) committed, e.g. violating the right to life by inflicting physical injury or infringing the right to privacy by the act of stalking.

To conclude, exceptionally identifiable aspects can generate exclusive categories. Offences in which minors have been either the victims or the offenders or the involvement of an offender who has been convicted before[7] are two distinctive features that should present a special category due to the key position they fulfil in most criminal justice systems.

3.1.2 Mandated areas

The EU bodies involved in criminal matters, Europol, OLAF and Eurojust, are competent to be involved in only a limited range of offences. Delineating the criminal acts that are included in the individual mandates of these bodies is important in order to define the restricted access rights they should be granted vis-à-vis the EU criminal records database. In the case of Europol, an additional distinction is made between Europol's competence regarding the creating of Analysis Work Files[8] (including intelligence concerning a specific theme or investigation[9]) and the functioning of Europol's computer TECS-system[10] (encompassing information on known and suspected criminals).

In addition to the mandated areas, the fact whether a crime was organised or not should establish the second field within this branch.

[6] For example every type of crime that has been committed by use of an organisational structure or by the use of violence.

[7] It is not relevant whether the offender concerned was convicted for the same offence or for a different offence.

[8] Art. 10–12 Europol Convention.

[9] B. Hayes, 'The Activities and Development of Europol, towards an Unaccountable "FBI" in Europe' (2002) *Statewatch* 4.

[10] Art. 7–9 Europol Convention.

A third field consists of all criminal acts affecting the European Community's financial interests. The fourth range of offences should be those involving two or more Member States. Clearly, a judgment related to a criminal act can receive several labels.

3.1.3 Framework Decisions

As Framework Decisions are intended to extend the level of harmonisation within the EU, the legal qualifications – e.g. fraud and counterfeiting of non-cash means of payment[11] and trafficking in human beings[12] – that are the subject of Framework Decisions (and proposals for Framework Decisions) delineate a relatively wide group of criminal acts. Due to the harmonisation effect throughout the Member States, this branch can define all criminal acts for which international recidivism can be taken into account by a judge ruling on a criminal offence.

3.2 Other search methods

In addition to the labelling technique, two search methods can be included in the decentralised model of an EU criminal records database. Contrary to the list of labels, these search methods do not require the creation of new rules or possibilities.

When creating an electronic link between all Member States' criminal records registers, it is obvious that searching this decentralised system can be performed by searching a particular name or case. Therefore, searches based on the specific data of a criminal case, e.g. the name of the offender,[13] date of birth, place of residence or the date the judgment was imposed, should be possible. This basic information is entered in national criminal record registers. Consequently, providing these searches does not entail supplementary rules to be imposed upon the Member States or their authorities.[14]

[11] Council of the European Union, Council Framework Decision of 28 May 2001 on combating fraud and counterfeiting of non-cash means of payment, OJ L 149, 2 June 2001.

[12] Council of the European Union, Council Framework Decision of 19 July 2002 on combating trafficking in human beings, OJ L 203, 1 August 2002.

[13] Means of identification, such as photographs, fingerprints, DNA or other, are not included. However, a statement indicating that the person's identity was duly verified and by which authority this was done, can be added.

[14] In order to avoid translation problems – other than the labels that are translated in all official languages of the EU – the translation software developed by Europol and operational since 2002 could be used.

Based on the concept of harmonisation, the Member States could evolve towards genuine EU qualifications of certain criminal acts. The difference between these qualifications and the labels should be clearly stated. Utilising a system of labels does not touch upon the national qualifications of the criminal offences, they are merely an umbrella indicator for a number of offences that have common characteristics. Introducing this third possible search method means that the EU qualifications can evolve to substitute these labels and can represent a common point of view of all Member States vis-à-vis the definition of a certain criminal act. Although this technique requires a high degree of harmonisation between all Member States, the definitions included in the annex to the Europol Convention can be an interesting foundation to start the discussion.

4. Contents of the criminal records database

The Mutual Recognition Plan introduces three possibilities in organising an exchange of criminal records information between the Member States, including the option of a genuine EU criminal records database. However, the document does not mention the content of such database. Although the national legislations of Member States are evolving at a swift rate, two documents are significant sources for determining which information should be inserted in the EU database, notably the Council of Europe Recommendation R 84(10)[15] and the study by the Institute for Advanced Legal Studies regarding money laundering and public procurement.[16]

The following paragraph will explain that the recommended model of an EU criminal records database should incorporate final judicial decisions related to criminal acts judged by a judge from a Member State regarding natural and/or legal persons.

4.1 Final judicial decisions related to criminal acts

Including intermediary decisions taken during a procedure in criminal matters would impede the efficient functioning of the international

[15] Council of Europe, European Committee on crime problems, *The Criminal Record and Rehabilitation of Convicted Persons*, (Strasbourg, Council of Europe, 1984), p. 55.

[16] Institute of Advanced Legal Studies, University of London, *Falcone Project JHA/1999/FAL/197; The Use of Criminal Records as a Means of Preventing Organised Crime in the Areas of Money Laundering and Public Procurement: The Need for Europe-wide Collaboration; Final Project Report*, (London: IALS, 1999), p. 100.

exchange of information. As is defined in the explanatory report to the Council of Europe Convention on the International Validity of Criminal Judgments,[17] the decisions that are final and enforceable in the state in which they have been pronounced are the exclusive substance of an EU criminal records database. Two exceptions to this rule can be justified, i.e. judgments in absentia and *ordonnances pénales.* Article 21(1) of that Convention states that judgments ruled in absentia and *ordonnances pénales* are subject to the same rules as enforcement of other judgments unless otherwise provided in the Convention. The explanatory report states on the one hand that this equalisation is made due to the high amount of judgments rendered in the absence of the sentenced person. On the other hand, *ordonnances pénales* are explicitly included in order to avoid the confusion caused by the interpretation that they would only be encompassed by the scope of the Convention on the Punishment of Road Traffic Offences.[18]

The relevance of this consideration lies in the fact that not every decision that is related to a criminal act is a judicial decision. Administrative decisions can also relate to a criminal act and can have significant consequences in several Member States.[19] It is important to note in this respect that disqualifications can in certain criminal legal systems (e.g. in Belgium) be an automatic consequence of a decision related to a criminal act without instigating a specific judgment. This practice does not necessarily result in the non-inclusion of automatic disqualifications in the EU criminal records system. Nevertheless, this is an issue that should be dealt with on a national level. When the national legislation provides that these disqualifications are inserted in the national criminal register, they can be part of the EU database.

An offence that is not classified as a criminal offence but is sanctioned with fines imposed by administrative authorities is identified in the German, Austrian and Portuguese criminal justice systems by the term *Ordnungswidrigkeit.* The Schengen Implementation Convention widens the scope of mutual assistance in criminal matters to proceedings brought by the administrative authorities in respect of offences that

[17] 'Explanatory Report on the European Convention on the International Validity of Criminal Judgments, 1970,' in E. Müller-Rappard and M.C. Bassiouni, *European Inter-state Cooperation in Criminal Matters* (ETS, no. 70, 1991), p. 39.

[18] Ibid., p. 41.

[19] For example the disqualification to drive a vehicle as a sentence for driving under the influence of drugs or alcohol or a disqualification to fulfil a certain professional position as a result of an offence connected to that specific profession.

are punishable in one of the two or in both contracting parties by virtue of being infringements of the rules of law where the decision may give rise to proceedings before a criminal court.[20] This particular provision is repealed by Article 2(2) of the Convention on Mutual Assistance in Criminal Matters of 29 May 2000. However, the content of the provision is copied in Article 3(1) of this Convention, widening the scope of mutual assistance in criminal matters between Member States. The phrase 'may give rise to' demonstrates that the fact whether – initially – the proceedings concerned fall within the scope of an authority competent in administrative or criminal matters, is irrelevant. However, it is essential that these proceedings may – at a later stage – be brought before a court that has jurisdiction in particular in criminal matters.[21]

Due to the decentralised organisation of the recommended model, only the administrative decisions that are inserted in the national criminal records registers can be included in the international exchange of criminal records information. Therefore, only the administrative decisions that are related to criminal acts can be the subject of the proposed EU criminal records database. In a number of criminal justice systems, the decisions described above are pronounced by different types of authorities. Amnesties and pardons can be ruled by governments or other institutions, although they are related to criminal acts. Therefore, the phrase 'decision related to a criminal act' is used to indicate decisions as a consequence of criminal behaviour irrespective of the type of authority that ruled the decision. Including decisions related to criminal acts regardless of the ruling authority embraces all convictions, acquittals, amnesties, pardons and revisions, decisions related to the confinement of mentally ill offenders and various security measures and finally decisions of military and juvenile courts.[22]

[20] Article 49 (a) of the Convention of 19 June 1990 applying the Schengen Agreement of 14 June 1985 between the Governments of the States of the Benelux Economic Union, the Federal Republic of Germany and the French Republic, on the gradual abolition of checks at their common borders.

[21] Council of the European Union, Explanatory Report on the Convention of 29 May 2000 on mutual assistance in criminal matters between the Member States of the European Union, OJ C 379, 29 December 2000. Similarly, the term 'conviction' is defined for the purposes of the current proposal of a Council Framework Decision regarding this subject. For the latest draft, see: Council of the European Union, 6372/07 Limite Copen 20, Proposal for a Council Framework Decision on the organisation and content of the exchange of information extracted from criminal records between Member States, Brussels, 16 February 2007.

[22] Council of Europe, *The Criminal Record and Rehabilitation of Convicted Persons*, pp. 17–19.

Decisions on conditional measures and conditional release should also be included as they are included in the national criminal registers of the majority of the Member States. The exchange of information with reference to conditional release and conditional measures is consistent with the provisions of the Council of Europe Convention on the Supervision of Conditionally Sentenced or Conditionally Released Offenders. The latter requires the transmission of these measures and conditions to the state that will implement them, which would be considerably facilitated when these decisions are inserted in the recommended model of an EU criminal records database. Similarly, administrative decisions that may be brought before a criminal court (e.g. measures concerning revocation or withdrawal of licences to carry firearms, measures concerning declarations of bankruptcy)[23] as referred to above, correspond with this categorisation.

The state in which the judgment is pronounced is not necessarily the state that keeps the information concerning the judgment (the depositary state). The information related to the judgment that should be incorporated in the recommended model of an EU criminal records database should comprise information concerning the depositary state.[24] The place of decision can be divided into the state of the decision, the region, the district, the state, the department, the city etc., depending on the geographic structure of the state concerned. In addition, the type of ruling authority – judicial or administrative authority – should be indicated.

4.2 *National and foreign decisions*

Under specific conditions,[25] the majority of Member States insert decisions related to criminal acts ruled in another state in their national criminal records register. The state in which the decision is ruled can be an EU Member State or a third state. In the case of a decision related to a

[23] Ibid., p. 19.

[24] This information consists of the state that holds the specific information regarding the decision and the identification number the decision was given within the national criminal justice system.

[25] For example, the offender should have the nationality of the state that includes the foreign decision in its criminal records register, the sentence should be compatible to the criminal justice system of the latter or a treaty or bilateral agreement should be concluded between the states involved requiring the insertion of this information. Council of Europe, *The Criminal Record and Rehabilitation of Convicted Persons*, pp. 19–20.

criminal act concerning a national of a Member State and ruled by an authority of a Member State, no objections can be formulated as this decision will be included in the EU database through the national register of the state in which the decision was pronounced.

In the case of a decision related to a criminal act concerning a national of a Member State and ruled by an authority of a third state, Article 22 of the Council of Europe Convention on Mutual Assistance in Criminal Matters covers the exchange of this information. This Article provides that states should exchange information regarding the decisions related to criminal acts that concern their nationals. The inclusion of decisions ruled in other states in the EU criminal records database is a direct consequence of this provision and is confirmed by Article 6 (8) (b) of the EU Convention on Mutual Assistance in Criminal Matters. However, in the case of a decision related to a criminal act concerning a national of a third state and ruled by an authority of a third state, the inclusion of this information in an EU database can not be endorsed.

4.3 Persons

The criminal liability of legal persons is an issue that has not been the subject of extensive harmonisation in the Member States. Dissimilarities between national provisions regarding the liability of legal persons can have important consequences on the exchange of information in criminal matters, especially in the fight against corporate crime. In accordance with the provisions of the EU Convention on Mutual Assistance in Criminal Matters, which calls upon the harmonisation of these rules in all Member States, the same should apply in the context of the exchange of criminal records information. Nevertheless, several steps have been undertaken in order to implement the criminal liability of legal persons.[26] As it is not the intention of the project and model that was recommended in its conclusions to amend national legislations, only the information that is included in the criminal register on a national level will be available through the EU criminal records database.

[26] The 1997 Action Plan to Combat Organised Crime pleads for the introduction of the principle in the context of organised crime. In accordance with the Mutual Recognition Plan, authorities of a Member State can collect fines imposed on legal persons of another Member State.

Information on natural persons who are involved in the creation and direction of legal persons[27] could be included in a national criminal records register and consequently it can be included in a EU model. Due to the fact that a set of data on legal persons[28] should be part of a criminal records register, the natural persons interconnected with its establishment and management can be added to this list and be part of the same register.

As the recommended model is intended to include only final judicial decisions, intermediary decisions are excluded even when they concern provisional measures. In the case of legal persons, provisional measures, such as the confiscation of an essential part of a its production line, can significantly affect the daily work of a company. Therefore, a separate register for intermediary decisions relating to legal persons is a feasible alternative.

4.4 Crimes

Given the divergent – and sometimes even incompatible – qualifications of crimes in the Member States, three options are open in order to make the recommended model feasible regardless of the dissimilarities between the criminal justice systems. First, the widest possibility is to include all qualifications, which would result in an unlimited access of Member States to each other's national registers. Second, restricting the amount of data and considering the good organisation of the EU database, a filter can be used as an alternative. The offences encompassed in the Annex to the Europol Convention are the most viable categorisation as operational definitions on a European level have been concluded for these criminal acts. A third possibility is the introduction of a genuine EU qualification of crimes. Although, the Europol offences can be a starting point, this technique requires an exceptionally high degree of harmonisation.

[27] The third recommendation of the so-called Millennium Strategy presented the possibility of a separate register of information on natural persons involved in the creation and direction of legal persons in the Member States. Council of the European Union, Limite Crimorg 36 Cor 1 6611/01, The prevention and control of organized crime – a European Union strategy for the beginning of the new Millennium, Brussels, 9 March 2000.

[28] Including the name, date and place of creation, the seat of the firm and its identification number in the national commercial register.

Nevertheless, the three options can be part of a phased strategy. This means that a first step could consist of the inclusion of all qualifications and in a second phase, the collection of qualifications could be managed and restricted by means of the labelling technique. Finally, the filtering method can result in the definition of EU offences.

5. Access and use of the criminal records database

Developing a vision on how to construct an EU criminal records database also means developing a vision on how to organise the access to and use of the register. In addition to the Member States' authorities (i.e. authorities concerned with criminal investigations) and the existing EU institutions, the access to the database by third institutions and third countries should also be considered.[29] Individuals should have the right to verify information relating to them by addressing the national competent authority of a Member State, which should address the authority maintaining the EU criminal records database.[30]

Requesting information from the criminal register of another Member State is a part of the judicial cooperation between Member States. Therefore, it is of profound importance that police authorities can only receive access after approval by a judicial authority. The EU institutions, Europol, Eurojust and OLAF can receive access that is limited to their specific mandate.

As Interpol has created internationally very significant databases, but is still dependent on the input by the states involved, a question arises regarding its ability to access the EU criminal records database. Regardless of the cooperation agreement Interpol concluded with Europol, the subject of Interpol's right of access to and use of the recommended model should be clearly regulated, possibly by means of a protocol to the 2001 cooperation agreement between Europol and Interpol.[31]

[29] The secrecy of the criminal investigation excludes the possibility of notifying the individual concerned of the disclosure of information.

[30] In the case of incorrect data included in the system or the inclusion of the information that is not in accordance with the requirements of the EU criminal records database, the state or authority that has entered the specific information should be obliged to correct or delete the data.

[31] Agreement between Interpol and Europol, 5 November 2001, www.europol.eu.int/legal/agreements/Agreements/8890.pdf.

The right to access and use by third countries regarding the recommended model, opens four options. The first and most restricted option is an absolute denial of admission to the database. This would leave third countries with the only alternative of traditional requests for information based on mutual legal assistance agreements, in order to obtain information available in the requested Member State's register. The second option, receiving a request for information sent by a third country could cause the requested Member State to provide all information available in its national register and in addition supply the requesting state with all contact data of the competent authorities of the states in which more information can be available. The third option is to give all information accessible in the recommended EU database to a third country by means of a Member State. This means that the latter state would, on behalf of all Member States, provide the requesting third country with all information it has access to in the database. This option would be tantamount to an indirect access for third countries. The fourth and widest option could be straightforward direct access to the recommended database for third countries. Nevertheless, both the third and fourth option require the regulation of specific conditions to ensure the flawless functioning of the exchange of information. Other conditions, such as a certain level of trust expressed in a bilateral agreement, can be added to the second and third option.

6. Vulnerable professions

The exchange of information regarding the criminal history of individuals between Member States, creates the opportunity to 'screen' people when they apply for professional positions in another Member State in a more meticulous way than a regular job interview. This can be of significant value in the context of employment to specific professions that are particularly vulnerable to the involvement of criminals. The vulnerability of these professions is generated by the manner in which the committing of certain offences is enhanced by employment in a particular environment or circumstances.

The professions that are defined are public professions in which trust is required for working in institutions that represent a state's authority (such as police and judicial authorities), educational professions in which trust is required for working with or close to minors (such as teachers or assistants in institutions for delinquents), medical professions in which trust is required for exercising positions such as doctor, nurse or therapist, financial professions in which trust is required for handling other people's financial resources (such as bankers and accountants), transport professions in which trust is required for transporting goods or people (such as pilots and chauffeurs of different types of vehicles) and trustworthy telecommunications professions in which trust is required for handling personal and non-personal data (such as website managers and internet service providers).

Due to the free movement of persons and services within the EU, it is not an option to award access to employers of these vulnerable professions. Nevertheless a certificate of non-conviction[32] could be used as a requirement which is limited to a declaration stating that the person involved has not been convicted of a crime before. Connecting this type of certificates to the aforementioned labelling technique creates the possibility of motivated requests. This means that an applicant for a vulnerable job/profession can obtain a certificate proving his state of non-conviction regarding that specific position.

7. Conclusion

In order to efficiently prevent and suppress (international) crime and penalise the offenders individually – and subsequently establish adequate judicial responses to international recidivism – in the Member States, knowledge of criminal records information available in other states is indispensable. Taking into account the national interests of all states and the legal, technical and financial efforts needed to implement a system of exchange of information, a decentralised system is the most feasible answer. This means that information on criminal records will remain in the national registers. An electronic link between them creates the opportunity for other states' authorities to find specific data. Making use of a centralised index of labels, representing the particular characteristics of final judicial decisions in criminal matters, by means of a labelling technique, facilitates the search for data within this pool of information. Judges within the Member States will thus be required to attach a specific label to every judgment in criminal matters they conclude.

[32] The requirement of this certificate of non-conviction should be made public together with the job offer in order to grant potential applicants the choice whether or not to apply.

In connection with certificates of non-conviction, the labelling technique will make motivated requests for detailed certificates of non-conviction achievable that can be used in the context of job applications in Member States without granting employers access to the register. Locating the EU database with Europol or the secretariat of the Eurojust–European Judicial Network as the maintaining authority means that no new secured technical facilities need be instituted.

One EU Convention signed and ratified by all Member States can encompass all necessary conditions to set up the network between the national systems, as well as encouraging international information exchange. Implementing the labelling technique can be done by a similar instrument. As a certain level of harmonisation will be required, Framework Decisions are the most adequate instrument for introducing the EU certificate of non-conviction and the system of international recidivism.

Notwithstanding the fact that a conferment of national sovereignty is uncalled for, the recommended model requires efforts and commitment from the Member States' authorities. However, considering the recommended model, a step-by-step-approach (with the current Council Decision[33] as a first step) is possible using different instruments for every step to take and the most feasible method of working when implementing a system that unifies all national criminal registers joining a decentralised approach with a centralised index.

The EU is currently gradually implementing the exchange of information extracted from criminal records. After careful research and debates on several possible options to establish the concept of an EU criminal records database, agreement was reached first on the principle of exchanging information extracted from criminal records. Its basic outlines – although motivated by urgency[34] – are included in a Council Decision of 2005[35] as the organisation and content of the exchange is at

[33] Council of the European Union, Council Decision of 21 November 2005 on the exchange of information extracted from criminal records, OJ L 322, 9 December 2005.

[34] See Council of the European Union, 10557/06 Limite Copen 65, Opinion of the European Data Protection Supervisor on the proposal for a Council Framework Decision on the organisation and content of the exchange of information extracted from criminal records between Member States (COM (2005) 690 final), 19 June 2006.

[35] Council of the European Union, Council Decision of 21 November 2005 on the exchange of information extracted from criminal records, OJ L 322, 9 December 2005 and Council of the European Union, 5463/1/06 Rev 1 Copen 1, Proposal for a Framework Decision on the organisation and content of the exchange of information extracted from criminal records between Member States, Brussels, 25 January 2006.

present the subject of separate proposal for a Framework Decision that will eventually repeal the 2005 Decision. Political agreement on this instrument is expected in the summer of 2007, even though the European Data Protection Supervisor has recommended that the entry into force of this Framework Decision should be delayed until the Framework Decision on the protection of personal data in the third pillar.[36] Due to the supreme importance of this instrument in the police and judicial cooperation in criminal matters, all eyes are now focused on the Council since debates in this area have proved to be particularly delicate and complicated.[37]

[36] For the latest draft, see: Council of the European Union, 6372/07 Limite Copen 20, Proposal for a Council Framework Decision on the organisation and content of the exchange of information extracted from criminal records between Member States, Brussels, 16 February 2007 and Council of the European Union, 10557/06 Limite Copen 65, Opinion of the European Data Protection Supervisor on the proposal for a Council Framework Decision on the organisation and content of the exchange of information extracted from criminal records between Member States (COM (2005) 690 final), Brussels, 19 June 2006.

[37] Council of the European Union, 7315/07 Limite Crimorg 53 Droipen 18 Enfopol 45 Dataprotect 10 Comix 267, Proposal for a Council Framework Decision on the protection of personal data processed in the framework of police and judicial cooperation in criminal matters, Brussels, 13 March 2007.

18

The European Criminal Record: Feasible or folly?

HELEN XANTHAKI

1. Introduction

The need to enhance the effectiveness of the process for the exchange of data from national criminal records is now widespread. However, proposals for a European Criminal Record (ECR) as a tool for achieving such effectiveness have been criticised mainly for an alleged lack of feasibility. Having discussed the legal, political and human rights requirements for feasibility of the ECR both at the EU and the national levels in previous chapters of this book, this chapter aims to focus on aspects of the ECR proposal that guarantee legitimacy and consequently feasibility of the proposal both as a legislative form and as legal substance.

2. Feasibility of the ECR proposal: The Sutherland criteria

Assessment of any legislative measure at the EU level is undertaken on the basis of the five Sutherland criteria:[1] need for action, choice of the most effective course of action, proportionality of the measure,

[1] 'The Internal Market after 1992: Meeting the Challenge', Report to the EEC Commission by the High Level Group on the operation of the internal market, SEC(92) 2044; also Supplement to European Report no 1808, 31 October 1992; Commission Communication to the Council and the EP, 'Follow-up of the Sutherland Report', COM(93) 361 final and SEC(92) 2227 fin; Opinion of the Economic and Social Committee, 5 May 1993 'On the Commission Communication on the Operation of the Community's Internal Market after 1992: Follow-up to the Sutherland Report', OJ C 201/59, 26 July 1993; Communication from the Commission, 'Follow-up to the Sutherland Report: Legislative Consolidation to Enhance the Transparency of Community Law in the Area of the Internal Market', 16 December 1993, COM(93) 361 fin.; Communication from the Commission to the Council, the EP and the ESC 'On the Handling of Urgent Situations in the Context of Implementation of Community Rules: Follow-up to the Sutherland Report', COM(93) 430 fin.

consistency with existing measures, and wider consultation of the circles concerned during the preparatory stages.[2]

The need for action in this area derives from the ineffectiveness of current mechanisms for mutual legal assistance in criminal matters[3] at an international level.[4] National criminal records have proven ineffective as inadequate, inaccurate and incomplete, especially with reference to crimes committed by foreigners in the jurisdiction or own nationals abroad,[5] even though mobility of persons, services and, consequently, crime in the EU has increased.[6] The problem presents itself in two dimensions. First, there are discrepancies in national criminal records which render understanding of foreign national data from criminal records difficult even in the few cases where language and legal system are not particularly foreign to the recipient of the data. There are three main areas of such discrepancy, namely the level of information available in the records, the types of persons with entries in national criminal records and the ground covered in these records.[7] Second, exchange of such data via current mechanisms of mutual legal assistance in criminal

[2] H. Xanthaki, 'The Problem of Quality in EU Legislation: What on Earth is Really Wrong?' 38 (2001) *Common Market Law Review* 651–676.

[3] United Nations Office for Drug Control and Crime Prevention, 'Report on the Expert Working Group on Mutual Legal Assistance and Related International Confiscation', 15–19 February 1993, Vienna at 2; also, S. Betti, 'New Prospects for Inter-state Co-operation in Criminal Matters: The Palermo Convention' 3 (2003) *International Criminal Law Review* 151–167, at 168; C. Fijnaut and M. S. Groenhuijsen, 'A European Public Prosecution Service: Comments on the Green Paper' 10 (2002) *European Journal of Crime, Criminal Law and Criminal Justice* 321–328, at 328; R. Ford, 'Judge Calls for EU Criminal Records System', *The Times*, 13 January 2007.

[4] J. Hatchard, 'Combating Transnational Crime in Africa: Problems and Perspectives' 50 (2006) *Journal of African Law* 145–160; D. Stafford, 'Mutual Legal Assistance in Criminal Matters: The Australian Experience' 17 (1991) *Commonwealth Law Bulletin* 1384–1390; L. E. Nagle, 'The Challenge of Fighting Global Organized Crime in South America' 26 (2002–2003) *Fordham International Law Journal* 1649–1715, at 1689.

[5] H. Xanthaki and C. Stefanou (1999), 'The Use of Criminal Records as a Means of Preventing Organised Crime in the Areas of Money-laundering and Public Procurement: The EU approach', European Commission FALCONE Study (Ref. No. 1999/FAL/197); in relation to the backlog of 27,000 entries to criminal records of UK nationals for crimes committed outside the UK, see 'Criminal Records: Backlog' [2007] *Hansard*, column 252: 10 January 2007.

[6] 'Final Report on the First Evaluation Exercise – Mutual Legal Assistance in Criminal Matters', OJ C 216/14-26, 1 August 2001.

[7] See H. Xanthaki, 'National Criminal Records and Organised Crime: A Comparative Analysis', in C. Stefanou and H. Xanthaki (eds.), *Financial Crime in the EU: Criminal Records as Effective Tools or Missed Opportunities* (The Hague: Kluwer Law International, 2005), pp. 15–42 at 40–41.

matters is plagued by the complex, often overlapping provisions of the – many and varied – relevant instruments at the national, international and EU levels.[8] Additional hurdles to effective and prompt provision of data from foreign criminal records are dual criminality[9] requirements and the multitude of grounds for refusal of mutual legal assistance,[10] problems in understanding the mutual legal assistance request and in responding to it in a manner procedurally permissible in the jurisdiction which receives the data.[11] The need for action in the area of EU criminal law is evident in existing EU measures which, unfortunately, have not come to full fruition as yet, i.e. the slow implementation of the 2000 MLA Convention[12] within a fragmented area of freedom, security and justice. These two phenomena lead to two aims for the ECR: harmonisation of data in national criminal records and prompt availability of data from all national criminal records within the EU. On the basis of these two goals one could state that the need for action in the field of data from criminal records is painfully audible.

Indeed, action can only take the form of a legislative intervention. Data from criminal records are sensitive data of EU citizens. Their treatment, maintenance and use touches on the human rights of EU citizens. As a result, any amendment to existing national laws referring

[8] Deciding which agreement facilitates the case most is a problem even within the EU: W. Schomburg, 'Are We on the Road to a European Law-Enforcement Area – International Cooperation in Criminal Matters – What Place for Justice' 8 (2000) *European Journal of Crime, Criminal Law and Criminal Justice* 51–60, at 54.

[9] J. Hafen, 'International Extradition: Issues Arising from the Dual Criminality Requirement' (1992) *Brigham Young University Law Review* 191–230 at 200; also, *United States* v. *Saccoccia*, 18 F.3d 795, 800 n.6 (9th Cir. 1994).

[10] 'Final Report on the First Evaluation Exercise. Mutual Legal Assistance in Criminal Matters', OJ C 216, 1 August 2001, p. 18.

[11] C. Gane and M. Mackarel, 'The Admissibility of Evidence Obtained from Abroad into Criminal Proceedings – the Interpretation of Mutual Legal Assistance Treaties and Use of Evidence Irregularly Obtained' 4 (1996) *European Journal of Crime, Criminal Law and Criminal Justice* 98–119; P. Tak, 'Bottlenecks, International Police and Judicial Cooperation in the EU' 8 (2000) *European Journal of Crime, Criminal Law and Criminal Justice* 343–360, at 346–348; J. Vogel, 'Combating International Organized Crime by International Cooperation: The German View' 70 (1999) *Revue International de Droit Pénal* 355–359.

[12] Council of the EU, 'Addendum to the I item note – Implementation of the Strategy and Action Plan to Combat Terrorism', Document No. 15266/06 ADD1 REV1, Brussels, 24 November 2006; T. Schalken and M. Pronk, 'On Joint Investigation Teams, Europol and Supervision of their Joint Actions' 10 (2002) *European Journal of Crime, Criminal Law and Criminal Justice* 70–82, at 70; A. Weyembergh and S. de Biolley, 'The EU Mutual Legal Assistance Convention of 2000 and the Interception of Telecommunications' 8 (2006) *European Journal of Law Reform* 285–300, at 298.

to such data can only take the form of a legislative text passed with the increased legitimacy and constitutionality safeguards offered by legislation.[13] In any case, most national provisions on criminal records are already provided for in national laws; their amendment could only be achieved through a text of equal value in the hierarchy of national and EU sources of law. Such an amendment would be required anyway, irrespective of whether the national data were to be accessed by additional foreign authorities or kept by an EU host body.

Proportionality of the measure refers to a balance between the aims to be achieved and the proposed means to be used.[14] In this case, the aims to be achieved are harmonisation of national data and facilitation of data from national criminal records. Leaving aside the debate as to the best form of action for the achievement of these aims, there is little doubt that the ECR can contribute both to harmonisation and facilitation. Indeed, as measure, the ECR goes only so far in achieving these aims without affecting adversely the human rights of EU citizens. In fact, the proposal for the ECR refers only to the data related to transnational crime thus delimiting the field of application of the proposed measure to its role as a tool for the combat of organised, transnational crime. This could not be said for the competing scenario of linkage of national criminal records, where all types of convictions and data on the past criminal life of EU citizens would become immediately accessible to all national competent authorities within the EU.

Consistency with existing measures is also obvious. The route to exchange of data from national criminal records has been open to EU national authorities for a few decades now via the mechanism of mutual legal assistance in criminal matters. The EU is pushing forward proposals aimed to strengthen the principles of mutual recognition[15] and the

[13] M. Fiorina, 'Legislative Choice of Regulatory Forms: Legal Process or Administrative Process?' 39 [1982] *Public Choice* 33–66.

[14] T. Gallas, 'Evaluation in EC Legislation' 22 (2001) *Statute Law Review* 83–95, at 85; H. Xanthaki, 'The SLIM Initiative' 22 (2001) *Statute Law Review* 108–118, at 114 and 115.

[15] Council of the EU, 'Programme of Measures to Implement the Principle of Mutual Recognition in Criminal Matters', OJ C 12, 15 January 2001 at 10; V. Mitsilegas, 'Constitutional Principles of the EC and European Criminal Law' 8 (2006) *European Journal of Law Reform* 301–323, at 314–321; V. Mitsilegas, 'The Constitutional Implications of Mutual Recognition in Criminal Matters in the EU' 43 (2006) *Common Market Law Review* 1277–1311; S. Peers, 'Mutual Recognition and Criminal Law in the EU' 41 (2004) *Common Market Law Review* 5–36; G. de Kerchove and A. Weyembergh, *Mutual Trust in the European Criminal Area* (Brussels: Éd. de

availability of data.[16] Relevant examples include the mutual recognition of final judgments in criminal matters,[17] measures 2–4 of the Council and Commission programme of measures to give effect to the principle of mutual recognition of decisions in criminal matters[18] and the draft Council Decision[19] aimed to facilitate information exchange against terrorism. In fact, the proposal for an ECR is a direct response to calls for the introduction of a unified format for application for data from criminal records and the establishment of a 'genuine European central criminal records office'.[20] If anything, the proposal for an ECR complies with and in fact strengthens the principles of mutual trust and of availability of data.

Wide consultation is the last of the Sutherland criteria for the acceptability of new legislative proposals at the EU level.[21] Consultation has been taking place and the Commission seems to be struggling with its choice of form for immediate access of national authorities to data from criminal records kept in other Member States. Nevertheless, on the basis of the analysis of national laws and their reception of the ECR proposal, it seems that from a substantive point of view national legal orders set five sets of strict conditions for the reception of the ECR.

First, the Framework Decision introducing the ECR must determine with clarity and accuracy the crimes which will fall within its field of application. This condition is put forward by the Austrian, Belgian, Greek, Slovenian, Spanish and UK experts that participated in the relevant IALS study. The minimal approximation of crimes and offences poses dangerous problems in the determination of equivalent offences within the legal orders of Member States. For this reason, the Framework Decision must refer to crimes with definitions that are not unduly at variance with or remote from concepts in national legal

l'Université de Bruxelles, 2005); P. Asp, 'Mutual Recognition and the Development of Criminal Law Cooperation within the EU', in E. J. Husabø and A. Strandbakken (eds.), Harmonization of Criminal Law in Europe (Antwerp-Oxford: Intersentia, 2005) 23–40, at 26.

[16] 'Hague Programme on Strengthening Freedom, Security and Justice in the European Union', OJ C53, 3 March 2005, p. 1; 'Action Plan Implementing the Hague Programme', OJ C 198, 12 August 2005, p. 1.

[17] See COM (2000) 495 final, 26.7.2000, section 5.

[18] See OJ C 12, 15 January 2001, p. 10.

[19] Proposal for a Council Decision on the exchange of information and cooperation concerning terrorist offences, 8200/04, Brussels, 5 April 2004.

[20] OJ C 12, 15 January 2001, p. 10.

[21] Standards for consultation in the EU were in introduced in 2003 via COM(2002) 704, 11 December 2002.

orders. The crimes falling within the competence of Eurojust could be utilised for this purpose.

Second, convictions for crimes in the ECR must have been reached under the ECHR and Article 8 in particular,[22] as this is an express condition for Austria, Germany, Greece, Ireland, Italy, Luxembourg, Spain and the UK. This would not pose difficulties for Member States whose traditions in respect of human rights seem to guarantee that there will be no grounds for exclusion of information on convictions.

Third, access to data of the ECR must be restricted, a condition necessary under Austrian, Belgian, French, German, Greek, Italian, Luxembourg, Spanish and UK national laws. As the purpose of the ECR is to combat organised crime, its use must be limited to functions and persons whose knowledge of the ECR is essential for the performance of their task in the fight against transnational and organised crime. Thus, at the national level only judicial and prosecution authorities are entitled to access. Further constricted levels of access may be offered to police authorities, tendering authorities, some professional associations (lawyers, notaries, accountants) and banking institutions for employees whose duties touch upon the prevention of organised crime as introduced by money laundering legislation. In view of the diversity of such authorities and associations, a mechanism for the authorisation of transmission of data to such bodies must be introduced, a necessity of Belgian, German and Italian law. Decisions on access requests must be issued within short deadlines in order to avoid unnecessary delays. Access to the data must also be allowed to subjects for their own records as required by Austrian, Belgian, French, German, Italian and UK law. This would pave the path for effective protection of ECR data as required by the 1995 Data Protection Directive and EU and international data protection standards. For the same reason the Italian model of indirect access to the data for tendering authorities, professional associations and banks could be effective and proportionate. At the EU level access must be awarded to Europol, the European Anti-fraud office (OLAF), the European Public Prosecutor (EPP) and the European Judicial Network. Access upon authorisation and for specific purposes only (such as employment at specific posts within the institutions or

[22] D. Ormerod, 'ECHR and the Exclusion of Evidence: Trial Remedies for Article 8 Breaches?' (2003) *The Criminal Law Review* 61–80; S. Farran, 'Recent Commission Decisions and Reports concerning Article 8 ECHR' 21 (1996) *European Law Review* 14–28.

participation in public procurement) must be awarded to all EU institutions, although it would be preferable to introduce indirect access though the subject.

Fourth, there must be judicial control over the host of the ECR. Control of the operations by an independent judicial authority, such as the EPP or Eurojust's Joint Supervisory Body (JSB), would enshrine data protection safeguards to the ECR. Periodic assessments of the work of the host institution by the supervisory independent judicial body and the European Parliament (EP) would enhance accountability and transparency.

Fifth, guarantees of quality and accuracy are necessary requirements for the reception of the ECR by Austrian, French, Spanish and UK law. A mechanism for the correction of ECR data could take the form of a body competent to decide on allegations of error. The EPP could be an ideal body for this purpose as the EPP's access to national criminal records and their data could be possible through the EPP's national officers, whose information would be up to date by the very nature of the EPP's role and tasks. In the meantime, however, Eurojust's JSB is equally suitable for this purpose, as its officers have access to the data in national criminal records and the capacity to control equivalence between entries in the national records and the ECR. Part of the quality of data in the ECR refers to the sixth condition put forward by Austria, Belgium, Spain and the UK, namely the introduction of erasure periods for the ECR. One option would be to erase convictions for the ECR as soon as national erasure takes place. However, this would maintain the existing inequality amongst EU citizens and their de facto discrimination on the basis of their nationality. It would also result in further fragmentation of EU criminal law. The second, and preferable, option would be to observe erasure periods introduced by data protection legislation on Eurojust: common erasure periods would contribute to harmonisation of the legal position of erasures in crimes where approximation has been achieved via existing EU laws.

3. The ECR: Feasible or folly?

The aim of this ambitious, yet topical, proposal is the establishment of a centralised ECR aiming to combat effectively the increasing problem of transnational organised crime within the EU. However, the introduction of the ECR is not problem free. The legality of such a measure could be seriously affected by human rights considerations, especially with regard to the protection of personal data. The balance between the necessity of the introduction of the ECR with the need to respect the rights of EU citizens rests on the conditions for the introduction of the ECR. It is, therefore, imperative to explore whether such a database can be constructed in a way which would not offend the privacy rights of the EU citizens while at the same time giving crime prevention authorities an effective weapon against crime. With these concerns at the forefront of analysis, prerequisites of legality are introduced with regard to the content of the ECR, access to the ECR, the suitable host of the ECR and the organisation of the proposed structure in a manner which could allow an unforced reception of the ECR by the legal systems of the Member States.

Nevertheless, the creation of yet another centralised unit in the area of EU criminal law will have political connotations, which may well impede the realisation of the proposals put forward in the study. Thus, it is equally imperative that the feasibility of the ECR is explored in order to ensure that the proposals put forward in this study are not only legally sound but also acceptable from the point of view of the current political will for the introduction of the ECR in the countries under study and at the EU level.

3.1 General principles governing the ECR

If the ECR is to be received by the national laws of the Member States and the accession countries, it must be introduced in a manner that will guarantee respect for the principles of legality, proportionality and necessity.

The ECR must comply with the principle of legality[23] and from a practical point of view this means that it must be established by law. The crimes included in the ECR must be introduced with clarity, precision and unambiguity.[24] The purpose of the ECR as a means of combating organised crime must be expressly introduced by law. The

[23] R. Tomasic, 'Towards a Theory in Legislation: Some Conceptual Obstacles' 6 (1985) *Statute Law Review* 84–105; for an analysis of legality in EU criminal law, see J. J. Piernas López, 'The Aggravating Circumstance of Recidivism and the Principle of Legality in the EC Fining Policy: nulla poena sine lege?' 29 (2006) *World Competition* 441–457; L. Moreillon and A. Willi-Jayet, *Coopération judiciaire pénale dans l'Union européene* (Munich-Brussels, Paris: Helbing and Lichtenhahn, Bruylant and LGDJ, 2005), p. 158; case C-382/92 *Commission* v. *UK* [1994] ECR I-2435.

[24] Case C-74/95 *Criminal Procedure* v. *X* [1996] I-6609.

Record must only operate to the extent expressly stipulated by the law of its establishment and allowed by national, EU and international human rights instruments.

The ECR must comply with the principle of proportionality balancing the pressing aim to combat transnational crime with the equally imperative need to respect the rights of citizens whose details will be included in the ECR.[25] It has been suggested that there are three applicable tests of proportionality in relation to new legislative proposals. Firstly, the measure must be appropriately and effectively aimed at a legitimate end, so that the relationship between means and ends is neither impossible nor unlawful. Secondly, the measure must be demonstrably necessary, in that no less restrictive means would achieve the same purpose. Thirdly, the measure must be proportionate or balanced, so that the injury or restriction to the individual caused by the act or measure should be offset by the gain to the public or the community as a whole.[26] In the case of the ECR the proposed database aims to harmonise data from national criminal records and make them immediately available to competent authorities in all Member States: the link between the ECR and its goals is both possible and lawful. Moreover, the ECR is necessary as all other efforts to achieve the same goal via mutual legal assistance mechanisms have failed. Furthermore, the ECR must balance the need of its establishment with the inevitable consequent delimitation of the rights of EU citizens. Thus, the ECR must contain exclusively data necessary for the achievement of its aim. Data in the ECR must only be used for lawful purposes.

The ECR must comply with the principle of necessity in relation to its contents and access to the data included in it. The necessity test has long been accepted as a crucial part of checklists for the justification of legislative proposals, especially in Germany and Austria[27] and subsequently in EU law.[28] The necessity test refers to a critical analysis of the legislative proposal addressing mainly the questions of 'how' or 'to what

[25] R. J. Currie, 'Human Rights and International Legal Assistance: Resolving the Tension' 11 (2000) *Criminal Law Forum* 143–181.

[26] T. St. J. N. Bates, 'UK Implementation of EU Directives' 17 (1996) *Statute Law Review* 27–49, at 32.

[27] E. Shäffer, 'Über Wert und Wirkungsmöglichkeiten von legistischen Richtlinien' (1991) *Österreichische Justizenzeitung* 1–3; O. Fliedner and C. Von Hammerstein, 'Neue Initiativen der Bundesregierung zur Verbesserung der Rechttssetzung (1990) *Zeitschrift für Gesetzgebung* 62–65, at 62.

[28] J. Scott and D. M. Trubek, 'Mind the Gap: Law and New Approaches to Governance in the EU' 8 (2002) *European Law Journal* 1–18.

extent' the new public responsibility should be created. Rarely does the question 'if' come into play.[29] Indeed, the necessity test in the case of the ECR refers mainly to the question of extent to which the EU and national institutions must stretch their resources with the new responsibilities assigned to them with the establishment of a new host for the ECR. The proposed database is placed with Eurojust, namely within an existing body as a means of limiting the resources necessary for the realisation of the proposed measure. In view of the increasing volume of transnational organised crime in the EU and the continuing failure of the EU to address the problem, the ECR solution passes the necessity test. Moreover, necessity of Community – rather than national – action[30] is supported by the transnational character of the problem and its solution: availability of data from all criminal records can only be achieved if a centralised EU database such as the ECR is put forward. After all, the ineffectiveness of national criminal records in transnational criminal cases constitutes the core of the reasoning behind the proposed ECR.

3.2 The host of the ECR

The ECR, as an EU-wide centralised database, must be placed with an EU host. Selecting a national host institution goes against the logic of the proposal, which promotes a centralised solution to the problem of discrepancies in national criminal records as accentuated by ineffective mutual legal assistance mechanisms. Moreover, the choice of a national host would take away a layer of security in the accuracy of the data maintained in the database and in the availability of the relevant data fully and promptly for all national competent authorities. Thus, the host of the ECR must be an EU body or agency.

The question is whether a new agency must be established for that purpose or whether the ECR can be placed within an existing EU body. Placing the ECR with a new agency or body created for this purpose would clash with the principle of necessity, as the resources devoted to the establishment of a new agency could not be justified on the basis of the achievement of the goals of the legislative proposal, at least not

[29] H. Schäffer, 'Evaluation and Assessment of Legal Effects Procedures: Towards a More Rational and Responsible Lawmaking Process' 22 (2001) *Statute Law Review* 132–153, at 137.

[30] J. Usher, 'Maastricht and English Law' 14 (1993) *Statute Law Review* 28–45.

easily. In other words, there would be no added value to the new agency, especially since Europol and Eurojust are competing for functions in the area of EU criminal law. Which of these two agencies can host the ECR?

Eurojust would be the agency of choice for this purpose on three main bases. First, Eurojust has the added advantage of a quasi-judicial nature,[31] a condition *sine qua non* for the legality and admissibility of data from criminal records before the national courts, at least in Belgium, the Czech Republic, France, Germany, Greece, Hungary, Ireland, Italy, Portugal and Spain.[32] Second, Eurojust possesses an existing mechanism for hearing appeals against the data to be included in the ECR, as required by the Charter of Fundamental Rights.[33] Its Joint Supervisory Body can serve as a point of dispute resolution from independent experts on issues arising from inaccuracies to the data included in the ECR. Third, recent data protection mechanisms in Eurojust guarantee adequate protection of the rights of EU citizens,[34] as provided for in Article 15 of the Eurojust Decision which refers exactly to data included in a national criminal record. Moreover, the Eurojust Data Protection Officer can strengthen the protection of data even further, especially with reference to access and use.

The character of Eurojust as a quasi-judicial body will be strengthened further if Eurojust is placed under the supervision of the European Public Prosecutor[35] in a *Corpus Juris* model.[36] This could also resolve the

[31] Moreillon and Willi-Jayet *Coopération judiciaire pénale*, p. 198.

[32] J. Sheptycki, 'Patrolling the New European (In)security Field; Organizational Dilemmas and Operational Solutions for Policing the Internal Borders of Europe' 9 (2001) *European Journal of Crime, Criminal Law and Criminal Justice* 144–158, at 154.

[33] OJ C 364, 18 December 2000.

[34] Rules of procedure on the processing and protection of personal data at Eurojust (text adopted unanimously by the college of Eurojust during the meeting of 21 October 2004 and approved by the Council on 24 February 2005), OJ C 68, 19 March 2005, p. 1.

[35] H. Radtke, 'The Proposal to Establish a European Prosecutor', in Husabø and A. Strandbakken (eds.), *Harmonization of Criminal Law in Europe*, at 103–118; A. Nikodem, 'The European Public Prosecutor: Waiting for Godot?' 44 (2003) *Acta Juridica Hungarica* 229–243; J. F. Kriegk, 'Le livre vert sur le ministère public européen: une avancée décisive dans la construction d'un espace judiciaire européen intégré' 123 (2003) *La Gazette du palais* 158–163; A. Perrodet, *Étude pour un ministère public européen* (Paris: LGDJ, 2001); H. G. Nilsson, 'Eurojust: The Beginning or the End of the European Public Prosecutor?' 3 (2000) *Europarättslig Tidskrift* 601–621.

[36] M. Delmas-Marty, *Corpus juris portant dispositions pénales pour la protection des intérêts financiers de l'Union européenne* (Brussels: Economica, 1999); J. Montain-Domenah, 'Le droit de l'espace judiciaire pénal européen: un nouveau modèle juridique?' 2 (2006) *Cultures and Conflits* 149–168 at 154; J. Spencer, 'The Corpus Juris Project: Has it a

current problem of fragmented and inadequate implementation of the Eurojust framework,[37] which endangers the body's effectiveness.[38]

3.3 Conditions imposed by the European Convention on Human Rights and the Charter of Fundamental Rights

The storage of data affects the life of EU citizens[39] as it clashes with their right to respect for private life introduced by Articles 7 and 8 of the Charter of Fundamental Rights[40] and Article 8 of the European Convention on Human Rights (ECHR) that forms part of EU law.[41] In its positive sense, the provision confers on every individual the right to respect for their private life. In its negative sense, the provision prohibits the interference with this right by public authorities. Exceptions can be made under strict conditions, namely that the interference is in accordance with the law, that it is necessary in a democratic society and that it is undertaken for, amongst others, the prevention of disorder or crime. The provision is supplemented by Convention ETS 108 of 28 January 1981 for the protection of persons in respect of automated

Future?' (1999) *Cambridge Yearbook of European Legal Studies* 355–372; B. Huber, 'Das Corpus Juris als Grundlage eines europäischen Strafrechts' (2002) *Palestra* 157–161; J. A. E. Vervaele, 'L'Union Europécne et son espace penal européen: les defis du modèle Corpus Juris' 81 (2001) *Revue du droit pénal et de criminologie* 775–799; S. Braum, 'Das Corpus Juris: Legitimität, Erforderlichkeit und Machbarkeit' 55 (2000) *Juristen Zeitung* 493–500; M. Delmas-Marty, *The Implementation of the Corpus juris in the Member States: Penal Provisions for the Protection of European Finances* (Antwerp: Intersentia, 2000–2001).

37 See 2005 Eurojust Annual Report, p. 15; also see Council of the EU, 'Addendum to the I Item Note – Implementation of the Strategy and Action Plan to Combat Terrorism', Document No. 15266/06 ADD1 REV1, Brussels, 24 November 2006 at 5.

38 H. Xanthaki, 'Eurojust: Fulfilled or Empty Promises in EU Criminal Law?', at 184 and 195; O. de Baynast, 'Eurojust, une avancée décisive' (2002) *Europe Magazine*, at 91.

39 The issue is not regulated by a single EU text as the Commission's attempt has so far failed: see 'Proposal for a Council Framework Decision on the Protection of Personal Data Processed in the Framework of Police and Judicial Cooperation in Criminal Matters', COM(2005) 475 final, 4 October 2005, Brussels; 2005/0202 (CNS).

40 Council Working Document 6316/2/01 REV 2 JAI 13; 2514th Council Meeting, Justice and Home Affairs, Luxembourg, 5–6 June 2003, Council Document 9845/03 (Presse 150) at 32.

41 On the application of the ECHR in EU law, see cases 4/73 *J. Nold, Kohlen- und Baustoffgroßhandlung* v. *Commission* [1974] ECR 491; 36/75 *Roland Rutili* v. *Ministre de l'intérieur* [1975] ECR 1219; 222/84 *Marguerite Johnston* v. *Chief Constable of the Royal Ulster Constabulary* [1986] ECR 1651; 249/86 *Commission* v. *Germany* [1989] ECR 1290; E. Askew-Renaud and K. Mirwald, 'Conference Report: A Critical Assessment of the EU Constitutional Treaty' 2 (2005) *Essex Human Rights Review* 79–86. The ECJ's adherence to the rights protected by the ECHR is also supported by the other EU institutions: Joint Declaration, OJ C I03, 27 April 1977, p. 1.

processing of personal data. The Convention came into force on 1 October 1985 and its purpose is to secure respect for every individual's rights and fundamental freedoms, and in particular the right to privacy with regard to automatic processing of personal data relating to them.

The question is whether data from criminal records qualify as private and, therefore, fall within the field of application of the ECHR and the Convention. The answer is found in Article 2 of the Convention that expressly defines private data as any information relating to an identified or identifiable individual.[42] Public information can fall within the scope of private life where it is systematically collected and stored in files held by the authorities. That is all the more true where such information concerns a person's distant past.[43] In any case, the storing of information relating to an individual's private life in a register and the release of such information come within the scope of Article 8(1) ECHR under *Leander* v. *Sweden*.[44]

Since data from criminal records are private in the sense of Article 8(1) ECHR, one wonders whether the practice of criminal records, even at the national level, might fall under the prohibition of interference by public authorities. Exceptions to the general prohibition rule can be found in Article 8(2) ECHR and must be interpreted narrowly.[45]

The basic principle of the legitimacy of storage of personal data is confirmed in *Klass*.[46] If it is not to contravene Article 8, such interference must be in accordance with the law, it must pursue a legitimate aim and it must be necessary in a democratic society in order to achieve that aim. The 'in accordance with the law' requirement demands that the impugned measure should have some basis in domestic law; it also refers to the quality of the law in question, requiring that it should be accessible to the person concerned and foreseeable as to its effects.[47] A rule is

[42] *Amann* v. *Switzerland* [GC], no. 27798/95 at 65, 16 February 2000, 30 [2000] *European Human Rights Review* 843.

[43] *Rotaru* v. *Romania*, no. 28341/95, 4 May 2000, BAILII [2000] *European Human Rights Review* 192.

[44] *Leander* v. *Sweden*, 26 March 1987, Series A no. 116, pp. 22 and 48; it must be noted that the case refers to secret registers.

[45] *Rotaru* v. *Romania*, no. 28341/95, 4 May 2000, p. 47.

[46] *Klass* v. *F.R.G.*, 6 September 1978, Series A, No 28, 2 [1979–80] *European Human Rights Review* 214; 1978 *Yearbook on the European Convention on Human Rights*. 622 (ECtHR): the case concerned the appropriateness of the German system of intercepting telephone communications.

[47] *Amann* v. *Switzerland* [GC], no. 27798/95, p. 50; C. Ovey and R. C. A. White, *Jacobs and White: The European Convention on Human Rights* (Oxford: Oxford University Press, 2006), p. 223.

'foreseeable' if it is formulated with sufficient precision to enable any individual, if need be with appropriate advice, to regulate their conduct.[48] Moreover, it is necessary to introduce explicit, detailed provisions concerning the persons authorised to consult the files, the nature of the files, the procedure to be followed or the use that may be made of the information thus obtained.[49]

3.3.1. The content of the ECR

The types of crimes included in the ECR are not an easy matter to resolve. In its proposal for the strengthening of data exchange the Commission opted for the linkage of criminal record databases in the Member States, thus allowing access of all competent national authorities to data concerning all types of entries.[50] Thus, national competent authorities in all Member States seem to be allowed access to information on sentences for all types of offences, including decisions of administrative authorities. This practice has been criticised by the European Data Protection Supervisor as disproportionate.[51] It would be difficult not to share this view. As the aim of the legislative proposal furthering the acquisition of data from criminal records is to combat transnational, organised crime, the availability of data must refer to transnational organised crime alone. Instead, the draft Framework Decision includes a long, non-exclusive, list of crimes which do not present a transnational and organised nature.[52]

Of course, the principle of legality requires precision in criminal legislative texts.[53] Thus, the constituting instrument of the ECR must identify expressly and exclusively the crimes included in the database. It is therefore necessary to identify the content of the ECR in detail.

[48] *Malone* v. *United Kingdom*, 2 August 1984, Series A no. 82, 7 [1985] *European Human Rights Review* 14, at 67 reiterated in *Amann* at 56.

[49] *Rotaru* v. *Romania*, p. 57.

[50] Council of the EU, 'Draft Framework Decision on Simplifying the Exchange of Information and Intelligence between Law Enforcement Authorities of the Member States of the EU', 6888/3/05, 27 July 2005.

[51] EDPS, 'Opinion of the European Data Protection Supervisor on the Proposal for a Council Decision on the Exchange of Information from Criminal Records' (COM (2004) 664 fin., OJ C58, 8 March 2005, pp. 3–6.

[52] Ibid., p. 6.

[53] L. Solan, 'Could Criminal Statutes be Interpreted Dynamically?' (2002) *Issues in Legal Scholarship* 1–25, at 3; *Kokkinakis* v. *Greece*, 25 May 1993, Series A, No 260-A, 17 [1994] *European Human Rights Review* 397, para 52.

As the ECR proposal must comply with the principle of subsidiarity,[54] the crimes included in the database must fulfil the condition of 'seriousness'.[55] This seems to exclude most of the grounds for exclusion from public tenders introduced in public procurement legislation. Unfortunate as this may be for the prevention of crime related to public procurement, it would be difficult to justify the inclusion of crimes related to professional misconduct in the ECR database. Regrettably, this aspect of organised crime must be dealt with separately.

The crimes included in the ECR must comply with the condition of transnationality as a requirement of the principles of subsidiarity, necessity and proportionality applicable in new EU legislative proposals.[56] This does not necessarily signify that data on crimes committed within one state would be excluded from the ECR. It merely means that the ECR must include crimes which inherently have an international nature, such as terrorism, money laundering, fraud of EU funds or counterfeiting of the currency (euro).

Moreover, as crimes and penalties are not standardised within the EU, the application of the principle of necessity requires that the ECR proposal makes use of existing EU instruments referring to crimes adversely affecting the EU's financial interests and the security of its citizens. One option

[54] Commission of the EU, 'Report from the Commission: Better Lawmaking 2005 pursuant to Article 9 of the Protocol on the Application of the Principles of Subsidiarity and Proportionality', COM(2006) 289 final, 13 June 2006, p. 8; P. Behan, 'Princip subsidiarity a proporcionality v tvorbe komunitarniho prava' 141 (2002) *Pravnik* 179–206; K. D. Henke et al., 'Subsidiarity in the EU' 41 (2006) *Intereconomics* 240–257; C. Ritzer et al., 'How to Sharpen a Dull Sword: The Principle of Subsidiarity and its Control' 7 (2006) *German Law Journal* 733–760; Cases 62/70 *Werner A. Bock* v. *Commission* [1971] ECR 897; *Bela-Muhle Josef Bergmann KG* v. *Grows-Farm GmbH & Co. KG* case 114/76 [1977] ECR 1211; 181/84 *R* v. *Intervention Board for Agricultural Produce, ex parte E. D. & F. Man (Sugar) Ltd* [1985] ECR 2889; case 118/75 *Watson and Belmann* [1976] ECR 1185; C-378/97 *Criminal Proceedings against Florus Ariël Wijsenbeek* [1999] ECR I-6207; C-161/96 *SudzuckerMannheim/Ochsenfurt AG* v. *Hauptzollamt Mannheim* [1998] ECR I-281; 181/84 *R* v. *Intervention Board for Agricultural Produce* [1985] 2889; C-280/93 *Germany* v. *Council* (Re Banana Regime) [1994] ECR I-4973, para 90; C-44/94 *R* v. *Minister of Agriculture, Fisheries and Food, ex parte National Federation of Fishermen's Organisations* [1995] ECR I-3115.

[55] J. Monar, 'Justice and Home Affairs in the EU Constitutional Treaty. What Added Value for the "Area of Freedom, Security and Justice"?' 1 (2005) *European Constitutional Law Review* 226–246, at 236 and 237.

[56] W. Perron, 'Perspectives of the Harmonisation of Criminal Law and Criminal Procedure in the EU', in Husabø and Strandbakken (eds.), *Harmonization of Criminal Law in Europe*, pp. 5–22, at 14–15; F. Longo, *The EU and the Challenge of Transnational Organised Crime: Towards a Common Police and Judicial Approach* (Milano: Giufrre, 2002).

would be to utilise the list of crimes falling within the competence of Eurojust. This choice would also facilitate the placement of the ECR at Eurojust. Another option would be to use the *Corpus Juris* model. The advantages of this second option lie with the wide acceptance that these crimes fall within the definition of organised crime, the recognition that these crimes damage the financial interests of the EU and the relative standard definition of these crimes, at least in the majority of Member States. The *Corpus Juris* crimes are also adopted in the proposal for the Directive of the European Parliament and the Council on the criminal law protection of the Community's financial interests[57] and in the Green Book on the establishment of a European Public Prosecutor. In addition to crimes harming the financial interests of the EU, the ECR must also include convictions for crimes whose combat is considered to be a priority for the EU for reasons of topicality or type of criminality, such as terrorism or paedophilia. It is important that widely accepted definitions for these crimes exist before they are included in the ECR introducing instrument.

Entries in the ECR must exclusively include convictions reached by final decisions of the national judiciary with the status of *res judicata* under the national laws of criminal procedure applicable to the jurisdiction where the decision is taken. Suspicions, opinions, personal assessments or information on current or incomplete investigations could not possibly be included in the ECR without clashing with the principles of legality, necessity and proportionality. The practice of exclusion of quasi-criminal sanctions of an administrative nature and data on judgments without the value of *res judicata* from data exchanges within the EU is common in EU legislative texts in the field. The principle is also applicable in the Commission's Draft Proposal for a Council Framework Decision on the organization and content of the exchange of information extracted from criminal records between Member States.[58]

3.3.2. Access to the ECR

The principle of necessity demands that access to the ECR is limited strictly to persons whose duties are facilitated by the information included to the ECR. The principle of proportionality requires that access to the ECR is limited to persons whose duties are facilitated to a degree that justify access to such sensitive personal data. The question, therefore, is which bodies within a democratic system need access to the ECR in order to prevent

[57] See OJ C 240 E, 28 August 2001, pp. 125–129.
[58] COM(2005) 690 final/2.5463/1/06 COPEN 1.

organised crime. These bodies must be introduced expressly, accurately and precisely in the instrument establishing the ECR. Their requests for access to the ECR must be reasoned and any information received by the ECR must be treated with strict confidentiality.[59]

Thus, direct access to the ECR must be awarded to national judicial and prosecuting authorities falling within the field of application of the 2000 MLA Convention and the Eurojust Decision. Access to police authorities might be justified only if it were made indirectly via prosecution authorities and only to high level police authorities specialising in serious, transnational and organised crime. Moreover, access must be allowed to Eurojust and the European Public Prosecutor. Furthermore, direct and immediate access must be allowed to the subjects themselves, whose requests need not be reasoned.[60]

Indirect access awarded under specialised agreements or memoranda for data exchanges could be offered to Europol and OLAF via reasoned requests to Eurojust made exclusively for the facilitation of the combat against organised, serious transnational crime.

Access to further agencies and bodies at the national and EU levels could be afforded indirectly and exclusively via the subject, following authorisation from the independent judicial supervisory body, be it the EPP or Eurojust JSB. Thus, such indirect access may be awarded to tendering authorities exclusively for the purpose of exclusion from tenders or to a few professional associations (lawyers, notaries and accountants) exclusively for the purpose of membership control, or to banks exclusively for the purpose of checks before offering employment in sensitive positions. Similarly, indirect access to the ECR may be awarded to the EU institutions exclusively for the purpose of employment checks in positions related to the prevention and combat of organised crime. These arrangements comply with national law requirements for access to national criminal records in the majority of Member States.[61]

[59] EDPS, 'Opinion of the European Data Protection Supervisor on the Proposal for a Council Decision on the Exchange of Information from Criminal Records', paragraph 9, p. 5.

[60] *Guerra and others* v. *Italy*, ECtHR, 26 March 1987 at 53; W. Hins and D. Voorhoof, 'Access to State-held Information as a Fundamental Right under the European Convention on Human Rights', 3 (2007) *European Constitutional Law Review* 114–126.

[61] Council of the EU, 'Council Decision on the Exchange of Information Extracted from Criminal Records – Manual of Procedure', COM(2004) 664 final, 6397/5/06 Rev 5, 15 January 2007.

3.3.3. Erasure periods

Since the rehabilitation of ex-offenders is a priority in the manner in which the ECR is to function, its constituting instrument must allow for the erasure of entries to the ECR. In view of the diversity of national criminal records in the EU and accession countries on this issue it is impossible to introduce erasure periods acceptable by all national laws. Until standardisation on this is achieved, the only manner in which this problem can be addressed is by stipulating erasure of entries to the ECR at the time that the same entries are erased from the national criminal records of the countries in which they are held. If they are held in more than one country, the shorter erasure period must apply.

3.3.4. Judicial supervision

Notwithstanding the quasi-judicial nature of the host of the ECR, there is a need to establish adequate and effective safeguards against abuse[62] of the ECR system. Indeed, the fundamental principle of the rule of law implies, inter alia, that interference by the executive authorities with an individual's rights should be subject to an effective control which should normally be assured by the judiciary, at least in the last resort. After all, judicial control offers the best guarantees of independence, impartiality and a proper procedure.[63]

Thus, there must be supervision of the ECR with reference to the accuracy of its data, the use of the data and access to the database. Compliance with Article 8 ECHR requires a minimum of supervision by an independent, rather than judicial, authority.[64] However, the majority of national laws require supervision by a judicial or quasi-judicial body.[65] Supervision of the work of Europol in relation to the ECR would be ideally placed with the EPP which, contrary to national prosecutors, is envisaged to be a quasi-judicial body.[66] Indeed, the EPP

[62] *Klass* at 22–23, paras. 49–50.

[63] *Golder*, 21 February 1975, Series A no. 18 at 16–17, para. 34.

[64] G. Heine, 'Changes in Criminal Law and Cooperation through, in particular, the Schengen Agreement and Europol', in Husabø and E. Strandbakken (eds.) Harmonization of Criminal Law in Europe, pp. 41–52, at 51.

[65] Council of the EU, 'Council Decision on the Exchange of Information Extracted from Criminal Records – Manual of Procedure'.

[66] 'Green Paper on the Criminal-law Protection of the Financial Interests of the Community and the Establishment of a European Public Prosecutor', COM (2001) 715 final, 11 December 2001, Brussels; C. Fijnaut, 'Criminal-law Protection of the Financial Interests of the Community against Fraud' (2000) *Delikt en Delinkwen* 972–988.

is envisaged to be an independent body with administrative organisation but equipped with judicial functions.[67] There is no doubt that under *Schiesser* v. *Switzerland*[68] the EPP would be considered a judicial body. However, until the EPP is established, the role of a judicial supervisory body for Eurojust as the host of the ECR can fall within the competence of its Joint Supervisory Body introduced by Article 23 of the 2002 Eurojust Decision. Eurojust already has the capacity and expertise to establish whether or not complaints brought before it concerning the accuracy of entries, the use and the access to the ECR are justified under EU and national laws.

3.3.5. The right to appeal

Moreover, citizens whose data are unlawfully or wrongly transferred must be awarded the right to appeal against the national authority that proceeded with the transfer or omitted to request erasure. Article 13 ECHR requires that persons whose rights and freedoms are violated must have an effective and arguable[69] remedy before national authorities.[70] Article 13 guarantees the availability at national level of a remedy to enforce the substance of the Convention rights and freedoms in whatever form they might happen to be protected in the domestic legal order. This Article, therefore, requires the provision of a domestic remedy allowing the competent national authority both to deal with the substance of the relevant Convention complaint and to grant appropriate relief – although Contracting States are afforded some discretion as to the manner in which they conform to their obligation under this provision. The remedy must be effective in practice as well as in law.[71] The authority hearing the complaint may not necessarily in all instances be a judicial authority in the strict sense. Nevertheless, as *Klass* clarifies, the powers and procedural guarantees an authority possesses are relevant in determining whether the remedy before it is effective.[72] As national criminal records authorities are already in compliance with

[67] Fijnaut and Groenhuijsen, 'A European Public Prosecution Service', p. 328.

[68] See ECHR *Schiesser* v *Switzerland*, 4 December 1979 A no. 43.

[69] F. Hampson, 'The Concept of an Arguable Claim under Article 13 of the European Convention on Human Rights' 39 (1990) *International and Comparative Law Quarterly* 891–899.

[70] *Çakici* v. *Turkey* [GC], no. 23657/94, § 112, ECHR 1999-IV; *Powell and Rayener* v. *UK*, ECHR Ser. A No. 172.

[71] *Wille* v. *Liechtenstein* [GC], no. 28396/95, § 75, ECHR 1999-VII.

[72] *Kopp* v. *Switzerland*, 25 March 1998, *Reports* 1998-II at 540, § 53.

Article 13, it is envisaged that appeals against the process, content and duration of data exchange with the ECR will be heard under the same process applicable to appeals against national criminal records. The provisions of Article 13 are reflected in Article 47 of the Charter of Fundamental Rights.

A similar structure of appeals must also be foreseen for appeals against the storage, content, access and erasure of data in the ECR that are not attributed to national authorities. Appeals against the ECR may be heard by the Eurojust JSB or the EPP, namely the supervisory bodies of the new structure. It is also possible that the new European Data Protection Supervisor (EDPS) could serve as an independent port of call for appellants. The question is whether the EDPS meets the criteria for classification as a judicial body. The answer is affirmative for four reasons. Firstly, the EDPS is established by law and is permanent,[73] the rule of law is applicable[74] and the procedure can be considered as *inter partes*.[75] Secondly, the EDPS is independent in that it is a third party in a dispute between the ECR and subjects, and the procedures for the EDPS's appointment and dismissal guarantee independence.[76] Thirdly, the EDPS's jurisdiction can be considered as compulsory, especially if the constituting instrument of the proposed ECR awards to the EDPS exclusive competence to hear appeals against the host institution. Fourthly, the EDPS has the legal expertise to hear disputes of a data protection nature. The EDPS meets the criteria for its classification as a judicial body[77] and thus could be considered a possible forum for appeals against the ECR and its host institution.

Appeals against these appeals must be placed within the current judicial structure of the Union and more precisely within the competence of the European Court of First Instance (CFI). This structure complies with the Additional Protocol to the ECHR No. 108, adopted in 2001. The Additional Protocol provides that decisions of such supervisory bodies must be appealed through the courts. The possibility of an appeal before a court against acts of EU bodies with binding legal effect

[73] Case C-54/96, *Dorsch Consult*, [1997] ECR I-4961, para. 23.

[74] App. 8790/79, *Sramek* v. *Austria*, 8 Dec. 1982, (1982) Series A-084, para. 71.

[75] Case C-110/98 to C-147/98, *Gabalfrisa*, [2000] ECR I-1577, paras. 35 and 36.

[76] Case C-53/03 *Syfait* [2005] ECR I-4609, para. 31.

[77] H. Hijmans, 'The European Data Protection Supervisor: The Institutions of the EC Controlled by an Independent Authority' 43 (2006) *Common Market Law Review* 1313–1342, at 1331–1332; also Case 222/86 *UNECTEF* v. *Heylens* [1987] ECR 4097, para. 14; Case 222/84 *Johnston* v. *Chief Constable of the RUC* [1986] ECR 1651, para.18.

is also supported by the principle of effective protection of EU citizens, also enshrined in Articles 6 and 13 ECHR.[78] Moreover, the possibility of extending judicial review under Article 230 EC to all acts of EU bodies with normative value has been well established.[79]

In practice, one would expect most appeals to be heard before the national courts, relieving the European courts from yet another cluster of cases. Appeals before the CFI require trial in Luxembourg with subsequent excessive expenses and inconvenience for the citizen. National courts are still more accessible for citizens and have a better appreciation of the data included in national criminal records. National cases are expected to form the bulk of disputes – after all, it is either the subjects or national agencies with disputed right to access that are most likely to have recourse to judicial action. In the fewer cases where an EU body seeks prohibited (in the first instance) access to the ECR or correction of ECR data, the CFI will be approached. The mechanism of preliminary rulings before the ECJ can be utilised by national courts unsure of the interpretation of the constituting instrument of the ECR. In this way the need for direct action before the CFI is further diminished.

For reasons of legality and democratic accountability the host institution for the ECR must report to the European Parliament (EP) on an annual basis. The EP must be informed on, amongst others, the number and topics of appeals against the host institution, the level on which the appeals have been resolved (namely administrative before the supervisory body or judicial before the courts) and on the outcome of these appeals. This is all the more important since the ECR, as indeed its host body Eurojust, is to be financed by the Community budget.

3.4 *Transfer of data to the ECR*

National laws are divided on the issue of the nature of the national authority which would transfer data to Eurojust as the host institution of the ECR.[80] Thus, it is sensible to allow the national law of each Member State to identify the national body that would transfer the relevant data to the ECR. This could belong to the executive (as is the

[78] Case C-50/00 P, *Unión de Pequeños Agricultores* v. *Council*, [2002] ECR I-6677, para. 39.

[79] Case 294/83, *Les Verts* v. *European Parliament*, ECR [1986] ECR 1339, para. 25.

[80] Council of the EU, 'Council Decision on the Exchange of Information Extracted from Criminal Records – Manual of Procedure'.

case in Germany) or the judiciary (as is the case in Greece). It is envisaged that competence to transfer data from national criminal records to the ECR would stay with the designated central national authority declared to the Council as the host of national criminal records.

The mechanism for the transfer of data from national criminal records to the ECR can be that of 'direct transfer', as envisaged in Article 15 of the 2000 MLA Convention, and sanctions must be imposed for unauthorised transfer and use of data, as provided by the OECD (1992) Recommendation concerning guidelines for the security of information systems. The provisions of Council Decision 2005/876/JHA of 21 November 2005 on the exchange of information extracted from the criminal record[81] are directly applicable in the case of the ECR. In particular, the own initiative principle of Article 2 suits the ECR structure perfectly.[82] Each central authority has the obligation to inform without delay the central authorities of the other Member States of criminal convictions and subsequent measures concerning nationals of those Member States entered in the national criminal record. Where the person concerned is a national of two or more other Member States, the information is transferred to each of these Member States, unless the person is a national of the Member State in the territory of which he has been convicted.

Should the Commission's Draft Framework Decision on the organisation and content of the exchange of information extracted from criminal records between Member States be passed,[83] then the ECR could be served by a consolidating instrument in this area of law. The draft Framework Decision is intended to create a solid, express and clearly defined regime for the transfer of data in the area of the third pillar mainly between designated competent national authorities.[84] In fact, the Commission's proposed standardised European format for the exchange of data could very well borrow its form from the ECR form for the maintenance of criminal data.

[81] OJ L 322/33, 9 December 2005.

[82] In fact, the Decision is seen as a step towards the ECR: EDPS, 'Opinion of the European Data Protection Supervisor on the Proposal for a Council Decision on the Exchange of Information from Criminal Records' (COM (2004) 664 final of 13 October 2004, OJ C 058, 8 March 2005 at 3–6 para. 4.

[83] COM(2005) 690.

[84] J. Macke, 'Exchange of Information on Criminal Records' 3–4 (2006) *Eucrim* 76–81, at 77.

3.5 *The instrument*

The selection of instrument for the establishment of the ECR is linked to the competence of the EU in the sphere of criminal law. After the recent environmental case[85] harmonisation of EU criminal law by use of first pillar instruments seems possible.[86] This creates fresh debates about spillover between pillars even outside the context of the Constitutional Treaty.[87] However, traditionally and historically, debates over the possibility of the use of *passerelle* referred to substantive criminal law.[88] Issues related to judicial cooperation in criminal matters have always been seen as reserved for harmonisation through third pillar instruments.

Nevertheless, it is also necessary to accept that the introduction of the ECR bears concerns related to the human rights of those whose data will be included. This is based on the subject matter of the ECR which touches upon both criminal law and data protection. It is, therefore, essential that the legal framework within which the ECR will function is identical in all participating countries. Deviations, partial exclusions or diversity of interpretation and implementation may affect the general effectiveness of the ECR as well as the full protection of the human rights of the citizens of the EU. It is for this reason that ideally the constituting instrument for the ECR is one guaranteeing at least a minimum of harmonisation on key issues. At the same time the current environment of fragmentation in EU criminal law requires a realistic approach to the ECR allowing for flexibility in the manner in which the desired strict minimum harmonised standards will be achieved.[89] These thoughts lead to the selection of a Framework Decision[90] as the constituting instrument of the ECR.

4. Conclusions

Although the idea of a centralised criminal record held at the EU level is rather new, the ECR is not envisaged to add further policing in the lives

[85] Case C-176/03 *Commission* v. *Council* [2005] ECR I-7879.

[86] S. White, 'Case C-176/03' (2006) *European Law Review* 81–93.

[87] S. White, 'Case C-176/03 and the Options for the Development of a Community Criminal Law' 3–4 (2006) *Eucrim* 93–99 at 99.

[88] J. Vervaele, 'The EC and Harmonisation of the Criminal Law Enforcement of Community Policy' 3–4 (2006) *Eucrim* 87–93.

[89] S. Peers, 'Mutual Recognition and Criminal Law in the EU: Has the Council Got it Wrong?' 41 (2004) *CMLRev* 5–36, at 8.

[90] G. Lysén, *EU Framework Decisions* (Uppsala: Iustus Förlag, 2006).

of EU citizens. Even currently, the data which will be included in the ECR are held by national archives; indeed, not all national entries will be included in the ECR. Currently, these data are available to national authorities of other Member States and accession countries through the large number of agreements imposing data exchange amongst national prosecuting, judicial and police authorities; indeed, the data available through the ECR are only a small part of those available to the national authorities through existing data exchange mechanisms. The agencies which will have access to the ECR already have access to the same data and the ECR will only allow access to such agencies. There is, therefore, nothing new or threatening for the rights of the citizens of the EU from the introduction of the ECR. If anything, EU standards for data protection are higher than those currently applicable in some Member States and certainly in the EU accession countries.

The ECR is an alternative mechanism of mutual judicial assistance between Member States, indeed one which will finally surpass the inherent problems of intergovernmental approaches and allow the Member States involved to have a solid EU backing behind the exchange data of a criminal nature for natural and legal persons residing in their countries as a means of preventing and combating organised crime.

Is the ECR feasible or folly? In the mind of this author it would be folly to choose any other option than ECR. Recent Framework Decisions in the area of exchange of information have facilitated the introduction of the ECR and have shown the way to a number of choices related to the database. Moreover, further discussion on the alternative intergovernmental approach has demonstrated that the hurdles to its application in practice are difficult to overcome. Even if these are set aside by Member States, the opinion of the EDPS on the disproportionality of exchange of data on all crimes remains like a Damoclean sword with possible judicial review consequences over the alternative choice of linkage of national criminal records. Perhaps the centralised ECR is more realistic than initially thought after all.

19

Conclusions

CONSTANTIN STEFANOU AND HELEN XANTHAKI

1. Recent developments

This book has examined in detail the proposal for the ECR and the conditions for its reception by the national legal orders of the Member States. The political feasibility of the ECR and its legitimacy from the point of view of human rights and civil liberties has also been explored. Recent developments in the area of mutual legal assistance and judicial cooperation in criminal matters have been presented and lessons from parallel relevant initiatives of the EU have been identified.

However, questions on the future of the ECR in legislative and political practice remain. In order to assess the future of the ECR one would have to provide updates on the current position with reference to relevant Commission initiatives. At the moment the Commission's proposal for a register of convictions is set aside. The indifference of Member States' delegations towards a central database, that would only include a mere listing of countries where convictions can be sought, has buried this proposal, hopefully for ever. It is very difficult to explain how the Commission possibly felt that Member States would undertake the expense of a centralised database for so little in exchange.

The ECR as a concept remains, albeit as a second stage solution, which will follow the initiative on the organisation and content of the exchange of information on criminal convictions. Member States find it difficult to subscribe to a central database, even one covering a limited range of crimes. At least at this stage.

What the Commission offers and indeed pushes forward instead is a different version of an ECR as described in the 2005 proposal for a Council Framework Decision on the organisation and content of the exchange of information extracted from criminal records between

Member States.[1] It is interesting to explore the state of affairs with reference to this initiative as a means of assessing the feasibility of this alternative route to the ECR.

In 2007 alone eight drafts of this proposal were discussed before the Council.[2] Two Presidencies this year have failed to secure agreement from all Member States despite their clear prioritisation of the matter.[3] Finland and Sweden have entered a general scrutiny reservation on the proposal, while a number of delegations have entered parliamentary scrutiny reservations.[4] Moreover, the Commission acknowledges that the Framework Decision is only a first step towards a legislative solution which will have to be completed by a second Council Decision on the electronic transfer of data.[5] In fact, the Commission accepts that a third step will most likely be necessary: via a process of commitology the technical details agreed in the second stage will have to be amended and adapted most probably via a new Council Decision.[6] The Commission's three-stage approach can only be viewed as a diplomatic repositioning on the difficult points of the original proposal: the Commission hopes that Member States can at least agree on the philosophy and main points of the initiative thus leaving the 'sore' yet crucial points of practicality for a later date when the pressure to proceed on the basis of a toothless Framework Decision will be evident.[7] Perhaps this is the time when the Commission will turn to the centralised ECR as a completion of the second stage of EU policy in the area of availability of data on criminal convictions.

However, Member States still fail to agree on a number of difficult issues. First, the field of application of the Framework Decision seems to be a rather contentious matter. A large number of Member States can only accept criminal convictions as falling within its field of application, whereas a small number of Member States require that administrative decisions are also included. France's suggestion to include administrative decisions so far as they are included in the national criminal records

[1] See COM(2005) 690 final/2; 5463/1/06 COPEN 1.

[2] See 11895/06 COPEN 86, 30–31 January 2007; 6372/07 ADD 1 COPEN 20, 5 March 2007; 7594/07 COPEN 38, 20 March 2007; 7594/1/07 REV 1 COPEN 38, 20 April 2007; 8628/07 CATS 33 COPEN 47, 20 April 2007; 9273/07 COPEN 55, 8 May 2007; 9442/07 CATS 50 COPEN 59, 21 May 2007; and 11601/07 COPEN 107, 16 July 2007.

[3] Council of the EU, 'Presidency Conclusions European Council 21/22 June 2007', Document 11177/07, Brussels, 23 June 2007, para. 30, p. 7.

[4] See 9442/07 CATS 50 COPEN 59, 21 May 2007, p. 1.

[5] See 7594/07 COPEN 38, 20 March 2007, p. 2. [6] Ibid., p. 3.

[7] See 7594/1/07 REV 1 COPEN 38, 20 April 2007, p. 4.

of the Member States, as well as the Swedish proposal to include decisions of public prosecutors have been rejected by the UK, Greece and the Commission.[8] Austria offered as a compromise the inclusion of a recital stating that Member States shall continue to be able to exchange information on convictions pronounced by public prosecutors or administrative bodies. Estonia, the Netherlands, Belgium, Poland and Greece support the Austrian proposal, whereas Spain, Hungary, Finland, France, Portugal and the UK oppose it.[9] The prevailing trend, however, is to delimit the field of application of the Framework Decision to criminal convictions and disqualifications.[10]

Second, the rules applicable to the erasure of information from criminal records are yet to be agreed. Member States had asked for the revision of Article 5 in order to allow the Member State of the person's nationality to update the information stored in criminal records within the deadlines applicable under the legislation of the Member State of conviction. This creates a dual deadline, one applicable to the erasure of criminal records for the rest of the Member States while the state of nationality may apply a different erasure deadline for internal use. Delegations have voiced concerns about this particular aspect of the proposal. Although most delegations seem prepared to accept one set of erasure deadlines for the retransmission of data to other Member States as opposed to the erasure deadlines for the internal use of data for the country of nationality, nevertheless the complexity of this dual regime has caused insurmountable obstacles to the agreement of the Framework Decision. The conflict between those wishing to impose the law of the state of conviction and those wishing to apply the law of the state of nationality remains.[11] However, an emerging prevailing trend imposes the sole application of the law of the state of conviction to all erasures.[12]

Third, disputes still exist with reference to the rules of transmission to third countries. The Commission proposal applied the law of nationality to the transmission of data to third countries. However, the majority of Member States objected to this possibility, as it would lead to the imposition of conditions on the provision of data that could not apply

[8] See 7594/1/07 REV 1 COPEN 38, 20 April 2007, p. 10.
[9] See 9273/07 COPEN 55, 8 May 2007, p. 4.
[10] See 11601/07 COPEN 107, 16 July 2007, p. 9 and para. 5 at p. 4.
[11] See 9442/1/07 REV 1, CATS 50 COPEN 59, pp. 3–4.
[12] See 11601/07 COPEN 107, 16 July 2007, p. 10.

under Article 13 of the 1959 CoE Convention. Thus, even for this purpose the law of the state of conviction seems to prevail.[13]

Fourth, the precise data to be transmitted under the Framework Decision remains undecided. Content of national criminal records is not standardised and the method of identification of citizens in entries within national criminal records is far from harmonised. Agreeing the elements of identification has proved impossible for the Member Sates. The latest solution offered by the German Presidency is a fragmented, unilaterally drawn list of different elements applicable variably in the instances of transmission, storage and retransmission.[14]

It is difficult to envisage an agreement, other than perhaps by use of the existing minimum common denominator, on these four issues by all Member States. A forward looking agreement would require immense compromise by Member States, even to the point of unconstitutionality. What remains to be agreed refers to the definition of a criminal conviction, the deadlines for erasure from criminal records, the data protection rules for retransmission, and the content of national criminal records. If Member States were indeed able to proceed on these points further than the current inefficient mutual legal assistance mechanisms, the result would be standardised – or at least harmonised – national criminal records. In essence, true harmonisation in the content and regulation of national criminal records would de facto solve the core problem of mutual legal assistance, namely the many discrepancies in the regulation of national criminal records at the national level. One could state, therefore, that the Commission went to all this trouble in exploring the legislative success of the criminal records linkage solution, only to reaffirm its inability to proceed beyond current mutual legal assistance mechanisms.[15] This is clearly demonstrated through the numerous discrepancies and intricacies of transfer of criminal data requests detailed in the latest version of the Manual of Procedure for the exchange of data from criminal records.[16] It can be argued that this is

[13] See 11601/07 COPEN 107, 16 July 2007, pp. 10–11.

[14] See 9442/1/07 REV 1, CATS 50 COPEN 59, pp. 5–8; also see 11601/07 COPEN 107, 16 July 2007, pp. 15–16.

[15] House of Commons European Scrutiny Committee, *Implementing the Hague Programme on Justice and Home Affairs: Forty-first Report of Session 2005–06* (London: The Stationery Office Limited, 2006), para. 22, p. 8.

[16] Council of the EU, 'Council Decision on the Exchange of Information Extracted from Criminal Records; Manual of Procedure', 11060/1/07 REV 1, COPEN 101, EJN 18, EUROJUST 36, Brussels, 22 June 2007.

yet another example of the Commission's frequently alleged inability to envisage the practical implications of its legislative priorities and legislative proposals.[17]

2. The concept of the ECR revisited

Few would doubt that national criminal records are only efficient within the boundaries of their jurisdiction. Even fewer would support the view that data from foreign criminal records are useless in the combat of transnational, organised crime. The question really is which form EU-wide availability of data from national criminal records will take.[18] This book and its editors are convinced that the inefficiency of national criminal records requires legislative action at the EU level in the form of the establishment of a centralised, Eurojust maintained, EU database with data on convictions for transnational crimes for all EU citizens. The proposal is not accepted universally and the prevailing view with the Commission at the moment seems to tilt towards the 'light' version of the ECR, namely the linkage of national criminal records as a means of immediate exchange of data on all criminal convictions for all crimes.

The choice between these two competing scenarios is ultimately a choice of competence and legal basis.[19] Linkage of national criminal records seems, at least prima facie, a rather ambitious initiative, as it involves exchange of data on all crimes. In contrast to this, the single-database centralised ECR involves the delimitation of crimes falling within the field of application of the new initiative to transnational organised crimes only. In other words, under the centralised ECR scenario availability of data on convictions can be immediate, secure, accessible and usable by EU and national authorities, but on limited types of crime only. Does the EU, especially post-'Reform Treaty', have the luxury of legitimacy to proceed with an initiative in the area of criminal law which will extend to all crimes?

The view of the editors is that this is not the case. Legal integration was never intended to cover all aspects of criminal law. In fact, the

[17] House of Commons European Scrutiny Committee, *The EU's Justice and Home Affairs Work Programme for the Next Five Years: Twenty-eighth Report of Session 2003–04* (London: The Stationery Office, 2004), para. 19, p. 10.

[18] See H. Leniston, 'What Prospects are There for the European Criminal Record' 19 (2006) *European Issues*.

[19] See Anne Weyembergh, 'Approximation of Criminal Laws, the Constitutional Treaty and the Hague Programme' (2005) *Common Market Law Review* 1567–1597, at 1568.

Reform Treaty will invite a much clearer delimitation of areas of legislative action, as the final collapse of the pillar structure will invite clearer subsidiarity tests even in the area of criminal law. So far, initiatives in the third pillar tended to have the extravagance of fragmentation,[20] which allowed them to hide behind the argument of intergovernmentalism. This prevailed when doubts about subsidiarity arose. What if the measure under scrutiny did not really reflect the need for necessarily EU legislative action? As long as Member States agreed unanimously, all concerns about subsidiarity and necessity were diluted.[21] The end of the third pillar and its intergovernmentalism will invite a rethink of this approach. Subsidiarity and necessity will now need to be demonstrated rather than deduced from unanimity. In this new environment the future for the current initiative of the Commission on data exchange on all crimes is now more uncertain than ever.

Moreover, the threat of judicial review of a legislative instrument extending transfer of data to all crimes remains, especially after the declaration of disproportionality of the measure by the EDPS. In fact, this threat seems to be strengthened in the post-Reform Treaty period, which seems to stay with enhanced judicial control in the area of criminal law triumphantly introduced by the now sidelined Constitutional Treaty.[22]

Furthermore, the final settlement of the relationship between EU and the ECHR will require stricter adherence to the ECHR criteria,[23] not only by Member States applying new EU legislative initiatives but by the EU itself at the legislative stage.[24] Thus, the jurisprudence of Article 8 ECHR and proportionality, legality and confidentiality acquire a central

[20] For the full picture of fragmentation in EU criminal law, see Council of the EU, 'Addendum to the "I" Item Note: Implementation of the Strategy and Action Plan to Combat Terrorism', 15266/06 ADD 1 REV 1 LIMITE, JAI 591, ECOFIN 399, TRANS 290, RELEX 801, ECO 173, PESC 1126, COTER 47, COSDP 922, PROCIV 235, ENER 274, ATO 132, DATAPROTECT 41, TELECOM 109, Brussels, 24 November 2006.

[21] See House of Commons European Scrutiny Committee, *The EU's Justice and Home Affairs Work Programme for the Next Five Years: Twenty-eighth Report of Session 2003–04*, paras. 56 (vii) and (viii), p. 20.

[22] See E. Guild and S. Carrera, 'No Constitutional Treaty? Implications for the Area of Freedom, Security and Justice', CEPS Working Document No. 231/October 2005, p. 4.

[23] See J. Kokotte and A. Rüth, 'The European Convention and its Draft Treaty establishing a Constitution for Europe: Appropriate Answers to the Laeken Questions?' 40 (2003) *Common Market Law Review* 1315–1345, at 1330.

[24] EU Network of Independent Experts on Fundamental Rights, 'Commentary of the Charter of Fundamental Rights of the EU', June 2006, http://ec.europa.eu/justice_home/cfr_cdf/index_en.htm, p. 97.

importance in the choice of legislative solution for the inefficiency of national criminal records. With specific reference to proportionality, it would be difficult to justify availability of data on convictions for all crimes at the EU level, when only transnational organised crime falls within the competence of the EU. Marrying the principles of privacy and rehabilitation of ex-offenders with a wide-ranging availability of data on all convictions would be a difficult task for the Commission. In fact, ensuring that privacy and rehabilitation are respected when data fall into the hands of foreign authorities, which are not equipped and are therefore unable to understand their meaning and significance under the national legal order of the originating state, would be almost impossible.

In essence, what is problematic with the interoperability of national criminal records lies in the nature of mutual legal assistance mechanisms in the last hundred years: inefficiency of data exchange is due to the necessary framework of safeguards needed for the protection of quintessential values such as defence rights, presumption of innocence, privacy and rehabilitation of ex offenders.[25] These frameworks are necessary for the constitutionality and legitimacy of actions or omissions of national authorities for the acquisition, access, use or provision of data from criminal records; thus, any effort to strengthen the exchange of data whilst stripping the process of admittedly inhibiting, yet necessary, safeguards seems doomed at the legislative, but mostly at the operational, level.

Thus, the choice of the EU in the area of data exchange is one between pursuit of ambitious goals via a tried and tested route, namely exchange of data on all convictions via a mechanism of mutual legal assistance, or pursuit of a relatively pedestrian goal via an innovative route, namely effective data availability on selected crimes via a centralised ECR. The second choice carries with it increased legitimacy based on limited EU competence, increased data protection levels based on existing and strengthened Eurojust mechanisms, and increased opportunity for legislative success.

It is therefore time for the Commission to abandon its majestic break with competence barriers and to reconcile itself to the welcome proportionality restrictions to its goals that would be imposed by the establishment of a centralised database of convictions concerned exclusively with transnational organised crime, maintained by Eurojust and entitled the 'European Criminal Record'.

[25] E. Denza, 'The 2000 Convention on Mutual Assistance in Criminal Matters' 40 (2003) *Common Market Law Review* 1047–1074, at 1069.

INDEX